LISTEN TO PUNK ROCK!

Recent Titles in
Exploring Musical Genres

Listen to New Wave Rock! Exploring a Musical Genre
James E. Perone

Listen to Pop! Exploring a Musical Genre
James E. Perone

Listen to the Blues! Exploring a Musical Genre
James E. Perone

Listen to Rap! Exploring a Musical Genre
Anthony J. Fonseca

Listen to Classic Rock! Exploring a Musical Genre
Melissa Ursula Dawn Goldsmith

Listen to Movie Musicals! Exploring a Musical Genre
James E. Perone

Listen to Psychedelic Rock! Exploring a Musical Genre
Christian Matijas-Mecca

Listen to Soul! Exploring a Musical Genre
James E. Perone

LISTEN TO PUNK ROCK!

Exploring a Musical Genre

JUNE MICHELE PULLIAM

Exploring Musical Genres
James E. Perone, Series Editor

BLOOMSBURY ACADEMIC
NEW YORK • LONDON • OXFORD • NEW DELHI • SYDNEY

BLOOMSBURY ACADEMIC
Bloomsbury Publishing Inc
1385 Broadway, New York, NY 10018, USA
50 Bedford Square, London, WC1B 3DP, UK
29 Earlsfort Terrace, Dublin 2, Ireland

BLOOMSBURY, BLOOMSBURY ACADEMIC and the Diana logo
are trademarks of Bloomsbury Publishing Plc

First published in the United States of America by ABC-CLIO 2021
Paperback edition published by Bloomsbury Academic 2025

Copyright © Bloomsbury Publishing Inc, 2025

Cover photo: Russia's punk band, Pussy Riot, conducting anti-Putin action
in front of the Kremlin, Moscow, Russia, January 20, 2012.
(PhotoXpress/ZUMAPRESS.com/Alamy.com)

All rights reserved. No part of this publication may be reproduced or transmitted
in any form or by any means, electronic or mechanical, including photocopying,
recording, or any information storage or retrieval system, without prior permission
in writing from the publishers.

Bloomsbury Publishing Inc does not have any control over, or responsibility for,
any third-party websites referred to or in this book. All internet addresses given
in this book were correct at the time of going to press. The author and publisher
regret any inconvenience caused if addresses have changed or sites have
ceased to exist, but can accept no responsibility for any such changes.

Library of Congress Cataloging-in-Publication Data
Names: Pulliam, June Michele, author.
Title: Listen to punk rock! : exploring a musical genre /
June Michele Pulliam.
Description: Santa Barbara : Greenwood, 2021. | Series: Exploring musical
genres | Includes bibliographical references and index.
Identifiers: LCCN 2020033566 (print) | LCCN 2020033567 (ebook) |
ISBN 9781440865725 (hardcover) | ISBN 9781440865732 (ebook)
Subjects: LCSH: Punk rock music—History and criticism.
Classification: LCC ML3534 .P84 2021 (print) | LCC ML3534 (ebook) |
DDC 781.6609—dc23
LC record available at https://lccn.loc.gov/2020033566
LC ebook record available at https://lccn.loc.gov/2020033567

ISBN: HB: 978-1-4408-6572-5
PB: 979-8-2162-5100-2
ePDF: 978-1-4408-6573-2
eBook: 979-8-2161-1199-3

Series: Exploring Musical Genres

To find out more about our authors and books visit www.bloomsbury.com
and sign up for our newsletters.

Dear Reader:
I am sorry in advance that I did not include
all of your favorite bands, in order, in this book.

Contents

Series Foreword	xi
Preface	xv
1 Background and History	1
2 Must-Hear Music	13
Against Me! *Transgender Dysphoria Blues*	13
Alice Bag: *Alice Bag*	15
Bad Brains: *I Against I*	18
Bad Religion: *Stranger Than Fiction*	20
Bikini Kill: *Pussy Whipped*	22
Black Flag: *Damaged*	25
Blondie: *Plastic Letters*	28
Buzzcocks: *Singles Going Steady*	32
The Clash: *London Calling*	35
The Cramps: *Songs the Lord Taught Us*	39
Crass: *The Feeding of the 5000*	41
The Damned: *Damned, Damned, Damned* (Expanded Edition)	44
Dead Boys: *Young, Loud, and Snotty*	46

Dead Kennedys: *Fresh Fruit for Rotting Vegetables*	49
Death: *For the Whole World to See*	52
The Dropkick Murphys: *Going Out in Style*	55
French Punk: *Punk 45: Les Punks: The French Connection*	58
Fugazi: *Repeater* and Minor Threat: "Straight Edge"	62
The Germs: *GI*	64
Gogol Bordello: *Super Taranta!*	67
Green Day: *Dookie* and *American Idiot*	71
The Jam: *In the City*	75
L7: *Bricks Are Heavy*	77
Las Vulpes: *Me Gusta Ser*	80
Me First and the Gimmie Gimmies: *Rake It In: The Greatest Hits*	82
Misfits: *Walk Among Us*	85
Mojo Nixon and Skid Roper: *Bo-Day-Shus!!!*	88
The Muffs: *The Muffs*	92
Pansy Division: *Deflowered*	94
The Pogues: *Rum, Sodomy, and the Lash*	98
Punk Christmas Music	101
Pussy Riot: *Kill the Sexist*	104
The Raincoats: *The Raincoats*	108
The Ramones: *Ramones* (Fortieth Anniversary Deluxe Edition)	110
Rancid: *. . . And Out Come the Wolves*	114
Richard Hell and the Voidoids: *Blank Generation*	117
The Runaways: *The Runaways*	121
The Sex Pistols: *Never Mind the Bollocks: Here's the Sex Pistols*	124

Shonen Knife: *Alive! in Osaka*	128
Siouxsie and the Banshees: *The Scream*	132
The Slits: *Cut*	135
Patti Smith: *Horses*	138
Social Distortion: *Hard Times and Nursery Rhymes*	142
The Stooges: *Raw Power*	145
Taqwacore	148
War on Women: *Capture the Flag*	151
Watch This! Documentaries, Feature Films, and Videos	154
Women in Punk	159
X: *Los Angeles*	164
X-Ray Spex: *Germfree Adolescents* (Reissue)	167
3 Impact on Popular Culture	171
4 Legacy	183
Bibliography	191
Index	249

Series Foreword

Ask some music fans, and they will tell you that genre labels are rubbish and that imposing them on artists and pieces of music diminishes the diversity of the work of performers, songwriters, instrumental composers, and so on. Still, in the record stores of old, in descriptions of radio-station formats (on-air and Internet), and at various streaming audio and download sites today, we have seen and continue to see music categorized by genre. Indeed, some genre boundaries are at least somewhat artificial, and it is true that some artists and some pieces of music transcend boundaries. But categorizing music by genre is a convenient way of keeping track of the thousands upon thousands of musical works available for listeners' enjoyment; it's analogous to the difference between having all your documents on your computer's home screen versus organizing them into folders. So, Greenwood's Exploring Musical Genres series is a genre- and performance group–based collection of books and e-books. The publications in this series will provide listeners with background information on the genre; critical analysis of important examples of musical pieces, artists, and events from the genre; discussion of must-hear music from the genre; analysis of the genre's impact on the popular culture of its time and on later popular-culture trends; and analysis of the enduring legacy of the genre today and its impact on later musicians and their songs, instrumental works, and recordings. Each volume will also contain a bibliography of references for further reading.

We view the volumes in the Exploring Musical Genres series as a go-to resource for serious music fans, the more casual listener, and everyone in between. The authors in the series are scholars, who probe into the details of the genre and its practitioners: the singers, instrumentalists, composers, and lyricists of the pieces of music that we love. Although the authors' scholarship brings a high degree of insight and perceptive analysis to the reader's understanding of the various musical genres, the authors approach their subjects with the idea of appealing to the lay reader, the music nonspecialist. As a result, the authors may provide critical analysis using some high-level scholarly tools; however, they avoid any unnecessary and unexplained jargon or technical terms or concepts. These are scholarly volumes written for the enjoyment of virtually any music fan.

Every volume has its length parameters, and an author cannot include every piece of music from within a particular genre. Part of the challenge, but also part of the fun, is that readers might agree with some of the choices of "must-hear music" and disagree with others. So while your favorite example of, say, grunge music might not be included, the author's choices might help you to open up your ears to new, exciting, and ultimately intriguing possibilities.

By and large, these studies focus on music from the sound-recording era: roughly the 20th century through the present. American guitarist, composer, and singer-songwriter Frank Zappa once wrote:

> On a record, the overall timbre of the piece (determined by equalization of individual parts and their proportions in the mix) tells you, in a subtle way, WHAT the song is about. The orchestration provides *important information* about what the composition *IS* and, in some instances, assumes a greater importance than *the composition itself*. (Zappa with Occhiogrosso 1989, 188; italics and capitalization from the original)

The gist of Zappa's argument is that *everything* that the listener experiences (to use Zappa's system of emphasizing words)—including the arrangement, recording mix and balance, lyrics, melodies, harmonies, instrumentation, and so on—makes up a musical composition. To put it another way, during the sound-recording era, and especially after the middle of the 20th century, we have tended to understand the idea of a piece of music—particularly in the realm of popular music—as being the same as the most definitive recording of that piece of music. And this is where Zappa's emphasis on the arrangement and recording's production comes into play. As a result, a writer delving into, say, new wave rock will examine and analyze the B-52's' version of "Rock Lobster" and not just the words, melodies, and chords that any band could sing and play and still label the result "Rock Lobster." To use Zappa's graphic way of highlighting particular words, the B-52's' recording *IS* the piece. Although they have expressed it in other ways, other writers such as Theodore Gracyk (1996, 18) and Albin J. Zak III (2001) concur with Zappa's equating of the piece with the studio recording of the piece.

In the case of musical genres not as susceptible to being tied to a particular recording—generally because of the fact that they are genres often experienced live, such as classical music or Broadway musicals—the authors will still make recommendations of particular recordings (we don't all have ready access to a live performance of Wolfgang Amadeus Mozart's *Symphony No. 40* any time we'd like to experience the piece), but they will focus their analyses on the more general, the notes-on-the-page, the expected general aural experience that one is likely to find in any good performance or recorded version.

Maybe you think that all you really want to do is just listen to the music. Won't reading about a genre decrease your enjoyment of it? My hope is that you'll find that reading this book opens up new possibilities for understanding your favorite musical genre and that by knowing a little more about it, you'll be able to listen with proverbial new ears and gain even more pleasure from your listening experience. Yes, the authors in the series will bring you biographical detail, the history of the genres, and critical analysis on various musical works that they consider to be the best, the most representative, and the most influential pieces in the genre. However, ultimately, the goal is to enhance the listening experience. That, by the way, is why these volumes have an exclamation mark in their titles. So please enjoy both reading and listening!

—*James E. Perone, Series Editor*

REFERENCES

Gracyk, Theodore. 1996. *Rhythm and Noise: An Aesthetics of Rock*. Durham, NC: Duke University Press.

Zak, Albin J., III. 2001. *The Poetics of Rock: Cutting Tracks, Making Records*. Berkeley: University of California Press.

Zappa, Frank, with Peter Occhiogrosso. 1989. *The Real Frank Zappa Book*. New York: Poseidon Press.

Preface

Punk rock is a reaction against bourgeois sensibilities and the music and popular culture industrial complex that decides what artists will be promoted and what is "cool" at the moment. The punk movement is not just confined to music either; it includes the written word and visual art. All are designed to overturn the model of art in which the general public appreciates work made by a talented few. Punk blurs the lines between artist and fan by encouraging anyone who has something to say to pick up an instrument, write, or create art and bypass the corporate gatekeepers to share that work with like-minded people. Because punk rejects corporate aesthetics that homogenize art so that it can be marketed to the lowest common denominator of consumers, it "was always intended to sound rough, unrefined, and under-produced" (Langerholc 2017). As a consequence, "most punk bands use the most basic instrumentation, with many punk bands only consisting of three members" (Langerholc 2017).

Punk culture is "nihilistic, pessimistic, anti-authoritarian and anarchic in its civil and political message; provocative, Dada-esque and theatrical in its artistic expression; and hedonistic, experimental and egalitarian in its social values" (White 2012). Punk promotes these ideas through its characteristic sound: the instrumentation is usually stripped down to guitar, bass, and drums; "songs are often played at a very fast tempo and include a great deal of emphasis on beats 2 and 4"; and "drumbeats are largely very simple and unadorned, except for the occasional super-fast fill" (Langerholc 2017). The songs are short, getting directly to the point, and "vocals are often shouted in a confrontational manner" (Langerholc 2017). Lyrical considerations often include politics, drug and substance abuse, general musings on life and the absurdities thereof, and sexuality, as opposed to romantic love. Many songs are written with the intent to shock, so punk is rife with profanities that often make the songs unsuitable for broadcast radio.

Punk rock began in 1976–1977 in London, New York, and France, and was influenced by the anti-capitalist and anti-authoritarian Situationist International collective as well as by the beatniks, Dadaism, surrealism, and the avant-garde movement. Punk's aim to shock "is an established part of avant-garde aesthetics" (Laing 2015, 96). Bad Religion front man Greg Graffin summed up punk as "the personal expression of uniqueness that comes from the experiences of growing up in touch with our human ability to reason and ask questions." It is "a movement that serves to refute social attitudes that have been perpetuated through willful ignorance of human nature," "a process of questioning and commitment to understanding that results in self-progress," and "a belief that this world is what we make of it" and that "truth comes from our understanding of the way things are, not from the blind adherence to prescriptions about the way things should be" (qtd. in Hiebert 2010). One way that punk refuted the status quo was by looking to "roots" music for inspiration. This roots music consisted of reggae, blues, and early rock and roll that predated the Beatles, which were the opposite of the progressive rock, pop rock, and disco that was a fixture of the 1970s popular music scene.

Too, punk aesthetics "made ugliness beautiful" (Malcolm McLaren qtd. in Hiebert 2010). Ripped clothing held together with safety pins, smeared makeup, and brightly colored mohawks were both shocking to the general public of the 1970s as well as the antithesis of glamour. The casual and even outrageous punk look showed that punks were unconcerned about fitting into mainstream society to become part of the workforce or make themselves attractive. Jon Savage, the author of one of the most definitive books about punk, *England's Dreaming*, explains that "punk's self-starter-D.I.Y. impulse was its most important consequence" (qtd. in Shea 2016). Without this impulse, punks would have never been able to share their relentlessly uncommercial music and ideas with the world. Punk's DIY attitude is what led punks to seize the means of production to start their own record labels to distribute their music, book their own concert tours, and communicate directly with fans as well as to create xeroxed zines and guerilla art. It is this DIY ethos that makes punk still relevant today, as new generations of musicians, artists, and fans are encouraged by other punks who have shared their work via informal and anti-corporate networks.

CHAPTER 1

Background and History

Punk rock is a musical genre that simultaneously emerged in the United States, the United Kingdom, and France in the mid-1970s, at a time "when youth in numerous Western industrialized countries struggled with feelings of alienation from the social, economic, and political forces around them" (Dunn 2011, 28–29). Punk was born of the "frustration with what many urban youths saw as the ineffectiveness of hippie-style liberalism" (St. John 2004). Punk's intellectual origins can be traced to France, "in the countercultural manifestos that appeared during and soon after the events of May 1968 in Paris," when student protests against capitalism, consumerism, traditional institutions, and American imperialism set off a general strike that even caused then president Charles de Gaulle to flee to Germany (Greene 2017, 123). Major figures of British punk, such as Malcolm McLaren, Tony Wilson, and Bernard Rhodes, were avid readers of the works of the Situationist International that inspired the May 68 protesters, "such as those by Guy Debord (author of *The Society of the Spectacle*), whose thoughts on personal freedom, the individual, and consumer society were a major political and social influence on the British punk scene" (Savage 1992, 27–32). The first punk festival was held, illegally, in the small French town of Mont-de-Marsan in 1976. Festival organizer Marc Zermati chose the remote location for the small festival to fly under the radar of French officials, who in the aftermath of the May 68 civil unrest had banned music festivals because they were places for young people to gather and perhaps plot to overthrow the government.

Ironically, punk did not take off in France the way it did in the United Kingdom and the United States, in part because it was unable to spark outrage among the old guard. However, punk's French influences could be seen in the emerging London and New York punk scenes. Punk's "theme of 'no future' was taken directly from the disenchantment and agitation of French youth in May 68," while its iconoclasm and the questions that it "posed as to the very essence of art (and anti-art) can be traced back to the French surrealists such as André Breton and the Dadaists of the early twentieth century" (Greene 2017, 123). In New York, key punk figures "were influenced by French literary and artistic figures, some of whom had their origins further back in time, but had been embraced by the French student counterculture of May '68" (Greene 2017, 123). Patti Smith, the godmother of punk, "was an avid reader of both nineteenth-century Symbolist poet Arthur Rimbaud and the more contemporary Jean Genet and used the works of both writers in her performances. Thomas Miller, better known as Tom Verlaine of the band Television, took the last name as an homage to Paul Verlaine, another French Symbolist poet, while the dandified look cultivated by Richard Hell owed a lot to the artistic bohemia of nineteenth-century fin de siècle Paris" (Greene 2017, 123). Both Smith and Hell "were involved in close relationships with the French multimedia artist Lizzy Mercier Descloux who was living and working in New York during the mid-1970s" (Goldman 2019; Hell 2013).

Both French and British punks "tended to view established social conventions" and institutions "as hypocritical obfuscations obscuring the brutality of real life," and "the original British punk scene both reflected and mocked the disintegration of British society in the late 1970s" (Dunn 2011, 28). Unemployment was high in the United Kingdom of the 1970s, and there was little class mobility. Also, the United Kingdom never experienced the postwar prosperity of the United States in the 1950s and 1960s, and some British cities still had rubble from buildings that had been bombed out during the war. American punks were not terribly different from their British and French counterparts. American society had also been changing since World War II. The civil rights movement, the anti-war movement, second-wave feminism, and the Stonewall riots challenged American institutions that subordinated nonwhites, women, and gays and lesbians and sent young men to die in Korea and Vietnam. Meanwhile, runaway inflation in the 1970s made the cost of living so expensive that families started to need two adult breadwinners. American youth were also fed up with hippie-style liberalism, which they saw as ineffective in bringing about any meaningful social change, and like their British counterparts, they felt alienated from the world, as consumer capitalism had appropriated authentic connections between people and repackaged them as mass culture.

Punk has been described as a genre that reclaimed what rock and roll was supposed to be about, such as listeners having serious emotional connections to their favorite artists and bands. The earliest punks grew up "with bands like the Beatles, the Who, and the Rolling Stones," who "fostered the now nearly antiquated idea that rock & roll was an intrinsic part of a young person's soul, an engine of social change and not just a consumer commodity" (Azerrad 2001, 7). That connection has been diluted "by pop's lowest common denominator approach"—where the music that is produced appeals to the broadest possible audience—as well as "impersonal stadium concerts and the unreality of MTV" (Azerrad 2001, 10).

> In 1976, two-thirds of the British record market was shared between six major transnational companies, and these companies had major overseas branches as well with licensing arrangements which would ensure access to every market of significance in the Western and Third Worlds. (Laing 2015, 9)

Big corporate music created "the classic transnational sound of the 1970s" exemplified by "the Swedish group Abba" (Laing 2015, 10). Another product of big corporate music was progressive rock, a genre that "emphasized the primacy of recorded music over live performance" and "equated musical excellence with a meticulous (and time-consuming, hence expensive) attention to detail in, and maximum use of the technical resources of the recording studio" (Laing 2015, 12). Punks looked to early rock and roll as well as the more contemporary pub rock scene for inspiration to create music that countered the alienation they experienced. Pubs were "one type of location in the mid-1970s where something like 'grass roots' might be discovered" with pub rock bands (Laing 2015, 16). Pub rock bands went "against the grain of contemporary rock" by looking to the past for inspiration in playing live music in small venues where audiences were more than passive consumers of music along the arena rock model. "Pub rock bands played music from, or inspired by, the golden age of rhythm and blues and rock 'n' roll" (Laing 2015, 17). The first punk bands used the dynamic performances of pub bands as a model to make music that disrupted the corporate music model of fans as passive consumers of music. Punk transformed audiences into "agents of cultural production" (Dunn 2011, 28–29). This transformation was brought about by artists who made music that was relentlessly anti-commercial by conventional measures, by developing alternatives to the big corporate music business, and by questioning the rock star model of artist as extraordinary genius who is distant from the common people who constitute his or her fans.

Punk rock songs and band names were the antithesis of mainstream music as well as pub rock. Pub rock was a reaction against progressive rock and the transnational sound, with its return to the basics of rock and roll and emphasis on live performances. However, both mainstream and pub rock songs stuck to "the well-established themes of love, dance," and "hard luck" (Laing 2015, 39). Because the word *punk* had previously been used to describe categories of people considered to be "rotten" and "worthless" in the eyes of mainstream society, punk bands looked "for qualities, objects, and activities" that were "despicable or disgusting and used them as band names as well as subject matter for their songs" (Laing 2015, 63). Punk band names included colloquial references to genitals or sex (e.g., Sex Pistols, Shonen Knife (boy knife), the Slits, the Muffs, Pussy Riot, Hole, Butthole Surfers, the Circle Jerks, Dicks); bodily functions or purification (e.g., Red Aunts, the Breeders, the Cramps, Germs, Rancid, the Hives, Garbage); drugs, alcohol, and dangerous substances (e.g., Strung Out, Everclear, My Chemical Romance, Agent Orange, Green Day); or outsiders, monsters, and death (e.g., Misfits, Pennywise, Leatherface, Dead Boys, Death). Musicians also took stage names that suggested they were despicable or disgusting, including Johnny Rotten and Sid Vicious of the Sex Pistols and Mojo Nixon, or that emphasized the artificial, such as Poly Styrene of the X-Ray Spex. Songs also followed this model: for example, the Dead Kennedys' "Too Drunk to F[—]" and "Nazi Punks F[—] Off"; L7's "Shitlist"; Bad Religion's "Infected"; Pansy Division's "Homo Christmas"; Jim Carroll's "People Who Died"; Against Me!'s "Unprotected Sex with Multiple Partners"; Dream Wife's "F[—] You Up," which they abbreviated to "FUU"; the Cramps' "Strychnine"; Pennywise's "F[—] Authority"; Hole's "Teenage Whore"; the Circle Jerks' "World Up My Ass"; and the Ramones' "I Wanna Be Sedated," to name a few.

Punk songs deconstructed and disrupted the paradigm of cis-het romantic love that is the subject of so many pop songs with lyrics of sexuality, "where the sexual is given precedence over the sentimental," and describe "lust, obsession, or disgust" as well as lyrics about nonheterosexual love (Laing 2015, 40). The Buzzcocks' "Ever Fallen in Love," written by lead singer Pete Shelley, who was bisexual, used gender-neutral pronouns to thwart attempts to make the song exclusively about heterosexual love. Other Buzzcocks songs that were about sex rather than love include "Orgasm Addict" and "What Do I Get?" Other songs attacked revered institutions such as the monarchy and organized religion (e.g., the Sex Pistols' "God Save the Queen," Bad Religion's "American Jesus") or any kind of government (e.g., the Sex Pistols' "Anarchy in the UK," the Dead Kennedys' "California Über Alles"), that remembered fallen revolutionaries (e.g., the Clash's "Spanish Bombs," which is about the soldiers who fought against fascism in Spain), or that called out racism, sexism, homophobia, or capitalism and consumerism, such as the Clash's "Guns of Brixton," about the 1981 riots in that city in response to the police's harassment of Black youth; L7's "Pretend We're Dead," about the cost of ignoring judicial assaults on women's reproductive freedom; Pansy Division's "That's So Gay," which calls out people who use this phrase; and Bad Religion's "21st Century Digital Boy," about a kid who "doesn't know how to live" but "has a lot of toys." The language used in many of these songs "drew on discourses which not only had been previously absent from popular song, but which had been excluded from the mainstream media discourse of society as a whole," such as the areas of pornography and obscenity (Laing 2015, 95).

"Since one of punk rock's avowed aims was disruption," most songs were not "in the playlists for the mainstream daytime programming," and any that got airplay at all were "relegated to the various 'specialist' rock programmes in the evenings or on weekends" (Laing 2015, 48). In the 1970s, radio's distancing of itself from punk rock "was reinforced by the 'moral panic' surrounding the music, its exponents and their audiences following the Bill Grundy incident in December of 1976" (Laing 2015, 48) in the United Kingdom, when Sid Vicious swore at the *Today* show host on live television during a peak viewing time.

Punk is subversive of existing hierarchal power structures both through overtly political music (e.g., the Clash, Bikini Kill, Pussy Riot, the Raincoats, Bad Religion, War on Women, the Slits, L7, X-Ray Spex) and through songs that challenge the nature of art and reality. For example, punk covers of others' work either repurpose existing music by performing it with irony (see the entire oeuvre of the super group Me First and the Gimmie Gimmies, who punkify very nonpunk songs, as well as Sid Vicious's version of Frank Sinatra's "My Way") or without (such as Shonen Knife's covers of the Ramones' music—the Japanese band so admires the New York City punk outfit that they have also been known as Osaka Ramones). As well, punks combine and repurpose other musical traditions and genres, such as the Celtic punk bands the Pogues, Flogging Molly, and the Dropkick Murphys, who play punk versions of older Irish music; gypsy and klezmer punk bands, who use Eastern European musical traditions as the foundation of their work; and the Angry Snowmen, who only play punk covers of Christmas music. The simplicity of most punk songs also encourages audiences to sing along with the band, which spreads infectious joy.

Another way that punk was different from previous musical genres and trends was that it showed people how to seize the "resources for agency and political expression" (Dunn 2011, 29). Punk's DIY ethos led to the development of alternative models of the music business, proving that "you could make a better connection with your audience without" a "big corporation to fund you, or even verify that you were any good" (Azerrad 2001, 10). Punks formed their own independent labels to promote their music without having to "heed the imperative of the hit parade" (Laing 2015, 19). Punk owed a debt to pub rock for this innovation; pub rock bands produced "their own discs, to be sold primarily at their own live performances" (Laing 2015, 20). However, the record labels of the punk era "were clearly distinguished from those earlier independents by their numbers, their size and their geographical locations. A catalogue of small labels published by *ZigZag* magazine in 1978 listed 120 companies with a repertoire of punk material, mostly with just a handful of titles and nearly all based outside London" (Laing 2015, 27). Moreover, "many of these labels were the vinyl equivalent to the fanzines which multiplied in the wake of *Sniffin' Glue*" (Laing 2015, 27). "By dispensing with the need for expensive productions, promotional staff and the other overheads of the chart-oriented companies," small record labels "could work to 'break-even' figures which could be as low as 2,000 copies for a single" (Laing 2015, 19). The California hardcore band Minutemen described their alternative model of promoting their own music as "jamming econo" (Azerrad 2001, 11). But jamming econo was more than just promoting your own music on a shoestring budget. Jamming econo allowed people to take charge of their own existence by changing their buying and working habits so that they were "beholden only to [themselves] and the values and people [they] respected" (Azerrad 2001, 11). As the Minutemen said in their song "History Lesson Part 2," "our band could be your life."

"Because punk also challenged the rock star model of the artist," punks weren't "consumers of the mass media," but instead, "agents of cultural production" (Dunn 2011, 28–29). Punk was formed in opposition to arena rock, which contrasted the superstars with their banks of technology on stage against the audience who had nothing but expensively acquired ticket stubs. "One effect of the earliest punk bands was to turn listeners into players" (Laing 2015, 103). Folk punk musician Billy Bragg tweeted that "the best think about punk was that anyone could get up and sing" (Bragg 2018). Bragg's statement shows how punk democratized art, in that the artist is someone who has something to say rather than someone who is extraordinarily talented. Because "punk meant an attitude towards musical performance which emphasized directness and repetition (to use more than three chords was self-indulgence) at the expense of technical virtuosity," artists did not have to be professional musicians to be in a band (Laing 2015, 22). In fact, many punks learned as they went along. For example, the members of the Runaways and Bikini Kill developed their musicianship as they developed their bands.

Punk audiences became active participants at shows both via conventional means, such as dancing, and unconventional ones, such as gobbing, or spitting, on each other. "Dancing had been one way of being active for an audience, and punk fans surging to the front of an auditorium to pogo responded in the same way as teds jiving in the aisles of the 1950s" (Laing 2015, 104). As well, punk bands encouraged participation at their shows through "provocation and goading" audience members, particularly through gobbing on them. Gobbing "was one ritual indulged in by both musician and audience: they spat at, and often on, each other" as a perverse gesture of intimacy (Laing 2015, 107).

Because the punk movement transformed how fans interacted with the music they loved, from the start, it was bigger than just music. The punk movement encouraged other types of artistic production as well. Punks self-published zines via mimeograph and Xerox machines and distributed them at shows, clubs, and record stores to communicate with like-minded people.

> Punk rock was the first musical genre to spawn fanzines in any significant numbers. The occasional surveys in the orthodox music press suggested that during 1977–78 there may have been over 50 appearing in all parts of Britain. As well as initiating the trend, [the zine] *Sniffin' Glue* played a pivotal role in establishing punk's self-image. . . . the cover of *Sniffin' Glue* 1 announced itself to be "for punks." It was the first time the audience rather than the music had been defined that way. (Laing 2015, 25)

Other punks created, accidentally or on purpose, their own fashion aesthetic: some punks wore safety pins in their clothing as a practical way to mend rips, and others wore fetish wear to shock bourgeois sensibilities or dyed their hair colors not found in nature as a way of demonstrating that they had no future in a world that offered only dead-end menial jobs that paid starvation wages—why bother looking presentable for a potential employer and committing to forty hours of soulless labor every week when you could just as easily squat in abandoned buildings and find (or shoplift) what you needed to live? Others, like designer Vivienne Westwood, created clothing that was a bricolage of clashing colors and styles. The "organizing principles" of this look "were those of binding and tearing. Far away from the flowing, loose clothes of the hippie era, nearly everything male and literally everything female was tight, holding in the body. At one level punk was joining a trend of the 1970s to bring 'above ground' the imagery of the machinery of 'bondage' and sadomasochism" (Laing 2015, 118). Fashion theorist Dick Hebdige characterized the punk look as what punk fashion designer Vivienne Westwood "called 'confrontation dressing' . . . [where] the rupture between 'natural' and constructed context was clearly visible. . . . The perverse and the abnormal were valued intrinsically . . . and placed on the street where they retained their forbidden connotations" (Hebdige 1979, 107–108).

Female performers and fans challenged orthodox rock practice in the male-dominated music business in three ways. They could dress like one of the guys, such as Gaye Advert (of the Adverts), who "opted for the leather jacket, wet-look trousers, and dog-collar style shared with male musicians" (Laing 2015, 115). Some wore an eclectic mix of clothing made from unlikely materials (such as Poly Styrene's dress made from a black tablecloth, which she topped with a battle helmet and wore with kitten heels) and used garish "cartoon" colors, such as fluorescent colors, that "cut against the colour coding for 'sexy' women performers" (Laing 2015, 115), or they confronted the idea of women as sex objects by wearing fetish wear, fishnets, see-through tops, miniskirts, stilettos with exaggerated heels, garter belts, and corsets. Punk visual artists, such as Banksy, make and share their work in public spaces without permission, or they set up spaces themselves, such as Reko Muse, the feminist art gallery that Kathleen Hanna of Bikini Kill created when her and a friend's photographs were taken down from an exhibit at Evergreen State University, where they were attending art school.

Most punks are left-leaning. Bands such as Pussy Riot, the Clash, Bikini Kill, Crass, Fugazi, Dropkick Murphys, Green Day, Death, L7, Against Me!, Pansy Division, the Slits, Gogol Bordello, and Bad Religion use their music to advocate for laborers and immigrants and against imperialism, fascism, racism, sexism, homophobia, and transphobia. Some band members are registered Democrats (e.g., Dropkick Murphys, Green Day), while others are affiliated with the Green or Libertarian parties (e.g., Jello Biafra of the Dead Kennedys). "Fat Mike" Burkett of

NOFX founded PunkVoter in the wake of the 2000 presidential election, whose winner had to be decided by the U.S. Supreme Court; the Clash headed the Rock against Racism events in London; L7 started the Rock for Choice series of concerts and were named Feminists of the Year by the Feminist Majority; and members of Pussy Riot spent two years in jail for their musical activism against Vladimir Putin's repressive regime. A small number of punk bands are politically conservative or even reactionary, such as Nazi and white supremacist punks. Johnny Ramone was a staunch Republican, which was a point of contention between him and his bandmates, particularly Joey Ramone. When the Ramones were inducted into the Rock and Roll Hall of Fame in 2002, Johnny said from the podium, "God bless President Bush, and God bless America." As well, "in late-1970s Britain, as the Clash were fronting Rock Against Racism, Oi! bands such as Skrewdriver were backing the National Front" (Lynskey 2004, "Meet the Pro-Bush Punks").

Today, punk is over forty years old. Many Year Zero bands have had their major works reissued by their labels in honor of their tenth, twentieth, thirtieth, and fortieth anniversaries. Several of these bands are also still touring and even making new music. But most importantly, punk is not dead. The Year Zero bands inspired new generations of punks, who have in turn inspired their own new generations of punks. The Raincoats, for example, inspired Kathleen Hanna and Toby Vail of the riot grrrl band Bikini Kill. In 2019, Vail and Hanna reunited with their old bandmates and played to sold-out shows in New York and Los Angeles, where their old fans came to their concerts with their children, who had grown up hearing Bikini Kill's music and could sing along. There are even children's books about punk rock, such as Eric Morse and Anny Yi's beautifully illustrated *What Is Punk?* and Jarrett J. Krosoczka's *Punk Farm* books, about a group of barnyard animals who form a band and go on tour.

Much of the punk aesthetic has also gone mainstream in the United States and Europe. When punks first started piercing themselves with safety pins and dying their hair with bold, unnatural colors and styling it in dramatic hairdos, like mohawks, they were so counterculture and shocking that they often could not find work until they changed their appearance. That is much different than how bright hair colors, piercing, and tattoos are perceived today, as those body modifications are entirely mainstream. Even doctors and lawyers are coloring their hair and getting tattoos.

Punk's longevity is due to how this genre continues to be relevant today. Punk has emboldened people to think of themselves as artists, and the internet has facilitated the ability to share songs and videos with like-minded people. Today, anyone with a cell phone can shoot a professional-looking video and record and edit sound with even the most basic computer. New punks also continue the genre's tradition of political activism. The riot grrrl band L7 started the Rock for Choice series of concerts. More recently, War on Women's second studio album, *Capture the Flag*, comes with a reading list of material about American imperialism and warmongering and how women's reproductive rights are being taken away. Fat Mike, of the hardcore band NOFX, started PunkVoter in 2002 to get young people registered to vote to lay the groundwork for regime change after George W. Bush sent American troops to war in Iraq after 9/11 based on faulty intelligence that Saddam Hussein had weapons of mass destruction and was connected with al-Qaeda. X played the first Farm Aid benefit concert in 1985. And Black Flag reunited in 2013 to play a benefit concert for cats.

Of course, because punk is over forty years old, much of it has now been commercially successful. Green Day, the Offspring, Against Me!, and Bad Religion, for example, were derided as sellouts for their commercial success in a 2015 article in *Noisey* (Ozzi), while older punk bands, such as the Ramones and the Raincoats, have developed wider followings long after their heydays as new generations of fans discover their music. Music sharing sites and streaming platforms such as Spotify, iTunes, and Pandora make it easier for fans to access the music of older bands who were never chart-topping artists.

Corporate conglomerates have also cashed in on punk by acquiring logos, names, and trademarks, which they repackage and sell to people who want to be edgy. For example, the retail chain Hot Topic, which specializes in marketing what they brand as "counterculture" clothing, sells "vintage" Ramone T-shirts to tweens and teens. Terminal C in Newark's Liberty International Airport sports CBGB LAB (Lounge and Bar) where travelers can drink a $20 craft beer and have a bowl of what must be Hilly Kristal's original (and terrible) recipe chili while listening to a low-volume soundtrack of acts that played at the famous Bowery punk club. CBGB LAB is certainly cleaner than CGBG ever was—the facility's walls are covered in graffiti wallpaper instead of actual graffiti. This was *Noisey*'s Eugenia Williamson's experience when she visited CBGB in 2016, as well as mine in 2019—the chili was so bad that I had to send it back. Or, if you prefer, you can have a $16 hamburger in Black Flag's old practice space (Koester 2013).

Punk festivals such as Warped Tour, Riot Fest, and Lollapalooza are also big business. The Warped Tour, for example, an annual event with free admission, lasted for twenty-five years. The tour shut down in 2018 when the festival's primary sponsor, Vans, pulled out in 2018 (Giordano 2018). The multiday punk and alternative rock Riot Fest has been held in Chicago every year since 2005. The traveling festival Lollapalooza was started in 1991 by the band Jane's Addiction. It continued until 1997 and was later revived in 2003. Since 2005, Lollapalooza has been taking place in Chicago's Grant Park. Satellite Lollapalooza festivals have also been held in Chile, Brazil, Argentina, Germany, and France since 2011.

Punk's longevity has transformed the meaning of the word *punk*. When Marc Zermeti first coined the word back in 1976, it was most often used to describe young people who are hoodlums or ruffians. Today, the term applies to things that are aggressively unconventional. Punk has endured and remained relevant throughout the years because it offers people an alternative to the homogenizing effects of global capitalism.

CHAPTER 2

Must-Hear Music

AGAINST ME! *TRANSGENDER DYSPHORIA BLUES*

Against Me! is best known for its anarchist and activist music, such as "Turn Those Clapping Hands into Angry Balled Fists," "I Was a Teenage Anarchist," and the anti-war "White People for Peace." It is also known because frontwoman Laura Jane Grace (née Thomas James Gabel) came out as transgender woman in a 2012 *Rolling Stone* interview, "Tom Gabel of Against Me! Comes Out as Transgender." Grace started Against Me! in 1997 in Gainesville, Florida. The band's name references Grace's difficult adolescence, when she was bullied in high school because she was one of the few punk kids and felt that the whole world was against her (AOL Originals 2014). Grace found solace in "anarchist punk rock and activist punk rock" because of its strongly feminist, anti-racist, and anti-homo- and transphobic stance (Gross 2017). The band's highest-charting album to date, *Transgender Dysphoria Blues*, was released in 2014, two years after Grace's coming-out *Rolling Stone* interview. Before her announcement, "Against Me! was a well-liked, top-of-the-middle-tier punk band that survived a brief flirtation with major-label stardom" (Caramanica 2014), and their music "only addressed gender issues in passing" (Thompson 2014). Today, "Grace is now almost certainly the highest-profile musician to transition, and her new album is part manifesto, part open letter to fans, her wife, and her bandmates" (Stewart 2014).

Although punk has always been a genre that challenges gender norms, *Transgender Dysphoria Blues* was unprecedented in how it narrated the difficulties of being transgender. Reviewer Petra Davis describes *Transgender Dysphoria Blues* as "a tough listen" because Grace openly describes her experiences before and during transition, which included daily threats of "rejection, humiliation, and violence" from people who felt threatened by the existence of trans people (2014). However, not everything on *Transgender Dysphoria Blues* is autobiographical: some songs recount the desperate experiences of other trans people, who self-harm, self-medicate with drugs and alcohol, and even resort to suicide to cope both with being rejected and brutalized by others and feeling that their bodies contradict their gender identities. Jon Caramanica remarks that the most shocking thing about *Transgender Dysphoria Blues* is not its content "but its polish. In places, it recalls far more anemically minded punk bands like the Gaslight Anthem, or even Green Day" (2014).

The album's first track, the anthem "True Trans Soul Rebel," indicates that *Gender Dysphoria Blues* is "a coming out record, first and foremost" (Thompson 2014). The song sums up what it is to be trans in a world where those who do not conform to binary gender roles are shunned, discriminated against, and even killed; they are "yet to be born" as their true selves, "but already dead." It describes the emotional turmoil experienced by trans people because they do not conform to binary gender roles, while offering the possibility that "it gets better" through its positioning on the album. In a 2014 interview, Grace remarked, "You become more brave about presenting femme" as you transition, "but you're still closeted, so you have nowhere to go" (Edwards 2014).

"Unconditional Love," "Drinking with the Jocks," "Osama bin Laden as Crucified Christ," and "Paralytic States" detail the multiple levels of violence experienced by trans people. The trans woman who is drinking with the jocks wishes that she "were just like them" in their ability to be comfortable with their own gender identities. "Drinking with the Jocks" emphasizes the performative nature of gender: the speaker is "winging my dick in my hands" and "laughing at the faggots," that is, any man that is perceived to have strayed from this narrow masculine paradigm. For the singer, fitting in with the boys is a type of self-inflicted violence in how she had to assume an identity that is repugnant to her sense of herself. "Unconditional Love," "Osama bin Laden as Crucified Christ," and "Paralytic States" chronicle the self-loathing that is the result of societal messages that people who do not conform to binary gender norms should not exist. "Even if your love was unconditional, it still wouldn't be enough to save me," the singer declares in "Unconditional Love" to describe her alienation.

"Osama bin Laden as the Crucified Christ" compares the violence against transgender people who will not conform to others expectations about their gender to the violence experienced by others due to their beliefs, including Christ, bin Laden, and Benito Mussolini and his girlfriend, Clara Petacci, who are referred to in the chorus: "You're gonna hang like Benito from the Esso rafters / Hang like Clara with her skull caved in." The comparisons to Mussolini and bin Laden are imperfect similes though, as neither are sympathetic figures. The transgender sex worker in "Paralytic States" commits the ultimate violence against herself when she cuts her wrists in a hotel bathroom, where she bleeds out, suffering the fate of many trans people, who are nearly ten times more likely to commit suicide than the general population—approximately 41 percent compared to 4.6 percent of the overall population in the United States (Haas et al. 2014).

Other songs are vignettes of life after Grace came out to the world as trans. In "FUCKMYLIFE666," Grace recounts her fears about the stability of her relationship with her wife, to whom she was married when she was Tom Gabel. "Black Me Out" explains Grace's strategy for dealing with those who will never accept that she is trans—she cuts these people out of her life. It is a fitting final track to the album, a coda to "True Trans Soul Rebel." In forswearing people who will never accept her, Grace is claiming her right to be herself. "Dead Friend" and "Two Coffins" are the two songs on *Transgender Dysphoria Blues* that are not about trans people. "Dead Friend" remembers Grace's friend Pope (John Paul Allison), who committed suicide when he was twenty-six, and "Two Coffins," written for Grace's daughter, contemplates the impermanence of life.

Transgender Dysphoria Blues was critically acclaimed as a groundbreaking album. It was ranked 109th on NPR's list of "The 150 Greatest Albums Made by Women" and described by reviewer Sarah Handel as "a milestone moment of a trans woman declaring her identity and articulating the highs and lows of her story" (2017). *Transgender Dysphoria Blues* made the lists of top albums of 2014 compiled by major music publications, including *Rolling Stone*'s "50 Best Albums of 2014" (15th), *SPIN*'s "The 50 Best Albums of 2014" (38th), *TIME*'s "Top 10 Best Albums of 2014" (4th), *PopMatters*' "The Best Albums of 2014" (6th), Noisey's "Top 25 Albums of 2014" (2nd), *Consequence of Sound*'s "Top 50 Albums of 2014" (6th), and "American Songwriter's Top 50 Albums of 2014" (20th).

ALICE BAG: *ALICE BAG*

Alice Bag (Alicia Armendariz) has been a notable figure of the Los Angeles punk scene since the 1977, when punk first came to her hometown. She was a founding member of the Latinx punk band the Bags

(1977–1980), which played the same venues as the Germs and the Runaways, and the band appears in Penelope Spheeris's documentary of the Los Angeles punk scene, *The Decline of Western Civilization*. Unlike the Germs, however, the Bags did not catch the interest of a record label who would record and distribute an album of their work to create a tangible artifact and solidify their reputation. During their brief time together, the Bags released only one single (though their collected works are now available on the 2003 album *All Bagged Up*). So it has taken nearly forty years for Bag to release a debut album. *Alice Bag* is a feminist analysis of the present day from the perspective of an older, queer woman of color.

Because the early Los Angeles punk scene was initially welcoming to women and people of color, Bag was inspired to form her own band with Patricia Rainone (later Pat Bag), who she met at an audition for a band that was to be manager Kim Fowley's next project after the Runaways fired him as their manager. Alice and Pat instead formed their own band, the Bags, taking the group's name and their noms de guerre from a gimmick they used during early performances, where they went on stage with brown grocery bags over their heads. Alice and Pat soon abandoned that practice after Darby Crash, the Germs' front man, ran up on stage and ripped the bags from their heads, but they kept the names. Alice (vocals) and Pat (bass) were joined by Craig Lee and Rob Ritter on guitar and Terry Graham on drums for their first gig at the Masque (Los Angeles) in 1977. The Bags' "live shows soon became legendary. The concerts were riotous affairs including altercations with celebrities" ("The Bags" 2007), and the band appears in punk documentary *The Decline of Western Civilization*. However, they are billed in *Decline* as the Alice Bag Band, as Pat Bag (Patricia Rainone) had left the band before this performance, taking the original band name that she had trademarked with her. But before *Decline* was released, the Bags had, in part, broken up because the Los Angeles punk scene was quickly being taken over by white suburban men who made the environment very unwelcoming for women and people of color. After the Bags disbanded, Bag "took a break from performing," but she was "always creating" (Agacki 2018). Bag and some of her friends formed the band Stay at Home Bomb, "a play on '50s housewife mom clichés" (Agacki 2018), and she has written three books to date.

Bag's debut album, *Alice Bag* (2016), is her most powerful work so far, "an amalgamation of stories and sounds from its creator's life" (Moreland 2016) that takes on a wide range of subjects, including domestic violence, GMOs, immigration, rape culture, lookism, homophobia, and the education-industrial complex. Bags describes her musical style as "punkchera," a combination of punk and the ranchera music that she grew up with ("Alice Bag" 2020). The album's first track, "Little Hypocrite," is a solid piece of rock that encourages the listener to "stop pretending," advice that applies to the other subjects in her songs, who are not so much pretending to be good but instead deeply programmed to behave in ways that are not in their own interests.

"He's So Sorry" mimics the musical style of girl groups from the 1960s (e.g., the Shirelles), including a sing-along chorus punctuated by castanets and a Phil Spector–like wall of sound. However, the subject of "He's So Sorry" is not a brokenhearted woman struggling to forgive her lover's perfidy, but a woman in an abusive relationship who is trapped by her dangerous ideas about romantic love as much as she is by her partner's violence. Bag's lyrics, sung in this girl group style, underscore how the conventions of heteronormative romance normalize the abuser's behavior just as he hits her: "Why do you push him away? / You know you want him to stay." The final scene video for "He's So Sorry" drives home what happens to women if they cannot get away from abusive partners—Bag and her bandmates croon the last chorus at the woman's grave after her lover has murdered her.

The ballad "Suburban Home" also examines how the conventions of heteronormative romance trap women in an "us where I used to be." In "No Means No," a date rapist has the meaning of this phrase explained to him by the female judge who rejects his pleas for leniency. Bag advises the younger subject of "Modern Day Virgin Sacrifice" to "look beyond the mirror" and "recognize [her] perfection." "Programmed" is derived from Bag's experiences as a student and a teacher, whose understanding of pedagogy is informed by theorist Paolo Freire, who views modern educational practices as suppressing critical thinking skills in favor of blind obedience to authority. Bag refuses her schooling, which taught to "color in the lines" and "spit back all their lies." The farmer in "Poisoned Seed" would rather "be up to his [neck] in weeds" rather than "water the poisoned seed," GMO crops that are genetically modified to resist broad-spectrum herbicides that are sprayed on the field to kill out competing plants. Using these seeds encourages agricultural practices that poison the ecosystem in which they are grown by killing off biodiversity.

In "The Touch I Crave," Bag responds to a homophobic critic who tells her that she is sinning when she does "what feels right." "Inesperado Adiós" ("Unexpected Goodbye") reflects the cruelty of the United States' current immigration policies. The song is based on Bag's experience helping a student's family get his father out of an immigration detention center (Moreland 2016). Bag's choice to sing "Inesperado

Adiós" in Spanish reflects that there are some situations that cannot be effectively translated: American whites have not experienced the horror of coming home one day to find a family member has been picked up by immigration officials to be deported.

Bag continues to record, tour, and write today. Her follow-up album, *Blueprint* (2018), has an impressive list of guest backup vocalists, including Spanish singer Martin Sorrondeguy of the queercore groups Los Crudos and Limp Wrist, Mexican American musician Lysa Flores, and Chilean American singer and poet Francisca Valenzuela on "Turn It Up" and Kathleen Hanna of Bikini Kill and Allison Wolfe of Bratmobile on "77," the number of cents that women earn in comparison to their male peers. However, *Blueprint* primarily consists of "upbeat rock and ambling ballads," although "77" and "Turn It Up" stand out as punk songs ("Alice Bag" 2020). Kathleen Hanna and Allison Wolfe appear with Bag in the video for "77," which they perform as a parody of the 1980 movie *9 to 5*, a comedy about female clerical staff being mistreated by their sexist boss. Setting the video in 1980 serves to remind viewers that the wage gap is not just a thing of the past. Bag also opened for Bikini Kill on their 2019 reunion tour. She has published an autobiography (*Violence Girl: East L.A. Rage to Hollywood Stage, a Chicana Punk Story*, 2011) and a memoir of her experiences in Nicaragua after the Sandinista revolution (*Pipe Bomb for the Soul*, 2015).

BAD BRAINS: *I AGAINST I*

Bad Brains is one of the inventors of hardcore punk. Bad Brains was formed in 1979 by guitarist Dr. Know (Gary Miller), vocalist H. R. (Paul D. Hudson), bassist Daryl Jenifer, and drummer Earl Hudson, H. R.'s brother. One of the few all-Black punk acts (in 1979 and today), the Washington, DC, band did not exhibit the "snotty strain of white male anger and discontent" of their peers (Aron 2018). Rather, Bad Brains' music, as described by Jenifer, is "the thinking man's punk" because it encourages "peace and love and positive mental attitude," a tenet of Rastafarianism that helps believers achieve happiness through becoming closer to Jah (Kirby 2015).

Bad Brains combines metal, punk, funk, and reggae to create music that is so "inherently complex" that it demands its audience's attention (Pickard 2016). The complex rhythms were derived from the band members' experience as the jazz-fusion combo Mind Power (1976–1979). The band members switched from playing jazz to punk after Jenifer introduced his bandmates to the music of the Dickies, Dead Boys, and the Sex Pistols (Kirby 2015); they were impressed with the "atypical progressions and feral movements" (Pickard 2016). Mind Power became Bad Brains in honor of the Ramones' song "Bad Brain."

The 1986 album *I Against I* has been described as "the band's first fully mature work" because of how it combines the group's diverse influences (Anderson n.d., "Bad Brains"). *I Against I* is a Rastafarian *Pilgrim's Progress* in how its songs ask and answer the questions of a spiritual pilgrim. The album's title track is a blistering condemnation of violence against other humans, a theme the band returns to in "Hired Gun," which is about a gangster who will never know peace because he is eternally on the run from the law. "House of Suffering" asks and answers the question, "How can there be a god when the world is full of suffering?": Jah's love is "inside the hearts of your own children." The House of Suffering is a human-made creation that humans can transcend with the realization that grace is stronger than doom. The newly enlightened subject of "House of Suffering" considers how he can use Positive Mental Attitude to enlighten others in "Re-Ignition." This project is expanded in "Let Me Help," which enjoins the listener to "rejuvenate more integrity. Universal all live as one" so to edify others. The love song "Sacred Love" exalts spiritual unions over physical ones: because "our love" is "sacred," the speaker tells his beloved to not "lust off [his] body" or "come to [him] as a whore" so that Jah will bless them the next day. *I Against I* appropriately concludes with a track that reminds listeners of the fate that awaits those who fail to "choose a divine light," "Return to Heaven."

Although Bad Brains' music expresses the Rastafarian belief in peace and love, the band's reputation for attracting rowdy fans to their shows soon got them shut out of DC-area clubs by owners who did not want their venues destroyed (an experience they recount in the song "Banned in DC"). As a result, Bad Brains relocated to New York City to find gigs, and they performed several times at CBGB. But in New York and on the road, the band continued to attract raucous crowds wherever they went. Musician Dave Harbour recalls a 1985 Bad Brains' performance in in Baton Rouge, Louisiana. The audience was filled with skinheads and fraternity boys whose moshing and fighting became indistinguishable once Bad Brains took the stage. After trying to eject some of the troublemakers from the venue, security "quickly realized they were outnumbered and left" (Harbour 2018).

Bad Brains' career has been interrupted several times by members' personnel problems. H. R. was arrested on a marijuana charge while the band was in the middle of recording *I Against I*, so his vocals on "Sacred

Love" were recorded from jail. The band was also kept apart by artistic differences. On occasion, H. R. refused to play at scheduled concerts and attend practice sessions when he and his brother Earl wanted to play reggae but Dr. Know and Jenifer wanted to play hard rock. Between 2015 and 2016, Dr. Know was on life support after a heart attack and organ failure, and H. R. suffered from debilitating headaches. However, both have recovered sufficiently to play a few gigs, including a short fortieth anniversary set at Chicago's Riot Fest in 2017.

Bad Brains has been eligible for induction into the Rock and Roll Hall of Fame since 2007, and they were nominated in 2017. However, the selection committee ultimately decided that Yes, Electric Light Orchestra, and Pearl Jam were more worthy of induction, to the chagrin of the band's fans. Bad Brains is the subject of the documentary *Bad Brains: A Band in DC* (2012), and the documentary *Finding Joseph I* is based on Howie Abrams and James Lathos's oral history of H. R.'s life.

BAD RELIGION: *STRANGER THAN FICTION*

The hardcore punk band Bad Religion is best known for its fast-paced three-part harmonies and songs that cover subjects such as racism, human rights, contemporary politics, science, and the media. Greg Graffin (vocals), Brett Gurewitz (guitar), Jay Bentley (bass), and Jay Ziskrout (drums) formed Bad Religion in 1980 while they were in high school. Although the band still records and tours today, Graffin has been the only constant member. Bad Religion's name and cross-buster symbol represent its founders' antipathy toward any type of dogmatic thinking, including religious fundamentalism, blind patriotism, and consumerism. *Stranger than Fiction*, Bad Religion's eighth studio album (1994), exemplifies the band's iconoclasm and desire for spiritual and intellectual sustenance in a plastic world.

Most of the songs on *Stranger than Fiction* are bleak portraits of modern life. The young subject of their best-known song, "21st Century Digital Boy," does not know how to go about living but has no shortage of toys provided by his parents as compensation for their emotional neglect of their child. "Incomplete" continues in this vein: the young subject is "the butt of the worst joke in history" and has no direction in life. "Television" is a "gentle and understanding" big brother, the boy's "connection to the world outside" that assures him that things will be okay. The video for "21st Century Digital Boy" blends the themes of all three of these songs: an infant sits in thrall to the blue glow of a huge television, and the band occasionally breaks through the static on screen to communicate with him. Romantic love is just another version of codependency in "Infected," where the speaker is "afflicted" while his partner is "addicted."

"Leave Mine to Me" and "The Handshake" scorn convention and conformity because they are the master's tools to control the masses. The existential "Leave Mine to Me" retorts that "you create your own reality" to those who would judge the speaker for his unwillingness to conform to religious and social dogma. "The Handshake" questions a gesture that represents civility and respect in our culture as nothing substantive; participants in this ritual merely hide their "restrained passion, mistrust, and bigotry" to enable the continuation of a world where "there's no harmony just class and race." "Individual" and "Inner Logic" deconstruct the mechanics of power that have hijacked our free will. Individuals "can't choose anymore" because they "command exception and accept dichotomy" ("Individual"), the tools that are used by governments to sort and control their populations, as described by philosopher Michel Foucault. The "automatons with business suits clinging to black boxes" ("Inner Logic") who have been conditioned to ignore their own inner logic are typical examples of the individual who only has the illusion of free will. However, the world described in "Stranger than Fiction" is the most terrible of all. As the world explodes into an apocalyptic calamity, "the windows are watching" while "the streets all conspire and the lamppost can't stop crying." Ultimately, the narrator pans life as the worst tome he has ever read.

Yet the songs on *Stranger than Fiction* are not without hope for humanity. The sarcastic tone of "Incomplete," "Better Off Dead," and "21st Century Digital Boy" indicate that their jaded subjects have a limited perspective on the world that makes it difficult for them to see a way out of their current predicament. The speaker of "Better Off Dead" offers a sarcastic apology to a jaded listener who is disappointed in a world that is not always entertaining or convenient: "The next time I create the universe I'll make sure we communicate at length" to ensure that this subject is not burned by the sun or disappointed by the moon. The speakers of "Hooray for Me," "Slumber," and "Tiny Voices" have more mature existential perspectives. While the speaker of "Hooray for Me" may be "unrespectable, never sensible, maybe incredible," and "so damned irascible," he does what he likes and invites the listener to imagine small amounts of time wherein you do not have to do anything that does not suit you. The speaker of "Slumber" reassures a young listener that his life is "historically meaningful and spans a significant time"; what matters most are the consequences of his actions. Our inner logic that the automatons with black boxes are so good at ignoring resurfaces in "Tiny Voices," the "screams of forgotten victims and the cries of innocence," along with a plea to be recognized and given recompense that lives on in the unconscious mind to remind us of our humanity.

Stranger than Fiction yielded four singles, including a rerecorded version of "21st Century Digital Boy" (originally released on *Against the Grain*, 1990) and "Infected," which were in heavy rotation on MTV and radio. Today, "Incomplete," "The Handshake," "Stranger than Fiction," and "21st Century Digital Boy" "remain some of the best-loved songs in the band's extensive catalog." (Weingarten et al. 2017). *Stranger than Fiction* is the only Bad Religion album to go Gold in the United States, and it appears at No. 18 on *Rolling Stone*'s "List of 50 Greatest Pop-Punk Albums." To date, Bad Religion has released sixteen studio albums and several compilations, including one Christmas album (*Christmas Songs* 2013), and is still releasing new music and touring today. Their original fans now attend shows along with their children.

Bad Religion's most recent album, *Age of Unreason* (2019), addresses the political climate in the age of Trump. The 2018 single "The Kids Are Alt-Right" and its accompanying video contrast today's alt-right youth with the children of the 1960s who protested racism, the war in Vietnam, and sexism instead of whining about their perceived loss of white male privilege. The song's title references the Who's 1965 anthem "The Kids Are Alright" (*Blabbermouth.net* 2018).

BIKINI KILL: *PUSSY WHIPPED*

Bikini Kill is a feminist punk band from Olympia, Washington. The band is known for its hardcore feminist lyrics and activism. Their body of work is relatively small: only three studio albums and two compilations. However, some of their singles were produced by punk luminaries such as Ian MacKaye of Minor Threat and Fugazi and Joan Jett. Bikini Kill played an integral role in starting the underground feminist punk riot grrrl movement: their song "Rebel Girl" is the unofficial riot grrrl anthem.

Founded in 1990 by Kathleen Hanna (front woman and songwriter), Tobi Vail (drums), Billy Karren (guitar), and Kathi Wilcox (bass), Bikini Kill quickly developed a reputation for creating women-centric environments at their shows with their "girls to the front" policy. They asked that men in the audience move to the sides to allow women in the coveted space at the front of the stage. Some men still make it uncomfortable for women to attend punk shows by aggressively moshing in the audience and even groping women who are at the front of the stage, where they can interact with the band. Hanna has been described as "one of America's greatest living rock performers," with a singing style similar to the X-Ray Spex's Poly Styrene (Frere-Jones 2012).

Bikini Kill was indirectly founded on the advice of Kathy Acker, author of the cult classic novel *Blood and Guts in High School*. Hanna met Acker at a writers' workshop in 1990 while she was an art student at Evergreen State University and doing spoken word performances. Acker advised the young Hanna to instead start a band to communicate her ideas because "nobody goes to spoken word, nobody likes spoken word," and "there's more of a community for musicians than for writers" (Marcus 2014, 47). The band's name is a reference to the 1967 B-film *The Million Eyes of Sumuru*, in which an evil woman attempts to achieve world dominance with her army of brainwashed, bikini-clad women that she dispatches to kill her enemies. Vale said that she liked the phrase "bikini kill" because it "encapsulated the nexus of sexiness and violence" (Marcus 2014, 47). Bikini Kill's songs are about "issues central to Riot Grrrl such as rape, domestic abuse, women's health, sexuality . . . and female empowerment" (Dunn 2011, 35).

"Rebel Girl," the band's best-known song, celebrates women's relationships with one another as empowering. Like many Bikini Kill songs, "Rebel Girl" works by subverting audience expectations of genre. The song's opening lines prepare listeners for what would seem to be a catty takedown of "that girl" who "thinks she's the queen of the neighborhood" because she "holds her head up so high." But the next lines of "Rebel Girl" do not slut shame this woman for falling outside the boundaries of normative femininity. Instead, the singer wants to be the Rebel Girl's "best friend" because she admires her attitude. Devin Faraci describes the lyric "that girl she thinks she's the queen of the neighborhood / I've got news for you. She is!" as "one of the most exciting, immediate and electrifying declarations of sisterhood" ever, "a battle cry for togetherness and friendship" (2013).

But the singer's feelings for the Rebel Girl are deeper than those in most women's same-sex friendships. The line that discusses tasting the revolution in the girl's kiss implies that perhaps the singer and the Rebel Girl are lovers. But that oversimplification of their relationship is destroyed by the singer's response to imaginary others who say that the Rebel Girl is a lesbian. Hanna responds with an affirmation, completing the sentence in the next line when she says that the girl is her best friend. In the song's final lines, where Hanna declares that she loves the Rebel Girl as she would a sibling, she is defying societal pressures that undermine women's bonds with one another. The Rebel Girl is that strong girlfriend that every woman should have because her example inspires other women to hold their heads up high and be there for each other.

Although "Rebel Girl" was never a top-selling single, it came in at No. 27 on *Rolling Stone*'s list of "Most Excellent Songs of Every Year since 1967." "Rebel Girl" was released as an EP, on the LP *Pussy Whipped*, and a single in 1993 and was produced by Joan Jett, who is featured on guitar and backing vocals. It is also musically and thematically representative of Bikini Kill's body of work.

Other songs on *Pussy Whipped* similarly challenge patriarchy and promote sisterhood among women: "Blood One" and "Tell Me So" explore how language is used to subordinate women. "Your alphabet is spelled with my blood," screams Hanna in "Blood One," defying language that is used to shape reality and control women. In "Tell Me So," she instructs a man who is looking at her to "take out a piece of paper" and "write everything down" so that he can read it back and possibly hurt her. In "Sugar," she refuses to "play girl to your boy" anymore and mimic her partners' fantasies until he takes care of her sexual needs, and she rejects a man's pressure to have sex with him in "Star Bellied Boy." "Alien She" contrasts the singer with the woman that she is expected to be: the alien she who is her "Siamese twin" wants her "to put the pretty, pretty red lipstick on." "Lil Red" reimagines Little Red Riding Hood as a woman who can protect herself instead of being a victim. She has "ruby red lips, the better to suck you dry," and "long red nails, the better to scratch out your eyes."

During Bikini Kill's eight-year career (1990–1997), harassment occurred at their shows by men who resented their feminism and their "girls to the front" policy. These hecklers shouted obscenities and threw bottles and even chains at the band as a way of enforcing their masculine privilege (Brockes 2014). Hanna was known for answering back midshow to hecklers and would even "wade into the audience and physically remove" them from the venue if they were too disruptive (Brockes 2014).

The band left Olympia for Washington, DC, in 1992 to find a base of operations that was more receptive of their art. Kathi Wilcox described DC in the 1990s as having "activist-friendly punk scene" with audiences that "understood the band perfectly" (Richards 2012). DC's environment was a marked contrast to other places, where they played to audiences "that had never heard rock songs about rape, domestic violence, empowerment and equality" (Richards 2012). When Bikini Kill toured outside of DC, however, they were increasingly harassed by anti-feminist men in the audience. The mainstream media contributed to this escalation by painting Hanna as a two-dimensional character, falsely labeling her as a victim of sexual abuse or recounting that she had worked as a stripper to discredit the band's feminist message, so the band had to issue a media blackout in 1993 (O'Falt 2013). Hanna recounts that "people hated us—and it was really, really hard to be in that band" (Burbank 2015). Nevertheless, Bikini Kill persisted in performing because they "wanted to make sure other girls found out about feminism" and how it was relevant to their lives (Brockes 2014).

Eventually, the band members became too burned out to perform: "Fiercely committed to punk's do-it-yourself ethos, the band became a cipher with no support system. No manager. No booking agent. Not even a roadie" (Richards 2012). They also had to remove hecklers because the venues they played had little or no security to do the job for them. Bikini Kill officially disbanded in 1997. Hanna went on to start the female electronic punk band Le Tigre and, later, Julie Ruin, a band that Wilcox also joined.

Even though Bikini Kill disbanded, the number of fans continued to grow. Documentaries about the band, such as *It Changed My Life* (1993) and *The Punk Singer* (2013), about Hanna as a musician and activist, cemented Bikini Kill's reputation as an influential punk band. "Summoned back to life by the boiling heat of today's political moment" (Rupert 2019), Bikini Kill reunited in 2019 to play several sold-out all ages shows in Los Angeles and New York City and Riot Fest in Chicago, where fans brought their children, who had grown up singing the lyrics to the anthems "Rebel Girl" and "Double Dare Ya" (Alexander 2009).

BLACK FLAG: *DAMAGED*

The California punk band Black Flag was "America's first hardcore band" (Robbins 2018), and they contributed "significantly to the development of this genre in the 1980s" (Kholi 2015). They also "played an essential role in the development and popularization of American punk" (Robbins 2018) and were one of several hardcore bands to play math rock, a type of music that is "is so uneven and rhythmically complex, that it feels mathematical in nature" (Schnipper 2017). Black Flag's sound is "a ferocious, edgy, and ironic amalgam of underground aesthetics and gut-pounding metal" (Erlewine n.d., "Black Flag"), which they were playing approximately fifteen years before "the fusion of punk and metal became popular" (Erlewine n.d., "Black Flag").

Founded in 1977 by guitarist and songwriter Greg Ginn, Black Flag was quickly widely regarded as the hardest-working band in punk due to their daily practice schedule and ceaseless touring to every area of the United States. The touring in particular helped Black Flag quickly build up an underground fan base, many of whom started their own bands after Black Flag showed them how to use a "DIY system of networking [with] likeminded bands" to "travel the country and promote music without booking agents or big time record labels" (Shaw 2014). Black Flag went through numerous personnel changes, as so many members were unwilling to adhere to Ginn's strict practice schedules or unable to devote the time to touring across the country, though Ginn stayed with the band until their breakup in 1986. Henry Rollins, the band's most famous vocalist, helped shape Black Flag's hardcore sound: his "furious bellow and barely contained ferocity was the missing piece the band needed to become great" (Dougan n.d.). Rollins joined Black Flag spontaneously during a 1981 New York performance, when he jumped from the audience to the stage to sing with the band: he remained as their lead singer until 1985 (Erlewine n.d., "Black Flag"). Like Washington, DC's Bad Brains, Black Flag found themselves blacklisted by clubs in their hometown (Los Angeles) because their fans had a reputation for trashing venues.

Damaged (1981), Black Flag's first studio album, is the best example of them as a hardcore punk band. Under Ginn's leadership, Black Flag's music quickly evolved on subsequent albums from hardcore to something else entirely, causing fans to complain that each successive album was a new thing entirely. Although *Damaged* did not receive a warm critical reception at the time of its release, it is now considered one of the definitive recordings of punk rock. *Damaged* was named twenty-fifth on *Pitchfork*'s "Top 100 Albums of the 1980s" (Carr 2002). *Pitchfork*'s Matthew Schnipper reflected that was an anomaly when it emerged in 1981 because "*Damaged* was such a leap forward for punk, the only point of reference was miles behind" (2017). But today, "thirty-five years on, *Damaged* still sounds absolutely berserk" (Schnipper 2017). Ginn's songs that he wrote for *Damaged* "while suffused with the usual punk conceits (alienation, boredom, disenfranchisement), were capable of making one laugh out loud, especially the protoslacker satire 'TV Party.' Extremely controversial when it was released, *Damaged* endured the slings and arrows of outrageous criticism (some reacted as though this record alone would cause the fall of America's youth) to become and remain an important document of its time" (Dougan n.d.).

Damaged's first track, "Rise Above," is an anthem about haters of every variety: "jealous cowards [who] try to control" and distort what the singer and his cohort have to say, while laughing at them behind their backs, unable to stop them. In "Police Story," the Los Angeles Police Department takes "the rights away from all the kids" who are "fighting a war that [they] can't win." *Damaged*'s title refers to everyone who is harmed by this world, a place that seems inherently bad, as it is represented in "Padded Cell": a "paradise fraud" filled with "straightjacket minds in line to be old." The sufferer of "Depression," who is going "boil over inside today," does not believe those who tell him that "things are going to get better"; the occupant of "Room 13" needs "to hang on" and begs someone else to keep him alive because he feels incapable of saving himself.

The speakers of "What I See," "Gimmie, Gimmie, Gimmie," "Damaged I," and "Damaged II" are paralyzed by a more generalized existential angst that is communicated through Rollins's primal scream-cum-vocals as well as the discordant throbbing noise that accompanies him. The speaker of "Gimmie, Gimmie, Gimmie" stands "here like a loaded gun waiting to go off"; yet, whatever he is asking for will not be sufficient to prevent him from ending up dead. The subject of "What I See" simultaneously wants "to live" while wishing he wouldn't because he needs to connect with his emotions, but he turns his "mind off" because feeling is too painful. The subject of "Damaged II" is so emotionally numb that he does not "even wanna see." The album's last track, "Damaged I," is autobiographical: Rollins sings, "My name is Henry and you're here with me now," reiterating the emotional pain on most of *Damaged*'s tracks. Other songs on *Damaged* describe subjects who self-medicate with alcohol ("Thirsty and Miserable," "Six Pack," and "No More"), television in "TV Party," or self-harm in "Life of Pain." "Spray Paint" is the most upbeat track on the album: it is a thirty-four-second song about the joys of free speech via vandalism.

Damaged almost never saw the light of day due to a dispute with the band's then label, Unicorn Records, a subsidiary of MCA. When Black Flag delivered their recording to Unicorn, the label refused to release the album because of its violent and profane (at the time) lyrics. But Ginn was undeterred and did an end run around Unicorn, releasing *Damaged* on his own label, SST records, to critical acclaim. Unicorn sued the band and SST to prevent them from using the name "Black Flag" and the band's trademark four black bars logo, which was Unicorn's intellectual property according to the band's recording contract. Black Flag would not regain the use of their logo or their name until Unicorn went bankrupt in 1983 and the rights reverted back to them. In the interim, Black Flag continued to tour and release more work via SST records, but their compilation album *Everything Went Black* had to be released under the names of the individual band members instead of "Black Flag" due to Unicorn's injunction.

After *Damaged*, Black Flag's sound evolved from hardcore to something so "heavily experimental, incorporating elements of jazz, blues, metal, math rock," that fans became angry because each successive album was "a new thing entirely" (Schnipper 2017). After six studio albums, several live albums, compilations, EPs and innumerable tours, Ginn decided to disband Black Flag and focus on promoting other bands on his SST label. But that was not the last of Black Flag. They reunited in 2003 and again in 2013 for benefit shows for cats, one of Ginn's favorite causes (Nichols 2003).

BLONDIE: *PLASTIC LETTERS*

Those who only know Blondie from their third studio album, *Parallel Lines*, more than likely do not think of them as a punk band. The singles from this album are better classified as New Wave, pop, or anything else that is not punk rock. "Sunday Girl" is a sweet and sad pop song, while "Heart of Glass," also known as the disco song, is as far from punk as a band can get. "Picture This," "I'm Gonna Love You Too," "Hanging on the Telephone," and "One Way or Another" have a punk-pop feel, but producer Mike Chapman gave *Parallel Lines* a commercial, overproduced sound that is the antithesis of punk. Too, all of Blondie's music draws on multiple genres, including 1960s pop, glam rock, rockabilly, blues, and New Wave, and is not as openly angry and defiant as that of their 1970s punk cohorts, such as the Sex Pistols or the Clash.

Further, Blondie does not look like a punk band, whose members typically dress in ripped T-shirts and jeans or fetish wear that identifies them as wholly anti-establishment. Front woman Deborah Harry looks like a modern-day pinup girl, with her full lips and trademark blonde hair that gives the band its name, and her male bandmates, with their black leather jackets and retro haircuts, look more like updated versions of juvenile delinquents, a style that became extremely fashionable in the early 1980s.

Blondie regularly performed at the New York club CBGB, the epicenter of the emergent punk rock scene of 1970s and 1980s New York, hosting acts that included the Ramones, Television, Richard Hell and the Voidoids, and Harry was the unofficial pinup girl of John Hillstrom's *Punk Magazine*, appearing in cartoon form in every issue. Blondie was the American counterpart of the British band Siouxsie and the Banshees, another early punk band with a female lead.

Graffiti artist Shepard Fairey's mural of Blondie at 316 Bowery in New York City, directly across from from the location of legendary club CBGB. Fairey, whose first art show was at CBGB in 1998, created the mural as a tribute to the club and one of its legendary performers. (Bigapplestock/Dreamstime.com)

Blondie's music is punk (as well as New Wave, 1960s pop, and glam rock, among others) in how Harry's performance of the songs subverts the conventions of gender and genre and destabilizes bourgeois sensibilities. So, for example, what seems to be a sweet pop love song (such as "Denis" or "Sunday Girl" from *Parallel Lines*) seethes with the emotions that are unsung by Harry but implied by her blonde sex kitten appearance and husky femininity, which communicate something more dangerous below the surface. The nameless nice girls who are the subjects of "Sunday Girl" and "Denis" cannot openly acknowledge their sexuality or only do so in the most innocent way to remain within their narrow gender role. "Sunday Girl" can only be patient rather than take direct action, because if she goes out with the guy she really likes, her parents will be upset. Yet, being a nice girl has a painful price for "Sunday Girl," whose guy is seen hanging out with another girl after "Sunday Girl" has turned him down for a date too many times.

In "Denis," the protagonist can only rhapsodize about her beloved's "eyes so blue" as a stand in for whatever else she might like about him. "Denis" is a cover of the 1963 single "Denise" by Randy and the Rainbows, in which a male singer blandly croons about his love for a girl in a straightforward pop song way. However, the singer's sex is important in both versions. In "Denise," the male singer's intentions might range from innocent teenage love to those of a cad because a man is not unsexed by any expressions of heterosexual desire. In Blondie's cover of the original, the meaning is altered by a female singer. As love culminating in marriage is still thought of as the crowning achievement of stereotypical womanhood, the stakes are higher, and the female singer's love for "Denis" is the perceived as the natural trajectory of a woman's life.

When Harry performed "Sunday Girl" on *Top of the Pops* (1978) and "Denis" in the band's video, she danced and dressed in a way that thwarted attempts to objectify her. The X-Ray Spex's Poly Styrene appeared on stage with braces on her teeth and a black garbage bag as a dress so she would not be perceived as a sex symbol. Harry, on the other hand, was conventionally glamorous, with her red lipstick and blonde hair, but she refused to perform as a stereotypical sex object. She did not so much dance during these performances but instead moved her hips and snapped her fingers in time to the rhythm. Lest anyone confuse her with the "Sunday Girl" that she sang about on *Top of the Pops*, Harry wore a suit and tie. For the band's video of "Denis," Harry dressed in a striped one-piece swimsuit similar to the one worn by the original Barbie, but she draped an oversized jacket over her right shoulder as a way of stopping any attempts to objectify her. She also disrupted objectification by looking directly at the camera rather than at a point outside of the frame, which broke the illusion of control.

Plastic Letters is a better representation of Blondie as a punk band than the better-known *Parallel Lines* because more of its songs have a harder edge. *Plastic Letters* did not enjoy the commercial success of *Parallel Lines*, and it was panned by critics because they really did not know how to classify Blondie's music. Kit Rachalis, writing for *Rolling Stone* in 1982, complained that *Plastic Letters* was "a B grade production" whose songs were garish and predictable, yet the reviewer seems to be genuinely confused about how Blondie fits into any musical genre, let alone punk. Rachalis was particularly annoyed by what she described as Blondie's celebration of seediness in "titles that scream headlines," such as "Bermuda Triangle Blues (Flight 45)," "Youth Nabbed as Sniper," and "Contact in Red Square" (Rachalis 1982).

What Rachalis failed to appreciate is that Blondie's "celebration of seediness" is an important component of punk. The desperate teen subject of "Youth Nabbed as Sniper" is not so different from the people in the Clash's "Police and Thieves" or "I Fought the Law": all feel that they are trapped by circumstances that can only be overcome through violence. That is the case in "Detroit 442," one of Blondie's punkier songs, in which the protagonist can only find freedom from the "concrete factory" where she works "on the plant assembly line" by cruising the streets of Detroit with Jimmy O (possibly Detroit-native Iggy Pop, whose real name is James Osterberg). "Detroit 442" is characterized by Clem Burk's hard drumming as well as James Destri's use of bass notes on the piano, giving the song a restless and angry feel.

An unlucky wealthy tourist disappears into the ocean in "Bermuda Triangle Blues (Flight 45)." The Bermuda Triangle is a mythical place over the Atlantic that supposedly sucks planes from the sky into a whirling vortex. It is an implacable natural force as powerful as the social and political forces that shape human lives. "Contact in Red Square" and "Cautious Lip" conjure up noir detective fiction, except the women in these songs defy the noir feminine stereotype of dizzy dames that need to be slapped, kissed, or rescued. Instead, the women in these songs are strong and dangerous women. The Soviet spy who is the subject of "Contact in Red Square" is a femme fatale on a mission from the Kremlin, while the speaker of "Cautious Lip" is biding her time until the person behind the cautious lip is vulnerable due to his overconfidence. The subject of "I Didn't Have the Nerve to Say No" will die before she lets someone who caught her in a vulnerable moment control her. The title character of the bouncy rockabilly song "Kidnapper" is about to discover that ransoming the thirteen-year-old girl that he has seduced and abducted was a bad idea. The girl "bitches like a brat," and the kidnapper is very likely to end up dead or in jail instead of rich.

Harry takes on a femme fatale persona in other tracks. The female subjects of "No Imagination" and "Love at the Pier" objectify men and toss them away after they have served their purposes. The speaker is not even able to be intimate with her imaginary partner, a stranger whose "tanned oily body" looks sinful, because when he takes a dip in the ocean to cool off, she walks away as she "saw [him] yelling." Because it is too hot outside, she leaves instead of finding a lifeguard to rescue him from drowning.

Plastic Letters is significant for Blondie because it was their first original release on Chrysalis Records, and it popularized the band in Europe while they were still mostly a cult favorite in the United States. The album shows a broad mix of styles, and most of the songs are three minutes or shorter. *Plastic Letters* shows the band's growth since the release of their self-titled debut album in 1976, and it placed them on the U.S. and U.K. charts for the first time. The album sold enough copies in the United Kingdom to be certified Platinum.

BUZZCOCKS: *SINGLES GOING STEADY*

The Buzzcocks were one of the earliest queercore groups, playing songs that were "bisexual" (Reynolds 2018), like the band's front man, Pete Shelley (Peter McNeish). Similar to other early British punk outfits, the future members of the Buzzcocks, Shelley and Howard Devoto (Howard Trafford), decided to form a band in 1975 after seeing a Sex Pistols show. Shelley and Devoto hit upon the band's name "from the chance conjunction of words in a magazine headline about the buzz-worthy TV show *Rock Follies*, a rock-biz satire featuring a tough-girl singer who cheekily addressed everyone as 'cock'" (Reynolds 2018). A year later, the Buzzcocks would tour with the Sex Pistols as their opening band and release their first EP, *Spiral Scratch*.

However, the Buzzcocks were not "a carbon copy of the music of Johnny Rotten." Although they "played with the same frantic amphetamine energy as [their] early punk cohorts," front man Shelley "belted out anthems of frustrated love and romance" (Swenson 2018) rather than anarchy or geopolitics. Their music was "anchored in catchy melodies that were directly influenced by the Beatles," and Shelley's "high-pitched voice was a direct contrast to Joe Strummer's bark or Rotten's acid screech" (Swenson 2018). Buzzcocks' guitarist, Steve Diggle, reflected how Shelley's songwriting "expanded what punk 'could be and what it could mean'" (Reynolds 2018) to influence later bands, such as Hüsker Dü, who brought "a sensitivity to American hardcore that hadn't been present prior," and created "a template that every C-86 and indie pop band that followed would owe a debt to" (McMahon 2018, "Pete Shelley"). When Devoto left the Buzzcocks before they became famous, Shelley became the band's front man and chief songwriter. Shelley was an unusual front man due to his "sheer ordinariness" (Reynolds 2018). When Shelley was seen "in the glitzy TV context of *Top of the Pops*" with "his open-neck button-shirts and slightly shaggy hair, he looked like neither a punk nor a pop star, but more like an office clerk on his lunch break. And he sang like one too" (Reynolds 2018).

It is commonly believed that Shelley took his stage name from the romantic poet Percy Bysshe Shelley: however, Tony Wilson, the founder of Factory Records, explains that Shelley's stage name had its origins in what his parents planned on naming him if he had been a girl (McMahon 2018). "That invocation of the she that he might have been connects to a genuine innovation that Shelley introduced to rock, and that reflected his fluid sexuality: the deliberate use of gender non-specific pronouns in love songs," a rhetorical trope that "would hugely influence later lyricists like Morrissey" (Reynolds 2018).

The band's third album, *Singles Going Steady* (1979), "would go down as [the Buzzcocks'] definitive statement" (Swenson 2018); today it is ranked No. 6 on *Rolling Stone*'s "List of 50 Greatest Pop-Punk Albums" (Weingarten) and No. 16 on *Pitchfork*'s "Best Albums of the 1970s" list (Plagenhoef 2004). Originally released in 1979, *Singles Going Steady* collects the band's singles that were unaffiliated with any of their prior albums. The album's first track, "Orgasm Addict" (1977), was their debut single, but it did not chart due to its frank references to masturbation and bisexuality, which got it banned from the airwaves by the BBC. Although the BBC's censorship of "Orgasm Addict" gave it credibility among punks, Shelley would later state that it was the only one of his compositions that he would "listen to and . . . shudder" (McMahon 2018, "Buzzcocks") with embarrassment.

Three tracks on *Singles Going Steady* illustrate how Shelley reinvented modern romance in his songs: "all the old kinds of romance are self-destructive because they don't take account of realities" (Reynolds 2018), Shelley explained in a 1978 interview in *NME*. Shelley's reinvention of modern romance "was a radical mundanity, using pained humor to sketch scenarios of humiliation, inadequacy and shortfall, coupled with melody that promised resolution or transcendence" (Reynolds 2018). The band's second single, "What Do I Get?," describes a state of "perpetual unfulfillment": the answer to the question stated in the title is "sleepless nights in an empty bed." The speaker of "I Don't Mind" is a "pathetic clown" who will "keep hangin' around." And the aim of "You Say You Don't Love Me" "is clarity achieved through a kind of positive disillusionment, serene acceptance of things as they are" (Reynolds 2018). "Ever Fallen in Love (With Someone You Shouldn't've)" continues the theme of unrequited love and is a fan favorite as well as the Buzzcocks' biggest U.K. chart hit. Originally released on *Love Bites*, "Ever Fallen in Love" is a "bisexual punk anthem" inspired by a man with whom Shelley lived for seven years, although Shelley's "use of gender-neutral pronouns meant the song really could be about anyone" (McMahon 2018, "Buzzcocks"). "Ever Fallen in Love" topped *NME*'s Songs of the Year list in 1978 and was later named by that publication as one of the Buzzcocks' ten best songs. It has been covered by bands as diverse as Fine Young Cannibals (whose 1986 single charted higher in the United Kingdom than the Buzzcocks' version), the Canadian punk bands Pup, and the emo band Thursday (McMahon 2018, "Pete Shelley") as well as by Roger Daltrey (The Who), David Gilmour (Pink Floyd), Elton John, Robert Plant (Led Zeppelin), and the Futureheads, who recorded the song together for a charity tribute to the late disc jockey John Peel. After Shelley's sudden death from a heart attack in December 2018, fans circulated a petition on Change.org to get people to download "Ever Fallen in Love" to make it No. 1 once again (Reilly 2018).

Other singles collected on *Singles Going Steady* include "Love You More," "Promises," "Everybody's Happy Nowadays," and "Harmony in My Head." "Love You More" and "Promises" deconstruct the clichés of erotic love. The speaker of "Love You More" is doomed from the beginning because he is "in love again." The speaker in "Promises" goes from saying "loving you is easy" to "loving you is not easy." The subject of "Everybody's Happy Nowadays" distances himself from the masses named in the title because he has become "tired of being upset, always wanting something I never could get." "Harmony in My Head" is one of the few songs sung by guitarist Steve Diggle, whose rough voice contrasts with the harmony he hears amid the "clattering shoppers" and the "neon signs that take your eyes to town." Most of the songs on side two of *Singles Going Steady* are the forgettable B sides of the singles from side one, uninspired rough drafts of the same ideas.

Before the release of *Singles Going Steady*, artistic differences among band members and escalating substance abuse on the part of all were tearing the Buzzcocks apart. These tensions reached critical mass after their label, United Artists Records, was bought by EMI, who wanted to release *Singles Going Steady* in the United Kingdom before the band delivered their forthcoming album, *Another Kind of Tension*. When the Buzzcocks refused to go along with this plan, EMI did not give them an advance to cover the recording costs of *Another Kind of Tension*. Rather than fight the record label for the money to record this album, Shelley decided to break up the band in 1981.

For a time, Shelley pursued a solo career that produced the hit electronic dance single "Homosapien," which was banned by the BBC for its veiled references to gay sex, but he was unable to follow that song's success with anything half as good. The Buzzcocks eventually reunited in 1990 with their final line up of Shelley and Diggle, who were joined by bassist Tony Barber and drummer Phil Barker to release the album *Trade Test Transmission* in 1993, but none of their albums after their reunion equaled their original work. Still, the Buzzcocks toured frequently after reforming and even opened for Nirvana's 1994 tour at Kurt Cobain's invitation.

THE CLASH: *LONDON CALLING*

The Clash (1976–1985) is one the Year Zero groups of punk rock, emerging on the London punk scene in the 1970s along with the Sex Pistols, the Slits, the Damned, the Jam, the Adverts, Siouxsie and the Banshees, and the X-Ray Spex. The founding members were active in other parts of the London music scene. Joe Strummer (John Graham Mellor) was in a pub rock band, the 101s, and got his stage name from his rudimentary strumming skills on the ukulele, which he played while busking on the London Underground. Mick Jones played guitar with the protopunk band the London SS, and future Clash drummer Nicky "Topper" Headon played with them for a week. Bassist Paul Simonon and sometime Clash drummer Terry Chimes tried out for the London SS but did not make the cut.

The Clash were "rebels with a cause" rather than "glorious nihilists" on the model of the Sex Pistols (Carson 1980), battling "the poverty of indifference with angry chords" (Hull 1979).The Clash's songs incorporated elements of reggae, rockabilly, dub, and R & B and tackled social decay, unemployment, racism, police brutality, political repression, and militarism (Erlewine n.d., "*London Calling*"). Fans often described the Clash as "the only band that matters" without realizing that the phrase was coined by their label, Epic, who used it in the band's promotional material. *London Calling* (1979), their third album, is acknowledged by critics as one of the most influential of all time (Christgau 1981, "1980 Pazz & Jop Critics Poll"; Christgau 1991, "Year of Lollapalooza"; Harvey 2019; Sinclair 2004; Partridge 2014; *Rolling Stone* 2012). For the album's fortieth anniversary, the Museum of London hosted an exhibition of the items from the band's personal archive related to *London Calling*, including draft lyrics, stage clothes, photos, and films.

London Calling was released after the Clash lost some of their anti-commercial credibility in the eyes of their fans after they allowed Blue Öyster Cult producer Sandy Pearlman to "drape their second album *Give 'Em Enough Rope* in the power-chord sheen of American rock" to market their music to American markets (Harvey 2019). The double album *London Calling* was the Clash's response to accusations that they had become sellouts. In this double album, the Clash signaled their "rejection of what other people thought the band should play or sound like" in how the band played the musical styles that most appealed to them (Harvey 2019).

The Clash's evolving musical style on *London Calling* was so eclectic that some critics described the album as "post-punk" rather than punk. They combined rockabilly, reggae, and ska with a wider range of styles, including "New Orleans R & B, pop, lounge jazz, and hard rock" (Erlewine n.d., "The Clash") to produce all "the shades of the Clash's music," ranging from "anger, passion, swagger, political fury, romantic heroism, anguish, dread, hope, innocence, humor and exhilaration" (Harvey 2019). Two of the three singles from *London Calling* became No. 30 on Billboard's 1979 Dance Club list: "London Calling" and "Train in Vain." "Train in Vain" is not surprising (also known as "Stand by Me"), as it is a love song. Some have described "Train in Vain" as singer and songwriter Mick Jones's response to the Slits' song "Typical Girls" (1979), which eschews heteronormative romance. Slits' frontwoman Viv Albertine was romantically involved with Jones and had broken up with him before he wrote the song. "Longing, tenderness and regret mingle in Jones' voice" in "Train in Vain" when he sings that "losing her meant losing everything, yet he's going to manage somehow" (Carson 1980). "Train in Vain" was a hidden track on the original version of *London Calling*, but it ends later versions of the album, which is appropriate in how the entirety of the album is about how "small battles as well as large ones," revolutions and love affairs, are "all part of the same long, bloody march" (Carson 1980).

"London Calling" is more typical of the Clash's work: written after the 1979 Three Mile Island nuclear disaster, it predicted an impending Anthropocene due to human misuse of technology. The third single from *London Calling*, "Clampdown," decries "the capitalist system that seeks to grind you down the minute you're old enough to start working" (Partridge 2014). "Lost in the Supermarket" similarly decries this system by focusing on "the emptiness of consumer culture" combined with "the loneliness of adolescence" (Partridge 2014).

"Spanish Bombs" is arguably *London Calling*'s best and most ambitious song. "Lost and lonely in his 'disco casino,'" vocalist Joe Strummer cannot tell whether the gunfire he hears outside is actually happening or just in his head. "Bits of Spanish doggerel, fragments of combat scenes, jangling flamenco guitars and the lilting vocals of a children's tune mesh in a swirling kaleidoscope of courage and disillusionment, old wars and new corruption," while "the evocation of the Spanish Civil War is sumptuously romantic: 'trenches full of poets, the ragged army, fixin' bayonets to fight the other line'." As in other Clash songs, "the heroic past isn't simply resurrected for nostalgia's sake" but, instead, to help us learn the lessons of the past "before we can apply them to the present" (Carson 1980).

"Death or Glory" parodies the oft repeated claim of most punk bands that they will never "sell out" by signing a record contract with the hopes of becoming rich, thereby compromising their own artistic integrity. While "every gimmick hungry yob digging gold from rock 'n' roll / Grabs the mike to tell us he'll die before he's sold," Joe warns us that those who sleep with nuns will eventually join the church. "The Guns of Brixton" sums up the Clash's revolutionary stance with its opening lines: "When they kick at your front door / How you gonna come?" He then asks whether people respond by putting their hands up or grabbing a gun. Sung by bassist Paul Simonon, "The Guns of Brixton" was described by *Billboard* as "the shining moment" of his career with the band in how "his monotone delivery speaks to the defiance, disaffection and paranoia pulsing through the skanking beat" of a mean ska song (Partridge 2014).

London Calling also includes three covers. "Brand New Cadillac" is an updated version of Vince Taylor's 1959 rockabilly tune. "Wrong 'Em Boyo" is a cover of the Jamaican rocksteady band the Rulers' cover of Lloyd Price's "Stagger Lee," a song that recounted a deadly 1895 St. Louis bar fight between Stagger Lee and Billy Lyons, which has now become the stuff of folklore. The Clash's updated version of "Stagger Lee" forges a connection "between rock and roll legend and the group's own politicized roots-rock rebel" (Carson 1980). The Clash's cover of Danny Ray and the Revolutionaries' "Revolution Rock" "celebrates the joys of this struggle as an eternal carnival" with a musical arrangement that includes an organ that spirals around Joe Strummer's vocals and a horn section that "totters, sways and recovers like a drunken mariachi band" (Carson 1980).

Other tracks on *London Calling* are so aware of genre conventions that the listener could be forgiven for believing that they too are covers rather than original songs. "Four Horsemen" sounds as if it could be "the movie soundtrack to a rock & roll version of *The Seven Samurai*" (Carson 1980). "Jimmy Jazz," which comes after "Brand New Cadillac," paints a "a Nelson Algren-like street scene" (Carson 1980) that seems to be from the same milieu occupied by Stagger Lee and Billy Lyons. "Rudie Can't Fail" is so full of brass and reggae rhythms that it could very well be the cover of a Jamaican dance hall song.

London Calling's cover was "a revolutionary strategy for a group that had sprung from the U.K. punk scene, which was all about disavowing the past" (Partridge 2014). The cover image of *London Calling* is a visual reference to the Clash's original name for the album, *The Last Testament*, "the idea being that this double LP would close a chapter in music history that had begun with Elvis Presley's RCA debut" in 1956 (Partridge 2014). On the cover of *Elvis Presley*, a black-and-white photograph of the singer meeting his audience for the first time is framed by his name, which is written in green and pink letters on the left side and bottom. In retrospect, this image represents Presley ushering in rock and roll as the record companies would understand it. The title of *London Calling*, written in pink and green letters, similarly frames a black-and-white photograph, but of Joe Strummer rather than Elvis, who is on the verge of smashing his guitar on stage to end rock and roll as everyone knew it.

After the release of the Clash's fourth album, *Combat Rock* (1982), it looked as if they were on the verge of "becoming the next Rolling Stones, reaping huge sales and critical adulation in the United States, and appearing at the giant US '83 festival in California" (Sweeting 2002). But the Clash was not "designed for the shopping malls and suburbs of heartland America" and "fizzled out after a depressing string of musical and personnel changes" (Sweeting 2002), despite Strummer's attempts to keep them alive. Headon was arrested in 1981 on heroin possession and fired from the band in 1982 when his addiction interfered with his ability to be a dependable band member. In the same year, Strummer disappeared for a month before the release of *Combat Rock*. When he resurfaced, he fired Mick Jones for his chronic tardiness and absenteeism from practices (Garcia 2012). As a result, the Clash's final studio album, *Cut the Crap* (1985), was musically "bland and erratic without Jones, who wrote most of the Clash's songs" (Ziegler 2009), as well as without a drummer—Clash manager Bernard Rhodes is credited with programming the drum machine on this album. Paul Simonon, with his contrapuntal ska/reggae-influenced bass lines, had also left the band to work on a new musical project.

The Clash finally dissolved in 1986. The original lineup appeared together on stage once more in 2000 to receive an Ivor Novello award for their outstanding contributions to British music, and the band members toyed with the idea of doing one more tour. However, Strummer's sudden death in 2002 from a congenital heart defect stopped all talk of a reunion. The Clash was inducted into the Rock and Roll Hall of Fame in early 2003 (*The Clash* n.d.), only a month after Strummer's death.

THE CRAMPS: *SONGS THE LORD TAUGHT US*

The American punk band the Cramps (1976–2009) were the progenitors of psychobilly, a genre that fuses rockabilly with hard rock and incorporates lyrics based on the sensibilities of schlocky horror and science films from the 1950s and 1960s. Their music employs fuzz and feedback characteristic of early 1960s surf music. The Cramps were created by the husband and wife team Lux Interior (Erick Purkhiser) and Poison Ivy Rorschach (Christine Wallace) in 1976. Their trademark musical style is manic-paced, jangling-guitar rockabilly laced with feedback and a menace, which is communicated by Interior's vocals. Interior's rapid-fire delivery of the Cramps' disturbing lyrics sounded like an auctioneer on amphetamines taken to singing his darkest thoughts.

The Cramps were one of the first bands to realize the potential of "punk rock as theater and spectacle" (Brown 2009). Interior frequently wore gender-bending costumes on stage and "evoked a lanky, proto-goth Elvis," while "Rorschach's boots, fishnets and bikini, coupled with her rugged and raucous guitar-playing, made her one of rock's most distinctive female icons" (Sweeting 2009). Their stage performance "upended the traditional rock band sexual dynamic of the flamboyant, seductive female and the mysterious male guitarist" (Brown 2009), which is demonstrated on the cover photo of *Songs the Lord Taught Us*: Interior's face is in the center, staring at the camera with a come-hither (so I can murder you) expression, and he wears bones for jewelry. Rorschach is positioned on the left so as to avoid an objectifying gaze as she looks at something outside of the frame. The Cramps' volatile and decadent live performances quickly made them regulars at CBGB.

Songs the Lord Taught Us (1980), the band's first full-length album, is "a gateway to a world that had largely been forgotten about by 1980" (Marszalek 2015). Their covers of rockabilly and psychedelic popular music from the pre-Beatles era are indistinguishable from their own songs, demonstrating the Cramps' fluency in "trash" culture from the 1950s and early 1960s. In those days, before streaming media and the internet, the Cramps' musical project educated younger listeners about alternative youth cultures that existed in a time period that most believe was homogenized and conformist.

Before *Songs the Lord Taught Us* was released, hearing these older songs was usually a matter of luck: one might catch them on late-night big-city radio stations where the DJs were allowed to play obscure music during an hour when few people were listening, or one might stumble upon this music in used record shops. The covers of this type of music played on *Songs the Lord Taught Us* are performed without irony, if only because the originals were already so outrageous, especially the Sonic's "Strychnine" (1965), a psychedelic protopunk song about the alleged health benefits of drinking the deadly poison. Dwight Pullen's "Sunglasses after Dark" (1958) is equally preposterous: a zoot-suited rockabilly enthusiast who wears sunglasses at night to look cool is cut up in a knife fight because he cannot see to defend himself. Other covers on *Songs the Lord Taught Us* include two rockabilly classics: Jimmy Stewart's "Rock on the Moon" (1959) and Johnny Burnette's "Tear It Up" (1954). The Cramps' cover of "Fever" more closely approximates Willie John Little's original R & B version rather than the better-known, but more sanitized version performed by Peggy Lee in 1958.

Tracks written by Interior or Rorscach on *Songs the Lord Taught Us* may have been channeled, as the album title suggests, from a few decades earlier rather than created, given how they could credibly pass as rock and roll from the pre-Beatles era due to their subject matter and sound—the Cramps' use of feedback and fuzz in their recordings contributes to the illusion that their music was from the past, when recording technology was less sophisticated. "I Was a Teenage Werewolf" references the 1957 B-film of the same name, with lyrics that make fun of its campy supernatural take on adolescence: a teen lycanthrope with "braces on [his] fangs" suffers "puberty rites and puberty wrongs." "TV Set" and "Zombie Dance" also exemplify the band's love of B-horror films from the 1950s and 1960s. The maniac speaker of "TV Set" cuts off the head of his victim, which he puts atop this appliance, and uses her eyeballs for "dials." Quite possibly, this is the same speaker as the one in "The Mad Daddy," whose general insanity is communicated via Interior's frenetic rockabilly vocals. "The Zombie Dance," with its imagery about the undead who "do the swim face down in the zombie pool," predicts the work of fellow horror punk artists the Misfits.

"Garbageman" is the Cramps' musical mission statement: the band comes out of the garage and along the driveway to deliver the refuse of the mind for the betterment of the listener. They describe themselves in this song as "one half hillbilly and one half punk" with "eight long legs and one big mouth," like a giant spider straight out of a B-grade science fiction film or the hippocampus, which can make you feel better when you are feeling down. The speaker of "Mystery Plane" is both alienated and perhaps part alien: he was left on planet Earth by his father, who is a UFO pilot, and he "can't identify with this world" because "square pegs don't fit into round holes." The Cramps invoke the spirit of alienated youth, particularly as represented in popular culture by James Dean, Marlon Brando, and Paul Newman.

"What's behind the Mask" is a B-movie version of *Phantom of the Opera*, where the speaker wants to know why he "can't see your face when I see what's in your pants?" and then wishes that he had remained ignorant after lifting the mask of his sexual partner. "I'm Cramped" might as well be an instrumental, as its lyrics are merely Interior occasionally singing, "I'm cramped," throughout a solid piece of rockabilly music that emphasizes their trademark musical style of substituting a second guitar and some creative percussion for the usual bass.

Although they never achieved commercial success, the Cramps were influential in the nascent punk movement. In the words of one reviewer, there would be no Misfits, no Damned, and no Rancid without the Cramps (im-dead 2005), who were "frequently imitated" but "never bettered" (Marszalek 2015). The Cramps continued to tour until 2009, when Interior died unexpectedly.

CRASS: *THE FEEDING OF THE 5000*

The British punk band Crass was "both inspired by and a reaction to liberal bands the Clash" (Dunn 2011, 27). Although Crass never sought (or achieved) commercial success, they were influential in the development of the anarcho-punk movement. "For Crass, the DIY, disalienation, and anti-status quo elements of punk were not just topics for songs, but a template for how one should live" (Glasper 2007), and band members worked to stay true to punk's original ideals. Crass never signed with a major label, and when the workers at a record pressing plant refused to fabricate their first album, *The Feeding of the 5000*, because of the blasphemous language on the track "Asylum," the band created its own label, Crass Records, to distribute and promote their music as well as the music of like-minded punks. Crass's DIY attitude "resonated with anarchism's core message of taking charge and directly addressing the immediate issues in one's life rather than asking for some governmental solution to a problem" (Dunn 2011, 32–33).

Crass also directly addressed important issues through contact with their fans. The band "would send fans leaflets (usually self-produced) on topics ranging from vegetarianism to environmentalism to nuclear disarmament," introducing "a slew of working-class punks to traditionally middle-class ideals," and their "records came elaborately packaged with dense screeds of polemic" (Aitch 2007). Crass was so effective at communicating these ideas to their fans that they were "courted by the KGB and the IRA (Irish Republican Army), and monitored at their Epping commune by MI5" (Aitch 2007), the British counterpart of the FBI.

Crass's music was so relentlessly anti-commercial that it can nearly be unlistenable at times. Their name aptly describes their lyrics, which used scatological and sacrilegious imagery to call out the hypocrisy of social and political institutions. Crass did not make music that might get them an invitation to perform on *Top of the Pops*, and no one could accuse them of selling out. Nevertheless, Crass's music was not nihilistic and transgressive, like that of the Sex Pistols, but instead a discourse on human rights that "was framed primarily as a critique of capitalism" (Dunn 2011, 32–33), specifically Prime Minister Margaret Thatcher's "free market" policies that stripped social safety nets from the poor (Dunn 2011). Much of Crass's music was about gender because the band "recognized that the liberal discourse around human rights privileged a particular account of human dignity and worth" that did not question "traditional gender roles and the subordination of women within a patriarchic family structure" (Dunn 2011, 32–33).

Crass's first album, *The Feeding of the 5000*, demonstrates their vision through songs that explain how people are controlled by social institutions such as the church, the state, and corporations. "End Result" discusses how consumer capitalism causes us to view people as products on a grocery store shelf whose contents are not safe for people to eat, as they might be bad for your health. These products are deliberately created by an unseen hand to be "a scapegoat of useless, futureless, endless, mindless ideas" to divert attention away from who has been turning individuals into products. Evading this unseen hand is impossible, as others are trying to brainstorm ways they can evade the attention of their figurehead—which isn't easy.

"They've Got a Bomb" elaborates on what is to be done with the defective products of "End Result." "They" will use their "tactical killing machine" to "smash the misfits who foul up their scene." "You Pay" is similarly pessimistic about exiting the system described in "End Result." Your taxes pay for "prisons," "wars," "lobotomies," "law," "their order," and "their murder," and there is no alternative to participation. The speaker in "Reject of Society" rejects "the silly rat race" that requires that she sweep up "the factory floor . . . from nine to four." "What a Shame" is similar to "End Result" in its focus on how social institutions will "fill you up with passive bullshit" to wear down people's resistance to being assimilated.

"Do They Owe Us a Living," "Asylum" (or "Reality Asylum"), "So What?," and "G's Song" critique capitalism's "assault on basic human rights" through institutional violence done to individuals via the process of habituating them to function as "good" laborers and citizens in the modern world (Dunn 2011). But the living that Crass is talking about is not a guaranteed basic minimum wage: like other anarcho-punk bands, Crass generally eschews "what they regarded as liberalism's faulty emphasis on government programs as a solution" (Dunn 2011). Those owed a living cannot be made whole through the damage done to their spirits via institutions such as school, where they do not give you much or treat you well, and you are labeled "different" to become the opposite of the norm.

Organized religion is presented as a form of structural violence in "Asylum" and "So What?" "Asylum" lambasts Christianity's graphic representations of Christ's crucifixion, which are meant to inspire pity and gratitude in believers, as only reproductions of someone whose body has been used to illustrate what happens to those who fight against the system. "So What?" observes that resisters will be "crucified as Jesus was" and made to be obedient unless they are able to deconstruct the institutional master narrative, which has "covered up the truth" and "didn't touch on the actual factual proof."

"G's Song" critiques income inequality exacerbated by Thatcher's austerity measures—"Got to suffer to get us moving / Say it's up to me and you"—while the wealthy have all that they need. "Securior," the name of one of the United Kingdom's largest private security companies of the twentieth century, describes how the wealthy and the powerful have their privilege enforced through private organizations whose employees are drawn from the military and law enforcement.

"Punk Is Dead" and "General Bacardi" call out the leaders of failed movements for selling out. "Punk Is Dead" seethes about how the punk movement has been appropriated by corporations and effectively defanged to become "schoolboy sedition backed by big time promoters," singling out the Clash for especial derision because they signed a contract with CBS. "General Bacardi" targets the hippie movement as a failed social revolution whose leaders are now sellouts who care little for anyone else: the hippies "talked of windmills and psychedelic dreams" and "formed little groups, like rich man's ghettoes." "Women" is a punk *Lysistrata*: in a world where men earn their place through war and women must trade their bodies for "men's money," which buys them security, listeners are enjoined to "fight war" against this system rather than "wars" between different factions of the same system. "Sucks" is the most anarchist song on *The Feeding of the 5000*. After calling out religion and politics, even anarchy is "not worthy of one's full faith."

The Feeding of the 5000 is one of the first punk albums to seriously espouse anarchist philosophy, and when it was released in 1978, its extreme sound made it a revolutionary recording.

THE DAMNED: *DAMNED, DAMNED, DAMNED* (EXPANDED EDITION)

Until recently, the Damned have not received the same attention given to other Year Zero punk bands, which is surprising given their longevity and impressive list of punk firsts. The Damned have been together continuously (except for a brief six-month breakup) since 1975 and are still touring today. They were the first punk band to release a single, the first U.K. band to tour the United States, the first to split up (in 1978), and the first to reform.

The Damned played gigs with their more famous contemporaries, such as the Sex Pistols and the Clash, and were regulars at New York's CBGB and the Masque in Los Angeles, where the impossibly fast tempo of their music influenced the West Coast hardcore scene. The Damned also had more working-class credibility than their Year Zero contemporaries: lead singer Dave Vanian (David Lett) and guitarist and bassist Captain Sensible (Raymond Ian Burns) worked as a toilet cleaner and a gravedigger, respectively, before they were able to support themselves as professional musicians (Rowley 2017). The Damned's other two founding members were drummer Rat Scabies (Christopher John Millar) and guitarist Brian James, who got his start in the protopunk bands the London SS and the Subterraneans and wrote the lyrics for the Damned's songs on their first two albums. Yet, the Damned have only recently received attention from music historians. They were the subject of the 2015 documentary *The Damned: Don't You Wish That We Were Dead?* and placed at No. 28 in *Rolling Stone*'s list of "50 Greatest Pop-Punk Albums" (Weingarten et al. 2017).

The Damned played their first gig in July 1976 at London's 100 Club, sharing the bill with the Sex Pistols. Their label, Stiff, rushed them into the studio that year to record what would be the first punk single, "New Rose," which was released just a few months before the Sex Pistols' "Anarchy in the UK." Their debut album, *Damned, Damned, Damned*, produced by singer and songwriter Nick Lowe, would be the first full-length punk album released by a British band. Yet, *Damned, Damned, Damned* was not commercially successfully when it was first released: "New Rose" was the only single from the album to chart in 1976.

Nevertheless, the Damned's punk firsts got them noticed that year by Malcolm McLaren, who asked the band to join his Anarchy in the UK tour, only to kick them off of it four days later (Rowley 2017). When the Anarchy in the UK tour came to Darby, the city refused to let the Sex Pistols play because of band's reputation for attracting venue-wrecking hooligans, which was fueled by their profanity-laden spat on British television with *Today* host Bill Grundy. Fellow tour members the Clash and Johnny Thunders and the Heartbreakers refused to play the Darby venue in solidarity with Pistols, but the Damned considered playing the gig anyway because working as professional musicians was better than returning to stultifying jobs that paid poverty wages. The other bands on the tour, however, viewed The Damned's hesitancy to boycott the venue as evidence that they were unpunk sellouts, and so McLaren dropped them from the tour. This rift with McLaren and other Year Zero bands combined with the Damned's later pop success contributed to how they were forgotten as one of the founding bands of punk whose early sound influenced such bands as the Germs, the Dickies, and Black Flag.

The Damned's debut album sped up the raw sound characteristic of the British Invasion bands of the 1960s, such as the Beatles and the Rolling Stones. The tempo of "New Rose" was so fast in this time before hardcore that people wondered whether the recording was sped up in studio. It was not. Instead, the raw and rapid sound of "New Rose" was the result of first takes with few overdubs that were recorded in just two days in the studio (Rowley 2017). The Damned's British Invasion influence is also apparent in tracks such as their cover of the Beatles' "Help" as well as their songs "Fan Club," "So Messed Up," and "Neat, Neat, Neat."

American influences are also apparent on *Damned, Damned, Damned*. "Neat, Neat, Neat" is barely two minutes long, and its "quick, fiery roar, with rough but right production from Nick Lowe," recalls Iggy and the Stooges (Ragget n.d., "Neat, Neat, Neat"). The manic tempo of "Neat, Neat, Neat" along with "Fish" and "See Her Tonight" predict the coming of hardcore. "See Her Tonight" is musically similar to the Germs' "Richie Dagger's Crime." Too, Vanian's sneering vocals could be American rather than British. On "Fan Club," for example, Vanian's deep, resonate voice is similar to that of Doors' lead singer Jim Morrison, and he sings the lyrics to "Born to Kill" with an American Southern accent.

But despite these influences, the tracks on *Damned, Damned, Damned* are as punk as anything produced by their Year Zero cohorts. The lyrics to "Born to Kill," "1 of 2," and "Stab Yor Back" are as nihilistic as anything produced by the Sex Pistols. Brian James's lyrics to "Fan Club" communicate boredom with fame before he has ever experienced it: very unpunk fans are "standing in the pissing rain" to wait for autographs from the band. "I Fall" obliquely references Satan as the original fallen angel who fought the good fight against a rigged system when it enjoins listeners to "be a falling angel" like the singer. The slower tempo of "Feel the Pain" along with "Stab Yor Back" are musical precursors to the Damned's transition to goth in the 1980s.

The Damned went on to commercial success as a goth band. Vanian was an ideal goth front man. His penchant for appearing on stage in chalk-white makeup and formal clothing gave him a vampire-like appearance, and his growling vocals made him sound like Bauhaus's Peter Murphy. At this time, the Damned's sound became synonymous with Vanian, as Brian James, Rat Scabies, and Captain Sensible left the band. During this period, three singles from the Damned's *Phantasmagoria* album (1985) charted in the United Kingdom, including "Grimly Fiendish." Their nonalbum single "Eloise" (1986), a cover of the Barry Ryan 1968 hit, became their highest-charting single ever, hitting No. 3 in the United Kingdom (*Official Charts* 2019).

To date, the Damned have released ten studio albums, nineteen live albums, and thirty-two compilations and are the subject of the 2015 documentary *The Damned: Don't You Wish That We Were Dead?* and the book *Smashing It Up: A Decade of Chaos with the Damned* (Tyler 2017). The Clash, the Sex Pistols, and the Heartbreakers have long ago broken up, but the Damned are still making music and touring with Vanian, who has been joined by Captain Sensible. Yet, they still have not received the recognition they deserve. On their 2019 tour, the Damned were actually the warm-up act for the younger band Rancid, who warmed up for the Misfits!

DEAD BOYS: *YOUNG, LOUD, AND SNOTTY*

The Year Zero band Dead Boys were so legendary for their on- and off-stage debauchery that when punk became mainstream, "the Dead Boys remained too tough to repackage for mass consumption" (Ludwig 2014). Their lineup consisted of lead guitarist Cheetah Chrome (Eugene Richard O'Connor) and drummer Johnny Blitz (John Madansky), who both left the protopunk group Rocket from the Tombs because they felt that the band's music was "a bit too comparable to art rock" (Prato n.d.); vocalist Stiv Bators (Steven John Bator), future member of Lords of the New Church; rhythm guitarist Jimmy Zero (William Wilden); and bassist Jeff Magnum (Jeff Halmagy). The five originally performed under the name Frankenstein, but the band never really caught on in Ohio in 1976, so they changed their name to Dead Boys, inspired by a line in their apocalyptic song "Down in Flames." They befriended Joey

Ramone when the Ramones did a show in Ohio and got him to arrange an audition at the Ramones' unofficial New York headquarters, CBGB. Soon after, CBGB proprietor Hilly Kristal briefly became their manager before they signed a record deal with Sire (Prato n.d.).

"Coming to the fore as the UK punk scene was starting to make ripples across the ocean, they took the vehemence and aggression of The Sex Pistols and applied it to American themes. In no sense politically motivated, where the British sung about 'No Future' the Dead Boys anthem was 'Nothing to Do'" (Punk 77 n.d.). The Dead Boys, who were influenced by bands such as the MC5, the New York Dolls, and Alice Cooper, "merged the UK punk look with a tough US street punk sound and nihilistic lyrics at odds with the artier sounds of Television and Patti Smith" (Punk 77 n.d.). They were a hit at CBGB. Lead singer Stiv Bators aped Iggy Pop with his on-stage antics, which consisted of cutting himself on stage and aggressive crowd-surfing.

The Dead Boys' debut album, *Young, Loud, and Snotty*, was released mid-1977. Soon after, they left New York to tour with the Damned, who had supported them during their time at CBGB. While, the Dead Boys were a hit with audiences in the United Kingdom, this success did not translate into commercial success for their debut album. In 1977, the press and the radio were afraid of punk rock, and while the outrage punks generated "could be used as publicity in the UK, the US was a different story and just didn't want to know" (Punk 77 n.d.). As a result, the Dead Boys' label, Sire, pressured the group to change their look and sound, resulting in their more commercial second album, *We Have Come for Your Children* (1978).

Bassist Jeff Magnum described the band's sophomore album as "awful," with "no bass" and inaudible guitars (McNeil and McCain 1996). Not surprisingly, *We Have Come for Your Children* was a commercial flop, and Sire dropped them from the label but still required the band to record a third album that they had been contracted to produce. However, lead singer Stiv Bators ensured that Sire would never be able to release the third album, the live *Night of the Living Dead Boys*: he sung off the mike during the recorded performance, which made the tape unusable. The Dead Boys broke up soon afterward in 1979.

Young, Loud, and Snotty is the Dead Boys' magnum opus. The recorded eleven songs "bridge early 1950s rock and roll and the punk movement that was evolving on both sides of the Atlantic" (Sullivan 2017). That bridge can be heard in "All This and More," with its growling guitars, vocals, and handclaps that give it the sound of classic 1970s rock. However, *Young*'s opening track, "Sonic Reducer," with its "H-bomb of an opening," signals the beginning of a new era. It opens with two guitar notes that fade into a distorted hiss that emerges from alternate channels before Bators' vocalizations (Sullivan 2017). "Sonic Reducer" is a classic punk outsider song, about someone who is so alienated from the world that he has built a bomb (the sonic reducer) to destroy the world. Sire released "Sonic Reducer" as the band's first single.

"All This and More" and "What Love Is" are anti-romance songs. "I don't need none of your two-bit machine love," sings Bators in "What Love Is," and he wants to "write on your face with my pretty knife." The homeless speaker of "Not Anymore" is too cold, hungry, and exhausted to be hurt anymore. "Ain't Nothing to Do" encapsulates the sentiment expressed in *Young*'s title: the speaker is bored and angry, ready to "beat up the next hippie" or "knock down the next old man" he sees. "The nihilism and choppy riffing of 'Ain't Nothing to Do' rival anything The Sex Pistols were doing over in Merry Old England" (Gil de Rubio 2017). In fact, guitarist Cheetah Chrome remarked that the Dead Boys "played a lot better than The Sex Pistols" and "had better songs" (Sullivan 2017). The Norwegian punk outfit Jeroan Drive later covered "Ain't Nothing to Do."

"Hey Little Girl" is the one track on *Young* that was recorded live at CBGB. "Caught with the Meat in Your Mouth" and "I Need Lunch" do not age well in the #MeToo era. "Caught with the Meat in Your Mouth" slut shames a female groupie, and "I Need Lunch" objectifies its female subject. Bators sings that he wants to be intimate with a girl and threatens that he will assault her if she tries to do more than serve him "lunch," or provide him with sexual gratification without commitment. "High Tension Wire" further objectifies women with the line "You're looking at me like I'm under the weather / But you'd crawl on your knees just to lick on my leather." "How extreme the Dead Boys music is depends on context. Certain rappers, death metal bands and hardcore punks have gotten into dark and violent lyrical territory that far surpasses what the Dead Boys were doing 40 years ago" (Sullivan 2017).

After splitting up, the Dead Boys reunited sporadically through the 1980s to perform the occasional gig. Bators tried his hand at acting, appearing in John Waters's *Polyester* and *Bill Fishman's Tapeheads*, which starred John Cusack and Tim Robbins as video music big shots, and he also pursued other musical projects with the 1980s New Wave group Disconnected and the Wanderers (who issued the lone album *Only Lovers Left Alive*) before joining ex-Damned guitarist Brian James in the goth-punk outfit Lords of the New Church.

Bators relocated to Paris, France, and before his death in a traffic accident in 1990, he had been attempting to assemble a punk supergroup that would have included Johnny Thunders and Dee Dee Ramone (Prato n.d.). Bators's life and death were the subject of the 2019 documentary *Stiv: No Compromise, No Regrets*. Chrome went on to do shows with the Stilettos with his own band, Cheetah Chrome and the Casualties, and tour with the notorious punk icon GG Allin. He also struggled with addiction before settling down to work at Nashville's Plowboy Records and writing his biography, *Cheetah Chrome: A Dead Boy's Tale: From the Front Lines of Punk Rock*.

After Bators's death, the remaining members of the Dead Boys reunited in 2005 to play a few reunion shows as well as a benefit for CBGB (Prato 2005), and in 2017, original members Cheetah Chrome and Johnny Blitz joined Adam Becvare (LustKillers, Black Halos, American Heartbreak) and guitarist Jason Kottwitz (Sylvain Sylvain and the Sylvains) to tour Canada for the forty-year anniversary rerelease of *Young, Loud, and Snotty*. The Dead Boys were featured in the 2013 movie *CBGB*, starring Harry Potter alum Rupert Grint at Cheetah Chrome. Chrome also has a cameo in the film. The Dead Boys are also featured in the documentary *D. O. A.: A Rite of Passage*, about the origins of punk rock.

DEAD KENNEDYS: *FRESH FRUIT FOR ROTTING VEGETABLES*

The Dead Kennedys was one of the first American bands to make a significant impact on the U.K. punk scene. Like the Clash, Crass, and the Sex Pistols, the Dead Kennedys' music was political, critiquing greedy capitalists and politicians and the "plastic suburban lifestyle" ("Dead Kennedys" 2001, 244). Their songs were Juvenalian satires laced with references to Nazism and the Holocaust. The Dead Kennedys' music combined "bright, slashing chords and hyperactive bass runs" with front man Jello Biafra's (Eric Reed Bouicher) "acerbic yodel-cum-snarl" (Deller 2011). Biafra's voice is one of the most distinctive in punk; his sneering delivery makes him sound like an American version of Sid Vicious.

The San Francisco band courted controversy beginning with their name and their first gig: their first live show was on November 22, 1978, the fifteenth anniversary of the assassination of President John F. Kennedy, which was viewed by mainstream Americans as a crass attempt to capitalize on a national tragedy Today, the band is best remembered for being tried for disseminating pornography to minors via their *Frankenchrist* album. During the Dead Kennedys' eight-year career (1978–1986), they released four studio albums.

Fresh Fruit for Rotting Vegetables (1980) is one of the first hardcore albums, "a hyper-speed blast of ultra-polemical, left-wing hardcore punk, and bitingly funny sarcasm" (Huey n.d., "Dead Kennedys"), which is the Dead Kennedys' signature statement. In it, Biafra spat out lyrics against conservatism, overreaching government authority, and capitalist greed in his sinister warble. "The thin production" on *Fresh Fruit* "dilutes some of the music's power, but the ragged speed-blur still packs a wallop, and the hooks cribbed from surf and rockabilly give it a gonzo edge" (Huey n.d., "Dead Kennedys"). While the songwriting was not consistent through the album, classics such as "Kill the Poor," "Let's Lynch the Landlord," "Chemical Warfare," "California Über Alles," and "Holiday in Cambodia" helped define the hardcore genre. "When Ya Get Drafted," "Let's Lynch the Landlord," and "Your Emotions" showcase the Dead Kennedys' "ability to blend upbeat, light-hearted music with sinister satirical lyrics" (Byrom 2005).

Many of these songs' themes are still relevant today. "Let's Lynch the Landlord" is a cheerful appeal to DIY with its catchy chorus "you know we can . . . lynch the landlord man" as a way of fighting back against a negligent owner who doubles the rent on his condemned property to increase his power and continue profiting off the poor. "When You Get Drafted" characterizes protests as a futile way of effecting political change because "what Big Business wants Big Business gets," including a war that kills the young because building bombs that blow cities off the map and building them back up again is profitable. The opening bass notes of "Holiday in Cambodia" "are some of the most sinister sounds punk rock ever produced" (Byrom 2005). The song "mocks the poor little rich kid who thinks he's got it bad" (Byrom 2005) with lines such as "You'll work harder with a gun in your back / For a bowl of rice a day." "Kill the Poor" is a punk version of Jonathan Swift's "A Modest Proposal," with its celebration of the neutron bomb rather than cannibalism as an effective solution to poverty.

References to Nazism and the Holocaust abound in many songs on *Fresh Fruit for Rotting Vegetables*. "California Über Alles" refers to Hitler's slogan *"Deutschland Über Alles."* The song warns listeners about the hippies, an army of "Zen fascists" coming to force everyone to "mellow out." Early punks despised hippies and the peace moment, which they viewed as politically ineffectual. "California Über Alles" compares hippies to Nazis who desire a totalitarian society, where Führer Brown (referring to then California governor Jerry Brown) will force children to meditate in school and everyone to "jog for the master race / And always wear the happy face." In this dystopia set in the near future of 1984 (a nod to George Orwell), resisters will be rounded up by the police, put in a camp, and showered with poisonous gas similar to the Nazis' use of Zyklon B "showers" in Auschwitz to murder Jewish captives. In "Let's Lynch the Landlord," when the tenants turn on the faulty ovens in their condemned dwellings, the building smells like Dachau, a Nazi extermination camp where the bodies of those killed were burned in crematory ovens.

The artwork on the band's fourth album, *Bedtime for Democracy*, makes similar connections between Nazi Germany and American groups such as the KKK, religious zealots, and opportunists who have overrun the Statue of Liberty. "Chemical Warfare" refers to a tactic banned by the Geneva Convention in 1929 that predicts the bioterrorism used today in Iraq and Syria.

These and other songs demonstrate the Dead Kennedys' nihilism. In "Forward to Death," the signer is so disappointed by the world that he is eager to die. In "Drug Me," the singer is both so in need of stimulation and overstimulated that he can only beg for everyone and everything to "Leave [him] alone so [he] can't see [himself]." "Your Emotions" addresses the postmodern condition where we are afraid of our emotions because they can make us into monsters. "I Kill Children" is one of the band's weaker songs. It was written by Biafra when he was eighteen and pondering the mentality of serial killers: Biafra's killer is a one-dimensional comic book villain who kills children because he "loves to see them die" and watches their mothers weep. Biafra claimed that the sentence "God told me to skin you alive," which is spoken before the opening of "I Kill Children," came from a Chick tract. "I Kill Children" along with "Stealing People's Mail" and "Funland at the Beach" primarily exist to shock bourgeois sensibilities. "Ill in the Head" and their cover of Elvis Presley's "Viva Las Vegas" are the weakest tracks on the album. The Dead Kennedys merely distort the corny title song from Presley's B-film of the same name via Biafra's shrill warble and a sped up tempo.

The Dead Kennedys made free speech history in 1986 as one of the first defendants prosecuted under newly revised federal obscenity laws championed by Tipper Gore to prevent minors from having access to excessively violent or explicitly sexual material. Their last album, *Frankenchrist*, contained a fold-out poster of H. G. Geiger's surrealistic painting *Landscape #XX*, which depicts rows of penises inside of vaginas.

The Los Angeles city prosecutor charged the Dead Kennedys with distributing pornography to minors after a parent complained that her son saw the offending material after purchasing the album. Members of the Dead Kennedys decided to "risk personal bankruptcy and fight the charges for the principal of free speech because they realized that their case would set a legal precedent affecting all musicians, artists, writers, film makers, and performers" (Kennedy 1990). The ensuing trial resulted in a hung jury and a Pyrrhic victory for the Dead Kennedys: Biafra was nearly bankrupt, and the ordeal had contributed to the band's breakup the previous year.

In the 1990s, former band members sued Biafra and his independent label, Alternative Tentacles, for withholding royalty payments. The court forced Biafra to hand over the rights to the majority of the Dead Kennedys' song catalog to his former bandmates. The band reformed in 2001 with other original members, including East Bay Ray (Raymond John Pepperell), D. H. Peligro (Darren Henley), and Klaus Flouride (Geoffrey Lyall), with former Dr. Know member Brandon Cruz replacing Biafra on vocals, and still tours today. Biafra has consistently refused to join his former bandmates.

To date, the Dead Kennedys have released four studio albums, two live albums, and an EP. They released a three-disc live compilation album in 2019, *DK40*, to celebrate the band's fortieth anniversary. The tracks come from three vintage shows in 1982 and 1985 (Prato 2019). The Dead Kennedys are the subject of the documentary film *Fresh Fruit for Rotting Eyeballs* (2005) as well as the books *Dead Kennedys: Fresh Fruit for Rotting Vegetables: The Early Years* by Alex Ogg and the 33 1/2 series volume *Dead Kennedys: Fresh Fruit for Rotting Vegetables* by Michael Stewart Foley.

DEATH: *FOR THE WHOLE WORLD TO SEE*

The American band Death (1971–1980) was a hard rock trio from Detroit, Michigan, whose music has been described as protopunk, or "punk before punk was punk," as well as the earliest example of Afro-punk. (Rubin 2009). Death consisted of David, Dannis, and Bobby Hackney, brothers who had been playing music together since they were children. *For the Whole World to See* (2009), the band's only album, was described by *New York Times* music critic Mike Rubin as "scorching blasts of feral ur-punk" which preceded the "all-black punk Bad Brains by five years" (Rubin 2009). Yet, Death is still virtually unknown by most punk fans because it took nearly thirty years for them to find a record label willing to produce and distribute *For the Whole World to See*, which they had recorded in 1974.

Death's story is typical of how punk was perceived by the music industry in the 1970s, particularly when the musicians were not white. Record executives thought that the Hackney brothers' musical style was too angry and too white for listeners to be marketable for audiences of any race. Their neighbors who heard their daily three-hour jam sessions in their parents' garage concurred. There "were so many voices around us trying to get us to abandon" playing rock and roll instead of Motown, recalls Bobby, that making music was a daily act of defiance (Rubin 2009). The Hackney brothers learned to play by imitating the R & B and funk that they heard on the radio in the 1960s and early 1970s. But their style would change after David saw an Alice Cooper show in Detroit in 1973. He was so impressed that he convinced his brothers to start playing hard rock. Other bands and musicians that inspired the Hackney brothers included the Who, Jimi Hendrix, and Iggy and the Stooges. These influences are evident in *For the World to See* in David's "propulsive guitar work," which was "derived by studying Pete Townshend's power-chord wrist technique" (Rubin 2009).

In 1974, Don Davis of Groovesville Productions allowed Death to audition and was so impressed that he put the band into the studio to make a demo tape with the intention of finding a record label willing to promote and distribute the band. That offer came from Arista Records in 1976, when Clive Davis promised the band a $20,000 contract on the condition that the Hackney brothers change their band's name to something less controversial and more marketable. But David, the oldest Hackney brother and the band's de facto leader, refused. For him, the band's name was not just a provocative moniker but a bigger part of his artistic vision: David wanted the band's music to show audiences that death was a necessary step in human spiritual evolution. Dannis and Bobby were open to changing the band's name to get a recording contract, but familial loyalty prevented them from overriding their elder brother's decision.

At the time, the brothers were in their late teens and early twenties and full of the cockiness of youth, so they believed that a better record deal would surely follow. But when that offer never materialized, the Hackneys convinced Don Davis to give them the master tapes from their studio session so they could press their own singles of what they believed was their strongest song, "Politicians in My Eyes," and promote themselves by distributing these records to Detroit radio stations in the hopes of getting enough exposure to attract another record deal. But that desperate effort at self-promotion failed; stations either did not play the single at all or only played it once or twice during nonpeak listening times.

By the beginning of 1977, the Hackneys were destitute, having spent all of their money to print five hundred copies of "Politicians in My Eyes." So when a distant relative in Burlington, Vermont, invited them to come visit for a two-week vacation, they ended up relocating there—in David's case, for several years and permanently for Dannis and Bobby. In Vermont, the Hackneys briefly played in the gospel band the 4th Movement, until David decided to return to Detroit. Dannis and Bobby moved on to other projects, including playing in a reggae band that was popular among local University of Vermont students. David, however, never really got over the failure of Death, and Bobby believes it was a contributing factor to his death in 2000 from lung cancer.

Death would have been consigned to the dustbin of history if Bobby's son Bobby Jr. had not heard "Politicians in My Eyes" at a party in San Francisco when it was played by a DJ specializing in obscure music. After Bobby Jr. recognized his father's voice, he located record collector Robert Cole Manis, who had acquired a copy of Death's single on eBay in 2001. At the dawn of the twenty-first century, "Politicians in My Eyes" had developed a cult following among fans of rare music, and Manis had paid $400 for his copy of the single. Manis soon became interested in helping the surviving members of Death distribute their first album and put them in touch with Chicago indie record label Drag City, who published *For the Whole World to See* from the master recording of their Groovesville session that had been sitting in a box in Bobby's attic for the past eight years. *For the Whole World to See* included reissues of the single "Politicians in My Eyes" and its B side, "Keep on Knockin'," as well as the remaining songs on the Groovesville session demo tape. Bobby Jr. and his brothers Julian and Urian formed the punk group Rough Francis to promote *For the Whole World to See* by performing covers of the songs on the album. The band's name was a tribute to their Uncle David, who before his death had recorded a single of his own music under his childhood nickname "Rough Francis," which he took as his post-Death stage name.

Rubin described *For the Whole World to See* as a "missing link between the high-energy hard rock Detroit bands like the Stooges and MC5 from the late 1960s and early '70s and the high-velocity assault of punk from its breakthrough years of 1976 and '77," which made the Hackneys "unwitting artistic kin to their punk-pioneer contemporaries the Ramones, Rocket from the Tombs, and the Saints" (Rubin 2009).

Other critics have also recognized the historical importance of *For the Whole World to See* as "the logical bridging of a lacuna [between hard rock and punk] rather than a before-its-time aberration" (Jurek 2018). The Hackney brothers are the subject of the documentary film *A Band Called Death* (2012).

THE DROPKICK MURPHYS: *GOING OUT IN STYLE*

The Dropkick Murphys are an American Celtic punk band from Boston who combine traditional Gaelic instruments, such as bagpipes, fiddle, tin whistle, accordion, mandolin, and banjo, with typical rock instrumentation. They play punk covers of traditional Irish, Welsh, and Scottish folk and political songs as well as their own compositions about drinking, politics, Irish-American culture, and working-class pride. The band got its name from Boston-area celebrity John E. "Dropkick" Murphy (1912–1977), a professional wrestler in the 1930s and 1940s who also ran an alcohol rehabilitation facility.

Although the Dropkick Murphys have been recording and continuously touring since 1996, they became more widely known in 2004 after the release of "Tessie," a cover of a song from the 1902 Broadway musical *The Silver Slipper*. "Tessie" was famously sung by fans of the Boston Americans (who eventually became the Boston Red Sox) during the 1903 World Series to rally their team to victory over the Pittsburgh Pirates. In 2004, when the Red Sox were in their first World Series in eighty-six years, the Dropkick Murphys released their cover of "Tessie" on EP to cheer their hometown team to victory. "Tessie" is still one of their highest-charting singles to date and is one of three songs played in Fenway Park after every Red Sox victory.

The song "Rose Tattoo," however, is better known in the United States. It was originally released as the lead single on the album *Signed and Sealed in Blood* (2013) and charted at No. 25 on *Billboard*'s US Hot Rock Songs in 2013. "Rose Tattoo" was rerecorded with vocals by Bruce Springsteen and released as a single to raise money for the victims of the Boston Marathon bombing in 2013.

The Dropkick Murphys' best-selling album, *Going Out in Style* (2011), is a representative sampling of the band's oeuvre, a mixture of covers of Irish standards and well-known songs about the downtrodden worldwide who stand up to injustice as well as their own compositions about Irish and Irish Americans in legend and history. *Going Out in Style* charted at No. 6 on the Billboard 200 list from 2011. Several tracks on *Going Out in Style* build on the stereotype of the Irish (and Irish

Ken Casey, lead singer of the Celtic punk band Dropkick Murphys, during a 2012 performance in Prague. (Yakub88/Dreamstime.com)

Americans) as scrappy, eternal underdogs, who love, mourn, drink, and fight with an intensity that makes them the antithesis of the comparatively passionless English or American WASPs. The title track is related from the perspective of an old man with no regrets in life who anticipates his wake, which will be celebrated in the Irish tradition of a booze-soaked party to send the departed off in glorious fashion.

The sentimental love song "1953" is in the tradition of other Irish ballads, such as "Peg o' My Heart," "Tessie," and "The Irish Rover." The characters of "Hang 'Em High" wait for a nameless enemy in an unknown battle, suggesting that, for the Irish, all fights begin and end in the same way. Although they were "outgunned and outnumbered," they refused to flee from "cowards," for whom there will be "no mercy, no quarter," because this opponent must pay for what they did wrong. The characters in "Deeds Not Words" battle a similar nameless enemy: "Where you gonna run to? where you gonna hide?" they taunt to an enemy who is dishonest and has this vengeance coming. "Cruel" is written from the perspective of someone who has had time to reflect on the rashness of his youth, when he was young and proud as well as hot-headed and stubborn. This speaker reflects that his "troubles won't end when [he's] saved by the bell" because he will "still answer to those [he] defiled."

"Hang 'Em High," "Deeds Not Words," and "Cruel" may seem like anthems that glorify mindless violence, as little information is given about the enemy or the context of the battle. However, the fighting Irish speaker of "Memorial Day," who enjoins listeners to take up arms to better their lives, puts into perspective why the Irish fight. It is a response to the diaspora created by English colonialism due to economic violence perpetrated against the poor by the wealthy. In the first verse, where the speaker enjoins the listener to "pick yourself up by your bootstraps" as a way of finding "a way out of your problems," he is not advocating rugged individualism, but rather reminding the listener of the power of the collective to fight the good fight, whatever the cause. "Take 'Em Down" also applies this spirit to unionizing. Those who do not stand up to the Goliaths of this world will suffer the life of someone who lives in fear of making mistakes.

Two songs tell the stories of Irish Americans whose lives have been ignored by most historians. "Broken Hymns" tells the story of Irish-American Union soldiers who were killed during the Civil War. Jimmy, the subject of "Broken Hymns," is dead, and his body is being returned to his grieving mother by train. It is unclear which battle Jimmy died in, but the date and place of his departure for war (April 1861, Brighton, Massachusetts) indicate that he may have been a member of the Irish-dominated Twenty-Eighth Massachusetts brigade led by Thomas F. Meagher, who believed that it was important for Irish Americans to fight for the Union cause as a way to counter anti-immigrant sentiment of the day that had been fueled by groups such as the Know Nothing party (Jones 2012). As Jimmy last wrote his mother a year to the day of his departure, he more than likely died in the Seven Days Battle near Richmond, Virginia, in July 1862, or the Battle of Malvern Hill on July 1, 1862. "The Hardest Mile" speculates about the fates of fifty-seven Irish immigrants who were lured to the United States in 1832 to build Mile 59 (Duffy's Cut) of the Pennsylvania Railroad. The workers were presumed to have died of cholera, as the work camp was hit hard by an epidemic that year. But 180 years later, seven bodies (six men and one woman) were unearthed near the site. The forensic evidence indicates that these people had been murdered rather than died of cholera, presumably by bosses who either did not want to pay them or who blamed the workers for bringing cholera to the camp (Phillip 2015).

Going Out in Style also includes two covers of well-known songs from another era. "Peg o' My Heart" (1913) was inspired by a popular musical at the time of the same name, in which the Irish Margaret "Peg" O'Connell is sent to England by her wealthy uncle to learn how to be a lady. Peg is looked down on by her English host family tasked with educating her for what they view as her lack of culture, but through a twist of fate, she becomes engaged to an English nobleman. The Dropkick Murphys' cover of "Peg o' My Heart" features vocals by Bruce Springsteen. "The Irish Rover" is an early nineteenth-century folk song about an impossibly large ship carrying an enormous amount of cargo and a colorful crew. After a seven-year journey, the ship gets lost in the fog before hitting a rock and sinking with all aboard, save the song's narrator. "Sunday Hardcore Matinee" extolls the joys of attending a punk show, which is described as both battle and musical experience. After the show, "your ears ring, your body aches" because you are "beaten, bruised and bloodied" from moshing rather than fighting. In this way, punk culture merges with Irish-American culture.

When the Dropkick Murphys are not touring or releasing albums (eleven studio albums to date as well as three compilations and numerous singles), they raise money for charity and support union causes and Democratic candidates. They have supported unions such as the AFL-CIO, the United Healthcare Workers, the Communication Workers of America, and the International Brotherhood of Electrical Workers and have their band T-shirts made by unionized American workers. In addition to raising money for the victims of the Boston Marathon bombing, they have collaborated with the Pablove Foundation, which raises money for pediatric cancer research. Bassist and lead singer Ken Cassey founded the Claddagh Fund in 2009 to support nonprofits serving children, veterans, and recovering addicts. In 2016, the band was honored by the Robert F. Kennedy Children's Action Corps for their charitable work (Fee 2016).

Not surprisingly, the Dropkick Murphys are also politically active, working with organizations such as PunkVoter to register young people to vote, and they took offense after learning that union-busting governor Scott Walker played their song "I'm Shipping Up to Boston" when he took the stage at the Iowa Freedom Summit in 2015. The band tweeted at the Republican governor to "please stop using our music in any way" (McMurray 2015).

FRENCH PUNK: *PUNK 45: LES PUNKS: THE FRENCH CONNECTION*

Punk did not begin in the United Kingdom but in France. The first punk festival was held in 1976 in the small French town of Mont-de-Marsan. Although attendance at this festival was small, between six hundred and fifteen hundred people (Briggs 2015, 144; Greene 2017, 125), being able to claim that you were at this event was "akin to having seen The Sex Pistols at the Lesser Free Trade Hall in Manchester on June 4, 1976, or a Velvet Underground gig in the 1960s" (Greene 2017, 125). Also, the few punk bands to play the festival, such as the Damned and Eddie and the Hotrods from England and Bijou and Little Bob Story from France, were outnumbered by the pub rock bands on the marquee. Festival organizer Marc Zermati, a French punk rock producer and owner of Paris's Open Market record shop, reportedly rejected the Sex Pistols for inclusion on the festival bill because he heard that they were not any good (Eudeline 2002, 14).

Organizing this festival was an act of defiance, as music festivals had been outlawed entirely by France's conservative president Giscard d'Estaing after the May 1968 demonstrations led by young people shut down the nation's economy for nearly two months, causing political leaders to fear revolution (*Underground* 2018). To avoid detection by the authorities, Zermati selected a bullfighting arena in Mont-de-Marson as the event's site. The small festival might have been forgotten if it had not been for the coterie of attending music journalists, led by Caroline Coon, who documented the event (Greene 2017, 125). The festival was enough of a success, however, to encourage Zermati to organize a second one in 1977, where the Damned were joined by the Clash (*Underground* 2018).

Punk's intellectual origins are also French, emerging from the countercultural manifestos of the May 1968 demonstrations (Greene 2017, 123). Punk's theme of "no future" was taken directly from the disenchantment and agitation expressed by French youth during these demonstrations. The protestors' "iconoclasm and questions posed as to the very essence of art (and anti-art) can be traced back to the French surrealists such as André Breton and the Dadaists of the early twentieth century" (Greene 2017, 125). Major British figures, such as Malcolm McLaren, Tony Wilson, and Bernard Rhodes, were influenced by this movement as well as the Situationist International, a group of avant-garde artists, intellectualists, and political theorists, such as Guy Debord (author of *The Society of the Spectacle*), "whose thoughts on personal freedom, the individual, and the consumer society were a major political and social influence on the British punk scene" (Greene 2017, 123).

The New York punk scene was also influenced by French literary and artistic figures that had been embraced by the French student counterculture of May 1968. Patti Smith, for example, "was an avid reader of both nineteenth-century Symbolist poet Arthur Rimbaud and the more contemporary Jean Genet and used the works of both writers in her performances. Thomas Miller, better known as Tom Verlaine of the band Television, took the last name as an homage to Paul Verlaine, another French Symbolist poet, while the dandified look cultivated by Richard Hell owed a lot to the artistic bohemia of nineteenth-century fin de siècle Paris" (Greene 2017, 123). McLaren wanted to name this new music New Wave, but Zermati prevailed with his name for this music, *punk*, a word that he believed captured the music's rebellious nature.

Despite punk's French origins, it did not catch on in France the way it did in England or the United States because its rebelliousness was just part of the French "tradition of resisting authoritarianism," which is still evident today (Hussey 2011). As well, "the French scene, which was centered mostly on [Zermati's] hipster record boutique Open Market in Paris, lacked the underground infrastructure of New York or London" (Reighley 2004). As a result, none of the French punk bands from this era achieved the same level of fame as their British or American counterparts. Many were unable to get the resources to produce albums of their work, and the only well-known song from that era sung in French was by the Belgian band Plastic Bertrand: "Ça Plane pour Moi" ("That's Cool for Me"). Soul and Jazz Records' compilation *Punk 45: Les Punks: The French Connection* provides a representative sampling of French punk and how it differed from its British and American counterparts. French punk is similar to British and American punk in how it looked to rock's early roots for inspiration: songs are short, and their instrumentation consists of an electric guitar, bass, and drums. However, French punks differ from their British and American counterparts by their willingness to incorporate electronica into their music by way of drum machines and synthesizers, creating electropunk. As a result, much early French punk is musically similar to American and British New Wave music.

Five of the songs on this compilation are by better-known French punk bands that did manage to produce albums, Marie et les Garçons (1976–1980) and Métal Urbain (1976–1980), and their artists' other musical projects, Electric Callas and Metal Boys. Marie et les Garçons' songs "Rein a Dire" ("Nothing to Say") and "A Bout de Souffle" ("Breathless") are characterized by the raw sound of early rock and roll combined with some of the experimental elements typical of New Wave. During their tenure, Marie et les Garçons opened for the X-Ray Spex at New York's CBGB before returning to Paris to back Patti Smith. Marie et les Garçons' vocalist, Marie Girard, went on to join the punk band Electric Callas. Their song "Kill Me Two Times" is musically similar to "Rein a Dire" and "A Bout de Souffle" in its stripped-down instrumentation that was typical of early rock.

The electropunk band Métal Urbain combines "gritty, blistering guitars and brutal confrontational vocals" with a drum machine and keyboards (Whitney 2004). Their founder, Eric Débris, was a fan of Brian Eno's work with Roxy Music, and he looked to "the unique potential of synthesizers to inject new sounds into the traditional rock-band setup" (Reighley 2004). Métal Urbain's other influences included Velvet Underground, MC5, the Stooges, and the New York Dolls (who played Paris in 1973), and their name was "was a nod to Lou Reed's *Metal Machine Music*" (Reighley 2004). In the late 1970s, Métal Urbain lacked a strong fan base in France, but they were better received in the United Kingdom, where they played "infamous London venues like the Roxy and the 100 Club" (Reighley 2004). The independent British label Rough Trade subsidized the pressing of ten thousand copies of "Paris Marquis," their second single, which quickly sold out in the United Kingdom. But, ultimately, Métal Urbain could not secure a bigger record deal in the United Kingdom (or in France): their "decision to perform in their native tongue limited their appeal with English-speaking punk fans" (Reighley 2004). Eric Débris and Charlie Hurbier recorded "Sweet Marilyn" with their spin-off band the Metal Boys. "Sweet Marilyn" is an excellent example of coldpunk, where the lyrics are delivered in a detached voice. The vocals are whispered rather than sung in this song.

Other examples of electropunk include A 3 dans le WC, KaS Product, the Dogs, Les Olivensteins, Asphalt Jungle, Gazoline, and Charles de Goal. KaS Product was "strongly associated with the French cold wave and electropunk movements" (*Post-Punk.com* 2019). The Dogs' cover of the Tremelos 1967 song "Here Comes My Baby" combines the raw energy of punk with rockabilly. Asphalt Jungle's brand of electropunk as demonstrated on their single "Planté Comme un Privé" has a distinctive New Wave sound. Charles de Goal's "Dans le Labyrinthe" ("In the Labyrinth") use of atonal notes is similar to the sound of American New Wave band Devo. Les Olivensteins' "Euthanasie" ("Euthanasia") uses the same bass lines as the one in American New Wave band the B-52s' "Planet Claire."

Other tracks on *Punk 45: Les Punks* have a classic punk sound. Calcinator's "Électrifié" ("Electrified") is an excellent example; the song's title seems to refer to the shimmering electric guitar chords that are part of its instrumentation. The distinctly punk sound of 84 Flesh, as exemplified on their song "Salted City," is reminiscent of bands like the Sex Pistols. The distorted guitar riffs of Angel Face's "Wolf City Blues" is reminiscent of hard rock acts like Jimmi Hendrix. The French bands on *Punk 45: Les Punks* who sing in English could be mistaken for American or British punk outfits from the same era. The Fantomes' "I Wanna Be Your Dog" is a credible cover of Iggy and the Stooges' punk classic. The Guilty Razors sing in English with what can only be described as a snotty American British accent. Their songs "Hurts and Noises" and "I Don't Wanna Be Rich" have the same phrenetic pace and feedback of their Year Zero counterparts. Warm Gun's "Breaking Windows," also sung in English, celebrates the joys of petty vandalism.

FUGAZI: *REPEATER* AND MINOR THREAT: "STRAIGHT EDGE"

To discuss Fugazi, it is also necessary to discuss Minor Threat, as the former was founded by Ian MacKaye, the front man of the latter until its dissolution in 1983, and the music of both bands was promoted by MacKaye's Dischord Records label. Not surprisingly, MacKaye's time in Minor Threat shaped Fugazi's sound—a smoother version of Minor Threat's hardcore that blends "elements of dub and reggae with high energy rock and punk/hardcore-styled guitars" (Edgar n.d.). After his time with Minor Threat, MacKaye's songwriting matured "away from the relentless buzz-saw 'loud fast rules' of hardcore punk toward more complex rhythms and dynamics" that characterize Fugazi's sound (Brace 1993).

Minor Threat was only together for four years, between 1980 and 1983, but the band was a major influence on the early punk scene in the United States. Along with Bad Brains and Black Flag, Minor Threat created hardcore punk. The band is also credited with starting the straight edge punk movement with their song "Straight Edge." Straight edge punks do not drink or do drugs, and some even abstain from sex and meat, to experience life in that most hardcore way of all, unfiltered. "Straight Edge" (released on the 1981 EP *Minor Threat*) describes a proto-straight-edged punk: he has better things to do than to do drugs and "pass out at the show." MacKaye recalls being repulsed by drugs and alcohol since the age of thirteen, after he saw friends getting drunk and high and committing petty crimes. He wondered whether this was what they would do for the rest of their lives (Azerrad 2001, 120). "Out of Step" (also on *Minor Threat*) similarly conveys MacKaye's straight-edge philosophy: "I don't smoke. I don't drink. I don't fuck. At least I can fucking think." His philosophy also abhors violence, which he views to be as senseless as excessively using alcohol and drugs, and he has asked fans to not slam dance at Minor Threat and Fugazi concerts because the practice often leads to fistfights (Azerrad 2001).

Minor Threat's sound was raw and primal. MacKaye shouted, rather than sung, lyrics against crashing drums and pulsating guitar riffs, and the songs were all so manic paced that it is sometimes difficult to hear what he is saying. Like MacKaye's straight-edged philosophy, Minor Threat's songs delivered their message without any musical niceties, such as tunefulness, that might make their music easier to listen to.

MacKaye formed Fugazi in 1987 with guitarist and vocalist Guy Picciotto, and their combined efforts created "a single voice, alternately barking and seductive, that defined '90s post-hardcore, if not the '90s rock underground itself" (Heller 2014). "Fugazi's sound is a progression on the loud-fast aesthetic practiced by funding member Ian Mackaye's former bands" ("Fugazi" 2001, 358), Embrace and Minor Threat ("Fugazi" 2001). The band's name is taken from Mark Baker's *Nam*, a collection of Vietnam War veterans' recollections about their wartime experiences. In the book, "Fugazi" was an acronym for "fucked up, got ambushed, zipped in[to a body bag]" (Brace 1993). "As with Minor Threat, the ideals behind Fugazi fed into the group's music, but the music itself is what made the most impact" (Heller 2014).

Fugazi's *Repeater* is widely regarded as the band's definitive album. It pulls together MacKaye and Picciotto's anti-corporate stance. The album's name describes how people are destined to repeat self-destructive behaviors until they realize how their actions are the result of global capitalism, which has blinded them to alternative ways of living as well as persuaded them that resistance to these forces is futile. In *Repeater*'s opening track, "Turnover," becoming alienated from one's body is a precondition for working people to get enough resources to live. "Repeater" continues in this vein while hinting at alternatives to the present system. MacKaye and Picciotto respond to someone who says that they need a job with an alternative to toiling at meaningless work to eke out a living: when they "need something [they] just reach out and grab it" in the way of many Year Zero punks, who squatted in abandoned buildings and took or found whatever they needed. MacKaye and Picciotto are not advocating victimizing others to live but, rather, in the truest punk fashion, resisting a system that only benefits a tiny minority at the expense of the many. They remind listeners that they are not interested in purchasing the popular products of consumer culture. Fugazi predates Chuck Palaniuk's screed against consumer culture in *Fight Club* by six years in their track "Merchandise." Their declaration that "you are not what you own" is a simplified version of Tyler Durden's exclamation, "You're not your fucking khakis" (Palaniuk 1996). "Greed" expresses this theme even more simply, while "Blueprint" offers mentorship in the punk way of living.

"Styrofoam," "Two Beats Off," and "Reprovisional" begin to answer the question at the heart of "Repeater," "Merchandise," and "Blueprint": how are people programmed to participate in a system that does not benefit them? "We are all bigots, so filled with hatred" that "we release our poisons like Styrofoam" because it was something written in a book. "Conflicting history tears us apart" in "Reprovisional." MacKaye wrote *Repeater*'s final track, "Shut the Door," after his friend and fellow musician Catherine Brayley died of a drug overdose. The oxymorons that MacKaye uses to describe his friend's self-destructive thinking, such as "I burn a fire to stay cool. I burn myself. I am the fuel," also apply to the self-sabotaging behaviors programmed into people in "Styrofoam," "Two Beats Off," and "Reprovisional."

Repeater was not a commercial success when it was released in 1990 and did not reach the Billboard 200 that year, but Fugazi's constant touring upon the album's release (250 shows in a year) boosted its sales to three hundred thousand by April 1991, an astounding number given that *Repeater* was released by MacKaye's independent label Dischord Record, which leaves it up to artists to promote their own work while giving them complete artistic control. Today, *Repeater*'s significance is better appreciated, and the album is frequently included in lists of top albums compiled by rock music publications such as *Pitchfork*, *SPIN*, and *Alternative Press*.

As well, Fugazi and Minor Threat are still important examples of how it is possible to be a successful artist without corporate sponsorship. Fugazi exemplified punk's DIY ethos by distributing their music through MacKaye's label, even after *Repeater*'s sales attracted the attention of record companies who would have signed the band, as well as by its insistence on playing venues that were accessible to all ages and cheap enough to let the band keep ticket prices below $10 (a promise they were able to keep during all but the end of their career). Fugazi went on "indefinite hiatus" in 2003 and have so far resisted fans' pleas for them to reunite, although band members still do play together when they are not working on other musical projects.

THE GERMS: *GI*

The Los Angeles punk band the Germs has been described as the "American Sex Pistols," not due to any musical similarity "but because both bands truly didn't know how to play their instruments and somehow became a huge success" (Jon 2017). In fact, the Germs set the "standard of anti-musicianship that made" other bands on the Los Angeles punk scene in the 1970s "seem polished by comparison" (Gold 2010). The Germs were also similar to the Sex Pistols in how the band's reputation for provoking mayhem got them banned from every venue in their hometown. By 1980, the Germs could only obtain bookings under the pseudonym GI, Germs Incognito. Yet, the Germs were a major influence on the nascent punk scene in the United States, and many music historians consider them to be the originators of hardcore punk (Sartwell 2002). The Germs' lead singer, Darby Crash (Paul Beaham), was the literal poster boy for the Los Angeles punk scene in the late 1970s: the movie poster for Penelope Spheeris' documentary of the Southern California punk scene, *The Decline of Western Civilization*, features a still of Crash passed out on stage. Finally, like Sid Vicious, Crash died young of a heroin overdose.

The Germs were formed in 1975 by Crash as part of his five-year plan "to make himself immortal" by starting a band with his friends that he would make into a "cultish, outrageous live act"; releasing "one great album"; and, finally, committing suicide "to secure his legend" (Adams 2008). His plan had "the timeframe of his hero David Bowie's apocalyptic anthem 'Five Years'" (Adams 2008). Crash was "a precocious and charismatic high school dropout who was fascinated by the idea of mind control and enjoyed trying to manipulate peers into doing his biding" (Mullen 2000). He had no difficulty convincing his high school friend Georg Ruthenberg and several other Hollywood-area girls to join his band and let him give them stage names. Ruthenberg became Pat Smear, and Teresa Ryan became Lorna Doom. Don Bolles, who kept his name, was the last to join the Germs as their permanent drummer.

The Germs quickly "became a resident band at the Masque, the hippest of all LA's underground clubs," where punk bands would try to outdo one another's outrageous behavior (Adams 2008). Channeling Iggy Pop, Crash would cut himself on stage and then draw a bloody circle on his chest to signify his cultish "Circle One," which represented the band and its followers. "Germs fans identified themselves with a cigarette burn on the inside of their left wrist; the burn had to be created by another fan" (Adams 2008). Crash wrote nearly all of the band's songs, "borrowing wildly from Nietzsche and Oswald Spengler, David Bowie and Freddie Mercury, Mussolini and Dianetics" to create "a narcotic kind of lyric that he believed might be a form of mind-control laced with despair and self-parody" (Adams 2008). During the Germs' chaotic live performances, Crash would either encourage fans to vandalize the venue, or the crowd would become angry and start to riot when Crash was too stoned or drunk to perform. By 1978, the Germs' "appearances were occasions of such mayhem that they were routinely broken up by riot police" (Adams 2008). Nevertheless, by the time the Germs recorded their one studio album, *GI*, the band's final lineup of Smear, Doom, and Bolles had gone from barely knowing how to play their instruments to being world-class rock musicians, making music that compressed "glitter rock and anarchy and teenage kicks and sun-bleached California disappointment" of the 1970s "into a single, pulsing dot of antimatter" (Gold 2010).

GI was a landmark album that would secure Crash's legacy with future generations, as per his five-year plan. The album was produced by Joan Jett, who was at the end of her career with the Runaways. *GI* "sonically documents the LA scene's relatively late punk flowering" and led the way for the coming generation of that city's hardcore punks (Empire 2008). *GI*'s first track, "What We Do Is Secret," describes young people's anger over how they are perceived by their elders, who have left them with no future: "We're aberrations, defects in a defect's mirror" who have "been here all the time." "Land of Treason" reprises this theme—"We're enemies of men. We are not desired"—and "Richie Dagger's Crime" elaborates on it. Richie Dagger is a young yet independent boy who is unpopular and alone. He is a thinly veiled version of Crash; his "life was such a mess and his friends weren't quite the best," but "he could set your mind ablaze with his sparkling eyes and visionary case." "Let's Pretend" and "The Other Newest One" are anti–love songs: "Love is a future that you still can't see" ("Let's Pretend"), and "You're not the first, you're not the last" ("The Other Newest One").

However, the best tracks on *GI* express Crash's generation's nihilism while mythologizing the Germs before they are even gone. Like X-Ray Spex's "Television," "Media Blitz" also characterizes the system as something that programs viewers, an undesirable fate. The result is a generation of young people who are "the red-eyed legends of the night before"; "We're the dead mind babies of the T.V. war." They can only secure a better future for themselves if they destroy the current system. "We Must Bleed" captures the existential panic precipitated by the modern world, where "the traffic's screaming, but we can't hear," and "the sounds, the metals" are driving everyone mad. This feeling is underscored by the sound of metal throughout the song. As a result, they have to literally cut themselves until they bleed to achieve relief from the resulting anxiety. "Dragon Lady" mythologizes Crash as the next cult figure: "You walk to the temple on the boulevard. You know the way in 'cause you're the son of God." Crash is this cult figure in "Shut Down (Annihilation Man)," where he declares that he has "got your minds" and "now I want your souls." In "The Slave," he describes achieving this control over others through his music, which makes listeners "writhe in the shackle" and twist their bodies "to the beat of the neuro-sutra can can." The Germs' performance of their songs turn Crash's poetic lyrics into subliminal messages, as Crash screams rather than sings them and often fails to speak into the microphone, leaving audiences to only catch parts of what he is saying.

After the release of *GI*, producer Jack Nitzsche took an interest in the band, and in 1980, he recorded six Germs songs for William Friedkin's film *Cruising* but ended up only using the track "Lion's Share" during a murder scene. In July of that year, the Germs broke up, and Crash went to London and hung out with Adam Ant's entourage before returning to Los Angeles with a Mohawk to start the Darby Crash band, which Smear described as being "like The Germs, but worse" (Acorn 2008). Less than six months after the Germs had broken up, Crash persuaded his former bandmates to do a reunion show, which they performed in December 1980 under the name GI to a sold-out crowd at the Starwood Hotel. Rumor has it that Crash's real motivation for the reunion show was to make money to purchase enough heroin to commit suicide with his girlfriend, Casey Cola. On December 7, Crash injected his girlfriend and himself with $400 worth of heroin. Cola survived, and Crash died; however, his self-mythologizing exit did not go according to plan. On December 8, 1980, the news of Crash's death was upstaged by the murder of John Lennon in Central Park.

The remaining members of the Germs would not reunite until nearly thirty years later when Rodger Grossman was making his 2007 biopic of the band, *What We Do Is Secret*. Grossman asked Smear, Doom, and Bolles to teach the actors playing the younger versions of themselves how to play the Germs' songs. Afterward, they performed a set with Shane West, who plays Crash in the film and looks and sounds remarkably like the iconic front man. The collaboration was so successful that the Germs decided to reform and tour with West as their new lead singer.

GOGOL BORDELLO: *SUPER TARANTA!*

Gogol Bordello's mission statement describes their music as "new mind-stretching combinations" of the world's folk music that incites "raw joy and survival energy" in their listeners. Gogol Bordello is not so much a band as it is a cabaret, the creation of Ukrainian ex-pat Eugene

Gogol Bordello front man Eugene Hütz (left) with Pamela Racine (right) and Yuri Lemeshev (back) on accordian during a 2012 performance in Luzhniki Statium (Moscow). (Yulia Grigoryeva/Dreamstime.com)

Hütz and musicians from all over the world who rotate in and out of the complex musical project, which has been touring and recording since 1999. Gogol Bordello is named after the nineteenth-century Ukrainian author Nikolai Gogol, who wrote in Russian about Ukrainian culture during the time when the Russian tsars augmented control of the region by outlawing the Ukrainian language and renaming Ukrainian cities with Russian toponyms. Hütz described Nikolai Gogol's work as "a kind of a smuggling operation" in how the author wrote about the Ukraine "with Russian words" to preserve his homeland's culture (Freeman 2008).

Gogol Bordello's musical mission is similarly a "smuggling operation" that slips Gypsy and Eastern European music into the English-speaking world "to make things exciting when they're not" (Freeman 2008). Gogol Bordello's unironic and "freewheeling use of the world's musical cultures," which "contain endless art-possibilities," is subversive in how it counters the postmodernist belief that "everything has been done," implying that making original art is impossible, according to the mission statement on Gogol Bordello's website. This belief discourages artistic exploration, which has already been suppressed by the popular culture industrial complex that privileges the work of a chosen few whose material can be profitably marketed to the masses. Gogol Bordello's music is sonically and linguistically varied, drawing on international traditions as well as being sung in languages other than English to create a blend of Eastern European folk melodies and African and Latin rhythms. The band incorporates congo drums, violins, guitars, and accordions into their music.

Gogol Bordello's subversiveness can only be understood by attending one of their concerts, which are more like the raucous second line of a parade, where the music transforms bystanders into participants who strut and sing with the band until they arrive at their destination. Audience participation is mandatory at a Gogol Bordello concert: the music invades the nervous system, tapping into an ancient bodily knowledge of the physical expression of joy. The audience does not need to know the dance steps; they are the dance. In this way, Gogol Bordello disrupts the modern model of happiness through the purchase of consumer goods. Art, following the punk model, can and should be made by everyone. It provokes the spontaneous eruption of joy. Because Gogol Bordello's music is best understood by experiencing them live, it is difficult to recommend an album or song that accurately represents their work. However, their fourth album, *Super Taranta!* (2007), covers a representative sampling of themes that are typical of Gogol Bordello's oeuvre.

The "taranta" in the album's title and its last track aptly characterizes Gogol Bordello's musical project, which is to cure "the jaded and irony-diseased" with "acts of music, theatre, chaos, and sorcery," according to Gogol Bordello's online mission statement. The word *taranta* references a dance invented by medieval Tuscan women that gave them momentary relief from the strict, patriarchal culture that tightly regulated their bodies. The taranta, or tarantella, is a rhythmic, sensual dance that women performed as an antidote to the venom of the "tarantole" spider, whose bite was reputed to make women distraught (*Masseria Faresalento Agriturismo* n.d.) Although the tarantole spider is a fictional creation, women in the Middle Ages were permitted to dance the taranta because their performance adhered to traditional gender roles. The church preached that women were inherently more frail than men, so when they danced with abandon while under the influence of the fictitious arachnid's venom, they were performing feminine frailty. The mostly instrumental "Super Taranta!" is an example of taranta-style music. Its upbeat tempo provokes modern listeners to dance as if no one is watching, neutralizing the disabling poison of bourgeois morality that makes people too embarrassed to use their bodies so freely in public.

"Supertheory of Supereverything," "Harem in Tuscany," "American Wedding," "Your Country," and "Alcohol" expose methods of social control so that they can be more effectively resisted. "Alcohol" is a drinking song that exults the beverage for enabling the user to "walk on burning bridges" and "fall in love with witches." "Your Country" exposes the geopolitical order as something unrelated to the will of the people. Nevertheless, this ever-changing global order cannot "prevent us from living most magical of lives." "Supertheory of Supereverything" questions all religious and political ideologies that classify and control people by categorizing them as either sex-addicted or suffering from schizophrenia. Such categories are used today to label people as undesirable immigrants into the United States. It is impossible to live a "decent life" in "Harem in Tuscany (Taranta)" because "the boots" of moral rectitude "are just too small." In the United States, the concept of *decency* is derived from the Puritans, who equated it with rejecting all pleasures of the flesh, particularly sex. In "Harem in Tuscany," Uncle Sadrino (Uncle Sam) leaves the United States for Tuscany to once again feel godlike, innocent, and free in this utopia. While some aver that Sadrino emerged from this harem less intelligent than when he went in, these narrow-minded critics equate intelligence to asceticism. The final chorus reveals that the Tuscan utopia is not limited to that geographical location, but it can be found anywhere with a culture that celebrates art and pleasure as sacraments. In the final chorus, Hütz recommends a "punk rock siesta in harem Carpathy," the region of the Ukraine where he was born, implying that this harem can be found in other parts of the world as well. These songs all explain why, for instance, "the word celebration just doesn't come to mind" in the case of an "American Wedding," which lacks a twenty-four-hour band and a three-day supply of vodka and herring.

Several tracks on *Super Taranta!* elaborate on Gogol Bordello's unique, joyful existentialism, such as "Ultimate" and "Zina-Marina." "Ultimate" poses the question, "if we are not here to do what you and I wanna do," then "why the hell are we even here?" And "Zina-Marina" points out that "it is easier to see evil as [an] entity" instead of a "condition inside you and me." The title of "Wonderlust King" is a malapropism of the word *wanderlust*, describing not just Hütz's immigrant adventures migrating from city to city but his love of wondering, of "hunting and gathering first-hand information / Challenging definitions of sin" and looking for the highest form of beauty. Other tracks illustrate Gogol Bordello's mission to "confront the jaded and irony-diseased" with their "chaotic and spontaneous" performances that are "alarming and response provoking." According to Gogol Bordello's website, "Forces of Victory" and "Tribal Connection" encourage listeners to view one another as members of one varied and glorious tribe, a "union of souls" ("Forces of Victory") of a "fun loving restless breed" ("Tribal Connection") that together can "turn frustration into inspiration" ("Tribal Connection").

Music itself is a powerful force to overthrow the existing order, as it is described in "Dub the Frequencies of Love." Dub music is an example of the sort of musical transmigration practiced by Gogol Bordello. Dub is a subgenre of reggae (a genre that influenced punk and ska) that remixes existing recordings to create original music. "My Strange Uncles from Abroad" elucidates Gogol Bordello's own musical transmigration taken from Hütz's ancestors. He gathered everything that they wrote to eventually share with "his strange nephews from abroad," who, in a future where those who are jaded have been cured, will have pure hearts because they were never told "to trust a plastic beat."

Gogol Bordello has released ten studio albums to date as well as six compilations and the 2005 EP *East Infection*. The band is the subject of the documentary *Gogol Bordello Nonstop* and has appeared in *Larger than Life and in 3D*, which is live concert footage from the 2009 Austin City Limits festival.

GREEN DAY: *DOOKIE* AND *AMERICAN IDIOT*

Green Day is one the of bands credited with reviving mainstream interest in punk in the 1990s after it had gone underground for about a decade to be replaced by alternative and grunge on the charts (Ramirez 2009). Childhood friends Billie Joe Armstrong and Mike Dirnt started Green Day in the San Francisco Bay area in 1990. Tré Cool joined the band as the permanent drummer after they recorded their first album, *39/Smooth* (1990). To date, Green Day has recorded twelve studio albums, sold more than eighty-five million records worldwide, won five Grammy Awards, and has been inducted into the Rock and Roll Hall of Fame.

Green Day's third studio album and major-label debut, *Dookie* (1994), was their breakout hit, bringing "the sound of late-'70s punk to a new, younger generation" (Erlewine n.d., "Green Day"). *Dookie* achieved diamond certification and is at the top of *Rolling Stone*'s list of the "50 Greatest Pop Punk Albums." Their seventh album, the rock opera *American Idiot*, shows that the band has matured from teen angst to a more complex existential crisis, which is played out through the character of Jimmy, both an adolescent Armstrong as well as an every-punk character.

NPR named *American Idiot* as one of the fifty most important recordings of the first decade of the 2000s, and it has achieved multi-Platinum status at this writing (Bolen 2009).

Green Day's early success was due to their single "Longview"; its video was in frequent rotation in 1994 on MTV and VH1, making it the first of Green Day's songs to become a major hit on American and international charts. Other singles followed that also rose to the top of American and international charts. The tracks on *Dookie* are representative of the band's adolescent sense of humor (band members were only in their early twenties when *Dookie* was recorded), as is the name of the album, which is also a colloquial term for feces. And it was the band's "unique brand of adolescent, self-denigrating humor" that made them so appealing when *Dookie* was released (di Perna 1994). "Longview" is about a case of ennui that is so debilitating that the speaker cannot even derive pleasure from masturbation. But the topic of the song is not what makes it remarkable, as most punk bands cover the theme of boredom, though in "fast, scrappy songs that convey the subject's stifling nature." "Longview," however, is played in a "shuffle rhythm, that lazy, swinging groove typically used by folks ranging from elderly bluesmen to lame dive bar cover bands," and guitars are absent from the verses, which emphasizes Mike Dirnt's playing of "what has since become the most recognizable punk bass riff of all time, a loping four-bar figure he came up with while tripping on acid" (Ramirez 2009). But what ultimately made "Longview" into Green Day's breakthrough hit were all of the swear words, claims *PopMatters*' AJ Ramirez, who could not "think of an earlier rock single that had to have so many words unsubtly censored for airplay," which made the song popular with teens who could easily fill in the muffled profanities.

The opening lines to *Dookie*'s second hit single, "Basket Case," are "the sort of instantly-quotable disaffection teenagers scrawl into their notebooks during class" (Ramirez 2012). Armstrong, who struggles with anxiety, has described "Basket Case" as characterizing anxiety and panic attacks as responses to the chaos in the world instead of just personal problems (Fricke 2014). Armstrong thwarts the listener's expectations of the singer in the song's third verse, where he references visiting a male prostitute. Armstrong, who identifies as bisexual, wanted to challenge listeners' expectations to show that "the world is not as black and white" as they might believe (Fricke 2014).

Other breakout singles from *Dookie* include "Welcome to Paradise," "When I Come Around," and "She." "Welcome to Paradise" was written about Armstrong's life after he moved out of his mother's house in

Rodeo, California, a working-class neighborhood surrounded by refineries and chemical plants on the outskirts of the wealthier Berkeley to become a squatter in an even worse part of town where gunshots could frequently be heard. "When I Come Around" has become "a punk standard for the ages" due to how "its riff puts a clever spin on a well-worn chord progression that makes it unmistakable" (Ramirez 2012). "She" is "sensitive without being soft; in between Armstrong's empathetic declarations of 'scream at me until my ears bleed, I'll take heed just for you,' the band is hammering away at its instruments with amped-up intensity" (Ramirez 2012).

Green Day's later albums, *Insomniac* (1995), *Nimrod* (1997), and *Warning* (2000), were commercially successful but too similar to *Dookie* to make much of an impression. The rock opera *American Idiot* (2004) demonstrated how the band had matured musically and intellectually. *American Idiot* is the story of Jimmy, a punk who is disillusioned with what life has to offer because he is coming of age during the contested presidential election of 2000, 9/11, and the Iraq War. Jimmy is a thinly disguised version of young Armstrong, with his turbulent family life in a dead-end working-class community, where the biggest diversions are to be found under the interstate or in a convenience store parking lot. In *American Idiot*, "Green Day nurtured a more blatant political consciousness which allowed for a refocusing of that anger towards less-juvenile purposes," such as protesting the Iraq War (Ramirez 2012). All three members of Green Day come from working-class backgrounds, "from the kind of families who bear a disproportionate amount of the tax burden of foreign wars, and whose children make up a disproportionate percentage of the forces who end up fighting them" (Pappademas 2014).

Five hit singles came from *American Idiot*, including its title track, "Jesus of Suburbia," "Holiday," "Boulevard of Broken Dreams," and "Wake Me Up When September Ends." "American Idiot" sets the story in the post-9/11 paranoid age, where a nation of American idiots is under the control of the media and accepting of the half-truths they are told to justify the Iraq War based on flimsy claims that the nation possessed weapons of mass destruction. The lyrics of "American Idiot" seem prescient years later after Russian interference in the 2016 presidential election.

"Jesus of Suburbia" establishes *American Idiot*'s story about Jimmy, who is also the Jesus of Suburbia and lives "In a land of make believe / That don't believe in me." Jimmy and his friends are the children of hypocrites who feed them lie after lie instead of any spiritual sustenance, so Jimmy leaves home in search of answers. "Jesus of Suburbia" and its musical counterpart on *American Idiot*, "Homecoming," are bookends that describe Jimmy's existential journey, and their structure is also similar; each is over nine minutes long and has five distinct musical movements. "Holiday" and "Boulevard of Broken Dreams" have a contiguous storyline, which is emphasized on the album by how the last notes of "Holiday" blend with the opening buzzing guitar of "Boulevard." "Holiday" is a rousing anti-war anthem in which Jimmy tells us that he begs "to dream and differ from the hollow lies" told by people such as "the president gas man" who has sent people like Jimmy away to die for oil in a foreign land. "Holiday" is "the band's fiercest invective," with its outrage and dismay at the state of the post-9/11 United States (Ramirez 2012). "Boulevard of Broken Dreams" is slow and contemplative, finding Jimmy walking alone and thinking about the ideas expressed in "Holiday." "Wake Me Up When September Ends," is a ballad that makes more sense in the context of the 2009 musical adaptation of *American Idiot*—a working-class youth joins the military to provide for his future family to the dismay of his pregnant girlfriend.

"American Idiot" is one of two songs from the album that have been repurposed by listeners to use for other protests. In 2018, British protesters encouraged their countrymen via social media to download "American Idiot" during the first two weeks in July so that it would top the U.K. charts when President Donald Trump was scheduled to make a state visit to meet with Prime Minister Theresa May and Queen Elizabeth (Wanshel 2018). "Wake Me Up When September Ends" was repurposed by blogger Zadi Diaz to protest the federal government's glacial response to Hurricane Katrina. Diaz's video montage of the human suffering in Katrina's aftermath is set to the song. Hurricane Katrina made landfall on August 29, 2005, but most of the footage that Diaz uses in her video was shot weeks after the storm, during a hot, muggy September that seemed endless to residents and rescue workers in New Orleans who were navigating the city without electricity or running water. In the background, President George W. Bush can be heard giving a public address in which he reassures residents that the "great city of New Orleans will be back." Green Day performed "Wake Me Up" later that year at a benefit for Katrina victims (Moss 2005) and again in 2006 in the Superdome with U2 before the New Orleans Saint's first game in the refurbished stadium ("Bringing the Music Back to New Orleans" 2007).

American Idiot was adapted for the stage in 2009 and had a 442-show run on Broadway before touring internationally. Green Day is the subject of Spotify's 2017 *Landmark: Green Day* documentary. The band also produced the documentary *Turn It Around: The Story of East Bay Punk*.

THE JAM: *IN THE CITY*

The Jam is a mod-revival punk band from Woking, United Kingdom, that was formed in 1972 by front man Paul Weller and some of his high school friends. Weller was a versatile musician who did backing vocals and played guitar, bass, and keyboards in addition to being the Jam's lead singer. In their early career, the Jam shared the angry outlook of many of their U.K. punk contemporaries, such as the Clash, the Sex Pistols, and the Slits, and used the same high-speed, stripped-down approach to their music. But on stage, the Jam did not look like a punk outfit: they performed in tailored suits instead of leather and fetish wear or ripped T-shirts and jeans. Weller was joined by Rick Buckler (drums, percussion) and Bruce Foxton (vocals, rhythm guitar, bass) for the band's first studio album, *In the City*.

In the City exemplifies the Jam's punk sound. The twelve songs on this album are rougher and shorter than on their later albums, and the sound relies on the efforts of the trio alone instead of drum machines and prerecorded sounds that characterize their later work, which is more New Wave than punk. *In the City*'s opening track, "Art School," is a punk manifesto for the genre, which was born of art school bands. "Art School" tells listeners that they do not need permission to do what they choose or go where they please because "any taste that [they] feel is right." In 1977, "any taste that you feel is right" critiqued the corporate gatekeepers of mass culture, who had replaced the social conformity of the 1950s with leftover hippie culture that was appropriated and repackaged by record companies and fashion marketers who told young consumers what type of music they should listen to and how they should dress. Weller describes the media as a brainwashing enterprise that controls people when they have no right to create the rules or judge others.

"I've Changed My Address," "I Got by in Time," "Away from the Numbers," "Sounds from the Street," and "Time for Truth" also decry conformity. The speaker in "I've Changed My Address" moves after his girlfriend expects them to get married because he does not believe in the institution of marriage. "I Got by in Time" reflects on how marriage itself has been changed in the past decade: "all the bonds you make between ya can be broken any time you want now." "Away from the Numbers" attacks the Jam's critics in the music business who questioned their punk authenticity, as the band came from the London suburb of Woking rather than Bromley, the suburb that was home to many other U.K. punk bands. "Numbers" refers to record sales, the barometer by which the music industry judges a band's success and legitimacy. In

"Time for Truth," the Jam tells off the same establishment types that the Slits, X-Ray Spex, the Clash, and the Sex Pistols held up for ridicule: "time for the young to stick together now," Weller sings, because the lawmakers, corporations, and older generation are "trying for a police state" to rule the bodies and minds of youth.

"Bricks and Mortar" is the only overtly political song on *In the City* in that it targets a specific social problem instead of offering a generalized critique of repressive institutions. The "bricks and mortar" of the title refers to urban renewal efforts in the United Kingdom in the 1970s that replaced old buildings with new construction. The government touted this type of urban renewal as progressive social change in the United Kingdom, which was in the midst of an extended recession and still visibly scarred by World War II. However, the urban renewal projects exacerbated poverty by displacing low-income residents; their old dwellings were torn down before any affordable housing was constructed for them. The new buildings that replaced the dilapidated structures also have a sinister quality: "windows and mirrors like a two-way glass" suggests the creation of a modern police state in the United Kingdom.

Other tracks on *In the City* reference earlier rock and roll and R & B from the 1950s and early 1960s, when people over thirty generally viewed this music as a threat to moral decency. The term *rock and roll* was originally used to describe African American gospel music and rhythm and blues. It refers to the swaying body movements of Black churchgoers listening to spirituals and is also a sexual analogy that characterizes the type of dancing people did to R & B in honky-tonks and juke joints. Religious conservatives considered this type of dancing to be indecent and even went as far as banning dancing altogether in some municipalities (as is famously portrayed in the 1984 film *Footloose*).

"Non-Stop Dancing" draws on the 1950s and early 1960s as a model of rebellion via dancing in ways that older people found so sexually suggestive that in 1956 Elvis was famously shot from the waist up when he appeared on the *Ed Sullivan Show* to avoid the ire of the FCC censors. (Gibson n.d.; Runtagh 2016, "Elvis Presley"). "In the City," the album's title track, predicts New Wave and revivalist rock and roll through the band's jangly guitars and treble-heavy sound that is reminiscent of British invasion music as it was originally heard on AM radio. "Takin' My Love" and "Slow Down" evoke the early Beatles, whose sound influenced many early punk musicians. "Takin' My Love's" title is similar to the Beatles' "All My Lovin'." "Slow Down" sounds more like early Beatles than any other Jam song, with lyrics that are pregnant with innuendo and squealing guitars, a sound perfected in the 1950s by artists such as Bo Diddly, Fats Domino, Buddy Holly, Elvis Presley, Janis Martin, and Larry Collins' 1958 "Whistle Bait," to name a few.

The Jam's cover of the "Batman Theme" also evokes the 1960s—the simple but unmistakable chords and lyrics were instantly recognizable to their contemporaries as the opening of the campy 1960s television show, with its over-the-top parodies of 1960s culture, and the Jams' punk gloss does not change the meaning of the original the way that other punk covers so famously transformed well-known songs, such as Sid Vicious's version of Frank Sinatra's "My Way" or the entire song catalog of Me First and the Gimmie Gimmies.

Of all the bands that emerged from the 1970s London punk scene, the Jam had the biggest impact on popular music in the 1980s. With each successive album, their sound moved away from punk toward a complex sound achieved with drum machines and layers of recorded vocals that could not be reproduced outside of the studio. The Jam's singles topped the British charts, making them superstars in the United Kingdom, but not elsewhere, as their music was too British to become popular outside of England. Nevertheless, their influence can be heard in later "British guitar pop bands of the '80s and '90s, from the Smiths to Blur and Oasis" (Erlewine n.d., "The Jam: Artist Biography").

Unlike most bands, the Jam ended their career at height of their popularity. In October of 1982, Weller abruptly decided that he was frustrated with the trio's sound and it was time for him to move on. However, instead of telling his bandmates in person about his decision to quit, Weller's father (The Jam's manager) relayed this message. Afterwards, the Jam did a quick farewell tour, and their last single, "Beat Surrender," topped the British charts that year. The Jam has been the subject of the documentary *The Jam: About a Young Idea* (2015).

L7: *BRICKS ARE HEAVY*

Donita Sparks and Suzi Gardner founded the feminist punk band L7 in 1985, later adding Jennifer Finch and then and Demetra Plakas, the band's third and permanent drummer. L7 created its own version of "cock rock" by "mixing traditional aspects of tough rough-and-roll bravado with overtly feminist lyrics and actions," covering subjects ranging from women's rights to control their bodies and be in public spaces without harassment to warmongering (Raha 2005, 182).

L7 has erroneously been associated with Seattle grunge of the 1990s, "even though Sparks and Gardner formed L7 in Los Angeles while both were working at the *LA Weekly*"(Raha 2005, 183). But that association is understandable given that L7's music has a grunge sound: L7's "cynical snarling" and "heavy droning guitars" are similar to the "heavy guitar sounds of grunge, which undoubtedly helped them lead a major label deal with Slash/Warner and a main-stage slot on the 1994 Lollapalooza tour" when grunge was popular. (Raha 2005, 182). Band members also sported a grunge look on stage; they dressed in jeans and T-shirts and sometimes wore heavy and smeared makeup. However, L7's stage look was cultivated to defy men's attempts to objectify band members, who made bold sexual expressions in their music in a scene that was not a welcoming place for women artists—their riot grrrl contemporaries Bikini Kill frequently dealt with hostile male audience members who would hurl bottles at the band while they were performing.

L7 is also notable for its feminist activism. The band organized the Rock for Choice concerts in 1991 with *LA Weekly* music editor Sue Cummings as an event that would allow musicians to show their support for women's reproductive freedom in North America, which was being chipped away by domestic terrorist bombings of clinics in the early 1990s as well as by politicians laying the groundwork for overturning *Roe v. Wade* with bills that chipped away at women's right to control their bodies as outlined in the 1973 Supreme Court decision. The Rock for Choice concerts continued annually through 2001 and featured other well-known bands and performers, including Hole, Liz Phair, Joan Osborne, Bikini Kill, the Bangles, Salt-N-Pepa, Melissa Ethridge, Sarah McLachlan, Kim Gordon, and Joan Jett (Raha 2005, 185). The Feminist Majority Foundation named L7 Feminists of the Year for their activism. L7 called attention to the dearth of female-headed acts at the 1999 Warped Tour by sending attendees a "love letter" in the form of a banner reading "Warped Needs More Beaver . . . Love, L7" that was flown over the heads of concertgoers (Raha 2005, 184).

Bricks Are Heavy, the band's third studio album, got L7 national attention with the single "Pretend That We're Dead," which peaked at No. 8 in *Billboard*'s 1992 alternative songs list. "Pretend We're Dead," one of the three singles from *Bricks Are Heavy*, describes what happens when women fail to be politically active. The bouncy 1980s-style pop tune is at odds with its biting lyrics, which urge the listener to "turn the tables with our unity" against a common enemy who is "neither moral nor majority." The speaker in "Everglade" is the sort of female punk fan that Bikini Kill had in mind with their "girls to the front" policy at their concerts. When she heads for the pit, at the front of the stage, a drunk man tries to attack her for occupying what is usually considered a "male-only" space. But Everglade uses her harasser's size against him: "on his own feet and hit the floor, Glade got to pushing and rolled him out the door." "Mr. Integrity" takes to task mansplaining punk purists. "Wargasm" is "fueled by crunchy power chords (like all L7 numbers) and unapologetically political (like most L7 numbers)" (Arnold 1992). "Wargasm" decries American military intervention overseas ("Wave those flags high in the air / As long as it takes place over there") and describes the bloodlust of hawkish citizens as being sexual in nature.

Several songs on *Bricks Are Heavy* tackle women's ambivalent relationship with anger, an emotion that is so antithetical to normative femininity that women are uncomfortable expressing it. The titular creature of "Monster" is the speaker's "insanity double" who she can depend on when things go sour to put her in touch with her anger, which will carry her through during these times. This "insanity double" is characterized as a "monster" because when women express their anger, they are characterized as out of control and irrational. Neither "Everglade" nor "Monster" charted in the United States, but both were popular overseas—"Everglade" reached No. 33 on the U.K. singles list. "Shitlist" similarly treats women's anger as an understandable response to people who have caused the singer to feel down or doubtful rather than a sign of their inherent instability. When the speaker of "Shitlist" "grabs [her] pen and write[s] out a list," she is taking powerful action by committing her anger to writing; her list reminds her to stay mad at people who have made her feel incapable or unworthy and reaffirms her own competence and worth. "Shitlist" did not chart, nor did it receive airplay, because the title and lyrics contain profanities.

"Diet Pill" tells a story of what happens when women are pressured to swallow their anger to conform to rigid gender roles that set them up for subordination. The song's opening phrase, "my diet pill is wearing off," is a line from John Waters' *Hairspray*, spoken by Edna Turnblatt when she is trying to indoctrinate her daughter, Tracy, into a limiting adult gender role by dismissing her desire to be something more than a domestic servant to a husband and children. Edna's "diet pills" give her the energy for domestic drudgery, but when these pills wear off for the speaker of "Diet Pill," she is no longer willing to endure this slavery.

Bricks Are Heavy was ranked No. 39 on *NME*'s list of the best albums of 1992 and No. 249 in *Spin Magazine*'s "The 300 Best Albums of the Past Thirty Years" list. *Bricks Are Heavy* was produced by Butch Vig, who had worked with Nirvana. "Where L7 differs from Nirvana, however, is in the clarity of its angry lyrics. There are no 'Oh well, whatever, neverminds' on *Bricks Are Heavy*. This is a band that knows exactly how it feels" about topics such as war, sexism, and American political apathy (Arnold 1992).

L7 has recorded six studio albums to date and been the subject of a concert film made by former Nirvana bassist Krist Novoselic (*L7: The Beauty Process*, 1998), a documentary about women in rock (*Not Bad for a Girl*, 1994), and band biopic (*L7: Pretend We're Dead*, 2016). L7 also played the band Camel Lips in John Waters's 1994 film *Serial Mom*, and their songs have been on the soundtracks of films and video games, including *Natural Born Killers*, *Tank Girl*, and *Grand Theft Auto: San Andreas*. L7 also created its own record label, Wax Tadpole, in 1999.

L7 disbanded in 2001, not due to a falling out among members but, rather, the chilly climate of the music industry towards all-female rock acts. The group reunited in 2014 after fans launched a Kickstarter campaign to raise money to make the band biopic *L7: Pretend We're Dead*. The anti-Trump "Dispatch from Mar-a-Lago" (2017) was the first new piece of music that the band had released in eighteen years.

LAS VULPES: *ME GUSTA SER*

Las Vulpes (the foxes) were the first all-female Spanish punk rock band. They formed in 1982, seven years after the death of dictator Francisco Franco, whose Catholic authoritarian regime had outlawed divorce, contraception, and abortion for decades. Las Vulpes' television performance of their song "Me Gusta Ser una Zorra" ("I Like Being a Whore") caused such a furor that it ended the band's career just as it was beginning. The television show's producers were prosecuted for obscenity because they had allowed the performance, and the band was harassed into breaking up two months afterward.

Las Vulpes' inception was typical of many punk bands: they started by playing covers songs by the Ramones and the Stooges. Band members Loles Vázquez, Mamen Rodrigol, Begoña Astigarraga, and Lupe Vázquez were attracted to punk because it is the music of protest, and Las Vulpes called out sexism in their work. The members of the Vulpes' desire for self-expression was particularly urgent, as they had all grown up in a country where dictator-for-life Francisco Franco had dissenters jailed or killed. After Franco's death in 1975, the government began to transition into a democracy that respected individual liberties. But when front woman Mamen Rodrigo sang in "Me Gusta Ser una Zorra" that she preferred sleeping with wealthy executives who would pay her and leave her in peace, she publicly challenged traditional ideas about romantic love and women's sexuality (Herrero 2013). This caused a furor in 1983, as Spain was still deeply conservative.

Las Vulpes were one of four Basque groups selected in 1983 by Carlos Tena to perform on his Spanish public television show *Caja de Ritmos* (*Rhythm Box*). Las Vulpes performed "Me Gusta Ser una Zorra," their overtly sexual take on the Stooges' "I Wanna Be Your Dog," during the show's early Saturday morning time slot, when families were watching (Herrero 2013). The four provocatively dressed young women who sang frankly about sex and ridiculed monogamy so jarred public sensibilities that the band became infamous overnight. Conservative journalists responded with editorials denouncing Las Vulpes and the producers of *Caja de Ritmos*, forcing Tena to resign as host and Spanish public television to cancel the show. Soon afterward, Spain's attorney general tried the producers for obscenity ("TVE Considera" 1983).

Public reaction to Las Vulpes' television appearance was harsher than it was toward the Sex Pistols' controversial television appearance on the *Today* show in 1976. The Pistols' profanity-laced tirade against *Today* show host Bill Grundy put an end to their upcoming tour after venue owners canceled their engagements because they were concerned by the Pistols' reputation for attracting violent fans. Public reaction to Las Vulpes' television appearance was violent because the four women's words and actions flaunted repressive gender norms. At one concert, band members were beaten up after the show by police officers who were part the government's harassment of the band (Herrero 2013). Earlier that evening, a right-wing group had chartered two buses to ferry members to Zamora to protest outside of where the band was performing that evening. When the band flew to Mallorca for a performance, airport security kept their luggage overnight and searched it drugs; the next day, the press published an erroneous claim that the members of Las Vulpes were drug traffickers (Alonzo 2008). In Bilbao, the police shut down their show on a technicality. Their performance at a Basuri prison, a festival organized by a prisoners' rights association, was similarly canceled at the last minute, this time by prison authorities, who claimed that the band might provoke a dangerous reaction among the incarcerated audience members.

After Las Vulpes' performance on *Caja de Ritmos*, the Madrid record label Dos Rombos cashed in on Las Vulpes' sudden infamy by releasing "Me Gusta Ser una Zorra" as a single, and without the band's permission, it added a second S to the band's name on the label in a typeface that made the two S's resemble the logo for the Nazi SS. The single's artwork only served to blacken Las Vulpes' reputation and fuel the release's sales. Dos Rombos' first run of "Me Gusta Ser una Zorra" quickly sold all seven thousand copies and produced a five thousand–copy second run a month later (Alonzo 2008).

Yet, the record sales did not change Las Vulpes' fortunes. Constant harassment so wore down band members that they broke up at the end of the summer of 1983. Members of Las Vulpes went on to be involved in other musical projects, and they briefly reunited twice. In 1985, Las Vulpes played a fundraising concert in Bilbao with several other bands. They reunited once more in 2005, this time as a tribute to band member Lupe Vázquez, who died in 1993. Their final concert produced Las Vulpes' only studio album, *Me Gusta Ser* (Exposito 2016).

ME FIRST AND THE GIMMIE GIMMIES: *RAKE IT IN: THE GREATEST HITS*

Me First and the Gimmie Gimmies are a super group whose shtick is performing punk covers of decidedly nonpunk songs, and their body of work is so intertextual that listening to them is as dizzying as watching a dog chase its tail. The Gimmies' fan site, *The Time Machine*, describes the band as so "unoriginal" and "lazy" that they have gone "beyond the known limits of punk laziness" because "everything about the band was stolen somewhere," from playing the material of others, taking the title of a children's book by Gerald G. Jampolsky and Diane V. Cirincione as their name, and appropriating art from other record covers to decorating their own merchandise. Even the Gimmies' interpretations of the songs they cover are stolen. The intros to their covers of songs such as "Sloop John B," "Mahogany," and "My Favorite Things" are riffs from other punk songs (the Ramones' "Teenage Lobotomy," the Germs' "Richie Dagger's Crime," and Bad Religion's "Generator," respectively).

Even the band members are "stolen" from other bands: Spike Slawson (Swingin' Utters, Filthy Thievin' Bastards, Re-Volts, and the ukulele-based cover band Uke-Hunt), Chris Shiflett (Foo Fighters), Joey Cape and Dave Raun (Lagwagon), and Fat Mike (also known as Michael John Burkett, NOFX). Fat Mike is also the founder of the indie label Fat Wreck Chords, which promotes the Gimmies' music.

But the Gimmies' repurposing of the materials of others is neither lazy nor unoriginal. Their songs recombine old, familiar source material into something new and original that is full of infectious joy. In this way, the Gimmies are like Gogol Bordello, whose mission statement declares that they recombine old material in a new way to prove that the postmodern idea that (original) art is dead is a lie. Critic Brett Callwood said that "the joy of Me First & the Gimme Gimmes [sic] is the fact that the musicians take songs that their fans likely wouldn't give any time to previously, and make them not only funny but enjoyable on a musical level" (2017).

Must-Hear Music   83

The supergroup Me First and the Gimmie Gimmies in a 2019 concert (left to right) with vocalist Spike Slawson (Swinging Udders, Lagwagon) on ukulele, Joey Cape (Lagwagon) on guitar, Chris Shiflett (Foo Fighters) on guitar, and Fat Mike (NOFX) on bass. The Gimmies repitore consists of punk covers of very unpunk pop and country songs. (Simone Re/Dreamstime.com)

Some of the band's official videos reinforce the Gimmies' commitment to punk's DIY ethos. For example, the video for "Danny's Song" opens with lead singer Spike Slawson outside of a bar, smoking a cigarette and loosening up to perform his karaoke set inside. Slawson plays the role of lounge lizard well, posing with a martini in his hand for the shaky hand-held camera that cannot even keep his face in the frame as he performs. "I Believe I Can Fly" is also set in a karaoke bar; the Gimmies perform their version of the song on the karaoke screen while costumed Gimmies and celebrities such as Paris Hilton, Bob Odenkirk, and Matthew Lillard take turns lip synching the lyrics. The Gimmies' cover of "I Believe I Can Fly" is so good that it will wipe R. Kelly's maudlin original version out of your brain. The Gimmies' video for their cover of George Gershwin song "Summertime" disrupts the audience's concept of the rock star as god through its use of the generic band video trope. The video is interspersed with shots of the band performing "Summertime" as a surfer punk song with footage of them wearing Hawaiian shirts and waxing surfboards, flying to concerts, and getting in and out of limos. The video subtly reminds the audience that rock stars are not born but made (most usually by wealthy record executives with the money to curate a musician into an income-generating brand). This public service announcement is important because it reminds the audience that they too can seize the means of production and make art.

Slawson as the Gimmies' lead singer reiterates punk's democratizing DIY ethos via his stage persona. He ends songs with "Yeah! Yeah!," which disrupts the audience's sense of having listened to a polished, professional piece of music. Slawson here is a karaoke singer instead of a professional musician, an amateur whose mundane existence is so enlivened through performance that he is reluctant to relinquish the mike to the next singer. This is not to say that the Gimmies are poor musicians—in fact, all are exceptionally accomplished musicians who are continuously involved in new projects. In this context, Slawson's amateur stage persona is one rooted in the word's original meaning, someone who is motivated to pursue an activity through his love of it.

Rake It In exemplifies the Gimmies' aesthetic, which is a reaction against the postmodern idea of the artist as someone who can only repurpose and repackage source material because everything new has already been created. Punk itself has always been a reaction against this elitist despair-inducing postmodern idea of art in that musicians and other types of artists have covered and otherwise repurposed the material of others as a means of self-expression. As a compilation album, *Rake It In* is self-conscious of the creative process. The band has repurposed and repackaged their own work to make an album with a title that mocks the crass materialism of the music business.

Rake It In also contains some of the Gimmies' best work. In addition to "I Believe I Can Fly" and "Summertime," the Gimmies cover "Take Me Home Country Roads" (John Denver), "The Times They Are a-Changin'" (Bob Dylan), "City of New Orleans" (Arlo Guthrie), "Sloop John B" (the Beach Boys), "Jolene" (Dolly Parton), "Uptown Girl" (Billy Joel), "Hats Off to Larry" (Del Shannon), "Rainbow Connection" (*The Muppet Movie*), "All My Loving" (the Beatles), "San Francisco" (Scott McKenzie), "Over the Rainbow" (Judy Garland, Israel Kaʻanoʻi Kamakawiwoʻole), and "Desperado" (the Eagles, Linda Ronstadt). The songs selected for inclusion on *Rake It In* demonstrate the Gimmies' virtuosity in their ability to cover folk, country, soft pop, classic rock, and even the Great American Songbook. The songs are also examples of what Slawson characterizes as AM rock, "that (bandwidth) . . . where you went when rock-and-roll was too scary or heavy for you. Where you could be assured that" the heaviest thing you would hear would be

Neil Diamond or Tom Jones (Callwood 2017). The Gimmies' covers of "Sloop John B," "San Francisco," and "Uptown Girl" are worlds better than the originals, and their cover of "Jolene" infuses the original with the bitterness that should have been in Dolly Parton's voice when she found herself begging a woman not to take her man. The Gimmies also communicate the absurd pettiness of the male singer's subject position in "Hats Off to Larry," the theme song of bitter exes everywhere.

The cover of "City of New Orleans," performed in a time when Americans travel long distances via plane instead of train, gives an uncanny quality to this song first popularized by Arlo Guthrie in 1972, when train travel already had a nostalgic feel to it. Slawson's vocals convey a sense of wonder at a type of travel that was so peaceful it was possible for babies to sleep in their mothers' arms and for old men to play cards in the club car while seeing houses, farms, and fields instead of the inside of airports after being searched by the TSA prior to getting bumped from your flight.

And would someone please take the Gimmies' sassy version of "Desperado" and use it as the theme song for the next film or streaming series about an antihero in the vein of *Breaking Bad* or *Better Call Saul*? It is not as if the Gimmies' work is unknown to producers; their work has been used in soundtracks for *The Wolf of Wall Street* ("Sloop John B"), *Shameless* ("I Only Want to Be with You"), and *Queer as Folk* and the video game *Tony Hawk: Shred* (both "Over the Rainbow").

To date, the band has released six albums, one live album (*Ruin Johnny's Bar Mitzvah*), and two compilations, and they continue to tour and record when time permits. The band members continue to be active with other bands and have occasionally invited other well-known punk musicians to fill in for them, including C. J. Ramone, Bad Religion's Jay Bentley and Brian Baker (also of Minor Threat), Chris Shiflett's brother Scott, and NOFX's guitarist Eric Melvin.

MISFITS: *WALK AMONG US*

The Misfits are an influential horror punk band whose fan base did not extend outside of the underground punk scene until their dissolution, when their front man Glenn Danzig became famous for his work with the metal band that bears his name. Danzig and Jerry Only (Jerry Caiafa) formed the Misfits in 1977, taking the band's name from the title of

Jerry Only, front man and bassist of the horror punk outfit the Misfits during a 2011 concert in Leipzeg, Germany. Only sports the devillock hairstyle he created, which became part of the Misfits signature look. (Katja Nykanen/Dreamstime.com)

Marilyn Monroe's last film. The Misfits' sound was a "darker and more sinister . . . punk-metal hybrid" (DeRosa 2005) that "willfully violated" many of the unofficial rules of the genre that were already "straightjacketing the scene" (Rachalis n.d., "Misfits: *Walk Among Us*"). Like other punk bands, the Misfits heavily relied on material from the 1950s and 1960s for inspiration, drawing from Elvis Presley and the Doors.

However, the Misfits were also more theatrical and musically over the top than their Year Zero cohorts. Their "look incorporated face paint, skintight costumes, Halloween-worthy paraphernalia, and hair sculpted into 'devil locks,' a radical deconstruction of the '50s rockabilly quaff," on the model of "the fiendishly dressed crooner Dave Vanian of The Damned" (Heller 2017). The Misfits' theatrics also owed a debt to Kiss and Alice Cooper, and their musical fascination with the "trash culture" world of horror and science fiction from the 1950s, 1960s, and 1970s is reminiscent of the Cramps' psychobilly. The cover and title of their debut album, *Walk Among Us*, alludes to this culture. *Walk Among Us* conjures up images of the placid, flesh-eating ghouls of George A. Romero's *Night of the Living Dead* as well as the science fiction classic *Invasion of the Body Snatchers*, where the aliens who walk among us take the forms of our friends and family. The album's cover features an image of the rat-bat-spider creature from *The Angry Red Planet* (or *Invasion of Mars* and *Journey to Planet Four*), and the spaceship hovering over this creature is taken from the film *Earth vs. the Flying Saucers*.

Because the Misfits emerged during a transitional period in the New York punk scene, they had trouble finding footing in an era somewhere between the Ramones and the nascent hardcore punk movement: "Where the first clique [of punks] had been artier and open to outrageous stagecraft, it wasn't receptive to a bunch of upstarts from the wrong side of the Hudson who dug sports and had the physiques of bodybuilders" (Heller 2017). As a result, *Walk Among Us* was not released by a record company capable of promoting their work until 1982, five years after they had been performing and had released several EPs on their own Plan 9 label as well as toured with the Damned on an abortive tour of the United Kingdom (which ended after Danzig was arrested in a bar fight and band member Joey Idol quit in disgust).

In *Walk Among Us*, "dark powers take the form of trash from the past and fears of the future." Danzig references the 1950s Nike missal project in "Nike-a-Go-Go" when he sings "death machine and man in love" and "rocket-blast fury with a manual sex drive" while straddling the overlap between J. G. Ballard's *Crash* and Stanley Kubrick's *Dr. Strangelove* (Heller 2017). Many tracks on *Walk Among Us* are derived from 1950s and 1960s horror and science fiction films. The creature of "20 Eyes," whose numerous orbs crowd his "human face," refers to *The Fly* (1958), and "I Turned into a Martian" is derivative of films such as *Invasion of the Body Snatchers* (1956), in which humans are hijacked by an alien consciousness. The character Vampira from *Plan 9 from Outer Space* (1956) is celebrated in the song bearing her name. "Devil's Whorehouse" alludes to another popular horror trope—Satanists and their depravities.

Three tracks on *Walk Among Us* celebrate the zombie from B-grade horror films of the 1950s and 1960s. "Night of the Living Dead" references Romero's 1968 classic of the same name, and "Space Zombies" was inspired by the 1968 film *Astro Zombies*. The undead are tired of their monotonous diets in "Brains for Dinner."

Several songs are from the viewpoint of the serial killer archetype popularized in slasher films such as Alfred Hitchcock's *Psycho* (1960) and Tobe Hooper's *Texas Chainsaw Massacre* (1973). The speaker of "Mommy Can I Go Out and Kill Tonight" is similar to *Psycho*'s Norman Bates in his devotion to his mother; he takes his victims from lovers' lanes and brings his mother souvenirs of his kills to demonstrate his devotion to her. The speaker of "Skulls" could be a member of the cannibal Sawyer clan of the *Texas Chainsaw Massacre*. "Last Caress" is a ghoulish love song to "sweet lovely death," whose speaker has already killed an infant and assaulted a mother and hopes to receive his last caress at the hands of the Grim Reaper. Danzig's passionate, sensual delivery of "Last Caress" is at odds with the dreadful subject matter. The speaker of "All Hell Breaks Loose" is the antagonist of nearly every slasher film. He declares, "Yea, who but me could write this book of cruel." "Hatebreeders" deconstructs the serial killer/maniac trope of the slasher film as someone who is born, not made, a killer: "It's in your blood and you can't shake it / Because you were bred to take it." "Hatebreeders" is lyrically similar to H. R.'s (Bad Brains) Dread-talk songwriting in its sparse verbal imagery.

Walk Among Us was not commercially successful during the band's six years together in its original formation, but it is better appreciated in hindsight. *Rolling Stone*'s list of the "50 Greatest Pop-Punk Albums" ranked *Walk Among Us* at No. 10, and *Rolling Stone*'s list of the "40 Greatest Punk Albums of All Time" placed it at No. 32 (Dolan et al. 2016).

As the Misfits were becoming exceptionally popular, they were also falling apart. They split up soon after *Walk Among Us* was released, fittingly dissolved on Halloween night 1983 after their annual performance at Detroit's Greystone Hall. The band was never able to tour as much as Danzig wanted to because Only and their guitarist, Doyle Wolfgang von Frankenstein (Paul Caiafa), worked for their father and could not afford the time away from their day jobs; the band also had difficulty keeping drummers. Although the Misfits' "live shows were visually stunning," their first incarnation "sucked musically"; they were never in tune and had a habit of smashing "their instruments eight measures into a set" (DeRosa 2005).

After the band's breakup, Danzig was sued by Only and von Frankenstein, who claimed he owed them a larger percentage of royalties. The Misfits reformed in 1995 after the parties reached an out-of-court settlement that allowed Only and von Frankenstein to perform and record as the Misfits and share merchandising rights with Danzig. The new incarnation of the Misfits is more heavy metal than punk. Glenn Danzig rejoined the band in 2016 and continues to tour today with Only and von Frankenstein—the band's original lineup.

MOJO NIXON AND SKID ROPER: *BO-DAY-SHUS!!!*

Mojo Nixon (Neill Kirby McMillan Jr.) is an American psychobilly/cow punk musician who is best known for his punk attitude that he brings to every project he is involved with as well as for his song "Elvis

Is Everywhere" that he performed in collaboration with Skid Roper (Richard Banke) on *Bo-Day-Shus!!!* Nixon's music is a mash-up of trash culture references and anarchist politics. Nixon does not so much write songs as he does rants or sermons. Nixon's music is more complexly instrumented than the usual punk sound; he incorporates brass and organ into many of his songs, which gives his music a gospel and bluesy dimension. His "broad, even extreme parodies conceal a sensibility concerned with maintaining and exercising personal freedom" (Brennan 2019).

Nixon became a musician as a teen, driving "his family crazy" by "banging on a drum kit in his basement" (Brennan 2019). At this time, he was also "developing the political consciousness that would later fuel much of his music. His budding activism got him arrested at fourteen when he protested local leash laws with the slogan "Free the Dogs." "In the police car afterward, young Nixon hummed MC5 songs and threatened the town's mayor" (Brennan 2019). After graduating from Miami University in Ohio in 1979 with a degree in political science, Nixon was an aspiring musician, and he moved to England in hopes of getting involved in the developing punk scene around the Clash. Nixon busked in the London Underground, "playing the music of Jerry Lee Lewis and Dion to survive" (Brennan 2019). Nixon returned to the United States in 1980 and enlisted in Volunteers in Service to America (VISTA), known as the domestic Peace Corps, and was sent to work in Denver. There, he continued making music and sang Woodie Guthrie and Leadbelly songs to unemployed folks he worked with.

Nixon also formed the punk band Zebra 123 while in Denver. When the group "staged a so-called Assassination Ball on November 22, 1980, the anniversary of the shooting of President John Kennedy," they were visited by the Secret Service because the band's posters depicted the exploding heads of Jimmy Carter and Ronald Reagan (Brennan 2019).

Nixon created his stage name after having what he refers to as the "Mojo Nixon revelation" while he was drinking on New Orleans's Bourbon Street. He hit upon the name Mojo Nixon, a combination of voodoo and bad politics, because "it's two words that shouldn't go together" (Holden 1990). Skid Roper is best known for his collaboration with Nixon between 1985 and 1989 as the duo's instrumentalist who played the washboard and the mandolin. After parting ways with Nixon, Roper has been involved with several other musical projects, which include the surf bands the Evasions and Skid Roper and the Shadowcasters.

Mojo Nixon became famous in the 1980s when he was "one of the most outsized personalities on college radio" (Huey n.d., "Mojo Nixon"). There he "won a fervent cult following with his motor-mouthed redneck persona and a gonzo brand of satire with all the subtlety of a sledge-hammer" that was "performed in maximum overdrive on a bed of rock-abilly, blues, and R & B" (Huey n.d., "Mojo Nixon"). Nixon's growing audience got him gigs as an MTV host as well as several small roles in movies, such as *Great Balls of Fire*, the biopic about musician Jerry Lee Lewis, as well as some extraneous media attention, such as debating Pat Buchanan on television on the subject of censorship. MTV made Nixon a star in 1988 by putting his video for "Elvis Is Everywhere" in heavy rotation. He was invited by the station to film a series of short rants that ran between commercial breaks and to be a periodic host for the channel and played gigs at the legendary club CBGB. His album *Bo-Day-Shus!!!* was his first album to make national charts on the strength of "Elvis Is Everywhere."

"Elvis Is Everywhere" "is a sly, raucous hymn/sermon to the King that identifies him as the 'perfect being' and claims that everyone has some of Elvis in him/her—save for the 'evil Anti-Elvis'" (Hochman 1987). "Released as Elvis-mania was peaking in August with the 10th anniversary of Presley's death, the song is working into something of a left-field hit" (Hochman 1987). Other songs on *Bo-Day-Shus!!!* written by Nixon build upon his gonzo redneck persona. In "I'm Gonna Dig Up Howlin' Wolf," Nixon threatens to "get me a big black bone" from the corpse of Chicago bluesman Chester Arthur Burkett with which he will "whomp on Ed Meese," Ronald Reagan's attorney general who famously led the Attorney General's Commission on Pornography and publicly declared that no children were going hungry in the United States. In "We Gotta Have More Soul," Nixon sings of reposing in his bed and listening to the radio, wishing to hear on this archaic device the type of music that has been replaced with "gutless, mediocre, mid-dle of the road sleep-inducin' homogenized pablum, background music for the slavery of daily drudgery." Nixon rails against drug testing as a violation of everything that the Founding Fathers stood for in "I Ain't Gonna Piss in No Jar," which references first lady Nancy Reagan's "Just Say No" campaign.

Other songs on *Bo-Day-Shus!!!* cover typical punk and country music fare, such as drinking ("Gin Guzzlin' Frenzy," "Positively Bodies Park-ing Lot"), partying ("Positively Bodies Parking Lot," "Wide Open"), and rules and their enforcers ("Wash No Dishes No More"). "Don't Want No Foo Foo Haircut on My Head" showcases Nixon's ability to combine his knowledge of popular culture and literature to ruminate on a topic. In one chorus, he works in references to Allen Ginsberg's "Howl" and *The Adventures of Rocky and Bullwinkle and Friends*: "Some of the best hair of my generation / Been destroyed by that evil stylin' mousse."

"The Polka Polka" and "Lincoln Logs" are the only two songs on *Bo-Day-Shus!!!* written by Skid Roper. Both lack Nixon's extended rant variety of lyrics as well as his scatological humor while capturing his maniacal absurdity. "The Polka Polka" parodies songs such as Little Eva's "The Locomotion" and the Midnighter's "The Twist," famously covered by Chubby Checker, that teach listeners a dance, while "Lincoln Logs" centers on nostalgia for a childhood toy.

Nixon's relationship with MTV came to an abrupt end in 1989 after the release of his and Skid Roper's next album, *Root Hog or Die*. Although the album was a success on college radio, MTV banned the video for his tabloid-themed "Debbie Gibson Is Pregnant with My Two-Headed Love Child," starring Winona Ryder, because Gibson was a big star on the network at the time and executives did not want to sour their relationship with the artist. Soon afterward, Nixon severed his relationship with MTV, and his collaboration with Skid Roper ended with their last album, *Unlimited* (1990). Afterward, Nixon embarked on a solo career, and he released several albums in the 1990s with his band the Toadliquors and made an album with the Dead Kennedys' front man Jello Biafra (*Prairie Home Invasion*) in 1994. Label problems helped decrease his visibility in the 1990s, but he continued to tour and record for a still-devoted fan base and worked in radio until retiring from touring in 2004 (Huey n.d., "Mojo Nixon").

Nixon then found a home on satellite radio as a DJ and talk show host. On his political comedy show *Lyin' Cocksuckers* (Sirius XM Radio), his interview subjects included Republican presidential candidates Rick Santorum, Mitt Romney, Herman Cain, and Michele Bachmann (Murphy 2012). He is a DJ on Sirius Satellite Radio's Outlaw Country, where his name and deep knowledge of the formats he plays are a draw for listeners, as well as their NASCAR show *Manifold Destiny*. Unlike terrestrial radio, which is governed by the FCC's decency rules and requires DJs to "stick to a song list and limit their between-tune patter to the weather or the virtues of a car dealership," satellite radio DJs can create radically new formats (McClain 2007). "Nixon found the liberty afforded by subscription-driven radio—including freedom from FCC indecency regulation—too good to be true" (McClain 2007). He is the subject of a forthcoming documentary *The Mojo Manifesto* (2020).

THE MUFFS: *THE MUFFS*

The American punk band the Muffs began as a collaboration in 1991 between Kim Shattuck (lead vocals and guitar) and Melanie Vammen (rhythm guitar), both former members of the all-female hard rock group the Pandoras. The Muffs began performing and recording in Los Angeles after being joined by bassist Ronnie Barnett and drummer Chris Crass. The band's music has been described as "distortion-laden bubblegum crunch and sweet '60s-inspired pop" (Freek 2000) that "took the sound of The Ramones" to create "catchy songs," with "acerbic lyrics aimed at a variety of targets" (Cocksedge 2013). Shattuck's vocals are reminiscent of other well-known female singers, such as Joan Jett, Kathleen Hanna, Liz Phair, and even Naoko Yamano, the lead singer of Shonen Knife. However, what made the Muffs more than a band that could play good punk-centric pop were the catchy melodic hooks of songs such as "Eye to Eye," "Lucky Guy," "From Your Girl," and "Every Single Thing," thanks to Shattuck's skillful lyrics. While the Muffs were "neither an overlooked gem of a band nor a beloved hitmaker," they developed enough of a following to complete a few more albums that were released on independent labels before going on hiatus in the mid-2000s.

The Muffs' self-titled debut album, released in 1993, captures their unique sound: distortion- and feedback-laden songs that are reminiscent of 1960s pop music with lyrics sung with a disarming earnestness. The songs on *The Muffs* deconstruct the heteronormative romantic idea as represented in pop and surfer rock of the 1950s and 1960s, in which women need the love of a good man to be complete and men demonstrate their devotion to their beloveds through behaviors that would be met with restraining orders today. The female subject of the songs on *The Muffs* is an independent woman who has no patience for overly dependent romantic partners and feels no remorse when she dumps them. However, this subject is also emotionally fragile at times, and the pain of unrequited love only contributes to making her feel more vulnerable.

"Lucky Guy," "Everywhere I Go," "Not Like Me," "Baby Go Round," "Another Day," and "Saying Goodbye" are about irritating partners and annoying suitors. The title of "Lucky Guy," a happy-go-lucky tune, suggests that this is a typical romance song about a man who finds the love of his life in a woman that he perceives as too good for him. But the lyrics are at odds with this stereotype; the speaker is a woman who has grown tired of her partner, whose good luck derives from how he is so devoid of ambition that he is content to fritter away his days despite having "a thousand things in front of him," which are perhaps opportunities that he should act on.

The lighthearted instrumentation of "Everywhere I Go" also contradicts the seriousness of the lyrics. In fact, the creators of an ad campaign for Fruitopia liked this instrumentation so much that they used its opening bars as the background music of a 1997 commercial for the product ("1997 Fruitopia Commercial" 2011). Yet, the lyrics are about a type of obsessive behavior that has been romanticized in popular music as evidence of deep devotion. The man, who is everywhere the speaker goes, is fraying her nerves, and being involved with him is not what she figured it would be like, as she has no privacy. She is "not afraid of [his] complete devotion now," but "if it ever gets out of hand," she is prepared to do what she has to do.

The subject of "Another Day" is another clingy, emotional vampire whose near constant presence makes the speaker "want to step on" him. Unlike "Everywhere I Go," "Another Day" is not musically at odds with the lyrics. It has a typical manic punk tempo that emphasizes how little the speaker cares for social conventions that relegate women to responding politely to men when they would rather be left alone. The subject of "Better Than Me" is a condescending mansplainer who prompts the speaker to observe that "from what you say and do / Don't you think there's something wrong with you?" The opening bars of "Not Like Me" have the elevated tempo more typical of most punk songs, which underscores the speaker's pragmatic and unsentimental attitude toward an incompatible partner that she wants to go away because he is "not like me."

In the breakup song "Saying Goodbye," the speaker has "better things to listen to / Than all" of this man's "ranting and raving" to her. Shattuck's tone contrasts with how this subject matter would be dealt with in a pop song. She neither delivers the lyrics in a weepy or regretful tone nor with the glee of someone who is insensitive to her partner's pain. The speaker of the breakup song "All for Nothing" is not angry and fed up with her partner, just sad that this relationship must end because her partner is stifling her. The speaker of "Baby Go Round" also lacks a typically feminine attitude about matters of the heart. She "does not seem to be all upset when her baby's running around" and is "doing all okay for a girl whose soulmate is in doubt." This is yet another example of how the Muffs resist heteronormative gender stereotypes that encourage women to participate in their own subordination. In the Muffs' music, a woman without a man is like a fish without a bicycle or, in other words, someone who is capable of living a rich, full life on her own because she knows what she wants and is not afraid to say what is on her mind.

But not all songs on *The Muffs* are about clingy and demanding men. The speakers of "Every Single Thing," "Eye to Eye," "I Need You," and "Big Mouth" are vulnerable women behind their tough exteriors. "Eye to Eye" and "I Need You" express a painful unmet need for love. The singer confesses in "Eye to Eye" that "her big ego" got in the way of the relationship with her partner. The resulting sadness is enough to "make [her] want to die." The hard-driving music of "I Need You" underscores the singer's painful unfulfilled desire. "Every Single Thing" reveals the fragility lurking behind a woman who is outwardly poised. In the post-breakup song "Big Mouth," a former lover reveals to others what she has told him in confidence. Yet, this man's ability to humiliate the speaker is limited since what he says "will come back to [his] big mouth." "From Your Girl" deconstructs how normative femininity sets up women for victimization. The speaker urges the male subject to not walk away from his girlfriend if he finds that "there's nothing to say" because "Anything [he wants] to do . . . she'll do it like a fool." Other songs on *The Muffs* include the thirty-five-second instrumental "North Pole" and "Stupid Jerk," an angry rant more than a song, which is performed by Mike Sanders rather than Shattuck. "Stupid Jerk" is a cover of an angry rant from the Angry Samoans, a band that Sanders started with his brother in 1978.

The Muffs disbanded in 2004 after the release of their fifth studio album, *Really, Really Happy*, but reunited again in 2014 to release *Whoop Dee Do*, which charted at No. 32 on *Billboard*'s "Heatseekers Albums" that year, and Burger Records rereleased *The Muffs* in 2015 with three bonus tracks.

PANSY DIVISION: *DEFLOWERED*

Pansy Division is the best known of the gay punk bands from the queercore movement of the early 1990s to emerged from a cadre of groups that included Team Dresch and God Is My Co-Pilot (Alston 2009). Singer, songwriter, and guitarist Jon Ginoli started Pansy Division in 1991 after feeling isolated "from both the dance-oriented gay scene and the similarly unvaried, hetero punk scene in San Francisco" (Torres 2015), so he put an ad in the alternative newspaper *SF Weekly* to connect with "gay musicians into The Ramones, Buzzcocks and early Beatles" ("Bio" 2018). Bassist and vocalist Chris Freeman was one of the people who answered Ginoli's ad, and they embarked on the musical project Pansy

Division, which defied cultural stereotypes about hyper-heterosexual male rock musicians as well as gay cultural stereotypes about rock music as something that would not interest the LGBTQ community ("Bio" 2018). Pansy Division "celebrates queerness with humorous songs that speak frankly about sex" and "takes aim at stereotypes about gay men" (Alston 2009).

When Ginoli and Freeman started Pansy Division, "gay people were underrepresented in the media and music," Ginoli told the *Chicago Tribune* in a 2016 interview (Dickinson). "The people who we thought were gay were not out or they were semi-out. But it was always a vague thing. We thought that the time had come to not be vague about it" (Dickinson 2016). There were no mainstream films or television shows with LGBTQ characters and few actors, musicians, or public figures who were openly non-cis-het. As the general public became aware of AIDS in the late 1980s, misconceptions about the disease emboldened homophobes to vilify gays as being responsible for its spread. And there was no It Gets Better Project to help LGBTQ youth understand that they are not aberrations but that their feelings are part of the normal spectrum of human sexuality.

Chris Freeman's biography on his website mentions that he had been on his own since he was sixteen after his parents kicked him out, presumably after they learned that he is gay, a fate suffered today by so many LGBTQ youth. When Freeman was a member of the band The Attachments, he was told that coming out would destroy his career (and that no one over thirty can have a career in music) (Freeman 2017). Too, "there was a lot of gay culture we couldn't relate to," recalls Freeman in forming Pansy Division. "We tried to invent a place for ourselves in it, an alternative for other queer misfits" (Freeman 2017). Having had the experience of being ostracized by other musicians for being gay and by other gays for being into rock, "we tried to turn our alienation into something positive," explains Ginoli about Pansy Division's musical project ("Bio" 2018). "We didn't want to be second-class citizens, so we didn't act like second-class citizens," stated Ginoli, and forming Pansy Division was one way that he and his bandmates were very assertive in their refusal (Dickinson 2016). Because the members of Pansy Division wanted to be "the ones who can say whatever we want to say," they refused to censor themselves and used "certain language and [sang] about certain subjects" that they had not heard other bands use before (Dickinson 2016). Soon Pansy Division had "built a passionate cult of gay kids who needed to hear lyrics that empowered them" (Alston 2009).

"Pansy Division's sound was influenced heavily by '70s-era punk bands like The Ramones and The Sex Pistols. Like those groups, Pansy Division keeps the songs short, sweet and snotty" (Alston 2009). Their early material was similar to their Lookout Records cohort in the early 1990s—"short, upbeat pop-punk songs with catchy choruses, jangly guitars, pop-friendly backing vocals. In short, fun, three-chord punk at its best" (Gerstenzang 2016). Their music celebrates queerness with humorous songs that speak frankly about sex and uses words that prevent most of their work from being played on commercial radio, which explains why they are not as famous (or infamous) as other punk acts. Instead, "Pansy Division has always been more cult than commercial" (Dickinson 2016).

Pansy Division put out a new album a year for six years and toured nonstop after signing with the independent label Lookout Records. Soon after Pansy Division became affiliated with this label, they caught the attention of their former Lookout labelmates Green Day, who asked Pansy Division to open with them during some of their 1994 *Dookie* tour, which introduced Pansy Division to mainstream audiences (Alston 2009). Pansy Division's reception to this larger, more mainstream audience was mixed, but their popularity soared as a result of their exposure via Green Day's *Dookie* tour, where they faced "thousands of high school kids each night," Ginoli recounts, which allowed them to reach a population of people who needed to hear their musical message and who otherwise might not have had the opportunity to hear Pansy Division in those early days of the internet and before streaming music services made a wide library of music easily available ("Bio" 2018).

Pansy Division's 1994 sophomore album, *Deflowered*, is an excellent example of them as a punk outfit. On *Deflowered*, Pansy Division is both raunchy and musically raw, while their later albums are so musically polished that the band's sound loses its punk feel. "Groovy Underwear" and "Beercan Boy" are frank declarations of male desire for other men that would not be considered terribly controversial if they were instead heterosexual objectifications of women's bodies. Compare, for example, the opening of Led Zeppelin's "Black Dog" to the lyrics of these two songs: from "Groovy Underwear," "Running shorts, thin as paper, barely dressed, nearly naked. Pulled down around your ankles, I'll make you spill out like an oil tanker," and from "Beercan Boy," "It's fat and wide. I can barely get my hand around it." "James Bondage" and "Negative Queen" are about types of gay men who would be familiar to Ginoli and Freeman in San Francisco. "James Bondage" needs no explanation, but the band aptly describes the "negative queen" as that man who "thinks he's Oscar Wilde, but he's Paul Lynde," the one who never says anything nice about people. "Body fascists"—"Ken dolls on steroids"—populate Los Angeles in "Fluffy City," an alienating and risible gay club scene. One man is so vapid that his brain literally lives between his legs.

The poignant "Denny," on the other hand, is told through the perspective of a young man dying of AIDS. Denny—and young men like him—is scorned by those who incorrectly fear that it is possible to contract AIDS just by being next to someone who is infected as well as those who view his illness as further justification for their homophobia. Denny is even more stigmatized by these sorts of people because, as a former sex worker, he epitomizes their worst stereotypes of gay men. Although Denny now watches his old videos and feels sad as he helplessly watches the footage in which he is infected, he is not going to leave this world without a fight. Instead, he has "HIV+" tattooed on his back in six-inch letters as well as a "skull and crossbones" tattooed on his forehead because he wants "them to see what they've done to me." The guilty party here is bigger than just those who made money distributing pornographic images of him; it includes all who want nothing to do with him now that he is infected as well the government, the medical community, and the pharmaceutical companies who waited so long before working to stem this crisis. By 1992, "HIV infection [had become] the number one cause of death among men aged 25–44 years" (Centers for Disease Control and Prevention 2001).

Other songs on *Deflowered* are either humorous public service announcements about how to be a good sexual partner, such as "Reciprocate" and "Kissed," or sweet ballads about gay men, such as "Rachbottomoff," about the first sexual experience of a shy young man who loves classical music. The last line of "Rachbottomoff" gives Pansy Division's sophomore album its title. The anti-bitter-ex "A Song of Remembrance for Old Boyfriends" honors former boyfriends "who now live with someone else" but are always with their former lovers as sweet memories. "Deep Water" is one of those Pansy Division songs that was written for the gay kids that Ginoli said needed to hear words of encouragement. "Deep Water" is told through the perspective of a gay teen who is trying to endure two more years of "a life of pain and fear" at home with an unsupportive family and peers. Even today, 40 percent of homeless youth are LGBTQ teens whose parents have kicked them out of their homes (National Coalition for the Homeless 2018).

Deflowered concludes with a punk cover of Pete Shelley's 1981 "Homosapien," which was banned by the BBC for its veiled references to gay sex. In 1994, changing decency standards made Shelley's lyric "homo superior in my interior" less shocking, and Pansy Division's cover is both a defiant and triumphant gay anthem. Pansy Division is also the subject of the 2008 documentary *Pansy Division: Life in a Gay Rock Band*. The band continues to tour and record today.

THE POGUES: *RUM, SODOMY, AND THE LASH*

The Pogues are the original Celtic punk band. Founded in 1982, their name derives from the Gaelic phrase *pogue mahone*, or "kiss my ass" in English. Their music "combines the instrumentation and tunes of traditional Irish music with the attitude and energy of punk" ("The Pogues" 2001). However, unlike American Celtic punk bands such as Dropkick Murphys and Flogging Molly, the Pogues' music is so deeply infused with Irish history and culture that listeners need a comprehensive set of liner notes to truly appreciate its complexity. The Pogues became known internationally after the Clash hired them as the opening act on their 1984 tour. At this time, "some of the Clash's political fury rubbed off, as the Pogues became vehemently anti-Thatcher" ("The Pogues" 2001). The Clash's Joe Strummer would later be a member of the band from 1992 to 1994.

The Pogues' 1985 album, *Rum, Sodomy, and the Lash*, is "a landmark work" on which the band both embraces and flees from tradition (Brennan et al. 2018). *Rum*'s tracks reference Irish mythology and revolutionaries and cover and revise folk songs about working-class heroes. The album's title is derived from a derisive description of the "traditions" of the Royal Navy that have been attributed to Winston Churchill. The Pogues' drummer, Andrew Rankin, suggested the title, as he thought the phrase "summed up life" in the band (Hurt 1985).

The album's opening track, "The Sick Bed of Cúchulainn," likens a nameless dying man to the Gaelic warrior Cúchulainn, who is cursed for attacking otherworldly women. The dying man fought the fascists during the Spanish Civil War (1936–1939): "Frank Ryan bought [him] whiskey in a brothel in Madrid," where he "decked some Fucking blackshirt who was cursing all the Yids." Frank Ryan led a contingent of Irish revolutionaries who traveled to Spain to help fight the Fascists (the Blackshirts) during the Spanish Civil War. The dying man was also a drunken brawler in his day; he once kicked the windows out of the Euston Tavern after he was denied service because he was too drunk. Now, as he is dying, he will sing a liberation tune to his allies of different races and ethnicities, with whom many Irish feel kinship because all have been colonized by the British (Moran 2005).

In the "rent boys serenade" (Deming n.d., "Rum, Sodomy, and the Lash"), "The Old Main Drag," a young Irish man goes to Piccadilly Circus (a favorite spot of hippies and hustlers in the 1960s) to trade his good looks for money or drugs, until he is assaulted by the police. He also receives "a swift one off the wrist," meaning that he was either paid to give another man sexual gratification or bought "a cheaper-than-usual shot of heroin that was injected in the lower forearm" (Moran 2005). All of these activities are overseen by a statue of Eros, the Greek god of love, which is the focal point of Piccadilly Circus. Shane MacGowan, who wrote "The Old Main Drag," had firsthand experience with being accosted by the police after he was arrested for stealing a chair from a pub (Moran 2005).

Rum also includes two instrumental tracks: "The Wildcats of Kilkenny" and "A Pistol for Paddy Garcia." The inhabitants of Kilkenny are renowned for being relentless fighters, as evidenced by the saying "to fight like Kilkenny cats" (Moran 2005). "A Pistol for Paddy Garcia" was composed when the band was writing the score for Alex Cox's 1987 film *Straight to Hell*, a parody of spaghetti Westerns. The song is written in the musical style of Ennio Morricone, a well-known composer of spaghetti Western soundtracks. Originally titled *A Pistol to Paddy Garcia*, *Straight to Hell*'s cast features members of the Pogues along with Elvis Costello, Courtney Love, and Dennis Hopper.

"A Pair of Brown Eyes" and "Sally MacLaenne" describe Irish pub culture. The speaker of "A Pair of Brown Eyes" is drowning his sorrows in drink after his girlfriend dumped him when he is chatted up by an old man, who one-ups his sorrows with his own horrific wartime experiences. "Brown Eyes" is similar to other Pogues' songs, which are filled with references to music that was popular in Irish pubs: the Johnny Cash song "A Thing Called Love" is playing on the jukebox (Moran 2005). The speaker of "Sally MacLaenne" now tends bar in the pub where he was born. Sally MacLaenne, whose virtues the speaker has come to appreciate, is not a woman but a type of stout (Moran 2005).

Four songs on *Rum* are covers of folk songs: "I'm a Man You Don't Meet Every Day," "Dirty Old Town," "Jesse James," and "Waltzing Matilda." The Pogues' version of the Scottish ballad "I'm a Man You Don't Meet Every Day" changes the wording of the original and puts the story in a modern and sinister context. In the original Scottish ballad, Jock Stewart is "a canny gaun man," Scots Gaelic for a "warily (canny) going (gaun)" or cautious man (Moran 2005). Jock demonstrates his easy-going nature in the original ballad when he talks of going for a shoot with his gun and dog next to the River Spay to hunt birds.

The Pogues' Jock Stewart is more sinister, an Irish version of Tony Soprano: Jock is "canny gun man," someone who is particularly skilled (canny) in the use of a gun. Because Jock has plenty of land and men who will fight for him, as well as money to share to pay for the drinks of others, he may be a gangster rather than a gentile landowner. Jock's disturbing nature is confirmed in the third verse, when he admits that he killed his dog for no particular reason, indicating that one cannot be at ease when drinking with him (Moran 2005).

"Dirty Old Town," about life in an industrial town, "is a cover of Scottish folk-singing giant Ewan MacColl, the brother-in-law of legendary American folk singer Pete Seeger and the father of singer-songwriter Kirsty MacColl, who joined the band on several songs" (Moran 2005). The American folk song "Jesse James" recounts the exploits of the Missouri bank robber who is represented in legend as a sort of Robin Hood who stole from institutions whose predatory lending practices left farmers homeless.

The folk song "Waltzing Matilda," which has been described as Australia's unofficial national anthem, does not refer to a woman but to a type of itinerant laborer who travels on foot (waltzing, from the German term *auf der walz*, to travel while plying one's trade as a craftsman). These laborers carried their possessions in bundles colloquially referred to as "matildas" that were a sort of de facto wives because their contents included items necessary for the waltzers' domestic comfort. "Waltzing Matilda" was "most likely written as a carefully-worded political allegory to record and comment on the shearers' strike" in 1894 against the ranchers. The strike culminated in the police murder of its leaders. Frenchy Hoffmeister, a swagman that police alleged was one of the strikers who had burned down a sheep shed to prevent the owners from bringing in scab laborers, was pursued by the police and found shot in the head. The official inquest alleged that Hoffmeister committed suicide rather than allow himself to be taken alive by the police. Modern historians, however, believe that Hoffmeister was murdered by the police in something more "akin to a Melbourne gangland assassination" (ABC [Australian Broadcasting Corporation] News 2010). Blatant discrepancies between witness accounts at the inquest point to a conspiracy on the part of police and lawmakers to cover up Hoffmeister's murder.

Other songs celebrate working-class heroes. The subject of "Navigator" is not a pilot but a "navvie," a laborer hired to work on massive construction projects, such as the English railway system. The navigators in this song are treated as disposable by their English bosses; after they passed away en masse by "landslide and rockblast," there is not even a sign to mark where they are buried deeply in the ground. The subject matter of "Navigator" is similar to the Dropkick Murphys' "The Hardest Mile," which is about a similar group of Irish railway construction workers whose deaths are similarly obscured.

Rum was certified Gold in the United Kingdom and France. It later placed at No. 440 on *Rolling Stone*'s list of "The 500 Greatest Albums of All Time" and No. 67 on *Pitchfork*'s list of "The Top 100 Albums of the 1980s."

PUNK CHRISTMAS MUSIC

Punk Christmas music subverts the commercialized idea of Christmas to return the holiday to its roots in Western and Northern European celebrations of Christmastide and Yule around the winter solstice. These celebrations were riotous affairs characterized by feasting and drinking during the darkest days of the year. Punk Christmas music celebrates the holiday as a time of raucous anarchy and childish delight in fleshly pleasures, and it depicts the lives of those for whom Christmas is not "that most wonderful time of the year" because they are in jail, broke, or brokenhearted. Punk covers of well-known Christmas songs also capture the DIY spirit of punk rock; most people know the words to Christmas songs and can sing along, which furthers the punk ethos about how music is not just something to be created and performed by a talented, privileged few but something that everyone can participate in.

Punk Christmas music can be traced to two events in 1977: The Sex Pistols' last show in the United Kingdom and the release of the Ravers' single "It's Gonna Be a Punk Rock Christmas." By December 1977, the Pistols had been banned from nearly every venue in the United Kingdom because their concerts incited melees among fans. The Pistols' final show in the United Kingdom was a benefit performance in Huddersfield for striking firefighters who were struggling to feed their children after being off the job for nine weeks. Although the Pistols did not play any Christmas songs at the Huddersfield benefit, the concert was a joyous celebration in keeping with the holiday's precapitalist roots as well as an act of generosity motivated by the Christmas spirt. Documentary filmmaker Julien Temple was present to film the gig, but his footage was not available to the public until the BBC aired it in its entirety in the documentary *Never Mind the Baubles* on Boxing Day (December 26) 2013. *Never Mind the Baubles* shows a side of the Pistols that most people were unfamiliar with: "Britain's most notorious punk band" putting on "daft hats" and being kind "to children" (Simpson 2013).

"It's Gonna Be a Punk Rock Christmas" is the first punk Christmas song, released by a little-known band described as the pioneers of Rocky Mountain punk. Formerly known as the Nails, in 1977–1978, the Ravers were always "the opening act for punk roadshows like the Nerves and the Ramones at Ebbets Field in Denver" (Kaufman 2000). "It's Gonna Be a Punk Rock Christmas" is an irreverent tune that drew on the Pistols' notoriety; it declares that "even Santa's gonna be a Sex Pistol for a day" and "the Queen will sing 'Anarchy in the UK'."

Punk Christmas music has developed into an important subgenre of punk in its own right and falls into two categories: punk covers of Christmas songs and original creations that mock the commercialism and forced cheerfulness of the holiday. Examples of punk Christmas covers include Stiff Little Fingers' "White Christmas," My Chemical Romance's "All I Want for Christmas Is You," the Dickies' "Silent Night," the Business's "Stepping into Christmas" (originally recorded by Elton John), SSD's "Jolly Old Saint Nick," the Misfits' "You're a Mean One, Mr. Grinch" and "Blue Christmas," and the Dandy Warhols' "The Little Drummer Boy." Bad Religion has released an entire EP of Christmas music. *Christmas Songs* is a collection of eight "high energy yet faithful renditions" of Christmas classics like "Hark! The Herald Angels Sing," "Little Drummer Boy," and "God Rest Ye Merry Gentlemen" that subvert "the expectations of listeners by performing the songs without irony" (Heaney n.d.).

Other bands create their own Christmas songs that treat the holiday as a time for indulgence in sex and intoxicating substances, sometimes to such a degree that the merrymaker lands in jail, or which contrast grim personal circumstances with the relentless cheerfulness of the season. The best-known example of this second type of original punk Christmas music is still the Pogues' 1987 "Fairytale of New York," which has become a Christmas classic in its own right. "Once censored by the BBC for its raw language" (Chilton 2015), "Fairytale of New York" is now one of the most played Christmas songs in the United Kingdom. It was voted the most popular Christmas song of 2019 in the United Kingdom (Beresford 2019). "Fairy Tale of New York" is an original Irish folk ballad in the tradition of the type of Celtic punk originated by the Pogues. It is a frame tale that opens with an Irish immigrant sleeping off a drunken binge in the NYPD drunk tank who begins to reminisce about his love gone sour after another man put in the cell with him sings a passage of the Irish folk song "The Rare Old Mountain Dew." "Fairytale of New York" is sung as a duet by Pogue's lead singer Shane MacGowan and the song's author, Kristy MacColl, who take the roles of a couple whose memories of their young love do not outweigh the bitter disappointment of the rest of their relationship. The Celtic punk band Dropkick Murhpys' "The Season's upon Us" is in the tradition of "Fairytale of New York" in how it represents family Christmas celebrations as alcohol-infused events destined to end in fighting, although the song is ultimately more lighthearted than "Fairytale of New York."

Other punk bands have produced anti-Christmas songs, such as Fear's "Fuck Christmas," NOFX's "Christmas Has Been X-ed," and Blink 182's "Happy Holidays You Bastard" and "I Won't Be Home for Christmas," where the speaker is spending the night in jail getting his "package unwrapped" by a guy named Bubba after he assaulted some Christmas carolers. Christmas is the season for fighting in both the Ramones' "Merry Christmas (I Don't Wanna Fight Tonight)" and MxPx's "Christmas Night of the Zombies." In the Ramones' video for "Merry Christmas," a couple has a violent fight during their own Christmas party before making up, and in "Christmas Night of the Zombies," the speaker's "face is green and the snow is red" because he is busy fighting the undead. Christmas is also the time for being brokenhearted in Rancid's "Xmas Eve (She Got Up and Left Me)" and Fall Out Boy's "Yule Shoot Your Eye Out for Christmas," where the best gift that the main character can hope for is that his former beloved not call him "when the snow comes down" because she is "the last thing [he] wants to see under the tree."

The Vandals' album of punk- and ska-infused Christmas songs, *Oi to the World!*, has something to offend nearly everyone. Songs include "I Don't Believe in Santa," "Christmas Time for My Penis," "A Gun for Christmas," and "Hang Myself from the Tree." Other punk Christmas songs are happier, such as the hardcore "Hooray for Santa Claus" by Sloppy Seconds, Impact's "Punk Christmas," and Showcase Showdown's "Ho Ho Ho Chi Minh" and "Merry Christmas, I Fucked Your Snowman." The first half of the Phenobarbidols' "O Holy Night" is a dead-serious rendition of the carol by the band's lead singer, who is accompanied by a piano. At the end of the carol, the band can be heard talking casually in the background before sneaking into the recording to play their punk rendition of the same song.

Pansy Division's "Homo Christmas" is humorous and salacious; the chorus, which declares "I want to be your Christmas present / I want to be your Christmas queer," frames verses that describe performing different sexual acts under the tree. Punk Christmas compilation albums include *Happy Birthday, Baby Jesus* and *Bollocks to Christmas*. The band Angry Snowmans, however, own Christmas. They only play punk Christmas music and describe themselves as "disgruntled, displaced Elves of the

North Pole who are telling the world about Santa's abusive practices" (*Angry Snowmans* n.d.). Their body of work includes the albums *Angry Snowmans* (2009), *What We Do Is Festive* (2011), and *Black Coal for Rotten Children* (2013).

Punk Christmas music has inspired bands to write music for other winter holidays. Shonen Knife has three songs that are particular to Japanese Christmas, a consumer-driven secular holiday imported from the West and celebrated on December 24 rather than December 25. It is oriented toward romantic couples rather than family. In their video for "Sweet Christmas," Shonen Knife makes the traditional Japanese Christmas cake, a sponge cake filled with cream and strawberries, and in "Space Christmas," the trio sings of Santa arriving on a "bison sleigh" (bison are the Japanese version of Santa's reindeer). The band also performs a Japanese cover of "All I Want for Christmas." Yidcore/klezmer punk bands have created irreverent Chanukah songs, including Yidcore's "Punk Rock Chanukah Song," Golem's "Freydele," Jingle Punks' "O Chanukah," and the queercore band Schmekel's "I'll Be Your Maccabee," which is reminiscent of Pansy Division's "Homo Christmas."

PUSSY RIOT: *KILL THE SEXIST*

The Moscow feminist activist punk art collective Pussy Riot became famous worldwide in 2012 for "A Punk Prayer" (also known as "Mother of God, Drive Putin Away"), a guerilla performance in two of the most important Russian Orthodox churches. The performance so incensed Russian president Vladimir Putin and Patriarch Kirill, the leader of the Russian Orthodox Church who is an ardent supporter of Putin, that three band members were beaten by the police and imprisoned for "hooliganism motivated by religious hatred," prompting international human rights protests against the Russian government ("Pussy Riot Found Guilty" 2012).

After Pussy Riot's sudden fame, people were surprised to learn that the band's entire oeuvre before this date consisted of six songs and five homemade videos with poor sound quality and that their music consisted of "simple riffs and scream-like singing" (Cautericci 2018). After Pussy Riot became a cause célèbre, they had access to resources that allowed them to create more polished videos that are sung in English rather than Russian, which gives them a wider audience. However, to date, Pussy Riot has not released any conventional albums (Mirovalev 2012). Instead, most of their songs and videos are available for download on many sites under the title *Kill the Sexist*.

Nadezhda Tolokonnikova (left) and Maria Alyokhina (right) of the feminist punk collective Pussy Riot in Moscow, 2014, at a rally opposing Russian military aggression against Ukraine. (Olegkozyrev/Dreamstime.com)

Pussy Riot was founded in 2011 with approximately a dozen members who rotate in and out of the group. Until 2015, band members always performed with their baklavas covering their faces, both to hide the identity of members from the police as well as to give Pussy Riot an everywoman quality that encourages others to become politically active. The group's musical themes include women's and LGBTQ rights and opposition to Putin's government and the Russian Orthodox Church, whose leadership supports the Russian president.

"A Punk Prayer" so provoked Putin and his supporters because it was performed on the altars of Christ the Savior Cathedral in Moscow and the Epiphany Cathedral in Yelokhovo. Christ the Savior Cathedral is "the main symbol of Christian Orthodoxy in [the] Russian Empire," and the cathedral in Yelokhovo housed Russian Orthodox clerics for sixty years after Christ the Savior was demolished by Stalin, not to be rebuilt until the 1990s after the dissolution of the Soviet Union. "Both sites represent transforming relations between State and Religion in Russia" (Velichko 2016). Band members Nadezhda Tolokonnikova, Maria Alyokhina, and Yekaterina Samutsevich were arrested and held without bail on blasphemy charges for the lyrics of "A Punk Prayer," which refer to Patriarch Kirill as a "bitch" and liken the Orthodox Church to feces (Velichko 2016). Tolokonnikova, Alyokhina, and Samutsevich were not permitted to see their children before they were sentenced to two years in prison (though Samutsevich was later released on probation). American and European Union leaders as well as Amnesty International denounced their imprisonment as disproportionate to their offenses (*BBC News* 2012). While Tolokonnikova was in prison, she corresponded with Slovenian philosopher Slavoj Žižek to discuss artistic subversion and political activism (Žižek and Tolokonnikova 2014).

Other songs and accompanying videos collected under *Kill the Sexist* are political protests that were released to coincide with significant events in Russia. In "Release the Cobblestones," the band recommends that Russians participate in the 2012 parliamentary elections by throwing "cobblestones during street protests because 'ballots will be used as toilet paper'." "Release the Cobblestones" was performed and uploaded to the internet on November 7, 2011, the ninety-fifth anniversary of the Bolshevik Revolution and a month before the Russian presidential election. Pussy Riot's prediction about how citizens' ballots were counted was prescient; international observers declared that Putin's 2012 landslide victory was fraudulent because the election's conditions were skewed in his favor (Organization for Security and Co-Operation in Europe 2012; Barry and Schwirtz 2012).

Many Russians shared this opinion. The election results triggered "the largest civil protests in Russia since the Soviet collapse" (Mirovalev 2012). "Kropotkin Vodka," released three days before the Russian presidential election, is named after Russian philosopher, activist, and revolutionary Peter Kropotkin (1842–1921), one of the founding fathers of anarchism. In the video for "Kropotkin Vodka," Pussy Riot starts small fires in expensive restaurants and boutiques before putting them out with fire extinguishers as they sing of "toppling the Kremlin bastards." The wealthy patrons in these establishments during Pussy Riot's guerilla performances appear to be deeply uncomfortable. "Death of Jail, Freedom to Protest" was recorded in mid-December of 2011 after the first anti-Putin protests, when the streets of Moscow rang "with cries of 'Russia Without Putin' and 'Putin Is a Thief'." Pussy Riot staged "Death of Jail" on the roof of a detention center where opposition leaders and activists were being held.

The three other songs on *Kill the Sexist* were performed after Putin's 2012 reelection. "Putin Zassal," which has been translated into English as "Putin Chickened Out" (Mirovalev 2012), "Putin Got Scared" (Flintoff 2012), and "Putin Is Wetting Himself" (Hilsum 2012), called for the occupation of Red Square and a popular revolt against Putin's regime. Eight members of Pussy Riot were detained by police after this performance. Pussy Riot staged "Putin Ignites the Fires of Revolution" on a Moscow apartment balcony across the street from the court where band members Tolokonnikova, Alyokhina, and Samutsevich were being sentenced to prison.

After Tolokonnikova, Alyokhina, and Samutsevich were released from jail in 2015, Pussy Riot broadened the scope of its work to critique police brutality and the Trump administration. Pussy Riot's fame surrounding "A Punk Prayer" gave them access to modest resources that have allowed them to improve the production value of their videos and emboldened band members to shed their trademark colorful baklavas and show their faces. Their videos are also now in English, which allows the band to reach a broader international audience. The video "I Can't Breathe" is named after the last words gasped by Eric Garner, an African American man who was choked to death by the New York City police after they detained him for selling loose cigarettes. In the video, Alyokhina and Tolokonnikova wear Russian police uniforms similar to those worn by law enforcement sent by Putin to quell protests of his 2012 reelection to a third term. The video "Make America Great Again" references Donald Trump's campaign slogan and was released in October 2016 on the eve of the U.S. presidential election. It envisions a dystopian future in which Trump's thugs enforce his values through shaming, torturing, and branding dissenters.

Some of Pussy Riot's newer music continues to critique Putin's regime, such as "Chaika" ("Seagull") (Pussy Riot 2016). In the video, band members dressed as Russian officials alternately devour huge meals and count money in between torturing hooded prisoners similar to those interrogated by the U.S. Army in the Abu Ghraib prison. Tolokonnikova takes a bath in blood in "Organs" as she denounces Putin's government. "Straight Outta Vagina" is a feminist parody of rap videos in which men glorify the objectification of women's bodies; the video celebrates the power of women to create life with its chorus, "Don't play stupid, don't play dumb / Vagina's where you're really from." Band members sing while surrounded by attractive young yes-men dressed in suits and high heels who mutely nod their heads in imitation of the sexualized and silenced interchangeable dancers in Robert Palmer's video for "Simply Irresistible."

Pussy Riot is touring internationally and continues to stage guerilla protests, such as the one in Russia when it was the host country for the 2018 World Cup. Four band members, including Tolokonnikova's husband, disrupted the match between Croatia and France by running onto the field while dressed as police. They were jailed for fifteen days for "violating the rules for spectators at sporting events and wearing police uniforms illegally" ("World Cup: Pussy Riot" 2018). Pussy Riot is the subject of the Russian British documentary *Pussy Riot: A Punk Prayer* (2013). Tolokonnikova published the 2018 book *Read & Riot: A Pussy Riot Guide to Activism*, which encourages readers to forgo the typical "write your lawmakers" and "get out and vote" type of protesting to engage in joyful political protest that "will make your government shit its pants" (Tolokonnikova 2018).

THE RAINCOATS: *THE RAINCOATS*

The feminist punk band the Raincoats started playing at "a time when the rock press didn't even know what women were" (True 2019). The Raincoats "challenged the patriarchy" with their songs about gender inequality, "subjects that are still timely today in the #MeToo era," and they influenced later generations of punk and alternative rock bands," including "Bikini Kill as well as Nirvana and Sonic Youth" (Chiu 2019). Although the Raincoats are a punk band, "little of what makes punk stereotypically 'punk' applies to them" because they wrote experimental songs that were "more adventurous" (Chiu 2019) in comparison to what their male contemporaries were producing. Their self-titled debut album, *The Raincoats* (1979), "sounds less like punk and more like folk song and nursery rhyme played at high volumes" (Powell 2013).

Like so many other British punk bands of the Year Zero era, Gina Birch and Ana da Silva, the founding members of the Raincoats, were in art school when they decided to form a band in 1977. This decision was the result of seeing the Slits and Patti Smith as well as the Clash and Subway Sect. When Birch first saw the Slits play a gig in London in 1977, she was "completely blown away" and felt that she had suddenly been "given permission" to start a band as well. Before then, it never occurred to Birch that she could be in a band, because, at the time, "Girls didn't do that." But when Birch saw the Slits perform, she thought, "This is me. This is mine" (Schemmer 2017). Birch and da Silva had little musical experience at the time beyond da Silva knowing "a few chords and folk songs on an acoustic guitar" and Birch liking to sing when she was alone (Schemmer 2017). When the two decided to form a band, da Silva went out and bought her first guitar, "an imitation Telecaster, for $25," and Birch purchased a "30 pound, brown Gibson-shaped bass that she spray-painted sparkly blue" because she thought that the bass would be easy to play (Schemmer 2017). Afterward, Birch and da Silva "recruited a rotating cast of friends to join the band, but the most well-known iteration of The Raincoats wasn't formed until 1978, with the addition of classical violinist Vicky Aspinall and former Slits drummer Palmolive" (Paloma Romero) (Schemmer 2017). That lineup recorded the Raincoats' first single in 1979, "Fairytale in the Supermarket," and their debut album.

Before they recorded their first album, the Raincoats toured extensively, learning their musicianship on stage, and the results were sometimes unpredictable. Birch recalls that audiences were often empathetic when their performances just "fell apart," but sometimes they were rude; journalist Danny Baker said of the band in *NME* that they were "so bad that every time a waiter [dropped] a tray, [they'd] all get up and dance" (quoted in Schemmer 2017). But this comment could have been due to the relentlessly anti-commercial nature of their music rather than their skill. *Vulture*'s Andy Beta describes the Raincoats' music as exemplifying a "fumbling democracy" where "no one instrument ever [takes] the lead" and "no one voice dominates the others shouting along" (2017). The Raincoats were also revered by their peers, such as the Sex Pistols' John Lydon. Lydon said in a 2009 interview that "all the books about punk have failed to realize" that all female and female-led bands, such as the Raincoats and the X-Ray Spex, were involved in the punk scene "for no other reason than that [they] were good and original" (Hodgkinson 2009).

The Raincoats is complex and "nonlinear," as noted band scholar Jenn Pelly has described it, "pitting discordant emotional experiences and sounds against one another." "Rather than contradictory, the effect precisely encapsulates the messiness of being alive" (Snapes 2017). *Pitchfork*'s Mike Powell said of album that it sometimes "feels less like premeditated music and more like séance captured on tape"; he describes Palmolive's drums as sounding like "cardboard boxes" and Vicky Aspinall's violin as resembling "the siren on a battery-powered ambulance" (2013). Yet, the threat of this music falling apart is what Powell says makes it so exciting. "With every tempo change and precariously structured arrangement, the thread holding the music together frays," and the Raincoats "gallop ahead with no clear indication that they will make it to the next chorus, let alone the end of the song" (Powell 2013).

"Fairytale in the Supermarket" was born out of Birch and da Silva's experiences living as squatters in London of the late 1970s, which allowed them to live as full-time punks without having to take day jobs. The line "no one teaches you how to live" both "underscores a simple fact of being a person" as well as captures "the essence of DIY culture"

(Pelly 2017). "No Looking" takes place between two lovers over morning coffee. The lyric "Went to fight dragons in the land of concrete" finds "mythical import in someone's daily commute" in "Adventures Close to Home" (Powell 2013). "Black and White" and "In Love" both attempt to truthfully represent romantic love: "all the classic symptoms of falling in love (loss of appetite, hallucinating the beloved's face wherever you go) are unsettlingly re-presented in terms of dysfunction, delusion, delirium. The implication is: who would WANT to be in love if this malady and constant haunting are the consequences?" (Reynolds 1996, "*Sex Revolts*," 331). "Off Duty Trip" is all too contemporary; it is about "a much-publicized rape trial in which a British Army officer received lenient treatment from a judge concerned about his military standing, and contextualizes that outrage within a larger view of women's objectification" (Powers 2017).

The Raincoats were not a commercial success during their heyday. Bassist Gina Birch said in an interview that "money and career were not things that were present in our thinking. Money and art didn't seem to go hand in hand, and we were definitely defiantly anti-commercialism" (Chiu 2019). However, over the decades, the Raincoats have cultivated a wider following, and they have influenced American indie musicians from Bikini Kill to Sleater-Kinney and Nirvana and are mentioned in films such as *10 Things I Hate about You* and *20th Century Women* (Beta 2017). In 2019, We Three Records released a fortieth anniversary edition of *The Raincoats*, and the band is touring. Gina Birch said of the Raincoats' debut album's late blooming, "It has a longevity perhaps because it is sometimes sounds woven together in an odd way, and it's very slight out-of-tuneness gives it a resonance that deepens and deepens over time!" (Chiu 2019). *The Raincoats* was ranked No. 74 on NPR's list of "The 150 Greatest Albums Made by Women" (Powers 2018).

In 2019, Gina Birch and Helen Reddington (the Chefs) released the documentary *Stories from She Punks*, which is based on interviews with early female punk musicians from bands that included the Raincoats, the Slits, the Au Pairs, and Dolly Mixture. The Raincoats are also the subject of a book by Jenn Pelly.

THE RAMONES: *RAMONES* (FORTIETH ANNIVERSARY DELUXE EDITION)

The American punk band the Ramones originated the early punk sound, which consisted of "short, loud, manic-tempoed tunes, hammered home with brute, primitive force" ("Ramones" 2002). The original quartet from Queens—Joey, (Jeffrey Ross Hyman, lead vocals), Dee Dee (Douglas Glenn Colvin, bass), Johnny (John William Cummings, guitar), and Tommy (Thomas Erdeyl, née Tamás Erdély, drummer)—"were troubled misfits who'd found a measure of salvation and solace in music" (Schinder 2008). Although they "revitalized rock and roll at one of its lowest ebbs, infusing it with punk energy, brash attitude and a loud, fast new sound," they "only achieved minor commercial success during their career," they never had a Top 40 hit, none of their albums went Platinum, and their first album, *Ramones*, took nearly forty years to sell enough copies to become Gold because "old-guard sorts . . . couldn't hear or didn't understand" their genius ("Ramones" 2002).

A line art illustration of the Ramones, with their seal logo that was designed for them by Autoro Vega, widely considered to be the "fifth" Ramone because he was the band's creative director and archivist. Vega designed the band's official seal to look like the one used by the president of the United States because he believed that the Ramones were as American as apple pie. (Ramavectroyer/Dreamstime.com)

As a result, The Ramones never played arena venues during their career because concert organizers could not count on selling enough tickets to cover expenses. Nevertheless, the band played "2,263 concerts—roughly as many as the Grateful Dead"—between 1974 and final show in Los Angeles on August 6, 1996. The Ramones also issued nearly an album a year during their twenty-two-year career, the first four "acknowledged classics" that provided "much of their live repertoire even into the Nineties" (Green 2014).

Yet, only today, nearly twenty years after the band broke up and all its members dead, are they celebrated for their influence on American punk. The Ramones now appear in lists ranking the all-time greats of rock, including *Rolling Stone*'s "50 Greatest Artists of All Time" and "25 Greatest Live Albums of All Time," and they were inducted into the Rock and Roll Hall of Fame in 2002. Twenty-first-century rock critics now recognize how the Ramones "crystalized punk's unruly attitude and musical aesthetic into an identifiable, accessible style that others could emulate and expand upon" (Schinder 2008).

The Ramones' sound "was a reaction to the sort of overproduced, bombastic music that was receiving airplay in 1974," such as progressive rock, with its lengthy guitar solos, disco, and bland pop tunes (Edelstein and McDonough 1990). The Ramones returned to the basics of rock—most of their songs consisted of voice, guitar, bass, and drums. Also, the Ramones' songs were short; "a Ramones set, especially in the early years, rarely lasted half an hour, and they might perform fifteen or more songs during the sonic blitzkrieg" (Green 2014). They "revered the music of the early to mid-Sixties, drawing upon the artful brevity of Top Forty radio in its heyday" to produce their own original sound (Green 2014). Their songs "maintained a hook-fueled sensibility rooted in" their love "for the vintage bubblegum and British Invasion pop they'd grown up with" and drew on "the worlds of comic books, horror films, girl groups and garage rock" (Green 2014).

In their performances, the only nod the Ramones gave to theatricality was to wear their hair in black pageboy bobs like the early Beatles, making it seem as if they were all brothers. Dee Dee's faux British accent and the band's name also alluded to the British Invasion. Dee Dee, who had taken the last name "Ramone" in homage to Paul McCartney's pre-Beatles stage name, Paul Ramon, persuaded his bandmates to adopt the surname as well. Other musicians who rotated in and out of the Ramones during their twenty-two-year career also took the surname Ramone as their stage name.

Johnny Ramone was indirectly responsible for one of the band's cornerstone sounds. After his bandmates decided that he would be better on guitar than bass, he was short on funds, so "he purchased a cheaper Moscato guitar instead of a Fender or Gibson." On this instrument, "Johnny built his style on furiously downstroked barre chords, playing with so much force that his fingers sometimes bled on stage" (Schinder 2008, 535). Joey, a tenor, was "a distinctive and supremely expressive vocalist" who was "adept at nailing the sincere sentiment that lurked beneath the twisted humor of his and Dee Dee's lyrics, which invoked existential confusion, mental illness, and romantic travail" (Schinder 2008, 535). Critic Scott Huey described Joey's vocals as the "signature bleat" that "was the voice of punk rock in America" (Huey n.d., "Joey Ramone").

Yet, lurking beneath the surface of a typical Ramones' song was "a unique sense of street-level surrealism that was manifested in the absurdist imagery and junk-culture aesthetic of their early lyrics and record sleeves" (Schinder 2008, 535). The simplicity and surrealism of a typical Ramones' song made their music subversive. Listeners cannot help but sing along with the band's catchy, upbeat tunes about sniffing glue, Bonzo traveling to Bittburg, and the joys of being sedated or beating on a brat with a baseball bat. These and other Ramones songs do not encourage drug use and violence but the cultivation of a punk zen aesthetic that invites listeners to contemplate, and even revel in, the absurdity of life.

The Ramones' eponymous debut album is the best example of their work. Its opening song, "Blitzkrieg Bop," is a representative introduction to the band's oeuvre. Inspired by the Rolling Stones and the Bay City Rollers, the song is a later-day version of sixties pop songs that instructed listeners in how to do a dance step, such as Little Eva's "The Loco-Motion," Chubby Checker's "The Twist," or Bobby Picket's "The Monster Mash" (Runtagh 2016, "Ramones' Debut LP"). Lyrically, "Blitzkrieg Bop" focuses on the frenzy that the Ramones incited in fans. Yet, the fictitious dance of the title has a sinister ring to it, with its obvious reference to Germany's martial strategy during World War II and its chorus of "Hey ho, let's go! Shoot 'em in the back now!" The next lines of the chorus suggest that the unbridled energy of the dancers could erupt into a riot. But in true Ramones' fashion, the song ultimately defies a coherent meaning. "Blitzkrieg Bop" has gone on to become included in several lists of top songs.

The next track, "Beat on the Brat," resists analysis. The song consists of the lyrics "beat on the brat with a baseball bat. Oh yeah, oh yeah, oh oh" sung repeatedly during its two-and-a-half-minute duration. The lyrics are rumored to have originated from Joey's witnessing a working-class mother in Queens physically discipline her unruly child. "Judy Is a Punk" is even more bleakly nonsensical. Judy goes to Berlin with her punk friend Jackie to join "the Ice Capades," where they will presumably die. As in most Ramones songs, the bleak lyrics of "Judy Is a Punk" are contrasted with the frantic, upbeat music.

The fourth track, "I Wanna Be Your Boyfriend," is as musically straightforward as the Ramones get. Joey croons, "Hey little girl, I wanna be your boyfriend," to a slower tempo characteristic of 1960s pop love songs. The song is a sort of stripped-down version of the Beatles' hit "I Wanna Hold Your Hand." "Havana Affair" is a song in the tradition of several Blondie tunes; the sensationalist lyrics pay homage to Cold War dime novels. The protagonist, who previously worked picking bananas, now finds himself on a Havana-bound PT boat, pressed into service "as a guide for the C.I.A.," where he will "spy on a Cuban talent show" after his arrival. Originally released in 1976, *Ramones* was remastered in 2016 with additional songs as well as different versions of tracks that appeared on the 1976 version. The remastered Ramones' songs include musical nuances that were not apparent to listeners who originally heard them on the radio or on the earlier versions of the albums.

The Ramones launched the grassroots punk rock movement in New York and London—"the Clash were among those who paid heed when the Ramones first toured Britain—and helped downsize rock from arenas and stadiums to the more sensibly scaled environs of clubs and neighborhood holes-in-the-wall" ("Ramones" 2002). As well, the band's frequent appearance at New York's CBGB club turned the venue from "a little-noticed hole in the wall into a cultural landmark" (Schinder 2008).

The Ramones' music has inspired at least forty-eight tribute albums (Prindle 2009), including the compilations *Gabba Gabba Hey: A Tribute to the Ramones* and *The Song Ramones the Same*, with tracks by L7, Mojo Nixon, Bad Religion, and the Dictators; *Brats on the Beat*, Ramones covers for kids performed by punk bands; and Shonen Knife's *Osaka Ramones*. The band is the subject of the documentary *End of the Century* and the books *The Ramones' Ramones* (Nicholas Rombus), *Why the Ramones Matter* (Donna Gaines), and *Hey Ho Let's Go: The Story of the Ramones* (Everett True). They also starred as themselves in Roger Corman's 1980 musical *Rock 'n' Roll High School*.

RANCID: ... AND OUT COME THE WOLVES

The Southern California punk outfit Rancid is one of the three bands credited with reviving punk in the 1990s (Green Day and Offspring are the others) Rancid's music is a unique combination of hardcore, ska, and reggae that is so faithful to these genres that listeners can be forgiven for believing that the band is playing covers of songs by 1970s "roots" artists who never became household names in the United States rather than their own original creations. Rancid was formed in 1991 by punk veterans Matt Freeman and Tim Armstrong, both former members of Operation Ivy, and Brett Reed. Rancid was one of the most commercially successful California punk bands of the 1990s. Lars Frederiksen joined the Rancid in 1993 to play with them on their sophomore album, *Radio, Radio, Radio* (1993). Their fourth album, *... And Out Come* *the Wolves* (1995), derived its name from the interest it generated from record company suits while it was still in the studio. *Wolves* is a representative sampling of Rancid's fluency in all three genres. . . . *And Out Come the Wolves* was warmly received by critics and fans, and it is Rancid's most commercially successful album to date. Its sales reached Platinum status in the United States, Gold in Australia and Canada, and Silver in the United Kingdom.

The songs on . . . *And Out Come the Wolves* are populated by a colorful cast of characters: criminals, junkies, and misunderstood young people who found their tribe through punk. The album's three hit singles are all uncannily similar to the reggae and ska from the 1970s that inspired the Clash, the Slits, and the Sex Pistols. The title of "Roots Radicals" is taken from reggae star Jimmy Cliff's "Roots Radical" and its line "you know I'm a radical," which refers to Cliff's Rastafarianism and Jamaican anti-colonialism.

The autobiographical "Roots Radicals" reflects how members of Rancid were influenced by reggae and ska as teens, listening to this music at home and going to punk shows. The speaker recounts taking the bus to punk shows as a gangly fifteen-year-old. During one of these trips, a song by well-known reggae musician Desmond Dekker plays on the bus's radio. The teen speaker has already been influenced by reggae with its "talk of revolution," which makes him declare in the chorus, "You know I'm a radical." "Roots Radicals" sounds as if it could be a song by a third-wave ska band like the Mighty Mighty Bosstones. But its self-conscious lyrics about how members of Rancid were influenced by ska and reggae show how their music is an example of cultural appreciation rather than appropriation. Rancid is not plagiarizing the music of other cultures, but instead is inspired by music from other cultures to create music describing their own struggles for agency.

"Roots Radicals" was released as a single in 1994, prior to the release of . . . *And Out Come the Wolves* the following year. "Time Bomb" and "Ruby Soho" were released as singles after the album hit the shelves. Like "Roots Radicals," "Time Bomb" could also pass as a cover of an older reggae or rocksteady song, with its Hammond organ and gangster movie imagery and ska iconography (Brannigan 2016); it tells the story of a twenty-one-year-old, sharp-dressed, Cadillac-driving drug dealer who is predictably shot to death by a rival. The track "Maxwell Murder" describes a similar character, a hit man whose exploits are sung about in a hardcore song is musically similar to the Germs' "Richie Dagger." "Time Bomb" is Rancid's highest-charting single to date, reaching No.

8 on *Billboard*'s "Modern Rock Tracks" to become the highest initial charting in the band's career. It is also credited with igniting a ska revival in the United States in the 1990s (Bray and Brennan 2017).

"Ruby Soho" has been described by critics as an "unabashed clone" of a Clash song, "down to the fast, bumping rhythm and shout-along chorus" (Piccoli 2003). The song's speaker is a musician who continues to tour because he has "seen his name on the marquee," something that his girlfriend, Ruby, does not understand, he believes, because of her reluctance to be away from him for long periods of time. While the speaker is far away from her, sitting in a room alone and listening to the reggae music from a party next door, he wonders whether he has made the right decision to leave Ruby, whose "heart ain't beatin cause she knows the feelin' is gone." "Ruby Soho" quickly became an MTV hit and such an iconic work of ska that Cliff covered it in 2011.

Many tracks on . . . *And Out Come the Wolves* are autobiographical, including the several breakup songs. In "Olympia, WA," Armstrong is in a post-breakup funk and hanging out on a corner with band member Lars Frederiksen. "Daly City Train" is a eulogy for a friend, referred to in the song as "Jackyl," an artist and a poet who overdosed. But Jackyl is not a poor victim of this world; instead, he is a junkie angel who always "maintained a sense of himself," unlike the people who are described in "As Wicked," such as the old man who looks through a dumpster for food and seems to be "like a machinist caught in the machine." Jackyl's early death is not something tragic so much as it is an event that saved him from the bad things in the world.

Other characters are also based on familiar types from punk culture. The punk bildungsroman "The Wars End" could just as easily be called "Portrait of the Punk as a Young Man": after Little Sammy's mother, who never understood him, "smashed his Billy Bragg record" to prevent him from hearing "that communist lecture," he leaves home. Armstrong adopts a faux British accent on "Junkie Man" to sing about another recurring figure in punk, the junkie. "Junkie Man" includes a passage of spoken word by Jim Carroll, which the punk musician and poet composed on the spot for the band (*MTV News* Staff 1995). Rancid used Carroll's line "and out come the wolves" from this passage as the title of their fourth album, as the phrase perfectly characterized the frenzied predatory behavior of rival record companies who wanted to lure the band from their label due to the excitement generated over the as yet unnamed album they were recording. Carroll's spoken word passage gave Rancid's 1995 album its name. (Rancid decided to remain with their label, Epitaph.)

"Disorder and Disarray" musically affirms Rancid's support for what is essentially the punk creed: thou shalt not sell out. "11th Hour" and "Avenues and Alleyways" are similarly part of the punk creed as much as they are sincere statements: thou shalt offer words of encouragement to the young. and thou shalt not be racist (or sexist or homophobic or classist) or even an asshole. "11th Hour" calls out to everyone who feels hopeless to see that they have the power to walk through "mountains of steel" if they realize their own mental strength. "Avenues and Alleyways" builds on this idea by focusing on the question posed in "11th Hour" as to who is in control: the media and those who benefit by controlling the narrative it fuels about race that "pit[s] cats against dogs." To jam this narrative, the speaker will treat people "of a different color" as his brother.

. . . *And Out Come the Wolves* was a commercial and critical success after its release in 1995, which led to Rancid playing *Saturday Night Live* ("Laura Leighton/Rancid" 1995) that year and the Lollapalooza Tour in 1996. The band is still touring and releasing albums today, with only one personnel change—in 2007, Branden Steineckert replaced Brett Reed on drums. They have been named one of the best pop-punk bands by *NME* (Beaumont 2017) and ska punk bands by the music website *Louder* (Fiorello 2015). Armstrong's success with Rancid allowed him to form the independent record label Hellcat Records, an offshoot of Epitaph Records, with Bad Religion's Brad Gurewitz.

RICHARD HELL AND THE VOIDOIDS: *BLANK GENERATION*

Punk musician and writer Richard Hell (Richard Lester Meyers) is the originator of the punk style. He was dressing in artfully ripped clothing held together with safety pins and sporting a Mohawk in 1974 in New York (Gendron 2002), two years before this look would be appropriated by impresario Malcolm McLaren to brand the Sex Pistols in the United Kingdom (McNeil 1996). Hell was a member of the seminal American punk bands Television, Neon Boys, and the Johnny Thunders (also known as the Heartbreakers or Johnny Thunder and the Heartbreakers) before forming Richard Hell and the Voidoids. All of these bands were regulars at the New York punk club CBGB.

After dropping out of his Delaware boarding school when he was sixteen, Hell came to New York as an aspiring poet whose nom de guerre was inspired by Arthur Rimbaud. Although Hell would go on to start his own publishing imprint, writing poetry in 1966 was insufficient to support him, so he turned to music as a more ruminative medium. Hell and his boarding school friend and fellow poet Tom Verlaine (Thomas Miller) started the Neon Boys, which morphed into Television and had the distinction of being the first band to play at Hilly Kristal's newly opened CBGB on the Bowery. Hell's intellectual progress consisted of defining himself as against, rather than for, things: he scorned the Beatnicks and their "insistence on spontaneity" and thought the hippies "were too soft"; and he believed that rock music "peaked in the 1950s" only to be corrupted and homogenized by the Beatles (Garner 2013).

Television "was a reaction against the downtown music scene," stripped down from "the showbiz theatricality of the glitter bands" and the "bluesiness and boogie," to make music that was "stark and hard and torn up, the way the world was" (Garner 2013). Hell visually communicated his worldview through the unique look that he cultivated during his time with Television, with his spiky haircut and torn clothes held together with safety pins that were equally functional and a fashion statement. His stage persona was edgy and energetic. When he became caught up in the music, he would hop around and dance, challenging the audience with his acerbic demeanor. While Hell's style reflected his life in New York in the slums of the Lower East Side, it was also "carefully constructed" (Finney 2012). Television inspired CBGB alumnae Patti Smith to form her own band, and she wrote Television's first review, which appeared in the *Soho Weekly News* (1974).

After a falling out with best friend Tom Verlaine, Hell left Television in 1975 before the band recorded their first album, but by this time, he had become "as an underground luminary" who "hovered on the brink of real stardom" during the second half of the 1970s (Garner 2013). Hell joined Jerry Nolan and Johnny Thunders (who had just left the New York Dolls) to form the Heartbreakers (not to be confused with Tom Petty's backing band of the same name), a band that had a reputation as playing just for "dope money" (Lester 2009). A year later, Hell quit the Heartbreakers to form his own outfit, the Voidoids, with whom he released two studio albums as well the early punk single "Blank Generation" (1976).

Hell and the Voidoid's first album, *Blank Generation*, takes its name from their wildly influential title track. "*Blank Generation* featured weird time signatures and playing that was almost jazzily complex—the Voidoids' lead guitarist Robert Quine studied compositional theory at music college—but the songs were short and sharp, and they rocked" (Lester 2009). *Blank Generation* received mixed critical reception upon its release in 1977. The *Village Voice*'s Robert Christgau gave it a B+, which he later revised to an A– (1979), but Dave Marsh, in the first edition of the *Rolling Stone Guide to Albums*, gave the album just two out of five stars (1979). In retrospect, *Blank Generation* is now "highly regarded by critics as one of the finest examples of early punk rock" as well as "the source of many of the themes and ideas that would come to define punk rock" (Finney 2012). In 2007, *BBC Music*'s Sid Smith described *Blank Generation* as a "thrilling and improbably poignant listening experience" that bottled up "the smell and feel of the whole NY CBGB era." Reviewer Michael Little pronounced that Hell was the only musician of his cohort asking the existential question: "Why should I bother living?" Hell's "grappling with this question" and the excellence of his band "are what makes 1977's *Blank Generation* such a seminal punk recording" (Little 2015).

The album's title track crystalizes Hell's nihilism that is exhibited throughout his work. Hell began writing and performing "Blank Generation" in 1975 with Television—CBGB habitué Andy Warhol described the song as one of Television's "defining numbers" (Finney 2012, 30)—and when Hell released it as a single with the Voidoids the following year, it was recognized from the beginning "as one of the most important tunes to the fledgling punk rock scene in New York" (Finney 2012, 32). The song's title "served as a label that helped galvanize the fans of punk" by providing "an identity and affiliation with a generation," which included its "disillusionment with rock 'n' roll at the time" (Finney 2012, 33). In 1978, Hell told rock journalist Lester Bangs that "blank was a line where you can fill in anything," and "the idea that you have the option of making yourself anything you want, filling in the blank," was uniquely powerful to his generation because it says that "I entirely reject your standards for judging my behavior" (Finney 2012, 33). The *San Francisco Chronicle*'s Michael Goldberg pinpointed why "Blank Generation" appealed to so many punks: it was "a punk anthem, a nihilist manifesto, a rejection of life itself" (Finney 2012, 33).

Several of lyrics in "Blank Generation" were taken from Theresa Stern's poem "After All I Wasn't Even Born"—Theresa Stern was a pseudonym for Hell's poetry collaborations with Tom Verlaine, which they self-published via mimeograph in the 1970s (*Pitchfork* 2004). The song was such a powerful punk statement that McLaren would direct the Sex Pistols to write and perform their own version; their song "Pretty Vacant" is more or less a rewrite of "Blank Generation," both structurally and lyrically, with its similar nihilist stance.

Hell also performed "Love Comes in Spurts" during his brief tenure with the Heartbreakers. The title is not a double entendre but a commentary about the erratic and painful nature of erotic love: "Love comes in spurts, in dangerous flirts, and it murders your heart." *AllMusic*'s Mark Deming makes a case for how the song "reflects the mind of a truly frustrated romantic" rather than the nihilism that critics say characterizes his music. "As Robert Quine's shrapnel-bursts of guitar explode around him, Hell spits, in a voice that splits the difference between rage and hurt" (Deming n.d., "Love Comes in Spurts"), that, at fourteen, he "was a child who wanted love that was wild." "Betrayal Takes Two" follows up on the frustrated romanticism of "Love Comes in Spurts." In the aftermath of a passionate affair, Hell reflects that "feelings will change—we're helpless they must," but "we like it that way—eliminates trust." The beloveds die in the ballads "The Plan" and "Another World." The speaker's true love dies in childbirth in "The Plan," leaving him to raise their daughter alone. "Another World" "has a funky feel, while Hell sounds as desperate as ever," singing about a dead lover (Little 2015).

"Liars Beware" and "Down at the Rock and Roll Club" tread ground that quickly became common tropes in punk. "Liars Beware" is the Voidoids' most political song on *Blank Generation*, calling out the ruling class as "liars," "highlife scum" who "keep [their] victims poor and dumb" but whose ulterior motives and shameless lies are no secret. "Down at the Rock and Roll Club" is "an old school, knock-down-drag-out party tune" that is "filtered through Hell's sense of being trapped and victimized, and always in the wrong place. He may say he's going to have some fun, but somehow it's doubtful; he may get drunk, but it's not going to provide him with either relief or release" (Little 2015).

Other tracks on *Blank Generation* are about Hell's drug addiction, which would nearly kill him after the Voidoids released their second album, *Destiny Street*, in 1982 (Lester 2009). Hell's addiction in "New Pleasure" makes him "too weak for life" and so numb that he is incapable of dressing himself. Hell's nihilism comes through in "Who Says?," which characterizes life as the greatest addiction: "Once born, you're addicted and so you depict it as good, but who kicked it?" Drug addicts, at least, are insulated from pain, thanks to drugs. The band's cover of Creedence Clearwater Revival's "Walking on the Water" addresses how Hell felt in those days when his addiction was so out of control that he thought he would die. When the speaker sees "a man walking on the water, coming right at [him] from the other side" while calling his name and telling him not to fear, he is terrified and runs. Hell's selection of a Creedence Clearwater Revival song to cover is ironic given that he had just bitterly denounced the countercultural ideals of the 1960s (Sokol 2017).

Soon after *Blank Generation*'s release, Hell and the Voidoids disappeared from music, in part due to Hell's heroin addiction, while punk was exploding in the United Kingdom and the United States. So when the Voidoids recorded their second and last album, *Destiny Street*, in 1982, it received scant critical attention because Hell "did not tour or cultivate an audience" and punk was being supplanted in the headlines by New Wave (Finney 2012). Too, during the recording of *Destiny Street*, Hell described himself as being so "insane and desperate and riddled with drugs" that he "didn't know how to make a record sound good" (Lester 2009). He would rerecord and rerelease his 1982 album in 2009 as *Destiny Street Repaired*.

Today, Hell pursues his literary and musical interests. He has written several poetry collections, novels, and a memoir, and he continues to record music (Sokol 2017). He is also the subject of the book *Richard Hell and the Voidoids' Blank Generation*, by Pete Astor.

THE RUNAWAYS: *THE RUNAWAYS*

In the decade of #MeToo, when women who came of age in the 1970s read the story of music impresario Kim Fowley and the five minor girls who would become the Runaways, it is hard not to become triggered. Fowley, who was credited with inventing the term "jailbait rock" (Vincent 2015), clearly abused his power as the Runaways' manager to enrich himself and rape then sixteen-year-old band member Jackie Fuchs (Jackie Fox) in 1977. Fowley (then thirty-six years old) drugged Fuchs with quaaludes after a show and then participated in her gang rape during an after-party in front of witnesses, including other band members (Cherkis 2015). Fuchs distinctly remembers making eye contact with her sister band members Joan Jett and Cherie Currie, who were also present (Cherkis 2015). That Jett and Currie would later deny witnessing the rape is a testament to how normalized sexual violence against women was in the 1970s, particularly in the rock scene (Lodi 2015; Roberts 2015).

Fuchs was so traumatized that she left the band just before they were to play the Tokyo Music Festival that would launch them to stardom in that country. She did not feel comfortable telling her story to the public until 2015, at a time when women more openly talked about being sexually assaulted and would soon demand a reckoning in 2017 after Ashley Judd and Rose McGowan made public how producer Harvey Weinstein sexually harassed them. Since then, other witnesses have corroborated Fuchs's account of the 1977 after-party. Currie quit the band soon after

Fuchs left, to be replaced by new member Vicki Blue. But in the end, the Runways would have the best revenge on Fowler: they would become a major influence on the emerging punk sound as well as an early example of an all-woman group.

The Runaways were created in 1975 by Fowler to be "male's heavy rock wet dream": a band of several beautiful young women dressed in "tight lycra, corsets, stockings and hot pants," which got them the attention of the music press for the way they looked rather than their musicianship ("The Runaways" n.d.). But the Runaways wrote their own songs and were excellent musicians, with Joan Jett's strong rhythm guitar; Lita Ford's heavy metal lead; Currie's growling, passionate vocals; Fuchs's driving bass; and Sandy West's explosive drumming (Chiu 2013). The band launched the successful solo careers of Jett and Ford and would influence later female punk bands, including L7, Bikini Kill, and Babes in Toyland. Although the band members did not describe themselves as feminists while they were together, "Their goals were certainly compatible with the goals of feminism in terms of promoting female power and equal rights for women musicians" (Chiu 2013). They "owned their sexuality" in their music and controlled how they presented themselves to audiences, despite how others, their manager included, viewed them. In retrospect, Jett "has identified herself as a feminist" and has become "a role model for other women in the music business" (Chiu 2013).

The band's self-titled debut album includes tracks that were at the time groundbreaking for female musicians: songs in which women sing about having sexual needs that are as fierce as men's and their willingness to act on them. The singer's subject position in the Runaways' songs was the antithesis of how women were characterized in popular culture, as passive objects of the male gaze who hoped and waited for the men they were interested in to initiate an encounter.

The Runaways opens with what has become their signature single, "Cherry Bomb." Both Fowley and Currie claim that the song was written on the spot as her audition song. "Cherry Bomb" is a sort of coming out song; the singer characterizes herself as "the girl next door" who will "have you and grab you until you're sore." In 1976, these lyrics were revolutionary in how they described an everywoman character as someone with sexual agency. But the chorus indicates that this woman is finally owning a part of herself that her parents and her culture believed did not exist. The song's title indicates that the singer might also be a virgin, as it references the phrase "losing your cherry," which is commonly used to describe the first time a woman has penile/vaginal intercourse. The song's simple lyrics and infectious chorus combined with Currie's canny and dangerous vocals helped make it one of the best-known songs from the 1970s. The single charted at No. 1 in Japan in 1976 and at No. 106 in the United States, but it has since become so iconic that Jett and Currie rerecorded it in 2010 for the video game *Guitar Hero: Warriors of Rock*.

Other songs that frankly describe women's sexual desire include "You Drive Me Wild," "Thunder," and "Lovers." And unlike "Cherry Bomb," these songs make no reference to the sex of the object of desire, which places greater emphasis on the female subject's desire and also breaks with heteronormativity because these feelings could be for anyone. The omission of gendered pronouns might be Jett's influence. Jett, who has refused to confirm or deny speculations about her sexuality, wrote "You Drive Me Wild" and "Lovers" with Fowley. In her cover of "Crimson and Clover," which she released in 1981 with her band the Blackhearts, Jett refers to the beloved with female pronouns. "Secrets" too lacks gendered pronouns in its description of love on the downlow. "Blackmail" describes another emotion that is considered to be incompatible with normative femininity: anger. In it, the singer promises that "you'll wish you were never born" because she will make you pay for "the life that you tore."

Other tracks on the album are more autobiographical, including "Is It Day or Night?" "Rock & Roll," and "American Nights." "Is It Day or Night?" depicts the confusion stemming from life on the road as a musician. The band describes their music and youth in "American Nights," where their "magic is young" because they have just gotten started and are "the queens of noise." This last phrase would be the title of their second studio album, *Queens of Noise* (1981), and its first track. "Rock & Roll" is a cover of a Velvet Underground song written by Lou Reed for their album *Loaded*, but the song's lyrics are particularly suited to the Runaways' collective stage persona. The song is related in the third person about Jenny, whose dull life was transformed when she heard rock and roll for the first time.

"Dead End Justice" could be about the band members if they had not had a career in music. It begins with Currie singing about being a sixteen-year-old blonde rebel girl who looks especially attractive in her tight jeans. But after she runs away with a fake ID to live on the streets and get drunk and high with the other "dead end kids," she is arrested for possession and sent to juvenile detention where, "behind bars, there's a superstar" who could sing and dance; however, these efforts are futile in jail. The song ends with a dialogue between Jett and Currie in which they plan their escape.

After Fuchs's and Currie's departures in 1977, Jett took over lead vocals and guitar, and Vicki Blue became the new bassist. They also promptly fired Fowley. This last action had the unintended consequence of voiding their contract with their label, Mercury/Polygram, who had agreed to promote the band based on its relationship with Fowler. The Runaways hired a new manager who had also managed Blondie and Suzi Quatro, but he could not help the group continue their musical career beyond one more studio album due to conflicts between band members or the consequences of their rock and roll lifestyle: drinking and taking drugs to excess made them undependable musicians. Jett later admitted to drinking so much in those days that she developed a heart infection (*Bad Reputation* 2018).

After four studio albums, the Runaways dissolved in 1979 and went on to careers as musicians or in the entertainment business. The band has been the subject of the documentary films *Edgeplay* (2004) and the biopic *The Runaways* (2010). The documentary *Bad Reputation* (2018), about Jett, also covers the Runaways in depth.

THE SEX PISTOLS: *NEVER MIND THE BOLLOCKS: HERE'S THE SEX PISTOLS*

The Sex Pistols are best known for their songs "Anarchy in the U.K." and "God Save the Queen" on their sole studio album, *Never Mind the Bollocks: Here's the Sex Pistols*. Their concerts, songs, and media appearances generated controversy, thanks in part to their manager, Malcolm McLaren, a provocateur who solidified their reputation for outraging bourgeois sensibilities. The original members of the Sex Pistols were singer Johnny Rotten (John Lydon), lead guitarist Steve Jones, drummer Paul Cook, and bassist Glen Matlock, who was replaced in 1977 by Sid Vicious (Simon John Ritchie). McLaren christened the band the Sex Pistols after hitting upon "the idea of a pistol, a pop-up, a young thing, a better-looking assassin" (Molon 2007, 76). The Sex Pistols were not the first punk band (the Ramones started their career in New York at the club CBGB in 1974), but they were one of the most important bands from the London punk scene in the 1970s due to their influence on the genre.

In keeping with the spirit of punk rock, the Sex Pistols were aggressively anti-commercial. Their songs were strident and laced with obscenities, and they covered topics that ranged from apathy, anarchy, and the British royal family to the Holocaust, guaranteeing that much of their music would not receive airplay because it violated decency

Must-Hear Music **125**

1967 Gibson Les Paul guitar owned by Steve Jones when he cofounded the Year Zero band the Sex Pistols in 1975. The photo on the right shows Jones in 1976 as he smashes the instrument against a wall of London's 100 Club, breaking its neck. The guitar was repaired but never playable again. (Usa Pyon/Dreamstime.com)

standards at the time. The length of the Sex Pistols' songs also made them unsuitable for airplay: most were under three minutes, which was too short for commercial radio. The Pistols' unique sound can be attributed to Rotten's vocals, described by *The Cambridge Companion to Singing* as an example of "naturalism," a style "so exaggerated, so distorted, as to be menacing" (Potter 2000, 35). Rotten's vocalizations are a sneering parody of a working-class British accent that can be heard "in his bizarre and typical upward-curving pitch-bend on the final syllable of a phrase" (Potter 2000, 35). Later punk singers, including Jello Biafra, front man for the Dead Kennedys, and Siouxsie Sioux, lead singer for Siouxsie and the Banshees, would imitate Vicious's singing style.

The Pistols also did not look and act the part of glamorous would-be rock stars: their hair was short and spiky, and their clothing was a combination of old T-shirts and bondage and fetish gear sold at McLaren and designer Vivienne Westwood's London boutique SEX. Rotten's teeth were so bad that they inspired his stage name, given to him by his bandmates due to his poor dental hygiene.

The band's on-stage behavior displayed contempt for their fans, other musicians, and even each another: The Pistols spit on and insulted audience members and frequently got into brawls with them as well as with members of other bands and each another during their concerts. Nevertheless, the Pistols' developed a following among young people in 1970s England, a nation that was mired in a crippling economic depression, because their angry music was more relatable to fans "who lived in council flats" than the commercially produced pop music that "was merely images pertaining to something mystical, devoid of reality" (Lydon 1993). Although the Pistols were only together for three years, they were sufficiently influential to have since been the subject of multiple music documentaries and books as well as the feature film *Sid and Nancy*, which speculated about the tumultuous relationship of Sid Vicious and Nancy Spungen. The band has since reunited several times after their break-up in 1978 to tour and record, and they were inducted into the Rock and Roll Hall of Fame in 2006, although the band, in typical Pistols' fashion, rejected the honor through a profanity-laced statement on their website (Brand 2006).

The Sex Pistols' began their career performing for art school audiences who were initially hostile to their music. Their debut gig in November 1975 at St. Martin's college was universally described as dreadful; the band's musicianship was inept, and band members got into a fistfight with another band playing the gig. The fisticuffs prefigured the atmosphere of later Pistols' concerts, which often ended in mayhem. During their first year, the Pistols built enough of a following to persuade Virgin/EMI to give them a contract. EMI released the band's first single, "Anarchy in the U.K.," in November of 1976, and it topped England's charts at No. 38. Music journalist Caroline Coon dubbed "Anarchy in the U.K." the epitome of the Pistols' "furious, venomous" sound (1976). EMI arranged for the band to tour in 1977 to promote "Anarchy in the U.K." and create a market for their forthcoming album, *Never Mind the Bollocks*. However, the tour ended before it began due to a profanity-laced exchange between Cook and the host of the *Today* show, Bill Grundy, during a live interview in December 1976, where Grundy goaded band members to get them to "to prove that these louts were a foul-mouthed set of yobs" (*The Guardian* [London] 1976). The incident magnified the Pistols' reputation for hooliganism, prompting the managers of the venues where they were scheduled to play to suddenly cancel their engagements.

But EMI had not completely given up on the Sex Pistols. In 1977, the label released the single "God Save the Queen" to coincide with Queen

Elizabeth II's Silver Jubilee in June of 1977 to trade on the ensuing controversy that the band's parody of England's national anthem would provoke. "God Save the Queen" describes the monarch as a moronic puppet of England's "fascist regime," a sentiment that was so offensive in 1977 that the BBC and the Independent Broadcasting Authority refused to play the single. The song did, however, resonate with the band's English fans: angry and cynical working-class youth for whom there was "no future in England's dreaming." That year, "God Save the Queen" reached No. 1 on *NME*'s charts and No. 2 on the U.K. singles charts.

The title of the Sex Pistols' debut album, *Never Mind the Bullocks*, was similarly offensive (the word *bullocks* is a vulgar British colloquialism for testicles). As a result, many record stores refused to carry the album, and it was left off the U.K. charts even after the reaching the No. 1 position in 1977. Banned from radio and most concert venues in the United Kingdom, the Pistols toured the United States to promote *Never Mind the Bullocks*, as they had developed fans in the United States. McLaren, however, did not book the Pistols in cities where their fans were most likely to reside but instead arranged for them to play most of their concerts in the American South, where the audiences were hostile to everything that the band stood for. McLaren's strategy was, as usual, to promote the band by generating notoriety for them.

Predictably, audiences in Atlanta, Memphis, San Antonio, and Dallas "were stunned, confused, angry, and amused" by the Pistols' performances, although the audience in Baton Rouge was remembered as being "the least outraged stop on the tour" in that no one got beat up by the police or run out of town, and Vicious received simulated oral sex while on stage (Cook 2013). The Pistols, meanwhile, were horrified by the U.S. gun culture and the level of violence compared to the United Kingdom. Cook recalls being "worried about being killed" while in the United States because the police near the stage had guns, an unfamiliar sight to Britons, where law enforcement officers do not carry firearms. In Memphis, Vicious was beaten up by guards hired by their American record label, Warner Brothers, to protect band members when he wandered away from the band's lodgings to procure some heroin and was mistaken for an intruder when he returned (Savage 1992, 446). The stress of the American tour exacerbated rifts between the band members, and the Pistols broke up on stage during their last show in San Francisco and went their separate ways.

Vicious embarked on a brief solo career, recording three covers of songs for the soundtrack to McLaren's mockumentary about the band, *The Great Rock and Roll Swindle* (1980, Julian Temple, Dir.), including one of Frank Sinatra's "My Way." Vicious's career abruptly ended after he was arrested in New York in October 1978 for murdering his girlfriend, Nancy Spungen, while high on heroin. In 1979, just twenty-four hours after Vicious bonded out of jail on this charge, the remorseful singer died from a heroin overdose.

Rotten reverted to his birth name, Lydon, and formed Public Image Ltd. with former Clash member Keith Levine. Cook toured with Iggy Pop, and both he and Jones did guest appearances and worked as studio musicians. The remaining band members, along with EMI/Virgin, sued McLaren for misappropriating the band's royalties.

The Pistols' original members, including former bassist Glen Matlock, have reunited three times since their 1978 break up in 1978, including their Filthy Lucre Tour in 1996, and again in 2007 to tour the United Kingdom and appear in European festivals in 2008.

SHONEN KNIFE: *ALIVE! IN OSAKA*

If you do not know who Shonen Knife is, you have probably at least heard one of their songs. This trio from Osaka, Japan, has been playing music and touring since 1981, when they were started by sisters Naoko (vocals and guitar) and Atsuko Yamano (drums) and Michie Nakatani (bass). Today, "though still virtually unknown in popular commercial music, they are legendary in underground culture" (Vallely 2017). Shonen Knife's music is unlike any other type of punk in that it is "unusually optimistic and sugary sweet" as well as devoid of political statements or cynicism about the human condition. Instead, like their idols the Ramones, Shonen Knife's music consists of catchy, sing-along tunes about topics that seem childish—sugary foods, all-you-can-eat buffets, dance parties in space, and Hello Kitty. Shonen Knife's sound is characterized by Naoko's jangly guitar and the band's sweet female harmonies that give their music the sparkly quality of 1960s girl groups combined with the energy of the early Beatles, another of their musical influences. Other musical influences include Black Sabbath, Kiss, the Crystals, and the Go-Go's, but especially the Ramones (Muther 2005). In fact, the band members admire the Ramones so much that they have performed as a Ramones tribute band under the name Osaka Ramones, and they have included covers of Ramones songs on many of their albums.

Shonen Knife first became popular outside of Japan in the late 1980s because of word-of-mouth recommendations of their work from other musicians. In 1987, they came to the attention of British DJ John Peel, who began playing their music on his BBC show. Kurt Cobain is credited

Must-Hear Music

Ritsuko Taneda on bass and Emi Morimoto on drums when Shonen Knife played in Cork, Ireland, in 2014. The Japanese punk band, also known as the Osaka Ramones, has been touring Europe and the United States since 1981. (Marcellofar/Dreamstime.com)

with introducing the band to American audiences. A huge fan of their music, Cobain asked the band to be the opening act for Nirvana's *Nevermind* tour in the United Kingdom after he heard them play in Los Angeles. Later that year, the band would have the first of its John Peel recording sessions. After the release of their second studio album, *Rock Animals* (1993), their video for the track "Tomato Head" was in heavy rotation on MTV in 1994 and was used in an episode of MTV's animated series *Beavis and Butthead* that same year. Later that year, Shonen Knife toured the United States and Canada on their own as well as with Lollapalooza, performing with Nirvana, Sonic Youth, and the Breeders, and contributed a cover of the Carpenters' "Top of the World" to the cover compilation *If I Were a Carpenter*.

Shonen Knife's music might sound distinctly unpunk given its sugary sweet sound as well as the apolitical lyrics of their original songs, which are more often than not about food, cats, or other subjects that conjure up the mod era of the 1960s. But the band's DIY ethos makes them punk, as does their relationship with their audiences. Shonen Knife is still touring today. They play small venues in the United States, where it is still possible to see the band in the front row after spotting them emerging from the ladies' room. They have a closer relationship with their audiences than other bands. But Shonen's lyrical simplicity is one element of their music that makes it so punk. This quality invites the listener to sing along and perhaps experience the most punk rock feeling of all—the joy of living in the present, freed from the confines of what came before and unconcerned about what comes next. This experience is a type of anarchy that is transformative; when you live fully in the present, you know what it feels like to be free of others' expectations. In this way, Shonen Knife is very much like their idols, the Ramones.

Another factor that makes Shonen Knife a punk band is how they repurpose American music to make their own creation—a type of music that bridges the gap between the two cultures. Shonen Knife is a band that demonstrates the fascination that the Japanese have with American bands whose lyrics, even if they are sung in Japanese, cannot easily be translated to another culture. American rock music has been popular in Japan since its beginnings, and some American bands, such as the Runaways, were more successful there than they were in the United States. Shonen Knife's songs, sung in imperfect English about both Japanese and American subjects, emphasize the process of one culture attempting to understand another.

Alive! in Osaka is a live compilation of some of the band's best songs, and it also captures the feeling of seeing the band in concert. Although Shonen Knife has been performing for nearly forty years, they are still an underground group that plays small venues on tour. On a stop in their *Alive! in Osaka* Tour in Denton, Texas (a small college town outside of Dallas), the small club was filled with approximately two hundred people who ranged in age from eight years old to people in their fifties. Most had heard of the band before the show and sang along to the songs. The band encouraged audience participation during their performance by selling kazoos before the show.

Shonen Knife's music does not sound like typical punk. Most of their songs do not have the typical hyped tempo of punk, nor do they cover subjects such as social justice or call out posers. Instead, their musical approach is closer to that of their idols, the Ramones, in that their songs are about pure joy. But where the Ramones celebrate the absurdity of life, Shonen Knife celebrates its wonder. As a Japanese band who has cultivated a following both in Japan as well as in the United States, several of their songs are about commonplace facets of American culture that fascinate the band members, such as all-you-can-eat buffets and barbeque parties, as well as elements of modern Japanese culture that appeal to Americans, such as Hello Kitty, sushi, and ramen. And so many of their songs are about food. Naoko Yamano, who writes most of the band's songs, says that she writes about food because she's "so ashamed to write about love," but "eating delicious food is (a) universal theme" (Rivera 2014).

Several tracks on *Alive! in Osaka* are metatextual pop songs that sound as if they were from the 1960s and 1970s; these include "Rock and Roll T-shirt," "Pop Tune," "Super Group," "Twist Barbie," "Jump into the New World," "Riding on the Rocket," "Move On," and "Pyramid Power." "Rock and Roll T-shirt," about an essential item of rock and roll material culture, has a harder bass line than other Shonen Knife songs, which gives it more of a 1970s rock sound characteristic of Black Sabbath or Bad Company than a 1960s pop group. The official video for "Pop Tune" attempts to recreate the early 1960s. The band members wear matching mod minidresses as they play in a studio with walls covered with sculpted birds whose design is characteristic of that era's modernism. The camera frames the band in such a way as to create a tryptic; each member is in her own separate cell, and the band's name appears in a pink mod font. The whole is reminiscent of early videos for pop groups such as the Monkees and the Beatles.

"Super Group" uncharacteristically tells a lengthy story about a generic "super group" whose "members are rock stars from 70s band." "Twist Barbie's" sound and subject matter could be a commercial from the 1970s for the Mattel doll, as it describes Barbie's characteristic blonde hairdo and blue eyes as well as her figure "Oh! Sexy girl." "Twist Barbie's" sound is reminiscent of go-go music. "Jump into the New World," "Riding on the Rocket," "Move On," and "Pyramid Power" have a similar mod sound and futurist theme that characterized pop music from the early 1960s. Their cover of "Cruel to Be Kind" fits in with these songs, as its original performer, Nick Lowe, wrote it in 1979 as a retro rockabilly piece of music.

Several songs are about food. "Banana Chips," "Sushi Bar Song," and "Wasabi" are simply about food, as are "All You Can Eat" and "BBQ Party," two American traditions that fascinate the band members. "Green Tangerine" was named after the fruit from the hometown of the band's current drummer, Risa Kawano (Reiley 2017). Others are more Japanese, such as "Bear up Bison," "Bad Luck Song," and "It's a New Find." "Bear up Bison" describes an animal that is common to Japan as well as the United States. In "Bad Luck Song," the lyrics say that if the song is "a monkey," then "it might be a good sign," as monkeys are associated with good luck in Chinese and Japanese culture. "It's a New Find" references both Japanese and American customs for shaking off malaise—"Feel in your pockets for something fun / Wash your socks and turn them inside out"—as well dressing up, getting a new haircut, and dancing. "Antonio Baka Guy," about a dark-skinned foreigner, is one of the band's oldest songs. It has their strongest punk and hard rock sound. with a throbbing base line like Deep Purple's "Smoke on the Water."

Shonen Knife's long-term success in Japan and the United States demonstrates how rock and roll become popular in Japan and has in turn influenced American rock. In some ways, their career parallels that of the Runaways, who were a bigger hit in Japan than they were in the United States. Shonen Knife's musical oeuvre also demonstrates another punk quality of their work—the blending repurposing of work from other cultures and musical genres to make new art, an ability that the gypsy punk band Gogol Bordello has perfected.

Finally, Shonen Knife's success can be understood through the bands that they have inspired. By 1989, so many punk and alternative bands had come to love Shonen Knife that they put together the tribute album *Every Band Has a Shonen Knife Who Loves Them*, consisting of covers of their songs by L7, Sonic Youth, Babes in Toyland, Lunachicks, and Red Kross. The Houston riot grrrl band Giant Kitty took their name from the Shonen Knife song of the same name.

SIOUXSIE AND THE BANSHEES: *THE SCREAM*

Siouxsie and the Banshees' sophomore album, *The Scream* (1978), exemplifies how the band was "helping establish the language of post-punk" while "punk was being formed" (Phillips 2018). The London band's earliest music is a gothic, avant garde expression of punk that was as influenced by the Talking Heads as it was the Sex Pistols, the group that Siouxsie Sioux (Susan Dallion) and her Banshees' bandmate Steven Severin (Steven Bailey) credit with introducing them to punk in 1975. Sioux and Severin were part of the Bromley Contingent, a term coined by music journalist Caroline Coon to describe the uniquely dressed fans of the Sex Pistols who followed the band from town to town. It was in this capacity that Sioux and Severin were involved with the infamous episode on Bill Grundy's *Today* show in December of 1976, when Sex Pistols' guitarist Steve Jones called the host a "dirty bastard" and a "fucking rotter" on live television after Grundy suggested an illicit rendezvous with Sioux after the show (Bennett 2016; "Transcript" 2004).

In 1976, Sioux and Severin decided to form Siouxsie and the Banshees, and they soon got their chance to play at a London punk festival sponsored by punk impresario Malcolm McLaren. Sioux became "as well known for her style as her voice" (Gregory 2017), with her dramatic eye makeup, "fetish clothing and fishnet, peek-a-boo shiny plastic bras, spiky stilettos, rubber stockings and swastika armbands" that made her a sort of "female Sex Pistol" (*Punk77* n.d., "Siouxsie"). Sioux's sartorial intent was not to objectify herself but, rather, "to show that erogenous zones are over rated" and that breasts "are no big deal" (*Punk77* n.d., "Siouxsie"). As part of the first coterie of London punk bands, she was instrumental in the development of the punk image. The Banshees' music reflected both "the chaos and grime of the city" but also found "the cold emptiness of the suburbs" (Phillips 2018). Sioux's fearsome atonal vocal pronouncements accompanied by a throbbing bass line and sharply ascending guitar notes characterize the tracks on *The Scream*.

The Banshees' second studio album, *The Scream*, was a seminal moment in punk and "marked the kick-off point for British post-punk, paving the way for everyone from Joy Division to Savages" (Phillips 2018), with music that was "angular, claustrophobic and goth before there was such a thing" (Gregory 2017). Most of the songs on *The Scream* were written by Banshees' guitarist John McKay, and the album's title is derived from Edvard Munch's painting of the same name. But the most notable feature of *The Scream* is Sioux's voice: she pierces listeners' hearts with her high notes, which pull "everyone into the future" (Gregory 2017). *Rolling Stone*'s Kurt Loder compared Sioux to a young Grace Slick (1979).

The Scream's opening track, "Pure," is not so much a song as it is a wordless sample of the Banshees' sound: a throbbing bass, a high-pitched guitar, and Sioux's scream-cum-yodel vocalizations. "Jigsaw Feeling" sonically illustrates the experience of alienation, feeling "total" one day and "split in two" on the next. The opening bassline lays down a predictable rhythm that is punctured by the high-pitched notes that Sioux hits to deliver the lyrics. "Overground" seems to come from beneath with a soft instrumental introduction that comes through on only one audio channel, as if it is being heard from a distant location, before the music swells to full volume to emerge overground.

The track "Carcass" sounds like a typical punk song and uses the same power chords that begin most Ramones songs. The lyrics of this anti-love song, however, are more goth than punk. They enjoin the listener to "be limblessly in love" as a way of embracing the pain and vulnerability that is an inevitable part of romantic love. Instead of struggling to avoid these feelings, the listener must give herself over to this pain and be "in love with the stumps, in love with the bleeding," and enamored with the pain. "Carcass" blends so effortlessly into the next track, a cover of the

Beatles' "Helter Skelter," that it is difficult to distinguish the two tracks, as both use the same guitar chords; Sioux's vocals are consistently disturbing and hypnotic.

"Mirage" is uncharacteristically tuneful, opening with a guitar riff that could be from a Psychedelic Furs song, which is not surprising given that in the nineties, during the band's last tour, they would be joined by one of that band's former guitarists. Yet, the song's melodious instrumentation sharply contrasts with its lyric exploration of a dizzying postmodern reality where "the image is no images; it's not what it seems."

Several tracks on *The Scream* examine how people are programmed to behave in ways that are contrary to their own interests. "Metal Postcard (Mittageisen)" references Nietzche's concept of the *Ubermench* as imagined by Hitler in its chorus: "Metal is tough, metal will sheen. Metal will rule in my master scheme!" "Metal Postcard (Mittageisen)" takes its name from German Dadaist John Heartfield's 1935 photocollage *Hurrah! Die Butter Ist Alle (Hurray! The Butter Is Gone!)*, in which a German family and their dog enthusiastically sup on metal chains and tools because their blind loyalty to Hitler has subverted their ability to act in their own best interests.

"Nicotine Stain" describes an insidious type of chemical warfare, where nicotine can be used to immobilize entire populations so that it is not necessary to go to war with them: if you "drop [cigarettes] on every country," then "all will be stone dead when the nicotine stain spreads." The creators of this perverse programming are scientists in "Switch," who "cross the wires and fuse humanities." However, this programming does not always work to make people behave in ways that benefit others to their own determent. The subject of "Suburban Relapse" escapes her programming while doing the dishes when she snaps," prompting her to question her sanity and wonder whether she should "throw things at the neighbors," "expose [herself] to strangers," or kill herself.

"Hong Kong Garden," the Banshees' first single, is included as a bonus track in the CD reissue of *The Scream*, where it is out of place with the other tracks on the album. "Hong Kong Garden," with its catchy hook, Asian guitar riffs, opening bars played on an electronic xylophone, was first aired during the Banshees' Peel Session in 1978 (Webb 2009) and became an instant hit, coming in at No. 7 on that year's U.K. singles chart and featured as the single of the week in *NME* and *Melody Maker*. Although "Hong Kong Garden" remains one of the Banshees' best-known songs, it also opened the band up to accusations of racism with the lines "Slanted eyes greet the bright sunrise, a race of bodies small in size." Sioux's "predilection for wearing swastika armbands on stage at the earliest Banshees' shows" only fueled this suspicion (Clerk 2016). Sioux, however, said that she wrote the song to channel her anger at the skinheads who used to hang out at the Christchurch Chinese take-out restaurant named in the song (Webb 2009). And while Sioux now regrets wearing swastikas, at the time, her intent was to defy bourgeois morality rather than to make any sort of anti-Semitic statement.

When *The Scream* was released in November of 1978, it received critical accolades from *Rolling Stone*, *NME*, and *Melody Maker*. The album was commercially successful as well, peaking at No. 12 on the U.K. album charts for the year. However, part of those sales were driven by enthusiasm for the band generated by the release of their single "Hong Kong Garden," which was released in August of that year while the band was in the studio recording *The Scream*. In a 2012 interview on BBC4, Sioux said that people who bought *The Scream* after hearing "Hong Kong Garden" were likely to be confused because the single was so stylistically different from the album (Sawyer 2012).

After *The Scream*, Siouxsie and the Banshees moved away from punk and post-punk toward New Wave, electronic, and dance music, as exemplified by hits such as "Kiss Them for Me" (*Superstition* (1991)) and "Peek-a-boo" (*Peepshow* (1988)), while their dark lyrics paved the way for goth music. After releasing eleven studio albums, the Banshees broke up in 1996 due to simmering tensions between band members that had festered. But they would influence a new generation of bands as diverse as Joy Division, Radiohead, PJ Harvey, Depeche Mode, the Smiths, and the Cure (Robert Smith was a former member of the Banshees).

THE SLITS: *CUT*

The all-female punk band the Slits "most directly challenged the gender hierarchies of British punk" (Cogan 2012, 122). The four members of the Slits were a varied and international bunch. Lead vocalist Ari Up (Ariane Daniela Forster) was from Munich, the granddaughter of the owner of *Der Speigel*. Her father had been a successful singer in Germany, and her mother would later marry John Lydon (Johnny Rotten) of the Sex Pistols. Ari Up was only fourteen years old in 1976 when she formed the band with Palmolive (and Kate Korus and Suzi Gutsy, who were later replaced by Viv Albertine and Tessa Pollitt). Palmolive, the Slits' drummer, left Franco's Spain in 1972 to come to London and received her stage name from Paul Simonon of the Clash, who could not pronounce her Spanish name, Paloma (Howe 2009). Albertine and Pollitt, on guitar and bass, respectively, were Londoners. Pollitt was born in

London and moved to Africa after the Slits disbanded for the first time in 1982.

The Slits are punk pioneers who were at ground zero of the punk movement in the United Kingdom in 1976 London, where they were among the inner circle of the Sex Pistols' fans and friends with Clash members Mick Jones and Joe Strummer. Their music incorporated elements of ska and dub, styles prevalent on the British scene, and encouraged their audiences to rebel against repressive gender roles that were the bedrock of bourgeois morality. Their first album, *Cut*, was not released until 1979, three years after they had been playing clubs regularly and had gone on tour with the Clash twice.

Cut was recorded during a ten-week Peel Session (live music sessions recorded for well-known BBC Radio 1 host John Peel), hit No. 30 on the U.K. charts, and was favorably received by critics. Greil Marcus later suggested that the Slits had rewritten the history of rock and roll in their debut performance at the Roxy in London. The Slits' music did not sound like anything else coming out of the New York or London punk scenes at the time. Bands like the Sex Pistols, the Clash, the Runaways, and the Ramones all returned to the basics of rock and roll—guitar, bass, and drums—to play compositions that followed the typical rock song pattern of verse, chorus, verse, chorus, bridge, verse, chorus. Instead, several of the Slits' songs sound like rounds, with the band members continuously repeating the chorus while Ari Up sings verses in between.

The Slits' music also has an angular, metallic sound to it. None of their songs have catchy tunes, and Ari Up can be painful to listen to at times. Palmolive's complex, up-tempo percussions woven through the songs create the illusion that the music on *Cut* is one big song rather than twelve individual compositions. Their musical style both incorporates the modern and experimental sound of New Wave and resists neat categorization. This musical strategy, which subverts the listener's expectations about what a song should be, lays the foundation for how the band subverts expectations of gender in multiple ways. *Cut* was not a commercial success in its time, but it has influenced new generations of musicians and just celebrated the fortieth anniversary of its recording.

The songs on *Cut* challenge dominant beliefs that women's subordination is justified by biology. Their songs "Typical Girls" and "Love and Romance" described femininity as a constructed social institution when second-wave feminism had just begun to reshape how people thought of gender. The "Typical Girls" are the essence of a type of normative femininity that persists today. These women participate in their own victimization because they are not creative people or rebels, and they are indecisive because they are too busy worrying about their bodies. Heterosexual relationships are inherently repressive for both "typical" girls and "typical" boys in "Love and Romance." The song represents heterosexual relationships as inherently oppressive for both parties: the typical girl in this song, in love with her typical boy, will "break [his] neck if [he] ain't home" when she calls him on the telephone every day. "FM" is one of the earliest songs about self-harm. The initials in the song's title stand for "frequent mutilation," which "transmits over the air, serving for the purpose of those who want you to fear." The Slits' capture perfectly the type of thinking that might persuade someone who self-mutilates to seek help, as this condition is most common among young women who have been victims of abuse or neglect or who have eating disorders or body dysmorphia.

Other Slits songs are more typical punk fare in their treatment of the difficulties of eating when you are too poor to buy food ("Shoplifting") or the distaste the band members and their audiences felt toward the prospect of going to a monotonous nine-to-five job ("Pay Rent"), which made it more difficult to be a creative artist. The subjects of "Instant Hit" and "Spend, Spend, Spend" each have their addictions. A boy in "Instant Hit," "set on self-destruct," uses heroin, and the speaker in "Spend, Spend, Spend" is addicted to shopping, which satisfies her feelings of emptiness.

The one song on *Cut* that does fit the model of a somewhat typical rock song is the band's cover of Marvin Gaye's "I Heard It through the Grapevine." However, when this song is sung by a woman, it takes on a different meaning. In Gaye's version, a man is bemoaning the impending defection of his (presumably female) beloved, and he even recounts advice that he got from his father: "People say believe half of what you see Son and none of what you hear." The singer laments that he heard through the grapevine that his beloved plans to leave him for someone else. When the Slits sing these lines, it sounds as if the speaker is a woman with a partner on the down-low, or perhaps a man as well. By not changing the pronouns of Gaye's song to imply a heterosexual love triangle, the Slits are subtly calling into question listeners' expectations.

Cut's provocative cover photo shows Albertine, Ari Up, and Pollitt topless and covered in mud (Palmolive refused to participate). Ari Up and Pollitt stare at the viewer, and Albertine looks to the side None of the women are smiling. The cover was created on the spur of the moment by the band, who "didn't want to be inviting the male gaze" (Sullivan 2013). The photo was shot in the rose garden outside of the studio where they had just recorded *Cut*. The band members "were egging each other on" and soon "sitting in the mud, smearing it over each other" (Irvine 2016). Because the band "wanted a warrior stance, to be a tribe," they "had to look confrontational and hard" to subvert the male gaze (Sullivan 2013).

Although the Slits made a significant contribution to punk, their career was cut short by institutionalized sexism. Male record executives, managers, and fellow musicians, who saw punk as an all-boys club, patronized and discouraged the band members. And when the Slits toured with the Clash, hoteliers denied band members accommodations due to their appearance; with their teased hair, fishnets, and stark makeup, the band members were seen as more threatening than the male punks they were traveling with. Other men felt so threatened by band members' dress and behavior, which fell outside of acceptable gender norms, even in the punk community, that they responded with violence. Albertine observed that "People didn't know whether to fuck us or kill us, because we looked like we'd come out of a porn magazine" (Petridis 2014). Ari Up was stabbed in the street twice in one year by strangers.

The Slits parted ways in 1982 after recording just three studio albums and doing a John Peel session, but in 2005, Ari Up and Pollitt reformed with new members. Albertine was unwilling to rejoin, and Palmolive had become a born-again Christian in the 1980s and was part of a Christian rock cover band with her husband, changing the lyrics of old Slits songs to ones in line with her newfound faith. The reformed Slits released a final studio album in 2009, *Trapped Animal*, before disbanding a final time in 2010 after Ari Up died of breast cancer. The Slits are the subject of the book *Typical Girls? The Story of the Slits* (Zoe Howe) and the documentary *Here to Be Heard: The Story of the Slits*.

PATTI SMITH: *HORSES*

The poet, songwriter, and singer Patti Smith is known as the poet laureate of punk for her music that is both introspective and outrageous. When Smith began playing at CBGB during the early days of punk, her music was very different from commercial rock, which was tied to the idea of the rock star who, because of his superior genius, had the right to inflict lengthy drum or guitar solos on his arena audiences. Like most punk musicians, Smith combines and repurposes sounds from previous genres into sonic bricolages, and is so excited by the beauty of the world that she cannot limit herself to one genre to express her sense of wonder. In fact, some of her recordings not only include multiple vocal tracks of her voice but have her singing several songs at once because her artistic vision is too intense to be contained by one melody.

For young Patti Smith, becoming an artist was the most punk rock thing she could do. Born into a family of devout Jehovah's Witnesses whose faith "strictly forbade any type of artistic expression" (Bockris and Bayley 1999, 27), she turned her back on organized religion. Her "battle with religion would become a major source of energy and inspiration for her as an artist" (Bockris and Bayley 1999, 28). She saw religion as something that necessarily excluded others who were not coreligionists. Art is the answer to religion, Smith believes, because it is inclusive and not based on dogma and rules that are impossible for people to follow.

As a young woman, Smith always felt that she was inherently different from her peers; she was too thin to be considered conventionally beautiful, and she completely rejected the stifling feminine gender role from the 1950s that she was expected to occupy, opting to be more androgynous in appearance. In high school, Smith was inspired by artists such as Modigliani and John Coltrane and poets and philosophers such as Arthur Rimbaud, Jean-Paul Sartre, and Jean Genet. Smith moved to New York City when she was a young adult, where she met a nineteen-year-old Robert Mapplethorpe, who would become the most important man in her life, even after they ceased to be a romantic couple after Mapplethorpe came out as gay. In the early days, when both were starving, Mapplethorpe and Smith inspired one another as artists. "Everything was always life or art" for Mapplethorpe and Smith, who spent all of their energy and meager financial resources on either one or the other (Bockris and Bayley 1999, 57).

Smith's freshman album *Horses* (1975) is widely regarded by critics as one of the most influential punk albums ever and would eventually earn Smith the unofficial title of the poet laureate of punk. *Rolling Stone*'s John Rockwell praised *Horses* for how it recognized "the over-whelming importance of words in [Smith's] work" (1976), while the *Village Voice*'s Robert Christgau said that it got "the minimal fury of [Smith's] band and the revolutionary dimension of her singing just fine" (1975). Critic Jonh Ingham favorably compared *Horses* to John Lennon's *Plastic Ono Band* (2014), while in *NME*, Charles Shaar Murray conceded that "first albums this good are pretty damn few and far between" after conquering his apparent distaste for Smith being a woman artist, which he thought would alienate some listeners who are not fans of "passive female intelligence" or who might become unnerved "in the presence of a powerful sexuality expressed by someone who they may not happen to find attractive" (1975). In *Horses*, Smith draws from her background as a poet and knowledge of French symbolism as exemplified in the works of Charles Baudelaire, William Blake, and Arthur Rimbaud (Shaw 2008, 4) as well as her love for beat poetry. Although *Horses* received virtually no commercial airplay because it was too unusual to be easily classified, by the end of 1975, it had made the lists of major albums of the year compiled by music publications (Smith 2009, 120) and sold over two hundred thousand copies in 1976 (Harry, Stein, and Bockris 1989, 137).

Horses' iconic cover photograph of an androgynous Patti Smith was shot by Mapplethorpe. The album opens with "Gloria," a song that exemplifies Smith's difficult relationship with organized religion. It opens with Smith's laconic declaration, "Jesus died for somebody's sins, but not mine." As the song progresses, the tempo speeds up as Smith sings about being smitten by Gloria, consumes her body and spirit in a shamanic experience. "Redondo Beach" recounts a fight that Smith had with her sister Linda, who stormed off afterward, leaving Smith to fear that she had been harmed. In this song, Smith remembers a story that she heard about a girl who committed suicide, her body eventually washing up at the beach after a similar quarrel—a fate that Smith feared for her sister when she briefly went missing after their disagreement.

"Birdland" describes a vision that Peter Reich had about his father, Wilhelm, the disgraced psychoanalyst, after his death. In the vision, Peter imagined that he saw the lights of a spaceship in the distance and that his deceased father was at the helm. The song captures the pathos of Peter Reich's grief: "He fell on his knees and looked up and cried out, 'No, daddy, don't leave me here alone'." Smith remembers growing up extremely poor in "Free Money," a time when her mother would imagine winning the lottery and everything she could do with the proceeds. In "Kimberly," Smith captures how an event such as the birth of a child feels to those who welcome it into the world, as one of those BC/AD moments, where time stops before everything will change. Smith recounts how it felt to hold her little sister Kimberly for the first time: "The babe in my arms in her swaddling clothes, and I know soon that the sky will split." Smith's imagery evokes stories of the birth of Christ as well as her own fascination with Joan of Arc, as in this moment, she feels like a misplaced version of this saint whose cause is her little sister peering at her.

"Break It Up" describes another of Smith's spiritual epiphanies; this one she experienced after visiting Jim Morrison's grave in Paris. She had a vision of the singer eternally bound like Prometheus. In the song,

Morrison is a stone angel, a reference to Morrison's song "American Prayer," in which he says, "Death makes angels of us all and gives us wings where we had shoulders smooth as raven's claws." In 2017, at Blues Fest, where she performed the entirety of *Horses*, Smith explained that "Break It Up" was written about "Doors front man Jim Morrison, and based on her recollection of her visit of Morrison's grave in Père Lachaise Cemetery in Paris, as well as a dream in which she witnessed Morrison stuck to a marble slab shaped as an angel, trying and eventually succeeding in breaking free from the stone with Morrison donning 'big white wings'" (Encalada 2017).

The main character in "Land" references another of Smith's heroes, poet and writer William Burroughs, and his character Jim from *The Wild Boys*. The hallucinogenic imagery in Smith's song follows her protagonist from an encounter with schoolyard bullies to death and rebirth through heroin (the horses of the title) and art. "Elegie," like all songs fitting this description, is both about the dead and the horror experienced by the living left behind.

Horses was born during Smith's two-month residency with the band Television at CBGB in March and April 1975. Her performances at the famous New York club helped put it on the map as a place where one could hear bands that would be famous in the future. Smith became so impassioned during some of her performances at CBGB that she shed blood on stage some nights. Meanwhile, "impressionable members of Blondie, Talking Heads, and Ramones [paid] close attention to her style," and "legends like Lou Reed and Andy Warhol [showed] up to absorb the band's sound" (Bockris and Bayley 1999, 119). Bob Dylan, who attended one of her CBGB shows, was indirectly responsible for Smith receiving a record contract after the two were photographed together by the *Village Voice*, which publicized Smith's work (Khanna 2007). The two would later become good friends.

Equally important was how Smith changed the way that women were perceived in the music business with her "high-minded poetry and ferocious stage presence" despite her refusal to identify as a feminist due to her mistaken belief that feminism is anti-male (Khanna 2007). Smith was inducted into the Rock and Roll Hall of Fame in 2007, won the National Book Award in 2010 for her memoir *Just Kids*, and collaborated with her son and daughter to write the theme song for the final episode of *Aqua Teen Hunger Force*. When Bob Dylan won the Nobel Prize for Literature in 2016, he asked Smith to travel to Stockholm to accept his prize. She sang his song "A Hard Rain's A-Gonna Fall" during the ceremony (Petrusich 2016, "Transcendent"). Smith has also been the subject of the books *Patti Smith's Horses* (Phillip Shaw) and *Patti Smith: A Biography* (Nick Johnstone).

SOCIAL DISTORTION: *HARD TIMES AND NURSERY RHYMES*

If some of the Greasers from *The Outsiders* managed to "stay gold" and form a band, it might look and sound a lot like Social Distortion. The Los Angeles punk band founded by front man and lead guitarist Mike Ness has continuously toured since 1978 (except for a two-year hiatus while Ness was in rehab). Social Distortion's original lineup consisted of Ness's schoolmate Dennis Danell on guitar, Brent Liles on bass, and Derek O'Brien on drums when they finally recorded their first studio album in 1983, *Mommy's Little Monster*. The band is best known for its anthem "Ball and Chain" as well as its cover of Johnny Cash's "Ring of Fire," which appeared on their self-titled first album with a major label, released in 1990.

Social Distortion was part of the nascent hardcore movement in their early days, playing with other Los Angeles–area punk bands, including the Adolescents, China White, and Shattered Faith. They were also featured in the seminal punk rockumentary *Another State of Mind* (1984). Their music can be described as angry and energetic, "a rough-hewn hybrid of punk rock guitar attack and rootsy melodies influenced by classic blues, country, and rockabilly," which is also why the band has never really caught on in the United Kingdom, as their music just sounds too American (Deming n.d., "Hard Times"). Social Distortion's music is not as political as that of other punk bands, although "Don't Drag Me Down" (off their fifth album, *White Heat, White Light, White Trash* (1996)) is a notable exception in how its lyrics describe racism and nationalism as "ignorance like a gun in the hand." The song's last verse seems to predict today's realities, in discussing a young person with a grandfather in the Ku Klux Klan: "Gonna go to the White House / And paint it black." In 1995, Social Distortion went on a two-year hiatus due to Ness's heroin addiction, reforming with newcomers after Ness completed rehab.

Hard Times and Nursery Rhymes is Social Distortion's quintessential album, demonstrating how the band's sound has matured over thirty-five years. *Hard Times* includes the addition of a Hammond organ to the band's usual two guitars, bass, and drums. Most of the songs on the album "exist in the world of cool cars, tough dames, and bad-luck guys who've been part of his regular cast of characters since the band's inception," and they are "tough, memorable, and solidly crafted"

(Deming n.d., "Hard Times"). The opening track, "Road Zombie," is the epitome of a Social Distortion song—"hard rocking with their characteristic double guitar sound." "Road Zombie" is an instrumental, which is atypical of the band. However, the lack of vocals allows the listener to better savor the band's typical sound—"twangy, hard-rocking double guitar work" that ranges "from electric blues to rockabilly to cowpunk to pure rock" (Moran 2002).

"California Hustle and Flow," "Gimme the Sweet and Lowdown," and "Still Alive" are autobiographical tunes. "California Hustle and Flow" "covers familiar territory for Social Distortion, with its blending of punk with electric blues" (Deming n.d., "Hard Times"). Ness could be singing about his younger self in the opening verse: "Running around like you're front page news / Lonely eyes and your motorcycle boots," in addition to a heart tattoo and dark black hair. This figure is one typical of many earlier Social Distortion songs, such as the subject of "Sick Boys" (*Social Distortion* (1990)), with his black leather jacket and faded jeans, who "rides a big motorbike" and is "always in trouble with the law." The third verse of "California Hustle and Flow" references Ness's battle with addiction. Ness is also in dialogue with his past self in "Gimme the Sweet and Lowdown"; he chides this person that he "should've made a better choice, listen to [his] inner voice." But now it is time for this younger self to restart and rejuvenate. "Still Alive," the final track, is a fitting conclusion to *Hard Times and Nursery Rhymes*. Ness is looking back at his career and declaring that he is "still alive" and "will survive."

"Diamond in the Rough," "Machine Gun Blues," "Far Side of Nowhere," and "Can't Take It with You" explore typical Social Distortion themes. The tough dames and down-on-their-luck guys who populate Social Distortion's music could be the subject of "Diamond in the Rough" in that they are somehow damagedand need affection. The gangster from 1934 who is the subject of "Machine Gun Blues," on the other hand, will never have the opportunity to experience this redemption; instead, he's "already done . . . public enemy number one," being pursued by the loved ones of those he has killed. "Far Side of Nowhere" celebrates the joys of being carefree and able to drive fast on a beautiful day and ride with a beloved where they "can run to the far side of nowhere / We can run 'til our days are gone." "Can't Take It with You" laments the futility of modern life; when you "work all your life, you've become a slave," and "there ain't no spending when you're in the grave."

Social Distortion's cover of Hank Williams's "Alone and Forsaken" demonstrates this artist's influence on Ness's writing. Lyrically, "Alone and Forsaken" treats a familiar Social Distortion theme: a lover cruelly rejected by his beloved. Williams's description of the ill-fated love affair is saturated in natural imagery that gives the events a sense of predestination. The lovers first come together in spring, when flowers are blossoming, grass is green, and golden meadows are thriving. But by the time summer rolled around, her "love like the leaves" has "withered and gone." Ness's raspy, jaded vocalizations enhance this sense of foreboding implied in the lyrics. He sounds like a man who is accustomed to being treated poorly by life, and so the present abjection is not terribly surprising. Williams's plaintive wail on the original contrasts sharply with Social Distortion's version in how he sounds like an innocent who was blindsided by the events chronicled in the song.

"Writing on the Wall" shares the lyrical theme of "Alone and Forsaken." It is about a beloved who has lost interest in her partner. The country/blues song "Bakersfield" captures the sound and themes of classic country music. A long-distance trucker is stuck in the title city, just eighteen hours away from his beloved, who might have changed the locks on their home while he has been away. The song's bridge is spoken rather than sung in the way of many of Johnny Cash's story songs. Like "Road Zombie," "Bakersfield" exemplifies the refinement of Social Distortion's sound. As the band has incorporated other musical genres into their music, such as blues and old-school country, it has not lost its punk edge. Blues and early country also began as DIY musical genres that were created to describe the realities of people's lives that were not addressed by commercial music.

The official video for "Gimme the Sweet and Lowdown" neatly sums up the themes covered on *Hard Times and Nursery Rhymes* as well as Ness's life. The video is a black-and-white cartoon that sums up Ness's life in six allegorical tattoos of the singer's idols, which appear on his arms one by one, until all lift up a near-dying Ness to allow him to escape the Grim Reaper. Joey Ramone when a young Ness is on the streets to escape a troubled childhood, appears and kicks him in the pants, setting him along the path of being a musician. Joe Strummer is Ness's comrade in arms, joining him to protest injustice. Johnny Thunders parties with Ness when he is living the fast life of a punk musician, and when his drinking and heroin addiction becomes so out of control that it destroys his relationships with partners and bandmates, Ness is joined by Billie Holiday, who died of a heroin overdose when she was just forty-four. Next, Hank Williams is playing guitar in a dive bar where Ness is acting out "Machine Gun Blues" before he is jailed with Johnny Cash, who is strumming his guitar in the cell that they share. In an early scene, Ness is literally trapped between the lucrative music business and death, tethered to the spot by a ball and chain, referencing one of the band's earlier hits of the same name.

Hard Times peaked at No. 4 on the *Billboard* 200 in 2011 and at No. 1 on *Billboard*'s chart for independent albums in the same year. It also charted in Germany, Sweden, Finland, and the United Kingdom.

THE STOOGES: *RAW POWER*

The Stooges are widely regarded as one of the most influential punk bands of all time, although they are often considered a protopunk rather than a punk outfit because they broke up two years before the Sex Pistols were calling for anarchy in the United Kingdom. But the Stooges invented the punk performance as it is known today. Iggy Pop (James Newell Osterberg) "stomped and writhed onstage like he'd just swallowed a live snake, rocking a dog collar years before Malcolm McLaren [manager of the Sex Pistols] thought to package music, nihilism, and fetish gear as a new youth subculture" (Berman 2016). During his performances, Pop sometimes smeared his chest with peanut butter or even bled after diving into the crowd face first while drunk or high.

Iggy Pop founded the Stooges in 1967 with brothers Ron (guitarist) and Scott Asheton (drummer) and Dave Alexander (bass) in Ann Arbor, Michigan, where Pop briefly attended the University of Michigan and worked in a record store. Ron is credited with coming up with the band's name "the Stooges (originally the Psychedelic Stooges) because, like" the more famous Howard brothers, band members felt that they were "not doing anything wrong"; yet, everyone was always picking on them (*Gimme Danger* 2016). As well, the Stooges' were playing punk, not protopunk. The Stooges were "raw, immediate, and vulgar," playing "grimy, noisy, and relentlessly bleak rock & roll" that contained elements of "the over-amplified pounding of British blues, the primal raunch of American garage rock," and even the psychedelic rock exemplified by the Doors, which made them an underground sensation in the late 1960s and early 1970s (Erlewine n.d., "The Stooges"). However, the Stooges were so musically out of step with the psychedelic 1960s that they were just too weird to achieve commercial success at the time. The Stooges' musical legacy would only be appreciated much later, after Pop had embarked on a successful solo career and the explosion of punk sparked interest in their work.

Early in their career, the Stooges secured a recording contract with Electra in 1968, through which they released *The Stooges* (1969) and *Fun House* (1970). But when both albums were commercial flops, the

Stooges were dropped by Electra, and the band broke up briefly in 1971, in part due to members' escalating drug use. David Bowie, who was a Stooges fan, befriended Pop and tried to resurrect the band's career by reuniting members and producing their third album, *Raw Power* (1973). *Raw Power* would eventually be one of the most influential rock albums of all time, in part due to guitarist James Williamson, who joined the Stooges in 1971. Williamson and Pop cowrote *Raw Power*'s songs—about half of them the day before they went into the recording studio with Bowie—and Williamson's guitar gave the recording a "swirl of sound that virtually drags you into the speakers," in the words of *Rolling Stone*'s Lenny Kaye, who reviewed the album when it was released (1973). *AllMusic*'s Stephen Erlewine commented that *Raw Power*'s "razor-thin audio and fierce attack helped kick-start the punk revolution"; yet, that "razor-thin audio" was not by design but instead the result of incompetent recording, and even producer David Bowie was unable to correct the audio by remixing the recording. In 1973, the "razor-thin" audio made *Raw Power* a commercial flop. Like the Stooges' earlier work, *Raw Power* would only be appreciated by fans in retrospect.

Twenty-four years after *Raw Power*'s release, *Los Angeles Times* music critic Robert Hilburn described the album as one of "the pivotal works in rock," linking "the brute force of The Who with the coming anarchy of the Sex Pistols and the raw self-affirmation of early grunge" (1997). In fact, the Sex Pistols later covered the Stooges' "No Fun" in 1976, and Pistols' lead singer Sid Vicious regularly performed "I Wanna Be Your Dog," "Search and Destroy," and "Shake Appeal" during his post-Pistols solo career. Former Smiths' guitarist Johnny Marr appreciated *Raw Power* for delivering "exactly what was on the cover: other-worldly druggy rock'n'roll, sex, violence" (Marchesse 2012). All of this is apparent in *Raw Power*'s eight songs.

Most of the tracks on *Raw Power* are lyrically sparse, demonstrating the Stooges' musical minimalism. The songs contain only enough words to evoke well-known musical genres and tropes. That is the case in the electric blues ballad "I Need Somebody," which opens with Pop singing that he is "your crazy driver, Honey I'm sure to steer you wrong" over a lazy bass riff and a squealing guitar. "I Need Somebody" "builds from a vague 'St. James Infirmary' resemblance to neatly counterpoint 'Gimme Danger,'" one of the Stooges' anti-love songs (Kaye 1973). All intimate relations between people hold the possibility of danger, which Pop embraces as an inevitable fact of life in "Gimme Danger." According to Pop, "Gimme Danger" and "I Need Somebody" were written at the behest of CBS, the label that produced *Raw Power*, whose management insisted that the album have a ballad for each side (*Raw Power* 1997, CD liner notes).

The lyrics to the anti-romance song "Your Pretty Face Is Going to Hell" (originally titled "Hard to Beat") sound like a rough draft of a Cramps' composition with their absurdist descriptions of erotic love: "Hallucination true romance. I needed love but I only lost my pants." The lyrically sparse "Penetration" "makes few qualms about its double entendre of a title" in how Pop wails and moans the title to "one of Williamson's aptly swaggering guitar licks" (Jordan M. 2017). "Shake Appeal" and "Search and Destroy" were the only two singles released from *Raw Power*. The minimalist lyrics of "Shake Appeal" are a psychedelic amalgamation of early rock and roll via the Beatles, while "Search and Destroy" communicates the anger of those who have been forgotten by society, such as the Vietnam vets who are suggested in the line "I'm a streetwalking cheetah with a heart full of napalm."

When *Raw Power* was released, the social contract forged during World War II between the government and veterans, workers and manufacturers was being shredded. American veterans of the Vietnam War were scorned when they returned and did not receive the level of support given to their fathers when they returned after World War II, and entire cities and their populations were plunged into poverty after manufacturers relocated to countries with cheaper labor. Pop, a Detroit native, witnessed this seismic shift in the American economy when the auto industry abandoned his hometown. Pop and Williamson express their pessimism about the band's future in "Death Trip" (*Raw Power* 1997, CD liner notes), while they herald the band's "back-from-the-grave resurrection" via the release of *Raw Power* in their title track, when Pop commanded a generation of glam-rock kids and biker-bar burnouts to "dance to the beat of the living dead" (Berman 2010).

After *Raw Power*'s release, the Stooges embarked on a disastrous tour of the United States to promote the album, which was charting poorly. The tour abruptly ended in February 1974 during their performance at Detroit's Michigan Palace. Pop was beaten up by a gang of bikers after challenging the entire audience to a fight, which is captured on the legendary bootleg album of the concert, *Metallic KO*—"you can actually hear hurled beer bottles breaking against guitar strings," said rock critic Lester Bangs of the recording. The Stooges' career as a band was over after the Michigan Palace melee. The performance solidified the band's reputation for attracting violent fans, which made it difficult to find concert venues where the owners were willing to let them play, a fate suffered by later punk acts, including the Sex Pistols and Bad Brains. Meanwhile, the weak sales of the Stooges' three albums made record labels unwilling to offer the band recording contracts.

After the Stooges' breakup in 1974, Pop accompanied Bowie on his 1976 European tour and embarked on his own successful solo act. Bowie produced Pop's solo albums *The Idiot* (1977) and *Lust for Life* (1977), and Pop cowrote Bowie's 1983 hit "China Girl." This finally allowed Pop to achieve a measure of financial stability and mainstream interest.

Stooges' bassist Dave Alexander died suddenly in 1975 due to complications caused by his drinking. Williamson went on to study calculus and become a vice president at Sony. The Stooges reunited again in 2003, playing festivals and releasing new material, and they were inducted into the Rock and Roll Hall of Fame in 2010 before breaking up for good in 2016 after the deaths of first Ron and then Scott Asheton of heart attacks in 2009 and 2014, and saxophonist Steve MacKay in 2015. After MacKay's death, Williamson announced that the band was no more, as only he and Pop remained. Pop, however, is still touring, and will receive a Grammy Lifetime Achievement award in 2020.

Iggy Pop and the Stooges have been the subjects of two documentaries, *Gimme Danger* (2016), directed by Jim Jarmusch, and *Stooge* (2017), which indirectly references the band via Robert Pargiter, who describes himself as the band's number one fan.

TAQWACORE

Taqwacore is both a cultural and a musical subgenre of punk. Taqwacores are Western Muslim youth who use punk as a medium to explore their faith, confront Islamophobia, and create a transnational Muslim youth culture. Michael Muhammad Knight coined the word *taqwacore* (a portmanteau of the Arabic word for "God consciousness" and the English word "hardcore") in his 2004 novel, *The Taqwacores*, in which a group of Muslim American punks formulate their own interpretations of Islam in opposition to the doctrinaire, fundamentalist versions that receive more media coverage. The characters in *The Taqwacores* live in a communal space apart from religious authorities, where they are free to decide for themselves what it means to be a Muslim. The antiauthoritarian nature of punk culture, which encourages people to think for themselves, reflects the characters' struggles to formulate their own spiritualties.

Knight, a convert to Islam, chafed against dogmatic interpretations of his faith that include strict rules about women, homosexuality, and alcohol. He saw punk music and culture as a way that Muslim youth could explore their faith because "punk has its own rules, which amount to saying 'fuck you'." The kind of Islam that Knight wanted "was a kind of "fuck you, I am a Muslim no matter what you might say" (Chaouch 2014). *The Taqwacores* begins with Knight's poem "Muhammad Was a Punk Rocker," which describes the Prophet's iconoclasm as his most punk quality.

Knight's antidogmatic Islam is exemplified by several of the characters in *The Taqwacores*, such as the Mohawk-wearing, pot-smoking Jenghis or the burka-clad feminist Rebeya. Jenghis's way of dressing and use of cannabis reject rule-bound interpretations of Islam, while Rebeya uses the anonymity of her burka to free herself from the scrutiny of the male gaze so that she can explore her faith in ways that fundamentalist Muslim societies would consider blasphemous. Under her burka, Rebeya redacts with a black Sharpie chapter 4, verse 34, of the Qur'an, which in most English translations recommends that men beat their wives; teaches during the communal house's coed DIY prayer services that Mary was also a prophet; and talks privately in her room with one of her male housemates. *The Taqwacores* was made into a film of the same name in 2010 and closely follows the plot of Knight's novel. The bands the Kominas, Secret Trial Five, Al-Thawra, and Vote Hezbollah were included in the film's concert scene.

The Taqwacores inspired the formation of several taqwacore bands, who used the book as "a manifesto for a new Muslim culture" that respects differences (particularly of sexual orientation), embraces gender equality, and challenges established Islamic traditions (Chaouch 2014). The first of these bands, the Kominas (Urdu for "scoundrel"), became a taqwacore outfit when Kourosh Poursaehi, a Texas teen of Persian descent, set to music "Muhammad Was a Punk Rocker" and sent the recording to Knight. Knight shared the recording with Boston musician Shahjehan Khan, a Muslim Pakistani American, who formed the Kominas with his friend Basim Usmani in 2004 because he was frustrated with how his peers treated him as if he and his people were personally responsible the terrorist attacks of 9/11. The Kominas begin describing their music as taqwacore after hearing Poursaehi's musical rendition of Knight's poem. The Kominas mix "punk sounds and attitude with Hindi lyrics, doses of bhangra and other south Asian beats" (Aitch 2007). Their "world-ranging sound and global politics" are reminiscent of the Clash, while their "sense of satire and mischief is reminiscent of the Dead Kennedys" (Aitch 2007). In fact, some members of the Kominas were previously in the band the Dead Bhuttos (named after the Pakistani political family of the same name whose influence in that country was similar to that of the Kennedys in the United States). The Kominas' first two singles, "Sharia Law in the U.S.A." and "Suicide Bomb the Gap," were released in 2005 via MySpace. These titles, along with others such as "Blow Shit Up" and "Pigs Are Haram," parody racist and Islamophobic post-9/11 stereotypes about Muslims. "Sharia Law in the U.S.A." likens fundamentalist Islamic law to the Patriot Act, and "Pigs Are Haram" refers to cops, not swine.

Islamic-inspired punk is not new. The British band Alien Kulture and the Texas punk outfit Fearless Iranians in Hell emerged in 1979 after the Iranian Revolution, and other groups soon followed, such as Fun-Da-Mental and Asian Dub Foundation. But the Kominas, along with Vote Hezbollah and the Sagg Taqwacore Syndicate, were the first to use the term *taqwacore* to describe their music. By 2007, there were enough taqwacore bands to allow the Kominas to organize a "taqwatour" of the American southeast. The documentary *Taqwacore: The Birth of Punk Islam* follows the Kominas, Al-Thawra (Chicago), Diacritical (Washington, DC), Vote Hezbollah (San Antonio, Texas), and Secret Trial Five (Vancouver, Canada) as they tour in a green school bus with the word "taqwa" painted on the front. The bands later played the South by Southwest music festival. Al-Thawra (Arabic for "the revolution") is a crust punk outfit from Chicago; the Sagg Taqwacore Syndicate is the project of R. "Saag" Harris, who played electronic eclectic hip hop from 2004 to 2007; and Vote Hezbollah, formed in 2005, took their name from Knight's novel. The all-female political punk band Secret Trial Five, from Vancouver, Canada, took their name from five Muslim men suspected of terrorism who are being held without charges in Canada.

Taqwacore angers both conservative Muslims and punk "fundamentalists." Conservative Muslims view taqwacore as blasphemous because, like most punk music, it is full of profanities and describes practices considered to be *haram* ("unclean"), including drug use and extramarital sex. When Secret Trial Five came to Chicago in 2007 to play a set at an event hosted by the Islamic Society of North America, they were prevented by the event's conservative organizers from finishing their set (apparently no one realized that Secret Trial Five was an all-female band). They did not approve of women singing in public, particularly women who are gender nonconforming, such as the band's lead singer, Sena Hussain, who describes herself as a Canadian Pakistani drag king. "Fundamentalist" punks, meanwhile, consider taqwacore's religious exploration to be antithetical to punk's broader antiauthoritarian stance. The Kominas' Basim Usmani explains that the band's biggest detractors are "anti-religious punks who cannot see any value in a religious heritage" (Aitch 2007).

Eighteen years after 9/11, taqwacore has disappeared from the punk scene. At present, the Kominas are one of the few early taqwacore bands who are still recording and touring, and they now describe their music as desi, a term used by Indian-Americans to describe South Asian music. The Kominas are the only taqwacore band whose work can be easily accessed via streaming music services such as Spotify. The curious must turn to YouTube to hear the work of Secret Trial Five or Vote Hezbollah. However, Secret Trial Five no longer wishes to be identified by the taqwacore label, which they feel limits their musical expression. Other bands, such as Vote Hezbollah and the Saag Taqwacore Syndicate, broke up before 2010. All that remains of them are a couple of abandoned MySpace pages and audio files uploaded to YouTube. However, a resurgence of taqwacore could happen given the level of present-day Islamophobia.

WAR ON WOMEN: *CAPTURE THE FLAG*

"War on Women isn't your typical hardcore punk band" begins a 2016 review (Westcott 2016). That is because the feminist band from Baltimore is fronted by a woman, and their songs are about feminist subjects, both of which are unusual in what is still a male-dominated genre. Front woman Shawna Potter talks about this in a *New York Times* interview with the optimistic title "Rock's Not Dead, It's Ruled by Women" (Coscarelli 2017). (It is not ruled by women, which is why I had to write a "Women in Punk" entry for this volume.) "There's actually very few people who do what War on Women do," Bikini Kill front woman Kathleen Hanna confirmed in an interview (Pelly 2018).

The coed Baltimore-based band was formed in 2011 by Potter and Harlan Brooks. They were joined by Jennifer Vito, Suzanne Werner, and Dave Cavalier and released their self-titled debut album in 2015. Their music has been described by critics as "eviscerating" (Pelly 2018), "frenzied" (Ozzi 2018), "incendiary" and "melodic" (Camp 2018), and lacking in "subtlety" (Breihan 2018). "Activism is prominently at the heart of their screeds against the systematic plagues of patriarchy, racism, and capitalism" (Pelly 2018). War on Women presents "female anger in a way that people are not used to," says Potter (Woolever 2018). While their music is "femme" and about what makes women angry, Potter says that as a musician, she is "not one of the boys" or "doing an impression of a male singer." She's herself, and she's "pissed" (Woolever 2018).

The band's name is both provoking and candid about their musical mission. Potter says that she is not "implying" that there is a war on women but "telling you" about this war and its multiple effects (Saunders 2015). When a heckler in Sweden asked her, "Why so angry, Baby?" Potter just looked at him and said, "There's a lot to be angry about, man" (Camp 2018). Potter credits musicians such as "Bikini Kill's Kathleen Hanna" as giving her "a language to talk about [issues of inequality], maybe even permission to show anger and frustration" (Camp 2018). Bands such as "Bikini Kill and the Slits contributed to what [Potter does] lyrically, sometimes poking fun at sexism, taking on a character, and using sarcasm, while expressing a very real anger" (Camp 2018).

Potter has built upon Bikini's "girls to the front" policy at shows. She has called out from the stage to "women, queers, femmes" to come to the front and "take up space" (Camp 2018) because, "For women, live hardcore shows can be physically violent and intimidating places, and it's often safer to stand near the back to avoid being struck by flailing limbs and flying bodies" (Westcott 2016). The usual setup marginalizes women, and "can sometimes result in women being treated as literal coat racks; I've been asked several times by men to hold their coat or backpack so they can jump unencumbered into the pit" (Westcott 2016). When fans approach Potter after shows, they tell her that "they have never been exposed to an aggressive band like War on Women," which simultaneously heartens and disappoints her because it means that these fans "haven't had the chance to see men and women on the stage, talking about gender equity with some aggression" (Case 2014).

"When they were starting out," War on Women described their sound as "Bikini Kill meets early Metallica" (Breihan 2018). On their sophomore album, *Capture the Flag*, War on Women makes it sound "as if those two strains always made sense together" (Breihan 2018). One reviewer described *Capture the Flag* as taking "every appalling headline, every new low in the name of patriotism, and every systemic problem" and "balling it into a fist" (Ozzi 2018). A handful of tracks on *Capture the Flag* "adopt the traditional markers of hardcore—aggression, d-beat rhythms, air-tight rage" (Pelly 2018). All use the "time-hardened hardcore technique of gang-shout vocals" (Breihan 2018) but with a difference: War on Women only uses women's vocals. This technique both gives women a literal voice and undermines the traditional musical model where the instrumentation is subordinate to the lead singer.

War on Women's previous material primarily focused on "street harassment and sexual assault—as exemplified by their best-known track 'Say It'" (Camp 2018), an anthem that "attacks the unfair dualities for women surrounding the context of rape" (Saunders 2015). *Capture the Flag* "takes aim at a broader range of targets," including Donald Trump's presidency (Saunders 2015). Trump, the subject of "Predator in Chief," has currently been accused of harassment, groping, and even rape by twenty-five women (Mindock 2019). The opening track, "Lone Wolves," was released a month after the Parkland, Florida, school shooting and describes "the terrorism of entitled, angry white men that isn't called terrorism" (Pelly 2018). Powell said that she almost named the song "Pulse," after the Orlando nightclub mass shooting. "YDTMHTL" makes it "life-affirming to empty your lungs" to sing the chorus: "You don't tell me how to live!" (Pelly 2018). On this song, the band is "not raging against the machine so much as blazing through the very water and air that keep capitalist heteropatriarchy alive" (Pelly 2018). Kathleen Hanna joins the band on vocals in "YDTMHTL."

On the mid-tempo "Silence Is the Gift," Potter sings that she will "never, never be a silent woman," indicating that women can resist when others encourage them to not speak out about what is important to them. The track "Divisive Shit" illuminates why women are culturally silenced: "the game is fucking rigged" because women "start out as the hopes of boys and end up as the fears of men." The title song, "Capture the Flag," explains that women can leverage men's fear of them as their "ammunition" because their "existence" is their "resistance." Other songs on *Capture the Flag* are about women's experience of physical and judicial violence against them. "Childbirth" provides concrete examples of what is happening because women's reproductive freedom is under threat by an onslaught of attempts to curtail and overturn *Roe v. Wade*. "Are all men terrified" that "all the women that they know will fuck somebody else and let his baby grow?" Potter asks, getting to the reality behind legislation that puts onerous burdens on women seeking abortions in the name of ensuring that they receive "safe" medical care. Powell calls out these lawmakers for leaving women and any children they bear against their will to die.

In "The Violence of Bureaucracy," the United States is complicit in another way that women's sexuality is brutally curtailed—via female genital mutilation in other countries—when we pull our troops out abruptly and leave no support behind. "Anarcha" exposes a little-known fact about the man who is honored as the father of modern gynecology, J. Marion Simms. Simms, a plantation owner, developed his knowledge of women's bodies by vivisecting his female slaves. "Anarcha" is one of the three named women that he experimented on; the names of the others were not recorded. The band's official video for "Anarcha" shows flashes of these three women along with bizarre gynecological diagrams of some of the horrifying medical procedures that Simms's performed on them.

"Pleasure and the Beast" encourages women to reclaim their own sexuality in the same way that "Silence Is the Gift" and "YDTMHTL" encourage them to reclaim their voices. Women's "existence should not be defined by any man," and they deserve to know themselves "before anyone else gets the chance." *Capture the Flag* ends hopefully with the track "The Chalice and the Blade." The song takes its name from the title of Riane Eisler's book of the same name, in which she corrects a popular assumption that patriarchy was the result of men discovering their own role in the reproductive process and subsequently putting an end to matriarchy and the worship of mother goddesses. In fact, patriarchy did not replace a female-led dominator model of society. Instead, patriarchy was promulgated by nomadic people who conquered agrarian societies that operated along a partnership model and understood men's role in reproduction. When Powell sings of modern people that "you need the mother to teach you how to behave," she is referring to the model offered by the ancient mother goddesses, where both men and women shared power. *Capture the Flag* comes with a sixteen-page companion workbook complete with a reading list to educate fans about the issues sung about on the album.

WATCH THIS! DOCUMENTARIES, FEATURE FILMS, AND VIDEOS

Punk rock developed alongside punk film. In Year Zero, aspiring filmmakers grabbed their Super 8s and made documentaries of bands that would later become part of the official history of punk. The punk movement also influenced many types of feature films, ranging from biopics to bildungsromans about fictitious punks to films that blended the conventions of established "trash" genres with punk aesthetics. The films in this entry are a representative sample of the different types of punk cinema.

Punk biopics dramatize the lives of real people, bands, and even places. Alex Cox's *Sid and Nancy* chronicles the last days of punk's original celebrity couple, the Sex Pistols' Sid Vicious (Gary Oldman) and his girlfriend, Nancy Spungen. Courtney Love (Hole), who originally vied for the role of Nancy, plays one of the couple's junkie friends (Grierson et al. 2019), and Iggy Pop and Slash (Guns N' Roses) have cameos. The film opens after Vicious has stabbed Nancy to death and is being taken into police custody. Upon its release, *Sid and Nancy* "was roundly panned by film critics and punk fans alike" as "messy and disjointed" (Osgerby 2014, 223–224). But fans and critics have since warmed to the film, and Oldman's performance as Vicious is masterful.

Roger Grossman's *What We Do Is Secret* (2007) depicts Darby Crash, the lead singer of the Germs, as a "sociopathic version of Jim Morrison" who regularly performed after "shooting up crystal meth, heroin, ketamine, or any other drugs he could find" (Yanick 2014). Shane West (who plays the late Crash, who died of a heroin overdose in 1980) was so convincing in his role that he went on to play gigs with the surviving members of the Germs (Yanick 2014).

Floria Sigismondi's *The Runaways* (2010) tells the story of how the all-female punk band was sexually exploited by their manager, Kim Fowley. Fowley recruits the four members of the Runaways because of their youth and sex to market as sexually available underage girls—lead singer Cherie Currie (played by Dakota Fanning) is so young that in the film's opening, she has just started her period. Michael Shannon, best known for his roles as the overzealous FBI agent in *Boardwalk Empire* and the sadistic bureaucrat in charge of the amphibian man in Guillermo del Toro's *The Shape of Water* (2017), convincingly plays Fowler as a raging narcissist with no remorse for how he exploited the four teen members of the Runaways.

Randall Miller's *CBGB* is a biopic about Hilly Kristal's Bowery night club that hosted hundreds of legendary punk acts. *CBGB* was criticized for lacking a "coherent plot and believable" and "enthusiastic actors" (Yanick 2014) and for omitting notable people and things (Jenkins 2013) from the story. However, some of these omissions were out of Miller's control, such as his inability to get permission for any of the Ramones' songs, so the actors who played band members had to perform covers of other works. Too, there is Alan Rickman's standout performance as Hilly Kristal; he presents the club owner as "an endearing slob" and "an authentic soul in an ersatz world" (DeFore 2013). Rickman (Severus Snape) is joined by another Harry Potter alum, Rupert Grint (Ron Weasley), who plays Cheetah Chrome (Dead Boys) and is a dead ringer for the signer in his youth. CBGB's story is related as a literal frame tale; frames of panels from John Holmstrom's *Punk Magazine* transition into significant scenes in the film.

Punk bildungsroman films follow the careers of fictional bands and musicians. Brian Gibson's *Breaking Glass* (1980) is one of the earliest examples of this type of film. *Breaking Glass* is a sort of punk *A Star Is Born* set in Year Zero London, where Kate (Hazel O'Connor) wants to make art for art's sake but is cynically manipulated by music business moguls along the way. *Breaking Glass* "deserves credit for being the only British punk-related film (apart from *Jubilee*) to center on a female protagonist" (Osgerby 2014, 221). The American films *Ladies and Gentlemen the Fabulous Stains* (1982) and *Times Square* (1980) are also about female punk musicians trying to break into the business.

Lou Adler's *LAGTFS* is full of real-life musicians, including members of the Sex Pistols, the Clash, and the Tubes, and stars Diane Lane as the band's front woman and Laura Dern as her cousin. Like *The Runaways*, "the feminist overtones [of *LAGTFS*] set to a soundtrack of punk-rock music, make the underrated film an important one, shedding light on how women are treated in the music business" (Cooper 2018). In Alan Moyle's *Times Square*, two women escape a mental clinic to live on the streets of New York, eventually forming the underground punk band the Sleez Sisters, who are "inspiration for the city's disillusioned teens" (Osgerby 2014, 221).

Other punk films are about the gritty lives of punks. Jack Hazan and David Mingay's 1980 film *Rude Boy* follows a young Brixton punk who quits his dead-end job to become a roadie for the Clash, encountering police brutality, racism, and corruption along the way. Hazan and Mingay's docudrama style is punctuated with footage of right-wing National Front rallies, "threatening police and other scenes portraying Britain as beset by social and political conflict" (Osgerby 2014, 212–213). Eventually, the roadie's "drunken boorishness alienates the band and earns him the sack—a personal decline that the film juxtaposes to the rise of a right-wing Conservative Party, the movie's doom-laden conclusion closing with Margaret Thatcher's 1979 election victory" (Osgerby 2014, 212–213).

Smithereens (1982), Susan Seidelman's "drama about a narcissistic, manipulative Jersey girl," offers a similarly bleak view of punks of New York's East Village (Grierson et al. 2019). Richard Hell plays "a poorman's version of himself, a hungry rock star who might periodically nod off before sex" (Grierson et al. 2019).

As the only two punks in ultraconservative Salt Lake City in 1985, Stevo (Matthew Lillard) and Heroin Bob (Michael Goorjian) "struggle to find themselves" in James Merendino's *SLC Punk* (1998). The film's humor comes from how they must "constantly explain their identities to family, friends, and society at large, who take their ripped clothes, mohawks, tattoos, and colored hair as signs of mental illness" (Distefano 2014). The ending, however, is absurd. Stevo decides that the punkest thing to do is "to get a job in the corporate world, with some vague notion of taking it down from inside" (Yanick 2014).

The runaway punks in Penelope Spheeris' *Suburbia* (1983) "build the kind of supportive, loving family they never had at home" (Grierson et al. 2019). The kids "squat in abandoned suburban tract homes, developing their own flawed version of a punk utopia" (Brennan 2016). "Spheeris cast real-life punks to play the kids—including the future Red Hot Chili Peppers bassist Flea—and included sets by scene luminaries like D. I., TSOL, and the Vandals, who do a great version of ['The Legend of] Pat Brown'"(Grierson et al. 2019).

The punks of *The Taqwacores* (2010) also live in a punk house, a collective of like-minded people who are each developing their own version of utopia based on their individual interpretations of Islam. *The Taqwacores* was adapted from Michael Muhammad Knight's 2002 novel of the same name, about a "then fictitious 'taqwacore' Islamic punk rock scene" (Murray 2010). Knight's novel "triggered a real-life musical movement," which the film dramatizes by bringing in the actual bands that it inspired. *The Taqwacores* "is moving and thought-provoking, both in its plea for universal inclusion and in the way Knight and writer-director Eyad Zahra seriously consider how sects within sects continue to bicker and belittle each other over the finer points of their beliefs" (Murray 2010).

Jeremy Saulner's *Green Room* (2015) asks the question, "What happens when a punk gig goes very wrong?" The band the Ain't Rights find out when they wind up broke while touring the Pacific Northwest and agree to play a skinhead bar in the middle of nowhere. Surprisingly, the band members' lives are not in danger for playing a cover of the Dead Kennedys' "Nazi Punks Fuck Off!" to their white supremacist audience but instead for witnessing a murder backstage. Patrick Stewart stars as the scary club manager.

Other punk films parody the conventions of B-film genres to make original art that does not take itself too seriously. The science fiction films *Jubilee* (1978) and *Repo Man* (1984) have since been released by the Criterion Collection, an organization that is dedicated to "publishing important classic and contemporary films from around the world in editions that offer the highest technical quality and award-winning, original supplements," according to the organization's website. *Jubilee* (Derek Jarman) examines "the despairing and angry mood of Britain in the mid-seventies" as it faces "economic recession, virtual war with the IRA, and an uncertain post-imperial future," which he felt was "epitomized by the subversive, ebullient energy and anger of punk and the Sex Pistols' controversial rendition of 'God Save the Queen'" in Queen Elizabeth II's Silver Jubilee year (Peake 2003). Queen Elizabeth I is taken into the future by her court astrologer John Dee to see that her kingdom is a "stark contrast to the Arcadian serenity" of her own time (Peake 2003). Queen Elizabeth II is dead, killed in a mugging, and London is a chaotic urban wasteland where gangs of punks run wild. *Jubilee* starred several punks and protopunks, including Jayne County (of the protopunk band Wayne County and the Electric Chairs), Adam Ant, Gene October, Siouxsie Sioux, and Steven Severin.

Alex Cox's *Repo Man* (1984) "represents a campy, film noir/sci-fi satire of Reaganite America" and "captures the energy and cynical edge of the early 1980s punk scene" (Osgerby 2014, 223). Los Angeles punk Otto (Emilio Estevez) is "wandering the streets alone and depressed after being fired from his dead-end supermarket job, getting dumped by his girlfriend and learning his parents have donated his college fund to a televangelist" when he is recruited by Bud (Harry Dean Stanton) to become an apprentice car repossession agent. The two repossess a 1964 Chevy Malibu with a top-secret cargo of radioactive aliens in the trunk. *Repo Man*'s soundtrack showcased the Los Angeles hardcore bands Black Flag, Suicidal Tendencies, the Circle Jerks, and Fear long before they hit the aboveground radar (Grierson et al. 2019).

Alex Cox's spaghetti western parody *Straight to Hell* (1987) is the third film in his punk trilogy (*Jubilee, Sid and Nancy*). It stars Joe Strummer (the Clash) and Courtney Love (Hole) and included cameos by Dennis Hopper, Grace Jones, Elvis Costello, director Jim Jarmusch, and members of the Pogues and the Circle Jerks. *Straight to Hell* was not a commercial success, but like other Cox films, it gained a cult status.

Dan O'Bannon's "mordant punk comedy" (Holden 1985) *Return of the Living Dead* purports to tell the "real" story behind the zombies in George Romero's classic *Night of the Living Dead* (1968). When several punks go to pick up their straight friend from his job at Acme Medical Supplies, the group is trapped after discovering a stored specimen—a corpse that was reanimated in the VA hospital after a secret military chemical accidentally leaked into the morgue. When the chemical escapes its container at Acme Medical Supplies, it reanimates the corpses buried in the cemetery next door, and the group spends the night fighting multiplying numbers of zombies in this gory dark comedy.

Roger Corman's punk rock musical *Rock 'n' Roll High School* (1979) is arguably "the most authentic punk movie" of all due to its silliness (Brennan 2016). *Rock 'n' Roll High School* is a hybrid of 1960s teen films, musicals, and absurdist comedy (Yanick 2014). The plot is simple: when the principal of Vince Lombardi High attempts to ban rock and roll outright, Riff Randall and her friends stage a coup, with the help of the Ramones, who play caricatures of themselves as "pizza-crazed punk rockers" (Yanick 2014). *Rock 'n' Roll High School* revels in its cheesiness and has a great soundtrack.

WOMEN IN PUNK

In her introduction *to Cinderella's Big Score: Women of the Punk and Indie Underground*, Marie Raha admits that "The 'women in music' category shouldn't even exist anymore" (2005, xiii). Yet, we still need this category because music industry gatekeepers are not signing up and promoting a representative sampling of the women who are making punk rock (Andrews 2014). Like men in punk, women have eliminated the middle man by starting their own labels and sharing their music with fans via the internet. Nevertheless, big corporate music labels still have an outsized influence in defining musical genres simply by what they choose to produce and promote.

Standard histories of punk also give fans the mistaken impression that the genre is a predominantly all-boys club. The bands that are most typically included in the genre's early canon, such as the Sex Pistols, Black Flag, the Clash, and the Ramones are all pale and male (Andrews 2014). When punk rock turned forty in 2016, and London planned events to celebrate the music that once infuriated its leaders, singer Viv Albertine of the Slits scrawled in permanent marker "where are the women?" on an exhibit's signage and then crossed out "the names of male driven punk acts and replac[ed] them with female driven ones such as Siouxsie and the Banshees and X-Ray Spex" (Shea 2016, "Hey Ho").

> [Yet] the early history of punk rock was full of memorable women, in the United States as well as Britain. New York had Patti Smith, Sonic Youth's Kim Gordon and post-punk dance bands Y Pants and ESG. The late-70s LA scene had been even more gender-balanced: Exene Cervenka of X and Alice Bag of the Bags were magnetic performers, and the Bangles and the Go-Go's cut their teeth in that scene before cleaning up their sound to go mainstream. Even in Washington, DC, in the early '80s, where the teenage band Minor Threat was seeding the shouty, sinewy, overwhelmingly male hardcore sound, the all-female group Chalk Circle paid tribute to European bands like Kleenex and the Au Pairs. (Marcus 1999, 48–49)

Even in the supposedly liberated 1970s, "it wasn't easy to be a woman in the early punk scene.... Although many punks had progressive politics, internalized gender bias was harder to eradicate," and "women had the tough task of both proving themselves and representing the

Some women in punk include (top to bottom, left to right) the New Age, "Animals and Men," 1976; Stef Petticoat, "The Petticoats," 1980; PragVec, "Expert," 1979; Drinking Electricity, "Subliminal," 1981; the Slits, "Man Next Door," 1980; Siouxsie and the Banshees, "Hong Kong Garden," 1978; Airmail, "No Human Feeling/In a Moment," 1979; Current Obsessions, "Faceless Rite," 1982; Amos and Sara, "Sara Goes Pop," 1982; Maximum Joy, "White and Green Place," 1982; and Y Pants, "Y Pants" (compilation) 1998. (Dimitris Kolyris/Dreamstime.com)

musicianhood of womankind" (Lee 2010). Many of the women that I have highlighted in this book, who toured with male punk bands and played the same venues as their brethren, were harassed on the road by fans and discriminated against by hoteliers, who were more willing to give lodgings to male punk musicians with a reputation for attracting rowdy fans than female punk bands. For example, when the Slits toured with the Clash, hotel managers were so threatened by their teased hair and fishnets that the band was denied accommodations. "When men wore the ripped, tight, dominatrix-inspired outfits characteristic of early punk, they were simply subverting the system—but when women donned similar attire, along with heavy black eyeliner, it became an excuse for sexual harassment" (Lee 2010). Meanwhile, "at shows, women musicians were ridiculed" and "targeted for thrown projectiles" (Lee 2010).

Las Vulpes, the first Spanish female punk band, were singled out for some of the most extreme harassment in their home country after performing their song "Me Gusta Ser Una Zorra" ("I Like Being a Whore") on national television. On tour, the police accused them of trafficking drugs, held their luggage at the airport for twenty-four hours, and beat them up at another concert venue. The harassment was so bad that Las Vulpes broke up two months later. Meanwhile, female punk musicians were either ignored or dismissed by the overwhelming male critics who wrote about music at the time. The few reviews that these critics did write about female punk musicians commented on the musicians' appearance as much as their music. Charles Shaar Murray, for example, writing for *New Music Express*, felt it necessary to temper his praise for Patti Smith's groundbreaking freshman album, *Horses*, with his inaccurate prediction that her music would alienate listeners who might feel threatened "in the presence of a powerful sexuality expressed by someone who they may not happen to find attractive" (1975). Predatory promoters like the Runaways' first manager, Kim Fowley, pandered to these critics by encouraging the four underage bandmembers who trusted him to dress and behave on stage like sex objects. Also, venues were not designed to accommodate female musicians. Even today, female artists have to relieve themselves backstage in urinals "because clubs weren't built with women stars in mind" (Ryzik 2018).

Nevertheless, they persisted. Women created some of the best punk rock of the early days. Like their male counterparts, women "picked up instruments they barely knew how to play and taught themselves quickly" and "formed bands that rapidly garnered fans" (Lee 2010). These women

> were sarcastic and mocked conventions of mainstream society that people rarely before questioned. They spoke of anarchy, riots, sexism and war as well as romance and friends. They had the audacity to curse on TV. They brought the safety-pin piercing, the dog-chain jewelry and the spray-painted circle-A (for anarchy) into the vernacular. In effect, they created a revolution that still has a lasting impact on music and culture today. (Lee 2010)

Women were attracted to punk for the same reasons that men were. It "gave young people who were not part of the mainstream a way to express themselves and be with like-minded individuals" and "offered an alternative to the status quo through which young people, particularly women, people of color, and members of the working class, were effectively silenced because they lacked access to platforms that would allow them to communicate their perspective to a wider audience beyond their circle of friends." Punk's DIY ethos was uniquely able to give women, people of color, and members of the working class this platform because it meant "that anyone and everyone could form a band and get up on stage to perform" or create and distribute a zine (Howe 2009, 3).

Female punk musicians "got up in front of hostile crowds to both prove they could play well and, for bands like Crass, X-Ray Spex, and the Raincoats, to offer salient feminist politics in lyric form" (Lee 2010). Poly Styrene said that "being in a band, saying what you want. It was better than being in a girl gang" (Simpson 2011, "An Optimist"). Women opened doors into other crucial parts of the scene as well, such as music journalism. Journalists such as Caroline Coon and Julie Burchill wrote articles and books about punk, documenting the movement in both photos and words. Coon also managed one of the best-known punk bands of all time, the Clash. Another woman, Vivienne Westwood, was one of the masterminds of punk fashion.

While women carved out a place for themselves in the early punk movement of the 1970s, the scene became less hospitable for women in the 1980s, particularly "on the West Coast, where hyper-masculine bands such as Fear and Black Flag became leaders of the new American punk scene" (Dunn 2011, 34). While "punk introduced vital strategies for resisting, reordering, and reworking these dominant codes of gender and sexuality, . . . the implicit feminist potential of women's punk subcultural resistance" was not made explicit until the riot grrrl movement led by bands such as Bikini Kill, L7, Bratmobile, Huggy Bear, Hole, Heavens to Betsy, Le Tigre, and the Gossip (Downes 2012, 208–209). Riot grrrl disrupted the conventional ordering of gender difference in punk subcultures: to provoke, politicize, and resist hetero-feminine girlhood. The riot grrrl movement brought "feminist perspectives to the forefront of punk culture," and prominent riot grrrl figures such as Kathleen Hanna and Alison Wolfe used both zine and music to tackle both "the sexist sentiments infiltrating punk and art scenes [and] the violent and homophobic attitudes that surrounded them" (Brooks 2017). "Riot grrrl refused to denigrate the feminine and instead created a visual and sonic spectrum of politicized girl signifiers within a subcultural punk context" (Downes 2012, 211). Kathleen Hanna and Tobi Vail formed Bikini Kill to spread feminism, and famously enforced a "girls to the front" policy at their shows to counter how men make women feel unwelcome at punk shows through subjecting them to violent moshing and sexual assault—Hanna would even wade into the audience to eject violent audience members.

Riot grrrl bands were also politically active. L7 and *LA Weekly*'s Sue Cummings organized the Rock for Choice series of concerts in 1991 to help the Feminist Majority Foundation raise money for their campaign to save *Roe* and educate a new generation of women about the need to become politically active. The enormously popular series of concerts continued throughout the United States until 2001, headlined by punk and nonpunk artists such as Iggy Pop, Bikini Kill, Liz Phair, the Offspring, Fugazi, Salt-N-Pepa, Rancid, Sarah McLachlan, and Melissa Etheridge.

Women continue to create and listen to punk music today. Notable all-female or female-fronted bands include Dream Wife, Go Betty Go, the Spinnerettes, the Interrupters, the Voids (hardcore), Skinny Girl Diet, Cayetana, Childbirth, Upset, Petrol Girls, Fight Rosa Fight, Downtown Boys, White Lung, War on Women, New Bloods, Sleater-Kinney, Drunken Butterfly, Skinned Teen, Team Dresch, Tribe 8, the Tuts, Tripppple Nippples, and Giant Kitty, a Shonen Knife–inspired band (Distefano 2018). Female hardcore punk bands include A Pretty Mess, War on Women, and the Voids (McDonnell and Vincentelli 2019; Goldman 2019). As well, female punks from previous generations, such as Shonen Knife and Patti Smith, continue to record and tour, while now iconic female punk bands, such as Bikini Kill, have reunited to reach a new generation of fans. Recent documentaries, meanwhile, examine women's contributions to punk, including Amy Oden's *From the Back of the Room* (2011) and the BBC's "Girls Will Be Girls" episode of *The Culture Show* (2014).

Even so, women continue to be harassed by men at punk and hardcore shows, and bands and fans ponder how to change this culture (Andrews 2014; Madani 2017; McCarthy 2015; O'Neil 2015; Sherman 2015; Sloan 2018; WHIMN 2017). "Alanna McArdle of Joanna Gruesome battles with sexist online trolls, Laura Jane Grace [of Against Me!] calls out the macho punk culture and both Syracuse, New York's Perfect Pussy and Vancouver's White Lung rage openly against the sexist boy majority" (Andrews 2014). And Poly Styrene, in her last year of life, was anxious about her daughter Celeste Bell's desire to have a career in music because she thought that the music industry was just as toxic for women in the twenty-first century as it had been in her day (Bell 2017).

X: *LOS ANGELES*

The Los Angeles punk band X combines punk's frenzy and electricity with country and rockabilly set to poetic lyrics sung by the band's two lead singers. X was formed in Los Angeles in 1976 by four transplants to the city: singer and guitarist John Doe (John Duchac), guitarist Billy Zoom (Ty Kindell), singer Exene Cervenka (Christine Cervenkova), and drummer D. J. Bonebrake (Donald J. Bonebrake). Doe had discovered punk rock after hearing Patti Smith's *Horses* and was eager to form a band. Zoom "had been playing rockabilly, blues, and R&B" in Los Angeles for years "and had backed Gene Vincent during the rockabilly icon's last shows" (Deming n.d., "X: Biography"). Zoom discovered punk via the Ramones and "wanted to play music that was fast, loud, and honest," so when he met Doe through a newspaper ad, the two began jamming together (Deming n.d., "X: Biography"). Doe met Cervenka at a poetry workshop, where they bonded over shared tastes in literature and started dating. When Doe read one of Cervenka's poems, he "thought it had the makings of a good song [and] asked her permission to sing it in the band he was forming with Zoom. Cervenka said she'd prefer to sing it herself, and before long, she was rehearsing with Doe and Zoom, with her enthusiasm compensating for her lack of musical experience" (Deming n.d., "X: Biography").

X's "speed, sartorial sensibility and nervous aggression were decidedly punk rock," while their "tightness and musical sensitivity (even in the early days) were a tacit challenge to the punk scene's prevailing ethos of D.I.Y. sloppiness" (Anderson n.d., "Johnny Hit"). Doors' keyboardist Ray Manzarek became X's producer, and he plays organ on *Los Angeles*. X is credited with putting "the L.A. punk scene on the map" (Deming n.d., "X: Biography"). They were the first Los Angeles punk band to be taken seriously by the music press on both coasts, playing "music that was as raw, passionate, and powerful as anything coming out of New York, London, or any other major city" (Deming n.d.). Their first two albums—*Los Angeles* (1980) and *Wild Gift* (1981)—were well received by critics and "sold remarkably well by small-label standards, helping establish Slash Records as a major independent label as well as defining the group's unique approach" (Deming n.d., "X: Biography").

The songs on *Los Angeles* are "the most typically punky" ones in X's repertoire (Peake 2019). *Los Angeles* has been described as "snapshot of a city and its punk subculture" ("100 Best Albums of the Eighties" 1989) and "the sound of youth culture gleefully racing toward oblivion" (Carr 2002). Slash Records produced *Los Angeles* for just $10,000. Upon its release, *Los Angeles* "received rave reviews from punk fanzines and the big-league music press" and was "an immediate success in the band's home town" (Deming n.d., "X: Biography"). As the album's reputation spread nationwide, it sold over fifty thousand copies—an impressive number for an album produced by an independent label.

X also cultivated fans outside of California thanks to the documentary *The Decline of Western Civilization*; director Penelope Spheeris gave X a lot of screen time in her chronicle of the Los Angeles punk scene. Doe and Cervenka married the year that *Los Angeles* was released, and they informed the lyrics of many of the songs on the album. The songs on *Los Angeles* describe the city in a noir style characteristic of writers like Dashiell Hammett, James M. Cain and Nathaniel West, chronicling the "flagrant inequality" that Cervenka described seeing in her adopted city, about which she and Doe wrote so compulsively, "because they had never seen anything quite like" it "or its punk-misfit culture" ("100 Best Albums of the Eighties" 1989).

"Sex and Dying in High Society" describes the lives of one of the city's wealthy, who got her money by "marrying [her] daddy with a different name." Now bored with her older husband, this woman has her maid burn her back with a curling iron because feeling that pain trumps all she knows of love. "The World's a Mess; It's in My Kiss" exemplifies Cervenka's beat-inspired poetry. Mark Deming characterized the song as sounding "like an urban apocalypse turned into a dance party" (Deming n.d., "The World's a Mess"). "Johnny Hit and Run Pauline" is a cautionary tale about the dangers that women face on the streets of the city. Johnny is a serial rapist high on heroin, shooting "all Paulines between the legs." At the end of his binge, Johnny awakens and is surprised to discover that he has killed his last victim, a woman he raped on a city bus. The song "is driven by a spare punkabilly beat and its title constitutes the entirety of its terse chorus" (Anderson n.d., "X: Johnny Hit").

Doe based the lyrics to the album's title track on a woman he knew who fled the city and had a nervous breakdown afterward. After she was in Los Angeles for a couple of years, Doe recounts, "she became more and more racist and stereotyping people" (Peake 2019). Doe's lyrics to "Los Angeles" bluntly capture the woman's transformation, and he wrote them for "shock value" to "show the dark side or underbelly of Los Angeles" (Peake 2019). Cultural theorist and X fan José Esteban Muñoz described "Los Angeles" as "a fairly standard tale of white flight from the multiethnic metropolis" that accurately depicted "the effect that the West Coast city had on its white denizens" (1997).

The title of the album's first track, "Your Phone's Off the Hook, but You're Not," captures the Ramones' sense of humor, while the lyrics that direct anger toward the deadbeat subject of the song characterize Blondie's biting anger. Cervenka's lead vocals deliver a perfect "first-person kiss-off" (Peake 2019). "The Unheard Music" is the longest track on *Los Angeles*, spanning almost five minutes. The song is "more restrained version of X's intelligent approach to punk's nihilism" and hints at the band's wide stylistic range (Phares n.d.) Cervenka and Doe's "eerie dual vocals emphasize [the song's] unsettling, detached lyrics" (Phares n.d.). It would become one of X's most covered songs. Elastica's Justine Frischmann and Pavement's Stephen Malkmus teamed up to cover a version for the film adaptation of Eric Bogosian's *Suburbia*, "suggesting that the song is as emblematic of the city's jaded counterculture as it is of X's thoughtful, poetic punk" (Phares n.d.).

Two heroin addicts in "Sugarlight" are "swallowing one bulb after another in the city of electric light" as the speaker's arm "is tied off, waiting to burn it down." The red-eyed speaker of "Nausea" will be "so sick" from binging on heroin that he or she will eventually "fall asleep in clothes," while the disaffected subject of the cover of the Doors' "Soul Kitchen" does not want to be on the street all night where "cars crawl past, all stuffed with eyes."

While X "never enjoyed the commercial breakthrough that many believed was their due," they were hugely popular in Los Angeles and "could successfully headline large outdoor venues like the Greek Theater" (Deming n.d., "X: Biography"). X's manager, Ray Manzarek, said that he "thought Exene [Cervenka] was the next step after Patti Smith" ("100 Best Albums of the Eighties" 1989). After the album's critical reception, "the same labels that had rejected the band were involved in a bidding war to sign them, and X was on its way to leaving a mark on the Eighties with a string of albums" ("100 Best Albums of the Eighties" 1989). The band released an album nearly every year up to 1987. But each successive album went away from X's punk roots. X's fifth album, *Ain't Love Grand* (1985), disappointed fans and critics with its "more polished sound," and "radio programmers and mainstream audiences paid little attention" (Deming n.d., "X: Biography"). Billy Zoom left X soon after because he was "disappointed with the band's failure to break through to a mass audience," and Doe and Cervenka divorced (Deming n.d., "X: Biography").

X replaced Zoom with Tony Gilkyson on guitar and recorded their sixth studio album, *See How We Are*, which received tepid critical reception. X went on hiatus afterward until the 1990s, after the success of

Nirvana's *Nevermind* made radio more receptive to more adventurous music. But when their next two albums (*Hey Zeus!* (1993) and *Unclogged* (1995)) got just "polite but not enthusiastic" reviews (Deming n.d., "X: Biography"), X announced that they were disbanding, again. They have since reunited several times to tour and rerecord or promote compilations of their work. X's original lineup reunited in 2017 ahead of a Grammy Museum exhibition of their work (Grow 2017, "X Look Back") and returned to the studio in 2019 to record the first new material together in thirty-four years (Willman 2019). X is the subject of the 1986 documentary *X: The Unheard Music.* Doe has written the memoir *Under the Big Black Sun: A Personal History of L.A. Punk.*

X-RAY SPEX: *GERMFREE ADOLESCENTS* (REISSUE)

The female-headed band X-Ray Spex was formed in 1976 by vocalist Poly Styrene (Marianne Joan Elliott-Said) and saxophonist Lora Logic (Susan Whitby), who first met in school, along with guitarist Jak Airport (Jack Stafford), drummer Paul "B. P." Hurding, and bassist Paul Dean. Styrene and Logic dropped out of school at fifteen and sixteen, respectively, to write songs and play music full-time. The X-Ray Spex's original sound quickly made them one of the most buzzed about bands on the London punk scene. Styrene's voice, simultaneously girlish and commanding, made declarations about feminism and postmodern consumer society that alienated humans from authentic experience. Logic's honking sax punctuated Styrene's musical declarations. Styrene was also notable for her cultivation of an anticelebrity image that challenged "the convention that female performers should be submissive and conventionally beautiful" (Simpson 2011, "The Spex Factor"). Styrene wore Day-Glo stage clothing, her teeth were girded in thick braces, and she did not wear cosmetics or deodorant. She famously declared that she "wasn't a sex symbol and that if anybody tried to make [her] one [she'd] shave [her] head tomorrow" (Murray 1978), which she later did in John Lydon's apartment just before the Rock against Racism concert in Victoria Park (Pelly 2017, "X-Ray Spex"). Logic left the band to join the Hare Krishna movement before the recording of *Germfree Adolescents* in 1977, and her saxophone parts were performed in session by other musicians.

Germfree Adolescents, the band's first studio album and the only one to be released with material performed and written by the original lineup, is widely held to be a punk classic ("1,000 Albums" 2007; Dimery 2005; Pelly 2017, "X-Ray Spex") as well as a feminist classic, particularly for the song "Oh Bondage, Up Yours!," which was not on the original version of *Germfree Adolescents*. "Oh Bondage, Up Yours!" is included in the reissue version of *Germfree Adolescents*.

Most of the songs on *Germfree Adolescents* describe postmodern subjectivity, a plastic world in which people's minds have been hijacked by the insidious messages of consumer culture to a degree that even free will is nothing more than a preprogrammed illusion. "Art-I-Ficial," "Obsessed with You," "Identity," "I Live Off You," "Plastic Bag," "The Day the World Turned Day-Glo," "Germfree Adolescents," "Age," and "Highly Inflammable" variously illustrate and critique postmodern subjectivity. "The Day the World Turned Day-Glo" describes the artificial, futuristic world of Styrene's present day, one viewed through a window covered with "nylon curtains," where the natural world has been eradicated and replaced with an "acrylic road."

The germ-free adolescents of the album's title track are similarly artificial and antiseptic in a time before the threat of AIDS required a latex curtain between intimate partners. There is a chance that you might get to touch this germ-free adolescent if you are wearing sterile gloves, but you will need to "rinse your mouth with Listerine and blow disinfectant in her eyes" because this culture has become so obsessed with cleanliness that artificial scents such as deodorant are preferable to any natural ones. "Art-I-Ficial" and "Age" similarly consider how natural is not normal or desirable in this world. The singer feels like she is putting on a mask when she puts on makeup, but "that's the way a girl should be in a consumer society." She must labor to keep this mask from changing as she gets older in "Age" or face the consequences of being shunned because she is no longer pretty enough to deserve love. An ideal girl is artificial in both the original and contemporary meanings of this word: both full of art as well as the antithesis of natural. "Highly Inflammable" denounces the obsession with fashion that Styrene loathed.

Humans have been persuaded to become indistinguishable from their plastic environment by the advertising industry described in "Obsessed with You." In this industry, people are reduced to symbols, "just a theme . . . another figure for the sales machine." The title sounds like a heteronormative romance ballad, which emphasizes how even romantic love has been manipulated by ad men into an unobtainable ideal to generate profits. The result is a collective identity crisis, where people have difficulty recognizing themselves in the mirror, as the reflection is unlike what is on television or magazines ("Identity") because all of these ads purporting to represent what is normal are driving people to insanity ("Plastic Bag"). Even the hierarchal social order that keeps so many in poverty is normalized via mass media, which perpetuates the ideas that we have to be taken advantage of ("I Live Off You"). This social order is normalized by those in power, who compare the situation to nature: "the cat eats the rat" because "the whole world lives off of everybody" ("I Live Off You").

But this contrived social order that commodifies and transforms all is not sustainable and could possibly have a frightening end, as described in "Genetic Engineering": "Genetic engineering could create the perfect race, . . . an unknown life-force that could us exterminate" by making workers into slaves. This clone's ability to work efficiently will be the end of our species, first putting laborers out of work and then eventually destroying our species after the inevitable singularity, an event described in contemporary speculative fiction in which AI become sentient and use their superior strength and intelligence to enslave the human race. "Genetic Engineering" is especially prescient in how it anticipates contemporary anxieties about AI. Styrene's introduction to "Genetic Engineering" connects it to Hitler's idea of a master race: after exclaiming the song's title, she counts down the band in German.

While X-Ray Spex offer a stinging critique of their world, they also hint at the possibility for resisting the massive social machinery. "Oh Bondage, Up Yours!" directly rejects subordinate gender roles. "Some people think little girls should be seen and not heard," Styrene states, in a quiet, girlish voice. Then she answers, "Oh bondage! Up yours!" in her characteristic punk battle cry. Bondage here does not refer to a sexual practice but the institution of gender itself, which is based on women's subordination to men. Styrene's requests to be bound and chained so she can be a slave exposes the end result of telling little girls that they should be seen and not heard.

The "Warrior in Woolworth" hints at others hiding in plain sight who are also subversive of the existing social order. The "rebel on the underground" or of "the modern town" may seem humble, but in reality, he is scheming about ways to thwart this order. Even those who are characterized as poseurs by establishment types who accuse them of liking to make others stare at them are revolutionaries in their "anti-art" stance. While "Establishments like a laugh" and find the poseurs entertaining, Styrene warns, "Overtones can be betraying." The chorus of "Plastic Bag" also hints at resisting the superstructures of consumer capitalism in 1977: "We're gonna show them all (the ad men and the politicians who try to control the population) apathy's a drag."

"Let's Submerge," "I Can't Do Anything," and "I Am a Cliché" each describe the punk scene. In the (literally) underground club of "Let's Submerge," "hades ladies are dressed to kill," and the people in the "subterranean . . . bottomless pit" receive "dagger glares from Richard Hell." "I Can't Do Anything" and "I Am a Cliché" parody outsiders who have written off punks as useless poseurs and illiterate hooligans. Styrene sings with mock seriousness of defending herself against Freddy, who "tried to strangle [her] with [her] plastic popper beads" before she "hit him back with [her] pet rat." "I Am a Cliché" is similar to "I Am a Poseur" in its reappropriation of terms of derision used to describe punks while also crystalizing the postmodern themes that predominate on *Germfree Adolescents*. In a world where everything original has been done before, it is impossible to be anything but a "cliché that you have seen before."

Styrene and Logic were attracted to the emerging punk genre in 1975 because it encouraged people to reject corporate popular culture by making their own art. Before her death in 2011, Styrene reflected that, in 1975, "being in a band, saying what you want, . . . was better than being in a girl gang" (Simpson 2011, "An Optimist to the Last"). But in 1979, Styrene started to feel that punk was changing "from liberating force to straitjacket" after the band was "pelted with tomatoes during a gig in Paris" (Simpson 2011, "An Optimist to the Last") by audience members who were enraged that X-Ray Spex had changed their sound. Styrene quit the band soon after and joined Logic in the Hare Krishna movement.

X-Ray Spex reformed briefly in the early 1990s, releasing the trilogy album *Conscious Consumer* in 1995, which was a commercial flop. The band was more favorably received in 2008, during a London comeback gig where they performed "Oh Bondage, Up Yours!" Styrene's daughter's band opened the show (Bell 2017). In 2010, Styrene recorded the single "Black Christmas," an alternative Christmas song, and was planning on releasing a new album, but she died in 2011 before that project came to fruition.

Styrene was the subject of a BBC documentary (*Who Is Poly Styrene?*) in 1979. Another documentary about the singer, *Poly Styrene: I Am a Cliché*, is in production. Also, a portrait of her by photographer Pennie Smith hangs in the British National Portrait Gallery.

CHAPTER 3

Impact on Popular Culture

Punk is a reaction against the mass culture industrial complex that decides what is culture, popular or otherwise, by selecting, financing, and marketing of artists whose work is likely to generate profits for shareholders. So, not surprisingly, punk also transformed how fans interacted with the music they love as well as how artists promoted their work. In the early days, because punk's sound and lyrics made it unsuitable for airplay, bands cultivated fans directly through constant touring and releasing their music on independent labels. This spirit of self-promotion is alive and well today.

The independent record labels that were a result of punk's DIY ethos played a significant role in shaping the genre over the decades. Some of these labels have now become giants in their own right, such as Epitaph, owned by Bad Religion's Brett Gurewitz, which has become "the largest punk label in America, and one of the largest independent labels in the world" (Heller 2014, "From Dischord to Lookout"). Fat Wreck Chords (owned and operated by Fat Mike of NOFX), Epitaph, and Dischord (a collective headed by Ian MacKaye of Fugazi and Minor Threat) "had just as much of an impact on the 1990s" (Heller 2014, "From Dischord to Lookout") as the music their owners made because the labels were able to support other up-and-coming bands. Lookout Records, started by musician Larry Livermore in 1987, built its success on Green Day's two pre-*Dookie* albums as well as the Operation Ivy discography. Lookout was home to other punk bands, such as Rancid, Alkaline Trio, Ted Leo and the Pharmacists, Screeching Weasel, and the Donnas, before it went bankrupt in 2012 due to mismanagement.

The profusion of independent punk labels also fueled various punk subgenres. Tim Armstrong of the ska/Oi! band Rancid, who owns the imprint Hellcat Records, used his label to "catapult Boston's street-punk champion Dropkick Murphys into the limelight," while New Red Archives, owned by Nicky Garratt of U.K. Subs, took off "with the success of the emo-tinged Samiam" (Heller 2014). Profane Existence, Deep Six, Six Weeks, and Prank promoted hardcore and crust punk bands, and Tooth & Nail and Solid State "led the Christian punk movement" (Heller 2014) of the 1990s. Meanwhile, TKO, GMM, and Vulture Rock "preserved the gruff, working-class punk" (Heller 2014) of their Year Zero forbears and brought street punk to bigger audiences. As well, "riot grrrl and queercore labels like Chainsaw and Mr. Lady—and their signees Team Dresch, the Butchies, and others—kept those subcultures thriving long after the riot-grrrl explosion of 1993 faded in the eyes of the mainstream" (Heller 2014).

The punk movement, with its emphasis on performers' passion rather than their virtuosity, encouraged others to pick up a guitar or drumsticks and make their own music as well as to create other types of art. Punks communicated with other like-minded individuals and expanded the genre's fans via self-published zines that they distributed at shows, clubs, and record stores. Zines are not magazines, and the word *zine* is not short for *magazine*. Magazines are produced for profit. Zines, on the other hand, "are proudly amateur, usually handmade" and reproduced via mimeograph or photocopy, "and always independent" (Heller 2013).

Zines were not original to the punk movement; they had precursors in science fiction fanzines and, later, rock fanzines. Punk, however, was "the first musical genre to spawn fanzines in any significant numbers" (Laing 2015, 25). Up through the 1990s, "zines were the primary way to stay up on punk and hardcore" in a time before the internet (Heller 2013). Zines "were the blogs, comment sections, and social networks of their day"; they contained artist interviews, record reviews, news briefs, opinion columns, ads for bands and records, best-of lists, classifieds, and "sometimes even flexi discs: floppy little records with exclusive songs from one or more of the bands covered" (Heller 2013). In short, zines were the music websites of their day, with everything from "listicles to think pieces to flame wars to music streams," just "by different names. And a bit slower" (Heller 2013).

Sniffin' Glue initiated the zine trend and "played a pivotal role in establishing punk's self-image" (Laing 2015, 25). The cover of the first edition of *Sniffin' Glue* "announced itself to be 'for punks,'" marking "the first time the audience rather than the music had been defined that way" (Laing 2015, 25). Mark Perry, the creator of *Sniffin' Glue*, was so inspired after seeing the Ramones that he went home and typed the first words of his zine, taking its title from the Ramones' song "Now I Wanna Sniff Some Glue." Perry "thought that if anything summed up the basic approach to the new music it was the lowest form of drug-taking" (Colegrave and Sullivan 2005, 153).

Illustrator John Holmstrom and future music journalist Legs McNeil created *Punk Magazine* (a zine despite the word "magazine" in the title) in 1975. McNeill hit on the title from 1970s police shows like *Kojak* and *Columbo*, whose titular characters called the bad guys they nabbed at the end of each episode "punks." McNeil said that he was "always running from the cops as a kid," and when they would catch him, they would say, "You're just nothing but a punk" (Colegrave and Sullivan 2005, 82). Within a few months of Holmstrom and McNeill starting *Punk Magazine* in New York, there was a huge demand for it in England. The London record shop Rough Trade ordered thousands of copies. Holmstrom and McNeil were trying to produce *Punk Magazine* as cheaply as possible, but the cost to ship their publication to the United Kingdom was so expensive that the zines sold for the equivalent of $10 apiece there, causing people to believe that the publishers were trying to rip off fans. When Rough Trade came up with the idea of photocopying everybody else's English fanzines, they put Holmstrom and McNeil out of business.

Slash was the first zine to document the Los Angeles punk scene. It was started in 1977 by Los Angeles native Melanie Nissen, a fan of British punk, and her boyfriend, Steve Samiof. "At 50 cents a copy, the large format fanzine/tabloid quickly became the essential source for information about L.A. punk" (Hannon 2017). Nissen and Samiof put out twenty-eight issues of *Slash* from 1977 to 1980, which included Nissen's photos of X, the Germs, the Alice Bag Band, the Screamers, and the Weirdos taken during nights at the legendary venues the Starwood and the Masque. The magazine's entire run has been anthologized in *Slash: A History of the Legendary L.A. Punk Magazine 1977–1980*. Several independent record labels from the 1990s also began as zines, such as Lookout, Ebullition, Profane Existence, and Second Nature (Heller 2014).

Punk zines played an important role in shaping the definition of punk. *Maximum Rocknroll*, a thick monthly printed on cheap paper with ink that came off on people's hands, was the de facto bible of punk by the 1990s. *Maximum Rocknroll* "is (and was) notorious for its passionate yet dogmatic view of what punk was supposed to be. Like factions of the Communist Party fighting among themselves, many inquisitions were led—and pogroms enacted" (Heller 2013). "Zines like *HeartattaCk* (the capitalized "H" and "C" stood for "hardcore") and *Profane Existence*" were zealous about punk's DIY ethos (Heller 2013). *HeartattaCk* was published by Ebullition Records, and the crust punk–oriented *Profane Existence* was published by the independent record label of the same name. *Punk Planet*, meanwhile, "straddled the divide between zine and magazine" by "upping the production values and professionalism of its design and content while doing its damnedest to embrace a broader definition of punk" (Heller 2013). *Cometbus*, on the other hand, was "painstakingly handwritten" but notable for its "collection of clear-eyed observations and sly, slice-of-life vignettes that bordered on literary greatness" (Heller 2013).

In the 1990s, "zines like *Gearhead*, *Slug and Lettuce*, and *Riot Grrrl* served as flashpoints for entire subcultures-within-subcultures, from rowdy garage-punks to vegan anarchists to, well, riot grrrls" (Heller 2013). Some zines, such as *Heavens to Betsey*, *The Official Kathleen Hanna Newsletter*, *Girl Germs*, and *Rancid News*, covered only one band. Others were written for female punks, such as *Conscious Clit*, *The Curse, A Girl's Guide to Taking over the World*, *Literal Bitch*, *Street Harassment: An Open Letter to Women and Girls*, and *Why Aren't Boys Called Sluts?*, or queercore fans, such as *Homocore* and *Outpunk*.

Punk's DIY ethos also spread to film. Many early punk documentaries were shot by amateur or up-and-coming directors on handheld Super 8 cameras, such as *The Slog Movie* (1982), *The Punk Rock Movie* (1978), *The Decline of Western Civilization* (1981), and *D. O. A.: A Rite of Passage* (1981). Teenaged filmmaker Dave Markey shot footage for *The Slog Movie* in Southern California's slam pits, capturing Henry Rollins singing his first show for Black Flag and the Circle Jerks headlining at the Whisky a Go Go. *The Punk Rock Movie* was the first film of director Don Letts, who shot footage of the Sex Pistols, Johnny Thunders and the Heartbreakers, and Wayne County and the Electric Chairs performing sets at the Roxy in London, where the filmmaker was a DJ at the time. Letts's footage is "grainy and gritty like the music it celebrates" (Lecaro 2015), a quality that calls attention to its director's very punk lack of artifice.

The Decline of Western Civilization was Penelope Spheeris's first feature film. Like Letts, she too makes her presence behind the camera known in the film; she can be heard asking questions to the hardcore bands and fans she is interviewing. Spheeris is also credited with "giving the women of punk rock their most reverent voice" (Lecaro 2015). *D. O. A.* was director Lech Kowalski's first feature film, which showed "the impact punk was starting to have on pop culture at the time and would for years to come" (Lecaro 2015). *D. O. A.* contains clips of Generation X, the Dead Boys, and Sham 69; its primary focus is the Sex Pistols' last tour of the United States. *D. O. A.* is best known for "its bizarre interview with Sid Vicious and girlfriend Nancy Spungen (in bed) just a few months before they died" (Lecaro 2015).

Punk's enduring popularity has drawn other filmmakers to document various scenes, such as Paul Reichman's *American Hardcore* (2006), which features American bands from the 1980s, such as the Circle Jerks, Minor Threat, Bad Brains, Black Flag, JFA, DOA, the Minutemen, SSD, Agnostic Front, 7 Seconds, and Gang Green. Christopher Collins's *UK/DK* (1983) is about the early British hardcore movement, Drew Stone's *All Ages* (2012) covers the Boston hardcore scene, and Ian McFarland's *Godfathers of Hardcore* (2017), produced for Showtime, explores New York's early 1980s hardcore scene and its musical inheritors.

Punk's Not Dead (2007) and *The Other F Word* (2011) are more concerned with the future of punk than documenting its past. In *Punk's Not Dead*, director Susan Dynner looks at the modern punk scene to answer the question of whether or not punk died in the 1980s or evolved. Andrea Blaugrund Nevins' *The Other F Word* looks at the lives of punk rock dads, including members of the Adolescents, Rancid, NOFX, Rise Against, and Bad Religion, who struggled to raise children while relentlessly touring. Don Letts and Jesse James Miller look at punk more broadly in the film *Punk: Attitude* (2005) and the four-part docuseries *Punk* (2019). Letts's *Punk: Attitude* goes back to the 1960s "to highlight punk's roots in bands such as New York's Velvet Underground and Detroit's MC5 and the Stooges" (Rettman 2019), while Miller's *Punk* "examines the conditions that created the genre and its enduring influence on music, fashion and culture" (Trakin 2019).

Other documentaries focus on notable punk figures and bands, including Todd Phillips's *Hated: GG Allin and the Murder Junkies* (1993); Sini Anderson's *The Punk Singer* (2013), about Bikini Kill and Le Tigre singer Kathleen Hanna; Jim Fields and Michael Gramaglia's *End of the Century: The Story of The Ramones* (2003); Julian Temple's *The Filth and the Fury* (2000), about the Sex Pistols; Deedle LaCour and Matt Riggle's *Filmage: The Story of Descendents/All* (2013); James Lathos's *Finding Joseph I* (2017), about Bad Brains lead singer H.R.; Don Letts's *The Clash: Westway to the World* (2003); Danny Garcia's *The Rise and Fall of the Clash* (2012); and Tim Irwin's *We Jam Econo: The Story of the Minutemen* (2005).

Just as punk rock was a reaction against homogenizing effects of the music industry, "punk fashion was anti-fashion," and the iconic punk look of ripped clothing held together with safety pins, garish cosmetics, and fishnet stockings were the DIY creations of other punks (Henry 1989, 2). "New" outfits were assembled from old school uniforms and thrift store detritus. They gave themselves choppy, ragged haircuts and dyed their own hair. Or they simply dressed down in ragged T-shirts and ripped jeans. The "organizing principles" of the punk look "were those of binding and tearing" (Laing 2015, 118). Unlike "the flowing, loose clothes of the hippie era, nearly everything male and literally everything female was tight, holding in the body . . . joining a trend of the 1970s to bring 'above ground' the imagery of the machinery of 'bondage' and sadomasochism" (Laing 2015, 118).

Designer Vivienne Westwood described the punk look as "confrontation dressing," where "the rupture between natural and constructed context was clearly visible" (Hebdige 1979, 107–108). Westwood's London boutique SEX sold items that would cause confrontations, including bondage wear along with T-shirts emblazoned with the slogans "Cambridge Rapist" or "Paedophilia," an image of Queen Elizabeth II with a safety pin through her nose, or two naked cowboys. Early punks in London and New York also "wore swastika symbols to shock and disturb the WWII generation" (Harris 2013). Siouxsie Sioux, who wore the swastika symbol in the early days of punk, explained that her generation "hated older people always harping on about Hitler, 'We showed him,' and that smug pride" (Harris 2013). Wearing a swastika in public was a sure way to be confrontational; older people would "go completely red-faced" when they saw someone wearing the symbol of the Third Reich, and, predictably, some punks were beaten up for this fashion choice (Harris 2013). Other influences on punk style included the Teddy boys of the 1950s, skinheads, greasers, Victorian fashion, and British school uniforms (Harris 2013). Punks wore brands of shoes that were favorites of Teddy boys and skinheads, such as Fred Perry, Doc Martens, and Ben Sherman (Harris 2013). The Ramones popularized what would become the uniform of punk fashion: black motorcycle jackets, shrunken T-shirts, beat-up skinny jeans, and Chuck Taylors (Harris 2013).

Punk fashion was a reaction against the emptiness of consumer culture as well as the bleak future ahead of so many young people in the late 1970s. In England, "punks were not only responding to increasing joblessness, changing moral standards, the rediscovery of poverty, etc. they were dramatizing what was to be called 'Britain's decline'" (Hebdige 1979, 87). American youth faced a similar situation in the mid-1970s during a time of rising unemployment and inflation. To protest their situation, punks on both sides of the pond presented themselves as society's garbage. Johnny Rotten of the Sex Pistols did this literally by wearing trash bags (Harris 2013). Richard Hell is credited with originating the style of ripped clothing held together with safety pins. Rumor has it that Hell appeared on stage one night dressed this way after his girlfriend got angry with him and cut up his clothing, which he had to reassemble with safety pins to go out that night.

Punk style, however, was different in the United Kingdom and New York. Punks in the United Kingdom wore shocking and garishly colored clothing as a way of rebelling "against a very entrenched class system," while punks in New York "stuck with the tried-and-true all-black everything" because punk in the United States "was more of an artistic movement" (Harris 2013). Also, in the United Kingdom, punks wore Royal Stewart tartan plaid, which was "the personal tartan of Queen Elizabeth II," because of its association with "the fashionable upper crust of British society in Victorian and Edwardian times" (Harris 2013). Punks reappropriated this plaid, wearing it in torn-up strips and as bondage wear as another way of giving the "middle finger to the established rulers of British society and showcase punk's dissatisfaction with the way things were" (Harris 2013). The British punk look was so shocking that by the end of the 1970s, punks and their style became a tourist attraction: "It took only a few years for punks and their style to become a tourist attraction" (Harris 2013). "Tourists would walk by and photograph punks and their clothes while they hung out in the Chelsea neighborhood" (Harris 2013).

Punk hair was an even stronger demonstration of the wearers' discontent with the status quo. Punk hair ranged from pompadours, like those worn by the greasers of the 1950s, to mohawks, to choppy home haircuts. This hair could be bleached nearly white or dyed black or other vivid colors not found in nature. Members of the Clash wore pompadours, and the Ramones wore identical Beatles-style long bowl cuts. Richard Hell's choppy DIY haircut would become a style "that many punks, including the Sex Pistols, would copy" (Harris 2013). Hell's cut was a reaction against the hippie, glam-rock, and disco generations and their androgynous long hair. New York City natives Tish and Snooky Bellomo popularized brightly colored hair in their New York boutique Manic Panic, which sold vintage clothing along with their own designs, brightly colored cosmetics, and the hair dyes that would eventually be marketed under their store's name (Hannon 2017). In the 1970s and early 1980s, punk hair was so outside of the mainstream it was incompatible with the dress codes of most workplaces, which was exactly the point: why bother being "clean cut" when the only jobs available were low-wage, dead-end gigs.

But punk style was more than just a reaction against the hippie movement, glam rock, and old people. Punk style was particularly liberating for female performers and fans in how it allowed them to challenge orthodox rock practice in the male-dominated music business in three ways. Women could dress like one of the guys, such as Chrissie Hynde of the Pretenders or Gaye Advert of the Adverts, who "opted for the leather jacket, wet-look trousers, and dog-collar style shared with male musicians" (Laing 2015, 115). Or they wore an eclectic mix of clothing made from unlikely materials, such as Poly Styrene's dress made from a black tablecloth, topped with a battle helmet and worn with kitten heels, and used fluorescent colors that "cut against the colour coding for 'sexy' women performers"(Laing 2015, 115). Or they could confront the idea of woman as sex object by wearing fetish wear, fishnets, see-through tops, miniskirts, stilettos with exaggerated heels, garter belts, and corsets. Punk performers who dressed this way, such as Siouxie Sioux, behaved in ways that were resistant to easy objectification.

Punk style evolved in the 1980s as a reaction to "the perceived artistic pretensions of the first wave of British punk" (Harris 2013) to adopt a more working-class, utilitarian look in opposition to "the increasingly flamboyant dress of punk's first wave" (Harris 2013). Hardcore punk was the driving force behind this change toward a simple, utilitarian style. The general outfit of choice consisted of T-shirts, workwear, and short hair instead of jewelry, spiky hair, and studded clothing that could do "serious damage to the wearer and others while moshing" (Harris 2013). Punk's anti-fashion ideals would later influence grunge.

Not surprisingly, punk also became part of haute couture. Zandra Rhodes was the first couture designer who put punk on the runway with her 1977 Conceptual Chic collection that "incorporated safety pins, black jersey, and fabric tears" (Harris 2013). Today, contemporary luxury designers, including Vivienne Westwood, are still influenced by punk style. Punk influence is evident in Rei Kawakubo's mid-1980s creations that "redefined the notion of shape and form" (Harris 2013). Gianni Versace designed a dress with large slits held together with safety pins, famously worn by Elizabeth Hurley in 1994. And in 2013, every model in Fendi's AW13 runway show sported a mohawk. A dress in this show that was made from shredded and reconstructed trash bags circles back to the trash bags Johnny Rotten wore in the 1970s (Harris 2013).

Punk also made several dive bars and crumbling theaters famous. The best known of these venues is New York's CBGB, Hilly Kristal's Bowery dive bar, adjacent to Skid Row, which opened in 1973 and is now widely acknowledged as the birthplace of punk due to the sheer number of punk bands who played there. The club's full name, CBGB & OMFUG, stands for Country, Bluegrass, Blues, and Other Music for Uplifting Gormandizers. "Both by location and music format, CBGBs appeared immediately doomed" (Cartwright 2007). However, CBGB soon became the center of a musical revolution due to Kristal's willingness to give new bands a place to perform. Bands gracing the stage included American acts such the Ramones, Blondie, Television, Patti Smith, Dead Boys, the Cramps, the Voidoids, the Misfits, Green Day, Hole, Social Distortion, the Runaways, Bad Brains, and Joan Jett and the Blackhearts as well as British punk bands, including the Damned and the X-Ray Spex. CBGB was eventually forced to close in 2006 due to a rent dispute.

London's 100 Club played a similar role in the birth of punk rock in the United Kingdom. The Oxford Street venue, which has been in existence since 1942, hosted the 100 Club Punk Special in 1976, a two-day event where luminaries of the emerging British and French punk scenes played, including Subway Sect, Siouxsie and the Banshees, the Clash, Stinky Toys, the Vibrators, the Damned, Buzzcocks, and the Sex Pistols. Sid Vicious, who had not yet joined the Sex Pistols and was the bassist for Siouxsie and the Banshees at the time, infamously blinded a girl during this event when he threw a glass at the Damned while they were performing. The glass shattered against a pillar, sending a shard into the eye of the girlfriend of the Damned's lead singer Dave Vanian (Robinson 2006).

The Masque (Los Angeles) and the 9:30 Club (Washington, DC) played pivotal roles in the early hardcore scene in the United States. Although it was only open for a year (1977–1978), the Masque was home to the Germs, along with the Go-Go's, the Cramps, Stranglers, Buzzcocks, the Damned, the Clash, the Circle Jerks, Dead Kennedys, Dead Boys, X, the Screamers, and the Skulls. The 9:30 Club in Washington, DC, was one of the premier punk venues on the East Coast in the 1980s. The club opened in 1980 in the old Atlantis nightclub and soon became a key stopping point for touring punk bands. Because so many DC-area punks were teens, the club allowed people as young as sixteen to enter. The 9:30 Club also hosted Sunday hardcore matinees. Teen Idles, Minor Threat, Fugazi, and Bad Brains were among the bands playing the 9:30 Club in the 1980s. Joan Jett even played the club in 2006, as did Hole in 2010, and Green Day performed a surprise set at the club in 2016. The 9:30 Club moved to a larger space in 1996, and its reputation continues to grow. The club is still open today and is the subject of the PBS documentary series *Live at 9:30*. *Rolling Stone* named the 9:30 Club No. 1 on its list of "The Best Big Rooms in America" (2013). "The landmark venue has been named Nightclub of the Year four times by Pollstar, and it regularly tops that industry journal's annual list of the top ticket-selling U.S. clubs" (Du Lac 2010).

Punk festivals have also played a vital role in both igniting the punk scene as well as perpetuating it for the past forty years. Early festivals were organized by small promoters and amateur event organizers, sometimes in defiance of the law, as was the case with the first-ever punk festival in 1976, in the small French town Mont-de-Marsan. At the time, music festivals had been outlawed in France in response to the May 1968 student riots. Later, in 1976, London's 100 Club held the two-day 100 Club festival, which is credited with jump-starting punk in the United Kingdom. The Deeply Vale festivals, however, held near Bury, England, from 1976 to 1981, are credited with inventing the punk festival scene. The free festivals were originally sponsored by a nearby commune and brought together punk and other types of music. The festivals went from three hundred attendees in 1976 who camped on-site for two days to an event attracting around twenty thousand fans and lasting six days. The BBC produced a television documentary about the Deeply Vale festivals in 2004, *Truly, Madly, Deeply Vale*, which is available on DVD. Canada's 1980 Heatwave festival was described as the punk rock Woodstock, but it had only one punk band in attendance, the Pretenders. Perhaps the festival billed itself in this misleading way because the Clash and the Ramones were scheduled to play. However, both bands cancelled their engagements. The hardcore Ieperfest has been held annually in Ypres, Belgium, since 1993. The festival's name is derived from the Dutch word for *Ieper*, which sounds very much like the town's French name.

Punk artists have also played an important role in festivals that support causes such as anti-racism, anti-sexism, and reproductive freedom. Many of the same bands who played the 100 Club festival went on to play the Rock against Racism concerts that were held in London from 1976 to 1979. The offshoot festival Rock against Sexism began in London in 1978, eventually migrating to the United States in the 1980 before shutting down in 1994. The riot grrrl band L7 organized the annual Rock for Choice series of concerts with the Feminist Majority Foundation "to mobilize the music community to protect abortion rights and women's health clinics" (Feminist Majority Foundation 2014). The concerts followed the model of Bob Geldorf's Live Aid concerts that raised money for victims of the Ethiopian famine. At the first Rock for Choice concert, organizers distributed "kits that told activists how to stage a

Rock for Choice benefit in their own towns" (Powers 1993). As a result, the series quickly became a multicity event and brought together second- and third-wave feminists. Punk bands headlining some of these concerts included Bikini Kill, Bad Religion, L7, Fugazi, Hole, Joan Jett, the Offspring, 7 Year Bitch, Lunachicks, Iggy Pop, and Rancid. Other punk festivals, such as the 1991 International Pop Underground Convention in Olympia, Washington, which featured Bikini Kill and Fugazi, got their punk credentials by focusing on the independence and DIY ethos of the artists who performed. The six-day International Pop Underground Convention was described by one reviewer as "a remarkable testament of musical self-preservation and fierce resistance to corporate takeover" (Margasak 1992). Olympia was also the location of the Yoyo A Go Go punk and independent music festival, which was held sporadically between 1994 and 2001.

Not surprisingly, several punk festivals are huge commercial events. The Warped Tour (also known as Vans Warped Tour due to the shoe company's longtime sponsorship) began in 1994 by focusing on alternative rock. By 1996, however, the festival had become associated with punk rock. Warped Tour has the distinction of being the longest-running traveling festival in North America, and by the 1990s, it had become so successful that the tour expanded to include destinations in Europe and Australia. However, after Warped Tour lost its main sponsor, Vans, festival promotors decided that 2020 will be the last. Riot Fest is arguably the most famous punk festival of the twenty-first century. The three-day music festival, which has been held in Chicago since 2005, began as a multivenue tour. By 2012, Riot Fest had become such a success that it grew to become an outdoor event, with additional festivals held at satellite venues in Denver and Toronto.

Over forty years after Year Zero, many elements of punk culture have been commercialized. The mall chain store Hot Topic sells overpriced "vintage" Ramones T-shirts to tweens, and CBGB has been briefly reincarnated as an overpriced eatery and bar in Newark's Liberty International Airport. But punk DIY ethos continues to inspire new generations to resist the popular culture industrial complex by making and sharing their own art.

CHAPTER 4

Legacy

The terms *post-punk* and *post-punk era* indicate that punk is dead. Tim Sommer narrowly defines the "Post-Punk era" (from 1978 to 1981) as "a time when a new generation of bands informed by punk actually lived up to the potential for creativity and artistic intimacy 'promised' by punk" (2016). Sommer's narrow definitions of *punk* and *post-punk* incorrectly indicate that punk and post-punk are moldering in their graves, having died with the end of the 1970s, and that punk never lived up to its promise of "creativity and artistic intimacy." As of this writing, punk is over forty years old. The work of influential Year Zero bands has been reissued in honor of punk's thirtieth and fortieth anniversaries, including the Raincoats' debut album, the Ramones' *It's Alive* and *Leave Home*, X-Ray Spex's *Germfree Adolescents*, and X's *Los Angeles*. Many Year Zero bands also continue to tour and make new music, including Misfits, the Damned, Bad Religion, Patti Smith, Iggy Pop, Alice Bag, and Social Distortion, while others, including Circle Jerks, the Dead Kennedys, and X, have reunited or reformed to play gigs.

Post-punk bands, or later punk bands (as I prefer to call them), are also a testament to the enduring legacy of punk. The term *post-punk* does not merely apply to punky music made after Year Zero, but rather, bands who are clearly influenced by punk to create even more experimental music. The Raincoats, for example, inspired Kathleen Hanna and Toby Vail to form the feminist group Bikini Kill. Post-punk, or newer punk bands, riffed on punk and made various subgenres, including Oi! punk (Rancid), hardcore (Germs, Fugazi, War on Women), Afro-punk (Bad Brains), Celtic punk (Pogues, Dropkick Murphys), gypsy punk (Gogol Bordello), cow punk/psychobilly (the Cramps, Mojo Nixon), riot grrl

(Bikini Kill, L7), queercore (Pansy Division, Against Me!), horror punk (Misfits), and the much-maligned pop punk (Green Day), just to name a few. Bands such as Green Day are described as post-punk because their music has the classic punk sound but is commercially successful.

The taqwacore subgenre of punk was not influenced by a specific band or genre. Michael Muhammad Knight's novel *The Taqwacores* imagines different types of Muslim American youth living in a punk house collective where all are free to explore their faith without the dogmatism of organized religion. For Knight's protagonists, being a young Muslim in the United States was the most punk rock thing of all. Knight's novel set off a wave of taqwacore bands, including the Kominas, Vote Hezbollah, and Secret Trial Five.

Many of these older punk bands, who have reunited or are still touring, appeal to a broader audience. When Bikini Kill reunited in 2019 and played sold-out shows in New York and Los Angeles, older fans brought their children, who had grown up hearing their music and could sing along with their parents to the lyrics. A 2018 Shonen Knife show in Dallas and a Social Distortion show in New Orleans had a similarly varied audience. I took my now adult daughter to both—she had grown up hearing their music—and I saw other parents and their children in the audiences at both shows. Older punks are cultivating a new fan base for the music they love via children's books, including Eric Morse and Anny Yi's beautifully illustrated *What Is Punk?* and Jarrett J. Krosoczka's *Punk Farm* books about a group of barnyard animals who form a band and tour.

While punk is not dead, its ability to shock is. In the 1970s, when English punks dyed their hair green and blue and orange and moussed it into spikes and mohawks, pierced their faces with safety pins, and wore garish combinations of thrift store finery and bondage wear, their style was so antithetical to social norms that they were unemployable, and tourists would flock to London to gawk at them. Today, hair in all shades of the rainbow, piercings, and tattoos have become so mainstream in the West that it is not unusual to see attorneys, professors, and physicians with nose piercings, visible tattoos, or even blue or green streaks in their hair. Punk designer Vivienne Westwood now produces haute couture. And words that were once considered so profane that the BBC would not allow them to be said on air are now tweeted by President Donald Trump. When the term *punk* was first coined by Marc Zermati in 1976, it meant a "young ruffian" or a "hoodlum." Today, something is "punk" or "punk rock" when it is aggressively unconventional, such as treating others with dignity and respect in a world of social media trolls.

Because much punk has become commercially successful during the last forty years, bands that include Green Day, the Offspring, Against Me!, and Bad Religion have been derided by punk purists as sellouts (Ozzi 2015). However, the commercial success of some punk bands has led to other bands being discovered by a new generation of fans and allowed for the delayed success of older acts. The Ramones only developed wider followings long after their careers were over as new generations of fans discovered their music at the Lollapalooza music festival. As well, music sharing sites and streaming platforms such as Spotify, iTunes, and Pandora make it easier for fans to hear older bands as well as albums and songs that are not, or never were, in the top 40. Before the internet, it was much harder to hear music that was not considered "suitable" for airplay. People who lived in big cities, at least, had a better chance of hearing old music or obscure music on late night radio programs or in independent music stores that sold used records.

The internet revived the career of the 1970s punk band Death, who did not even have a chance to get their music before the public on their own because they could not find a record company to promote them or radio stations to give their self-produced single airplay. Death broke up soon afterward. Forty years later, one of the bandmembers' children went to a party and heard what he thought was his uncle's voice singing on a record the DJ was playing. The DJ had acquired one of the few copies of Death's self-produced single on eBay. Soon after, the remaining members of Death rediscovered the tapes from their own professional recording session in an attic and reformed under the name Rough Francis to play Death's music for a younger generation of fans who could appreciate that the band was ahead of their time.

Not surprisingly, many large corporations have merchandized punk as much as possible, purchasing logos and trademarks to merchandise them in retail stores. For example, the chain Hot Topic sells a variety of "edgy" apparel and accessories, including but not limited to Ramones T-shirts, to their young demographic. And while the legendary CBGB club shuttered its doors in 2006, you can still visit the CBGB LAB (Lounge and Bar), which is located in Terminal C in the Newark Airport. While there, you can purchase food items and expensive beers and listen to musicians who once graced the stage of the infamous Bowery nightclub. Of course, the CBGB LAB is much cleaner than the original club, but you can still find graffiti, thanks to the specialized wallpaper in the facility. Such was the experience of *Noisey*'s Eugenia Williamson when she made the pilgrimage to the restaurant in 2016 as well as mine in 2019. Or, if you prefer, you can head over to Black Flag's former practice space and have an overpriced hamburger (Koester 2013).

Punk festivals such as Warped Tour and Riot Fest are big business. Warped Tour was an annual event with free admission and featured acts such as Against Me!, Adolescents, Bad Religion, Buzzcocks, Circle Jerks, the Damned, the Distillers, the Donnas, Flogging Molly, Go Betty Go, Gogol Bordello, Green Day, Joan Jett and the Blackhearts, Lunachicks, Me First and the Gimmie Gimmies, the Misfits, the Muffs, My Chemical Romance, NOFX, the Offspring, Rancid, Social Distortion, the Suicide Machines, Suicidal Tendencies, and the Vandals. The tour finally came to a close in 2018 after Vans, the man sponsor, withdrew its support (Giordano 2018). Chicago's Riot Fest is an annual three-day event that features punk, alternative, and hip-hop. Riot Fest began as a multivenue festival, but in 2012, it moved to an outdoor event and later expanded satellite events in Denver and Toronto. Punk bands that have played Riot Fest include Bad Brains, the Misfits, the Dead Milkmen, Descendents, Gogol Bordello, the Offspring, Iggy and the Stooges, Joan Jett and the Blackhearts, Bad Religion, Rancid, Blondie, NOFX, Billy Bragg, Social Distortion, Patti Smith, Smoking Popes, the Vandals, and Bikini Kill. Nevertheless, corporate merchandising of punk has not diluted its viability as a model of resistance to conformist societies, totalitarian leaders, and global capitalism.

Over the past forty years, punk has flourished because the genre's primary tenet is to use art to disrupt the status quo and give the marginalized a voice. In punk's early days, many punk outfits also gave their time to causes that were important to them. The Sex Pistols, the Clash, and X-Ray Specs played the Rock against Racism concert in London, and the Pistols later played a Christmas benefit show to raise money for striking firefighters who had been off the job for five weeks. Later bands have continued this tradition of activism. X played the first Farm Aid benefit concert in 1985. The members of L7 were named Feminists of the Year by the Feminist Majority Foundation for starting the Rock for Choice series of concerts. Fat Mike, of the hardcore band NOFX, started PunkVoter in 2002 to get young people registered to vote and lay the ground for regime change after George W. Bush sent American troops to war in Iraq after 9/11 based on faulty intelligence that Saddam Hussein had weapons of mass destruction and was connected with al-Qaeda. And Black Flag reunited in 2013 to play a benefit concert for cats.

Some punk band members are registered Democrats (Dropkick Murphys, Green Day), while others are affiliated with the Green or Libertarian parties (Jello Biafra of the Dead Kennedys). A small number of punk bands are politically conservative or even reactionary, such as Nazi or white supremacist punks. Johnny Ramone was a staunch Republican, which was a point of contention between him and his bandmates, particularly Joey Ramone. When the Ramones were inducted into the Rock and Roll Hall of Fame in 2002, Johnny said from the podium, "God bless President Bush, and God bless America." And "in late-1970s Britain, as the Clash were fronting Rock Against Racism, Oi! bands such as Skrewdriver were backing the National Front" (Lynskey 2004, "Meet the Pro-Bush Punks"). The 2015 movie *Green Room* depicts the horrors that a fictional punk band endures when they are on the road and play a white supremacist punk venue in rural Oregon to make enough money to get home. Bands such as Bikini Kill, Crass, Fugazi, Dropkick Murphys, Green Day, Death, L7, Against Me!, Pansy Division, the Slits, Gogol Bordello, and Bad Religion continue to use their music to advocate for laborers and immigrants and against imperialism, fascism, racism, sexism, homophobia, and transphobia. War on Women's second studio album, *Capture the Flag* (2018), came with a reading list meant to raise their fans' consciousness about American imperialism and warmongering and present-day threats to women's reproductive rights.

Punk has also flourished internationally because the genre lends itself to social protest. Chinese punk musician He Yong's 1994 song "'Garbage Dump' is celebrated as China's first punk song" (Steen 2011, 137). "Garbage Dump" recollects the 1989 Tiananmen Square massacre in Beijing, when the government sent tanks and troops to violently suppress thousands of prodemocracy student protestors. Afterward, the Chinese government suppressed information about the massacre, including how many were killed (estimates range between hundreds and thousands). Today, the Chinese government has so successfully censored information about the Tiananmen Square massacre that, in 2015, only fifteen out of one hundred Chinese students could identify the iconic "Tank Man" photograph that shows a lone protester standing up to a line of tanks (Lim 2015). In 1994, the Chinese government thought that Yong's video for "Garbage Dump" was so threatening to the social order that they banned it, not just for its references to the Tiananmen Square massacre but for its graphic depiction of "how the Chinese government actively and forcefully shapes its citizens' consciousness" (Jaivin 2016).

The Soviet government felt similarly threatened by Western rock music, specifically punk. In 1983, Yuri Andropov "declared war on

Western pop music as 'a dangerous ideological pollution among Soviet youth'" and sent out the KGB "to control what music was played in local discotheques," which played Western music because young pop music consumers "preferred Western music hits to Soviet ones" (Zhuk 2011, 149). This campaign against punk began with "confusing reports in Soviet periodicals" that characterized British punks as neofascist skinheads. As a result, "all Western music that was associated with the punk movement and used fascist symbols" was banned in the Soviet Union. During this time, anyone who sported what the KGB described as punk fashion that merely consisted as "'shaven temples' were arrested on the streets of Dnipropetrovsk during 1983–85" (Zhuk 2011, 157). Ironically, the Soviet ban included bands like the Clash, who collaborated "with British Communists in their struggle against racism and neofascism" (Zhuk 2011, 150).

Three decades after the fall of the Soviet Union, the punk collective Pussy Riot used their performances to protest Vladimir Putin's authoritarian leadership of Russia, a style that he derived from his time in the KGB when Russia was part of the Soviet Union. Pussy Riot's guerilla performance "A Punk Prayer" (or "Mother of God, Drive Putin Away") in two of Russia's most important Orthodox churches so incensed Putin that three band members were beaten by the police and arrested for "hooliganism motivated by religious hatred" (Elder 2012, "Pussy Riot Sentenced").

Punk is also flourishing in South Korea. When South Korea opened its borders to the world in the mid-1980s, its citizens had nearly forty years of music to catch up on, leading to a rock resurgence. "Bands like Crying Nut and No Brain effectively introduced Korea to punk rock," and today, "the genre is undergoing a creative revival" (Singh 2018) in a country where the young are "forced to deal with the pressures of conforming to the country's repressive conservative ideals, compulsory military service for all men, and an increasingly right-wing, power hungry government" (*Vice* Staff 2009). Straight-edge punk is especially popular in South Korea due to its out-of-control drinking culture that "makes European bingers look like they're solemnly celebrating mass with the Pope" (*Vice* Staff 2009). As a result, "being straight-edge in Korea is a pretty potent life decision" (*Vice* Staff 2009).

But punk's most enduring legacy is not its music but its attitude about art. Punk values passion over virtuosity. From the beginning, the punk movement encouraged people to think of themselves as artists and to make art in all forms from whatever they could find to express themselves. Punk is not the only musical movement to encourage people without formal training or corporate sponsorship to express themselves through art. The rap and folk genres similarly encourage people who do not necessarily think of themselves as artists to make art as a means of expression and political protest. In the early days of punk, people shared their art through guerilla concerts held in art schools, pubs, and public places, whether or not they had formal permission to be there; through mimeographed zines; and through homemade fashion. Bands aggressively promoted themselves by continuously touring and selling singles they had paid to press to audience members. The digital revolution has allowed artists to cut out the corporate middleman to share their art with like-minded people. Today, anyone with a cell phone can shoot a professional-looking video as well as record and edit sound with even the most basic computer and share their work with the world via the internet. As a result, more than ever, punk is living up to its promise of creativity and artistic intimacy.

Bibliography

ABC [Australian Broadcasting Corporation] News. "Waltzing Matilda an Odd Cold Case." February 12, 2010. https://www.abc.net.au/news/2010-02-12/waltzing-matilda-an-old-cold-case/329506.

Abrams, Howie, and James Lathos. *Finding Joseph I: An Oral History of H.R. from Bad Brains*. New York: Lesser Gods, 2016.

Abreu, Amelia. "Southern Comfort." *Dallas Observer*. February 8, 2001. https://www.dallasobserver.com/music/southern-comfort-6392950.

Acker, Kathy. *Blood and Guts in High School*. New York: Grove Press, 1984.

Acorn, Gordie. "The Death and Afterlife of an LA Punk." *The Guardian*. August 23, 2008. https://www.theguardian.com/music/2008/aug/24/popandrock1.

Adams, Tim. "The Death and Afterlife of an LA Punk." *The Guardian*. August 23, 2008. https://www.theguardian.com/music/2008/aug/24/popandrock1.

Adato, Allison. "Crash and Burn: The Most Untimely Death of a White-Hot Germ." *Los Angeles Times*. December 3, 2000. http://articles.latimes.com/2000/dec/03/magazine/tm-60392.

Agacki, Dan. "'I Never Left Music. I Was Always Creating': An Interview with L.A. Punk Legend Alice Bag." *Milwaukee Record*. July 10, 2018. https://milwaukeerecord.com/music/i-never-left-music-i-was-always-creating-an-interview-with-l-a-punk-legend-alice-bag.

Aitch, Iain. "'Why Should We Accept Any Less Than a Better Way of Doing Things?'" *The Guardian* [London]. October 19, 2007. https://www.theguardian.com/music/2007/oct/19/popandrock.

Albertine, Viv. *Clothes, Clothes, Clothes. Music, Music, Music. Boys, Boys, Boys.: A Memoir*. New York: Thomas Dunne Books, 2014.

Albertine, Viv. *To Throw Away Unopened: A Memoir*. New York: Faber and Faber Social, 2018.

Alexander, Rae. "For Children at the Bikini Kill Reunion, 'Revolution Girl Style Now' Is Finally a Reality." *KQED*. May 1, 2009. https://www.kqed.org

/pop/111468/for-children-at-the-bikini-kill-reunion-revolution-girl-style-now-is-finally-a-reality.

"Alice Bag: The Chicana Punk Who Rioted before Riot Grrrl." *NPR: Latino USA*. March 25, 2016. https://www.npr.org/2016/03/25/471874609/alice-bag-the-chicana-punk-who-rioted-before-riot-grrrl.

Alice Bag: Official Website. n.d. Accessed July 7, 2019. https://alicebag.com.

"Alice Bag: Los Angeles Is a Diverse Metropolis, and Our Punk Scene Was Ddiverse." *Guitar Girl Magazine*. September 6, 2020. https://guitargirlmag.com/interviews/alice-bag-los-angeles-is-a-diverse-metropolis-and-our-punk-scene-was-diverse/.

All Ages: The Boston Hardcore Film. Drew Stone, dir. 2012.

"AllMusic Best of 2017: Favorite Punk Albums." *AllMusic*. n.d. Accessed August 5, 2020. https://www.AllMusic.com/year-in-review/2017/favorite-punk.

Alonzo, Raúl. "Vulpess." *Lafonoteca*. July 5, 2008. http://lafonoteca.net/grupos/vulpess.

Alston, Joshua. "Pansy Division's Punk Beat Smashes Gay Stereotype." *Newsweek*. April 10, 2009. https://www.newsweek.com/pansy-divisions-punk-beat-smashes-gay-stereotype-77433.

Ambrose, Joe. *Gimme Danger: The Story of Iggy Pop*. London: Omnibus Press, 2008.

Ambrose, Joe. *Moshpit: The Violent World of Mosh Pit Culture*. London: Omnibus Press, 2001.

American Hardcore. Paul Reichman, dir. 2006.

"American Songwriter's Top 50 Albums of 2014: Presented by D'Addario." *American Songwriter*. November 24, 2014. https://americansongwriter.com/american-songwriters-top-50-albums-2014/2.

Anderson, Mark, and Mark Jenkins. *Dance of Days: Two Decades of Punk in the Nation's Capital*. New York: Akashic Books, 2003.

Anderson, Rick. "Bad Brains: I Against I." *AllMusic.com*. n.d. Accessed July 19, 2018. https://www.AllMusic.com/album/i-against-i-mw0000189123.

Anderson, Rick. "X: Johnny Hit and Run Pauline." *AllMusic*. n.d. Accessed December 20, 2019. https://www.AllMusic.com/song/johny-hit-and-run-pauline-mt0031788087.

Anderson, Rick. "X: White Girl." *AllMusic*. n.d. Accessed December 20, 2019. https://www.AllMusic.com/song/white-girl-mt0012350770.

Anderson, Stacey. "Dropkick Murphys Tell Gov. Scott Walker, 'Stop Using Our Music.'" *Billboard*. January 25, 2015. https://www.billboard.com/articles/news/6450875/dropkick-murphys-scott-walker-stop-using-our-music.

Andrews, Charlotte Richardson. "Punk Has a Problem with Women. Why?" *The Guardian* [London]. July 3, 2014. https://www.theguardian.com/music/musicblog/2014/jul/03/punk-has-a-problem-with-women-why.

"Andy Warhol's Interview." 1975. The Richard Hell Papers; Series 3, Sub E; Box 9; Folder 635. The Fales Library Special Collections. New York University. http://dlib.nyu.edu/findingaids/html/fales/hell/dscref604.html.

Anesiadis, Alexandros. *Crossover the Edge: Where Hardcore, Punk and Metal Collide*. London: Cherry Red Books, 2019.

The Angry Red Planet. Ib Melchior, dir. 1959.

Angry Snowmans. n.d. Accessed July 10, 2018. https://angrysnowmans.bandcamp.com.

Another State of Mind. Adam Small and Peter Stuart, dirs. 1984.

Antifos, Rania. "Someone Turned Donald Trump's Handwritten Notes on the Impeachment Hearing into a Ramones Song." *Billboard*. November 20, 2019. https://www.billboard.com/articles/news/8544377/donald-trumps-handwritten-impeachment-hearing-ramones-song.

Antonia, Nick. *Too Much, Too Soon: The Makeup Breakup of the New York Dolls*. London: Omnibus Press, 2011.

Apar, Corey. "Pansy Division: *The Essential Pansy Division*." *AllMusic*. n.d. Accessed July 21, 2018. https://www.AllMusic.com/album/the-essential-pansy-division-mw0000532346.

Arcand, Rob. "Legendary L.A. Punk Band X Announce New Reissues of 4 Classic Albums, Now Available to Stream." *SPIN*. July 28, 2018. https://www.spin.com/2018/07/x-4-classic-albums-reissue-fat-possum-stream.

Arnold, Gina. "Bricks Are Heavy." *Entertainment Weekly*. June 19, 1992. https://ew.com/article/1992/06/19/bricks-are-heavy.

Aron, Nina Renata. "It's Been Nearly 40 Years since Bad Brains Shattered Stereotypes about Punk Rock—And Black Music." *Timeline*. February 1, 2018. https://timeline.com/bad-brains-shattered-stereotypes-about-punk-rock-and-black-music-3659aafcc9cc.

"The Art of Punk—Black Flag." *YouTube*. June 11, 2013. https://www.youtube.com/watch?v=N0u04EqNVjo.

Astor, Pete. *Richard Hell and the Voidoids'* Blank Generation. New York: Bloomsbury, 2014.

Auslander, Philip. *Performance: Visual Art and Performance Art*. New York: Taylor and Francis, 2003. 46.

Azerrad, Michael. *Our Band Could Be Your Life: Scenes from the American Indie Underground, 1981–1991*. New York: Little Brown, 2001.

Babey, Ged. "Pussy Riot—*Kill the Sexist*—Album Review." *Louder Than War*. August 6, 2012. https://louderthanwar.com/pussy-riot-kill-sexist-album-review.

Bad Brains: A Band in DC. Ben Logan and Mandy Stein, dir. 2012.

"Bad Religion Takes Down Alt-Right Movement with New Single, 'The Kids Are Alt-Right.'" *Blabbermouth.net*. June 20, 2018. https://www.blabbermouth.net/news/bad-religion-takes-down-alt-right-movement-with-new-single-the-kids-are-alt-right.

Bad Reputation. Kevin Kerslake, dir. 2018.

Bag, Alice. *Violence Girl: East L.A. Rage to Hollywood Stage, a Chicana Punk Story*. Port Townsend, WA: Feral House, 2011.

Baker, Mark. *Nam: The Vietnam War in the Words of the Men and Women Who Fought There*. New York: Berkley, 1983.

Bamseom Pirates Seoul Inferno. Jung Yoon-Suk, dir. 2017.
A Band Called Death. Mark Christopher Covino and Jeff Howlett, dirs. 2012.
Bangs, Lester. *Psychotic Reactions and Carburetor Dung: The Work of a Legendary Critic: Rock 'N' Roll as Literature and Literature as Rock 'N' Roll.* New York: Anchor Books, 1988.
Bangs, Lester. "Richard Hell and the Voidoids." In *The Rolling Stone Record Guide*, 2nd ed. Edited by Dave Marsh and John Swenson. New York: Random House, 1983.
Baranovitch, Nimrod. *China's New Voices: Popular Music, Ethnicity, Gender, and Politics, 1978–1997.* Berkeley: University of California Press, 2003.
Barber, Chris, and Jack Sargeant. *No Focus: Punk on Film.* London: Headpress, 2006.
Barker, Emily. "The 500 Greatest Albums of All Time: 100–1." *NME*. October 25, 2013. https://www.nme.com/photos/the-500-greatest-albums-of-all-time-100-1-1426116.
Barry, Ellen and Michael Schwirtz. "After Election, Putin Faces Challenges to Legitimacy." *The New York Times*. March 5, 2012. https://www.nytimes.com/2012/03/06/world/europe/observers-detail-flaws-in-russian-election.html.
BBC News. "Pussy Riot Jail Terms Condemned as 'Disproportionate.'" August 18, 2012. https://www.bbc.com/news/world-europe-19302986.
Beaumont, Mark. "The 16 Best Pop-Punk Bands of All Time." *NME*. January 20, 2017. https://www.nme.com/blogs/nme-blogs/best-pop-punk-bands-1943797.
Beaumont-Thomas, Ben. "Lorna Doom, Bassist with Cult Los Angeles Punk Band Germs, Dies." *The Guardian*. January 17, 2019. https://www.theguardian.com/music/2019/jan/17/lorna-doom-germs.
Beeber, Steven Lee. *The Heebie-Jeebies at CBGB's: A Secret History of Jewish Punk.* Chicago: Chicago Review Press, 2006.
Begrand, Adrien. "X-Ray Spex: Germ Free Adolescents." *PopMatters*. August 9, 2005. https://www.popmatters.com/xrayspex-germfree2005-2496118827.html.
Bejgrowicz, Tom, and Jeremy Dean. *Scream with Me: The Enduring Legacy of the Misfits.* New York: Harry N. Abrams, 2019.
Belenky, Biju. "Never Mind the Sex Pistols . . . It Was the Damned Who Pioneered UK Punk." *Vice*. November 22, 2016. https://www.vice.com/en_us/article/8gxkz3/never-mind-the-sex-pistols-it-was-the-damned-that-pioneered-uk-punk.
Bell, Celeste. *Dayglo!: The Poly Styrene Story.* New York: Omnibus Press, 2019.
Bell, Celeste. "My Mum, the Punk Pioneer: Poly Styrene's Daughter Remembers the X-Ray Spex Leader." *The Guardian* [London]. April 28, 2017. https://www.theguardian.com/music/musicblog/2017/apr/28/my-mum-the-punk-pioneer-poly-styrenes-daughter-remembers-the-x-ray-spex-leader.

Bennett, Jon. "What Happened When the Sex Pistols Appeared on the Bill Grundy Show." *Louder*. December 2, 2016. https://www.loudersound.com/features/in-december-1976-the-sex-pistols-appeared-on-the-bill-grundy-show.

Bennett, Samantha. *Siouxsie and the Banshees' Peepshow (33 1/3)*. New York: Continuum, 2018.

Beresford, Jack. "The Pogues' 'Fairytale of New York' Voted UK's Most Popular Christmas Song of 2019." *Irish Post*. December 5, 2019. https://www.irishpost.com/news/pogues-fairytale-new-york-voted-uks-popular-christmas-song-2019-174832.

Berger, George. *The Story of Crass*. London: Omnibus Press, 2006.

Berman, Judy. "How Iggy and the Stooges Invented Punk." *Pitchfork*. October 4, 2016. https://pitchfork.com/thepitch/1312-how-iggy-and-the-stooges-invented-punk.

Berman, Stewart. "Iggy and the Stooges Raw Power [Legacy Edition]." *Pitchfork*. April 14, 2010. https://pitchfork.com/reviews/albums/14125-raw-power-legacy-edition-raw-power-deluxe-edition.

Bernière, Vincent, and Mariel Primois. *Punk Press: Rebel Rock in the Underground Press, 1968–1980*. New York: Abrams, 2013.

Bernstein, Jon. "Rise Above: Will Donald Trump's America Trigger a Punk Protest Renaissance?" *The Guardian*. December 15, 2016. https://www.theguardian.com/music/2016/dec/15/protest-songs-hip-hop-punk-black-flag-trump.

"The Best Albums of 2014." *PopMatters*. December 22, 2014. https://www.popmatters.com/188860-the-best-albums-of-2014-2495578571.html.

"The Best Big Rooms in America." *Rolling Stone*. April 26, 2013. https://www.rollingstone.com/music/music-lists/the-best-big-rooms-in-america-141825/surf-ballroom-in-clear-lake-iowa-170435.

Bestley, Ron, and Alex Ogg. *The Art of Punk: The Illustrated History of Punk Rock Design*. London: Omnibus Press, 2012.

Beta, Andy. "How a British Post-Punk Group Influenced Entire Generations of Rock Bands." *Vulture*. November 21, 2017. https://www.vulture.com/2017/11/the-lasting-influence-of-the-raincoats.html.

Beyond the Screams: A US Latino Hardcore Documentary. Martin Sorrondeguy, dir. 1999.

"Bio." *Pansy Division*. 2016. https://pansydivision.com/bio/ https://pansydivision.com/bio.

Birch, Will. *Cruel to Be Kind: The Life and Music of Nick Lowe*. Cambridge, MA: Da Capo Press, 2019.

Blakinger, Keri. "On Bradley Nowell's Birthday, Here's How Six Sublime Songs Show Their Enduring Relevance Today." *New York Daily News*. February 22, 2016. https://www.nydailynews.com/entertainment/music/sublime-songs-maintain-relevance-today-article-1.2540323.

"Blondie." *Rock and Roll Hall of Fame*. 2006. https://www.rockhall.com/inductees/blondie.

"Blondie: 'Sunday Girl' (1978)." *YouTube*. September 9, 2013. https://www.youtube.com/watch?v=oJLMfFJT9ac.

Bloom, Madison. "Germs Bassist Lorna Doom Dead at 61." *Pitchfork*. January 17, 2019. https://pitchfork.com/news/germs-bassist-lorna-doom-has-died.

Blum, Jordan. "United States of Rage and Love: Green Day's *American Idiot*—Introduction and 'American Idiot.'" *PopMatters*. September 2, 2014. https://www.popmatters.com/185074-united-states-of-rage-and-love-green-days-american-idiot-introductio-2495623192.html.

Blush, Steven. *American Hardcore: A Tribal History*. Port Townsend, WA: Feral House, 2001.

Bockris, Victor, and Roberta Bayley. *Patti Smith: An Unauthorized Biography*. New York: Simon and Schuster, 1999.

Boden, Sarah. "Meet Gogol Bordello: Gypsy-Punk Oddballs Bringing the Sexy Back." *The Guardian* [American edition]. June 14, 2008. https://www.theguardian.com/music/2008/jun/15/worldmusic4.

Bolen, Bob. "The Decade's 50 Most Important Recordings." *All Songs Considered*. NPR. November 16, 2009. https://www.npr.org/2009/11/16/120326033/the-decades-50-most-important-recordings.

Bordowitz, Hank. *Turning Points in Rock and Roll*. New York: Citadel Press, 2004.

Bovey, Seth. *Don't Tread on Me: The Ethos of '60s Garage Punk*. Abingdon, UK: Routledge, 2006.

Boxer, Sarah. "Art of the Internet: A Protest Song Reloaded." *New York Times*. September 24, 2005. https://www.nytimes.com/2005/09/24/arts/art-of-the-internet-a-protest-song-reloaded.html.

Brace, Eric. "Punk Lives! Washington's Fugazi Claims It's Just a Band. So Why Do So Many Kids Think It's God?" *The Washington Post*. August 1, 1993. Accessed September 25, 2020. https://www.washingtonpost.com/archive/lifestyle/style/1993/08/01/punk-lives-washingtons-fugazi-claims-its-just-a-band-so-why-do-so-many-kids-think-its-god/6c56fef5-780a-4a6e-8411-8c6b407e1eed/.

Bradshaw, Peter. "*The Taqwacores*: Review." *The Guardian* [London]. August 11, 2011. https://www.theguardian.com/film/2011/aug/11/the-taqwores-review.

Bragg, Billy (@BillyBragg). "The best think about punk was that anyone could get up and sing. You kept the oiks out while you and your mates became stars. Think of all the working class kids whose potential was turned away at the door." *Twitter*. February 5, 2018. https://twitter.com/billybragg/status/960616505883885569.

Braidwood, Erica. "The Best Female-Fronted Punk Bands." *NME*. July 2, 2018. https://www.nme.com/blogs/best-female-fronted-punk-bands-2344471.

Brand, Madeleine. "Sex Pistols' Steve Jones: Just Saying No." *NPR: Day to Day*. March 13, 2006. https://www.npr.org/templates/story/story.php?storyId=5259850.

Brannigan, Paul. "The Top 10 Best Rancid Songs." *Louder*. August 17, 2016. https://www.loudersound.com/features/the-top-10-best-rancid-songs.

Bray, Ryan, and Collin Brennan. "Rancid's Top 10 Songs: 'Time Bomb.'" *Consequence of Sound*. June 8, 2017. https://consequenceofsound.net/2017/06/rancids-top-10-songs/7.

Bray, Ryan, and Len Comaratta. "All Access: An Oral History of DC's 9:30 Club, as Told by Ian MacKaye, Henry Rollins, Bob Mould, and Many Others." *Consequence of Sound*. May 18, 2014. https://consequenceofsound.net/2014/05/all-access-an-oral-history-of-dcs-930-club.

Breaking Glass. Brian Gibson, dir. 1980.

Breihan, Tom. "Album of the Week: Dropkick Murphys *11 Short Stories of Pain and Glory*." *Stereogum*. January 3, 2017. https://www.stereogum.com/1918097/album-of-the-week-dropkick-murphys-11-short-stories-of-pain-and-glory/franchises/album-of-the-week.

Breihan, Tom. "Album of the Week: War on Women *Capture the Flag*." *Stereogum*. April 10, 2018. https://www.stereogum.com/1990586/album-of-the-week-war-on-women-capture-the-flag/franchises/album-of-the-week.

Breihan, Tom. "VH1 100 Greatest Songs of the '00s." *Stereogum*. September 29, 2011. https://www.stereogum.com/826992/vh1-100-greatest-songs-of-the-00s/franchises/list.

Brennan, Collin. "Five Films That Got Punk Right (According to Actual Punk Bands)." *Consequence of Sound*. April 11, 2016. https://consequenceofsound.net/2016/04/five-films-that-got-punk-right-according-to-actual-punk-bands.

Brennan, Collin. "Rancid's Top 10 Songs: 'Olympia, WA.'" *Consequence of Sound*. June 8, 2017. https://consequenceofsound.net/2017/06/rancids-top-10-songs/9.

Brennan, Collin, Lior Phillips, and Michael Roffman. "The 50 Albums That Shaped Punk Rock." *Consequence of Sound*. January 7, 2018. https://consequenceofsound.net/2018/01/the-50-albums-that-shaped-punk-rock.

Brennan, Gerald E. "Mojo Nixon." *Encyclopedia.com*. November 5, 2019. https://www.encyclopedia.com/education/news-wires-white-papers-and-books/nixon-mojo.

"A Brief History of Zines." Duke University Libraries. Accessed January 3, 2020. https://library.duke.edu/rubenstein/findingdb/zines/timeline.

Briggs, Jonathyne. *Sounds French: Globalization, Cultural Communities and Pop Music, 1958–1980*. Oxford, UK: Oxford University Press, 2015.

"Bringing the Music Back to New Orleans." *ABC News*. July 26, 2007. https://abcnews.go.com/GMA/Playlist/story?id=2486887&page=1.

Brockes, Emma. "What Happens When a Riot Grrrl Grows Up?" *The Guardian* [London]. May 9, 2014. https://www.theguardian.com/music/2014/may/09/kathleen-hanna-the-julie-ruin-bikini-kill-interview.

Brockmeier, Siri C. *"Not Just Boys' Fun?": The Gendered Experience of American Hardcore.* Master's thesis, University of Oslo, 2009.
Brooks, Katherine. "First Riot Grrrl Exhibition Explores the Lasting Impact of the Punk Feminist Movement." *HuffPost.* December 6, 2017. https://www.huffpost.com/entry/alien-she_n_3908938.
Brooks, Katherine. "Punk Icon Kathleen Hanna Brings Riot Grrrl Back to the Spotlight." *Huffington Post.* November 29, 2013. https://www.huffpost.com/entry/kathleen-hanna-punk_n_4351163.
Brown, August. "Lux Interior Dies at 60; Founder, Front Man of Punk Band the Cramps." *Los Angeles Times.* February 4, 2009. https://www.latimes.com/local/la-me-lux-interior5-2009feb05-story.html.
Brown, Lyn Mikel. *Girlfighting: Rejection and Betrayal among Girls.* New York: NYU Press, 2005.
Browne, David. "American Idiot." *Entertainment Weekly.* September 24, 2004. https://ew.com/article/2004/09/24/american-idiot.
Brownstein, Carrie. *Hunger Makes Me a Modern Girl: A Memoir.* New York: Riverhead Books, 2016.
Buckler, Rick, and Ian Snowball. *That's Entertainment: My Life in the Jam.* London: Omnibus Press, 2015.
Burbank, Megan. "Rebel Girl, Redux." *Portland Mercury* [Portland, OR]. April 3, 2015. https://www.portlandmercury.com/portland/rebel-girl/Content?oid=15463567.
Burchill, Julie. *"The Boy Looked at Johnny": The Obituary of Rock and Roll.* London: Pluto Press, 1978.
Burr, Ty. "'Strummer' Illuminates the Man and Music." *Boston Globe.* November 6, 2007. http://archive.boston.com/ae/movies/articles/2007/11/09/strummer_illuminates_the_man_and_music.
Bush, John. "Sublime: Artist Biography." *AllMusic.* n.d. Accessed December 19, 2019. https://www.AllMusic.com/artist/sublime-mn0000486047/biography.
Buskin, Richard. "Blondie: Hanging on the Telephone." *Sound on Sound.* 2008. https://www.soundonsound.com/people/blondie-hanging-telephone.
Byrom, Cory D. "Dead Kennedys: *Fresh Fruit for Rotting Vegetables.*" *Pitchfork.* December 9, 2005. https://pitchfork.com/reviews/albums/2626-fresh-fruit-for-rotting-vegetables.
Byrom, Cory D. "Pansy Division: *The Essential.*" *Pitchfork.* March 5, 2006. https://pitchfork.com/reviews/albums/6149-the-essential.
Cahill, Greg. "Hoist a Pint: The Pogues Come Roaring Back with Reunion Tour and Five Sea-Worthy Reissues." *Metroactive.* 2010. http://www.metroactive.com/bohemian/10.04.06/pogues-0640.html.
Cain, Haley. "Alice Bag on Getting Older, Being Brash, and How Artists Can Fight Back against Trump." *Bust.* Accessed July 30, 2020. https://bust.com/music/194834-alice-bag-interview.html.
Callwood, Brett. "Anger Is Energy for Alice Bag." *LA Weekly.* March 8, 2018. https://www.laweekly.com/anger-is-an-energy-for-alice-bag.

Callwood, Brett. *MC5: Sonically Speaking: A Tale of Revolution and Rock 'n' Roll*. Detroit, MI: Painted Turtle, 2010.
Callwood, Brett. "Me First and the Gimme Gimmes Play Trash Music." *Westwood*. May 4, 2017. https://www.westword.com/music/spike-slawson-says-me-first-and-the-gimme-gimmes-plays-american-schlager-8974815.
Callwood, Brett. *The Stooges: Head On*. Detroit, MI: Wayne State University Press, 2011.
Camp, Zoe. "War on Women: Pissed-Off Feminist Punk Band Aims for 'Lasting Impact.'" *Revolver*. June 4, 2018. https://www.revolvermag.com/music/war-women-pissed-feminist-punk-band-aims-lasting-impact.
Campbell, Jonathan. *Red Rock: The Long, Strange March of Chinese Rock & Roll*. Hong Kong: Earnshaw Books, 2011.
Cantrall, Liz. "L7: 'Dispatch from Mar-a-Lago.'" *Spin*. September 29, 2017. https://www.spin.com/2017/09/l7-dispatch-from-mar-a-lago-stream.
Canty, Ian. "Pure Hell: *Noise Addiction*—Album Review." *Louder Than War*. January 19, 2016. https://louderthanwar.com/pure-hell-noise-addiction-album-review.
Caramanica, Jon. "Gender Politics Wiggles into a World Guys Staked Out." *New York Times*. January 10, 2014. https://www.nytimes.com/2014/01/11/arts/music/against-me-with-laura-jane-grace-rings-in-a-new-album.html.
Carlson, Matt. "The Muffs: Biography." *AllMusic*. n.d. Accessed July 24, 2018. https://www.AllMusic.com/artist/the-muffs-mn0000893383/biography.
Carlson, Zach, and Bryan Connolly. *Destroy All Movies!!!: The Complete Guide to Punks on Film*. Seattle, WA: Fantagraphic, 2010.
Carr, Eric. "The Top 100 Albums of the 1980s." *Pitchfork*. November 21, 2002. https://pitchfork.com/features/lists-and-guides/the-top-100-albums-of-the-1980s.
Carson, Tom. "Album Reviews: *London Calling*." *Rolling Stone*. April 3, 1980. https://www.rollingstone.com/music/music-album-reviews/london-calling-2-252761.
Cartwright, Garth. "The Birthplace of Punk." *The Guardian* [London]. September 1, 2007. https://www.theguardian.com/commentisfree/2007/sep/01/birthplaceofpunk.
Case, Wesley. "War on Women: A Co-Ed Feminist Punk Band for All." *Baltimore Sun*. April 4, 2014. https://www.baltimoresun.com/entertainment/bs-xpm-2014-04-04-bal-war-on-women-interview-04-2014-story.html.
Cautericci, Christina. "I Think Trump Could Be Useful." *Slate*. May 25, 2018. https://slate.com/news-and-politics/2018/05/pussy-riots-nadezhda-tolokonnikova-on-trans-rights-trump-and-the-activist-messiah-complex.html.
Centers for Disease Control and Prevention. "Update: Mortality Attributable to HIV Infection among Persons Aged 25–44 Years—United States, 1991 and 1992." *Morbidity and Mortality Weekly Report*. May 2, 2001. https://www.cdc.gov/mmwr/preview/mmwrhtml/00022174.htm.

Chaouch, Rebecca. "Taqwacore: Punk Piety for Young Muslim Rebels." *Huffington Post*. November 24, 2014. https://www.huffpost.com/entry/islamic-punk-rock_n_6180074.

"Chart History: The Clash: London Calling." *Billboard*. June 23, 2018. https://www.billboard.com/music/the-clash/chart-history/TLP/song/314748.

Che, Cathy. *Deborah Harry: The Biography*. London: Andre Deutsch, 2013.

Check, Sound. "Pure Hell: How Four Black Kids Changed the Face of Punk in the 70's." *Afropunk*. January 3, 2017. https://afropunk.com/2017/01/pure-hell-how-four-black-kids-changed-the-face-of-punk-in-the-70s.

Cherkis, Jason. "The Lost Girls." *HuffPost*. July 9, 2015. https://highline.huffingtonpost.com/articles/en/the-lost-girls.

Chick, Stevie. *Spray Paint the Walls: The Story of Black Flag*. Oakland, CA: PM Press, 2011.

Chilton, Martin. "Fairytale of New York Is the True Sound of Christmas." *The Telegraph* [London]. December 21, 2015. https://www.telegraph.co.uk/music/what-to-listen-to/fairytale-of-new-york-is-the-true-sound-of-christmas0.

Chiu, David. "The Raincoats and the Slits, Punk Legends, on Their Debut Albums Turning 40." *Forbes*. November 21, 2019. https://www.forbes.com/sites/davidchiu/2019/11/21/the-raincoats-and-the-slits-punk-legends-on-their-debut-albums-turning-40/#2309e88730fb.

Chiu, David. "The Runaways: Rock and Roll Provocateurs." *CBS News*. June 18, 2013. https://www.cbsnews.com/news/the-runaways-rock-and-roll-provocateurs.

Chow, Andrew R. "Target's CBGB Tribute Draws Backlash, Followed by an Apology." *New York Times*. July 25, 2019. https://www.nytimes.com/2018/07/25/arts/music/target-cbgb-east-village.html.

Christagu, Robert. "Christgau's Consumer Guide." *Village Voice*. February 26, 1979. *RobertChristgau.com*. https://www.robertchristgau.com/xg/cg/cgv2-79.php.

Christagu, Robert. "Consumer Guide—Patti Smith: *Horses*." *Village Voice*. December 1, 1975. *RobertChristgau.com*. Christgauhttp://www.robertchristgau.com/xg/cg/cgv12-75.php.

Christagu, Robert. "The 1980 Pazz & Jop Critics Poll." *Village Voice*. February 9, 1981. *RobertChristgau.com*. https://www.robertchristgau.com/xg/pnj/pjres80.php.

Christgau, Robert. "1980 Pazz & Jop: The Year of the Lollapalooza." *Village Voice*. January 4, 2019. https://www.villagevoice.com/2019/01/04/1980-pazz-jop-the-year-of-the-lollapalooza.

Christgau, Robert. "The 1992 Pazz & Jop Critics Poll." *Village Voice*. March 2, 1993. *RobertChristgau.com*. https://www.robertchristgau.com/xg/pnj/pjres92.php.

Christgau, Robert. "Pazz & Jop 1997: Dean's List—*Sublime*." *Village Voice*. February 24, 1998. *RobertChristgau.com*. https://www.robertchristgau.com/xg/pnj/deans97.php.

Chrome, Cheetah. *Cheetah Chrome: A Dead Boy's Tale from the Front Lines of Punk Rock*. Beverly, MA: Voyageur Press, 2010.
Cinquemani, Sal. "Review: Green Day: *American Idiot*." *Slant*. September 21, 2004. https://www.slantmagazine.com/music/green-day-american-idiot.
Claassens, Carina. "Unraveling the Punk Culture of South Africa's Modern Youth." *Culture Trip*. September 1, 2017. https://theculturetrip.com/africa/south-africa/articles/unraveling-the-punk-culture-of-south-africas-modern-youth.
The Clash. n.d. Accessed August 1, 2020. http://www.theclash.com/gb/home.
"The Clash." *Rock and Roll Hall of Fame*. n.d. Accessed August 1, 2020. https://www.rockhall.com/inductees/clash.
"Clash Star Strummer Dies." *BBC News*. December 27, 2002. http://news.bbc.co.uk/2/hi/entertainment/2600669.stm.
The Clash: Westway to the World. Don Letts, dir. 2000.
The Class of 1984. Mark L. Lester, dir. 1982.
Clerk, Carol. *Kiss My Arse: The Story of the Pogues*. London: Omnibus Press, 2006.
Clerk, Carol. "The Making of 'Hong Kong Garden' by Siouxsie and the Banshees." *Uncut*. May 27, 2016. https://www.uncut.co.uk/features/making-hong-kong-garden-siouxsie-banshees-77065.
Cochrane, Lauren. "Poly Styrene, Rock's Original Riot Grrrl, Plans to Bondage Up Christmas." *The Guardian* [London]. December 3, 2010. https://www.theguardian.com/music/2010/dec/04/punk.
Cocksedge, Rick. "The Muffs: *The Muffs*." *PunkNews.org*. July 2, 2013. https://www.punknews.org/review/12067/the-muffs-the-muffs.
Cogan, Brian. *The Encyclopedia of Punk*. New York: Sterling, 2010.
Cogan, Brian. "Typical Girls? F[—] Off, You Wanker! Re-Evaluating the Slits and Gender Relations in Early British Punk and Post-Punk." *Women's Studies* 41 (2012): 121–135.
Colapinto, John. "Green Day: Working Class Heroes." *Rolling Stone*. November 17, 2005. https://www.rollingstone.com/music/music-news/green-day-working-class-heroes-245468.
Colegrave, Stephen, and Chris Sullivan. *Punk: The Definitive Record of a Revolution*. New York: Thunder's Mouth Press, 2005.
Collins, Cyn. *Complicated Fun: The Birth of Minneapolis Punk and Indie Rock, 1974–1984—An Oral History*. St. Paul: Minnesota Historical Society Press, 2017.
Conaton, Chris. "The Muffs: *Blonder and Blonder* (Reissue)." *PopMatters*. May 26, 2016. https://www.popmatters.com/the-muffs-blonder-and-blonder-reissue-2495432856.html.
Control. Anton Corbijn, dir. 2007.
Cook, Alex V. "Throw Something at 'Em: The Sex Pistols in Baton Rouge." *Alex V. Cook—Author, Journalist, Critic, Teacher* (blog). January 11, 2013.

http://alexvcook.blogspot.com/2013/01/throw-something-at-em-sex-pistols-in.html.

Coon, Caroline. "The Sex Pistols." In *Rock She Wrote: Women Write about Rock, Pop, and Rap*, 93–104. Edited by Evelyn McDonnell and Ann Powers. New York: Dell, 1995.

Cooper, Sabrina. "The 35-Year-Old Punk-Rock Feminist Film Relevant Today." *Lenny*. February 5, 2018. https://www.lennyletter.com/story/the-35-year-old-punk-rock-feminist-film-relevant-today.

Corchran, Nina. "Alice Bag: *Blueprint*." *Pitchfork*. March 27, 2018. https://pitchfork.com/reviews/albums/alice-bag-blueprint/.

Cornwell, Hugh, and Jim Drury. *The Stranglers: Song by Song*. London: Bobcat Books, 2011.

Coscarelli, Joe. "Rock's Not Dead, It's Ruled by Women: The Round-Table Conversation." *New York Times*. September 1, 2017. https://www.nytimes.com/2017/09/01/arts/music/rock-bands-women.html.

Costa, Mindy. "Heavy Weather: The Troubled Career of the Raincoats." *The Guardian* [London]. November 5, 2009. https://www.theguardian.com/culture/2009/nov/05/the-raincoats-reform.

Cotter, Robert Michael Bobb. *The Complete Misfits Discography: Authorized Releases and Bootlegs, Including Recordings by Danzig, Samhain and the Undead*. Jefferson, NC: McFarland, 2019.

"The Cramps." In *The Rolling Stone Encyclopedia of Rock and Roll*, 3rd ed., 219–220. Edited by Holly George-Warren and Patricia Romanowski. New York: Fireside, 2001.

Croland, Michael. *Oy Oy Oy Gevalt! Jews and Punk*. Santa Barbara, CA: Praeger, 2016.

Cross, Michelle. "Pansy Division: *Absurd Pop Song Romance*." *AllMusic*. n.d. Accessed July 21, 2018. https://www.allmusic.com/album/absurd-pop-song-romance-mw0000051029.

Cubarrubia, R. J. "Ian MacKaye Approves Urban Outfitters' Minor Threat Apparel." *Rolling Stone*. July 31, 2013. https://www.rollingstone.com/music/music-news/ian-mackaye-approves-urban-outfitters-minor-threat-apparel-76158.

"*The Culture Show*: 'Girls Will Be Girls.'" *BBC Two*. 2014. https://www.bbc.co.uk/programmes/b048s4tj.

Currie, Cherie. *Neon Angel: A Memoir of a Runaway*. New York: It Books, 2010.

Daily, Chris. *Everybody's Scene: The Story of Connecticut's Anthrax Club*. Harrisburg, PA: Butter Goose Press, 2009.

"The Damned." In *The Rolling Stone Encyclopedia of Rock and Roll*, 3rd ed., 234. Edited by Holly George-Warren and Patricia Romanowski. New York: Fireside, 2001.

The Damned: Don't You Wish That We Were Dead? Wes Orchoski, dir. 2015.

The Dandy Warhols. "Little Drummer Boy (1994)." *YouTube*. December 2, 2008. https://www.youtube.com/watch?v=ZuaiLIUQz5M.

D'Angelo, Mike. "*CBGB*." *AV Club*. October 10, 2013. https://film.avclub.com/cbgb-1798178258.
Davidson, Eric. *We Never Learn: The Gunk Punk Undergut, 1988–2001*. New York: Backbeat Books, 2010.
Davies, Matt. "'Do It Yourself': Punk Rock and the Disalienation of International Relations." In *Resounding International Relations: On Music, Culture, and Politics*, 113–140. Edited by Marianne Franklin. New York: Palgrave, 2005.
Davis, Petra. "The Body Is Not Gender: Laura Jane Grace of Against Me! Interviewed." *The Quietus*. March 26, 2014. https://thequietus.com/articles/14834-against-me-laura-jane-grace-interview.
De Fen. "A Stroll Down Memory Lane with Kenny Stinker Gordon of Pure Hell." *Punk Globe*. n.d. Accessed August 13, 2018. https://www.punkglobe.com/kennystinkergordoninterview0511.php.
"Dead Kennedys." In *The Rolling Stone Encyclopedia of Rock and Roll*, 3rd ed., 244–245. Edited by Holly George-Warren and Patricia Romanowski. New York: Fireside, 2001.
The Decline of Western Civilization. Penelope Spheeris, dir. 1981.
DeFore, John. "*CBGB*: Film Review." *Hollywood Reporter*. October 11, 2013. https://www.hollywoodreporter.com/review/cbgb-film-review-647782.
Deller, Alex. "Dead Kennedys *Fresh Fruit for Rotting Vegetables* Review." *BBC*. 2011. Accessed July 28, 2018. https://www.bbc.co.uk/music/reviews/6v6m.
Deming, Mark. "The Damned: 'Neat, Neat, Neat.'" *AllMusic*. n.d. Accessed November 2, 2019. https://www.allmusic.com/artist/the-damned-mn0000138520/songs.
Deming, Mark. "Ever Fallen in Love?" *AllMusic*. n.d. Accessed December 17, 2018. https://www.AllMusic.com/song/ever-fallen-in-love-mt0005937422.
Deming, Mark. "*Hard Times and Nursery Rhymes*." *AllMusic*. n.d. Accessed July 1, 2018. https://www.AllMusic.com/album/hard-times-and-nursery-rhymes-mw0002086199.
Deming, Mark. "Love Comes in Spurts." *AllMusic*. n.d. Accessed February 17, 2019. https://www.AllMusic.com/song/love-comes-in-spurts-mt0012472335.
Deming, Mark. "*Rum, Sodomy, and the Lash*." *AllMusic*. n.d. Accessed August 2, 2018. https://www.AllMusic.com/album/release/rum-sodomy-and-the-lash-mr0000088555.
Deming, Mark. "TV Party." *AllMusic*. n.d. Accessed July 27, 2018. https://www.AllMusic.com/song/tv-party-mt0004738207.
Deming, Mark. "X: Biography." *AllMusic*. n.d. Accessed December 20, 2019. https://www.AllMusic.com/artist/x-mn0000960690/biography.
Deming, Mark. "X: The World's a Mess; It's in My Kiss." *AllMusic*. n.d. Accessed December 20, 2019. https://www.AllMusic.com/song/the-worlds-a-mess-its-in-my-kiss-mt0012347112.
Dempsey, Jacob. "War on Women—'Capture the Flag': Album Review." *Post Trash*. May 15, 2018. http://post-trash.com/news/2018/5/14/war-on-women-capture-the-flag-album-review.

DeRosa, Jon. "Stuck in Lodi." *Pitchfork*. March 7, 2005. https://pitchfork.com/features/article/5982-stuck-in-lodi.
Desolation Center. Stuart Sweezey, dir. 2018.
di Perna, Alan. *Green Day: The Ultimate Unauthorized History*. Beverly, MA: Voyageur Press, 1994.
Diaz, Zadi. "Hurricane Katrina—Wake Me Up When September Ends—Green Day." *YouTube*. August 14, 2006. https://www.youtube.com/watch?gl=SN&page=1&hl=fr&v=BlmaCBn1djk.
Dicker, Jarrod. "Interview of Greg Ginn of Black Flag." *Stay Thirsty Media*. March 4, 2010. https://www.staythirstymedia.com/news/43/335-greg-ginn.html.
Dickinson, Chrissie. "Pansy Division Celebrates Turning 25 by Kicking Out the Jams." *Chicago Tribune*. May 16, 2016. https://www.chicagotribune.com/entertainment/music/ct-pansy-division-ott-0520-20160516-story.html.
Diggle, Steve. *The Buzzcocks: Harmony in My Head—Steve Diggle's Rock 'n' Roll Odyssey*. London: Helter Skelter Publishing, 2003.
Dimery, Robert. *1001 Albums You Must Hear before You Die*. London: Cassell, 2005.
Distefano, Alex. "The 10 Best Punk Rock Movies." *Village Voice*. August 27, 2014. https://www.villagevoice.com/2014/08/27/the-10-best-punk-rock-movies.
Distefano, Alex. "10 of the Best Contemporary Female-Fronted Punk Bands." *LA Weekly*. August 24, 2018. https://www.laweekly.com/10-of-the-best-contemporary-female-fronted-punk-bands.
Divaman. "Blondie: *Plastic Letters*." *Sputnik Music*. February 27, 2017. https://www.sputnikmusic.com/review/73034/Blondie-Plastic-Letters.
D. O. A.: A Rite of Passage. Lech Kowalski, dir. 1981.
Doe, John, and Tom DeSavia. *More Fun in the New World: The Unmaking and Legacy of L.A. Punk*. New York: Da Capo Press, 2019.
Doe, John, and Tom DeSavia. *Under the Big Black Sun: A Personal History of L.A. Punk*. New York: DaCapo Press, 2017.
Dolan, Jon, et al. "40 Greatest Punk Albums of All Time." *Rolling Stone*. April 6, 2016. https://www.rollingstone.com/music/music-lists/40-greatest-punk-albums-of-all-time-75659.
Donnelly, K. "British Punk Films: Rebellion into Money, Nihilism into Innovation." *Journal of Popular British Cinema* 1 (1998): 111–112.
Dougan, John. "Black Flag: *Damaged*." *AllMusic*. n.d. Accessed July 27, 2018. https://www.AllMusic.com/album/damaged-mw0000198777.
Downes, Julia. "The Expansion of Punk Rock: Riot Grrrl Challenges to Gender Power Relations in British Indie Music Subcultures." *Women's Studies* 41 (2012): 204–237.
Dresch, Donna. "Chainsaw." In *Rock She Wrote: Women Write about Rock, Pop, and Rap*, 74–75. Edited by Evelyn McDonnell and Ann Powers. New York: Dell, 1995.

Driver, Richard. "Dropkick Murphys: 11 Short Stories of Pain and Glory." *PopMatters*. January 16, 2017. https://www.popmatters.com/dropkick-murphys-11-short-stories-of-pain-glory-2495403752.html.

"Dropkick Murphys: Chart History." *Billboard*. n.d. Accessed December 19, 2019. https://www.billboard.com/music/dropkick-murphys/chart-history/TLN.

Du Lac, J. Freedom. "Misfits, New Wave Icons and Giant Rats: A History of D.C.'s 9:30 Club." *Washington Post*. April 18, 2010. https://www.washingtonpost.com/wp-srv/special/artsandliving/930-club-turns-30.

Du Plessis, Michael, and Kathleen Chapman. "Queercore: The Distinct Identities of Subculture." *College Literature* 24(1) (February 1997): 45–58.

Dudes. Penelope Spheeris, dir. 1988.

Duncombe, Stephen, and Maxwell Tremblay, eds. *White Riot: Punk Rock and the Politics of Race*. New York: Verso, 2011.

Dunn, Kevin. "'Know Your Rights': Punk Rock, Globalization, and Human Rights." In *Popular Music and Human Rights*, vol. 1, 27–38. Edited by Ian Peddie. London: Routledge, 2011.

Earth vs. the Flying Saucers. Fred F. Sears, dir. 1956.

Eastea, Daryl. "Blondie *Parallel Lines* Review." *BBC Music*. 2007. https://www.bbc.co.uk/music/reviews/mf54.

Eddy, Chuck. "Music Review: '. . . And Out Come the Wolves.'" *Entertainment Weekly*. September 8, 1995. https://ew.com/article/1995/09/08/music-review-and-out-come-wolves.

Edelstein, Andrew J., and Kevin McDonough. *The Seventies: From Hot Pants to Hot Tubs*. New York: Dutton, 1990.

Edgar, Elton. "Six Underrated 90's Bands That Should Be in the Rock & Roll Hall of Fame." *Spinditty*. n.d. Accessed September 25, 2020. https://spinditty.com/artists-bands/Five-90s-Bands-Destined-For-The-Rock-Roll-Hall-of-Fame.

The Edge. "100 Greatest Artists: The Clash." *Rolling Stone*. December 2, 2010. https://www.rollingstone.com/music/music-lists/100-greatest-artists-147446/the-clash-91542.

Edgeplay: A Film about the Runaways. Victory Tischler-Blue, dir. 2004.

Edwards, Gavin. "Laura Jane Grace's Fresh Start: Inside Against Me!'s New 'Blues.'" *Rolling Stone*. January 21, 2014. https://www.rollingstone.com/music/music-news/laura-jane-graces-fresh-start-inside-against-mes-new-blues-246593.

Egan, Sean. *Love with a Passion Called Hate: The Inside Story of the Jam*. Warsaw, Poland: Askill, 2018.

Egerdahl, Kjersti. *Green Day: A Musical Biography*. Santa Barbara, CA: ABC-CLIO, 2010.

Eisler, Riane. *The Chalice and the Blade: Our History, Our Future*. New York: HarperOne, 1988.

Elder, Miriam. "Pussy Riot: 'Things Have Changed, but Our Desire to Protest Remains.'" *The Guardian* [London]. December 26, 2012. https://www.theguardian.com/music/2012/dec/26/pussy-riot-protest-interview.

Elder, Miriam. "Pussy Riot Trial 'Worse Than Soviet Era.'" *The Guardian* [London]. August 3, 2012. https://www.theguardian.com/world/2012/aug/03/pussy-riot-trial-russia.

Elderfield, Jonathan. "Touring Sites from London's Punk Rock Scene, 40 Years Later." *Seattle Times*. April 6, 2016. https://www.seattletimes.com/life/travel/touring-sites-from-londons-punk-rock-scene-40-years-later.

Elliott, Debbie. "Gogol Bordello: Music from 'Gypsy Punks.'" *NPR: All Things Considered*. April 29, 2006. https://www.npr.org/templates/story/story.php?storyId=5371385.

Ellis, Iain. *Rebels Wit Attitude: Subversive Rock Humorists*. Berkeley, CA, and New York: Soft Skull Press, 2008.

Empire, Kitty. "Our Pop Critic on the Germs." *The Guardian*. August 23, 2008. https://www.theguardian.com/music/2008/aug/24/popandrock1.

Encalada, Javier. "Patti Smith: The Mother of Punk Gave Jim Morrison His Wings." *Northern Star*. April 18, 2017. https://www.northernstar.com.au/news/patti-smith-the-mother-of-punk-gave-jim-morrison-h/3166811.

Encarnacao, John. *Punk Aesthetics and New Folk: Way Down the Old Plank Road*. Abingdon, UK: Routledge, 2013.

End of the Century: The Story of the Ramones. Jim Fields and Michael Gramaglia, dirs. 2003.

Ensminger, David A. *Left of the Dial: Conversations with Punk Icons*. Oakland, CA: PM Press, 2013.

Ensminger, David A. *The Politics of Punk: Protest and Revolt from the Streets*. New York: Rowman & Littlefield, 2016.

Ensminger, David A. *Visual Vitriol: The Street Art and Subcultures of the Punk and Hardcore Generation*. Jackson: University Press of Mississippi, 2001.

Epting, Chris. "Dead Boys Legacy Very Much Alive Thanks to Cheetah Chrome." *HuffPost*. November 1, 2017. https://www.huffpost.com/entry/dead-boys-legacy-very-much-alive-thanks-to-cheetah_b_59f24bf7e4b06ae9067ab764.

Eremenko, Alexey. "Shonen Knife: *Genki Shock!*" *AllMusic*. n.d. Accessed July 17, 2018. https://www.AllMusic.com/album/genki-shock%21-mw0000714099.

Erlewine, Stephen Thomas. "Bad Brains: Artist Biography." *AllMusic*. n.d. Accessed June 22, 2018. https://www.allmusic.com/artist/bad-brains-mn0000075264/biography.

Erlewine, Stephen Thomas. "Bad Religion: Artist Biography." *AllMusic*. n.d. Accessed July 20, 2018. https://www.allmusic.com/artist/bad-religion-mn0000062823/biography.

Erlewine, Stephen Thomas. "Black Flag: Artist Biography." *AllMusic*. n.d. Accessed July 27, 2018. https://www.AllMusic.com/artist/black-flag-mn0000091650/biography.

Erlewine, Stephen Thomas. "Buzzcocks: Artist Biography." *AllMusic*. n.d. Accessed December 16, 2018. https://www.AllMusic.com/artist/buzzcocks-mn0000629564/biography.

Erlewine, Stephen Thomas. "The Clash: *London Calling*." *AllMusic*. n.d. Accessed June 23, 2018. https://www.AllMusic.com/album/london-calling-mw0000189413.

Erlewine, Stephen Thomas. "Green Day: Artist Biography." *AllMusic*. n.d. Accessed June 24, 2018. https://www.AllMusic.com/artist/green-day-mn0000154544/biography.

Erlewine, Stephen Thomas. "The Jam: Artist Biography." *AllMusic*. n.d. Accessed July 3, 2018. https://www.AllMusic.com/artist/the-jam-mn0000084053/biography.

Erlewine, Stephen Thomas. "The Jam: *Snap!*" *AllMusic*. n.d. Accessed July 3, 2018. https://www.AllMusic.com/album/snap%21-mw0000190336.

Erlewine, Stephen Thomas. "L7: *Hungry for Stink*." *AllMusic*. n.d. Accessed June 12, 2018. https://www.AllMusic.com/album/hungry-for-stink-mw0000116419.

Erlewine, Stephen Thomas. "Rancid: *Let's Go*." *AllMusic*. n.d. Accessed July 25, 2018. https://www.AllMusic.com/album/lets-go-mw0000120605.

Erlewine, Stephen Thomas. "The Stooges: Artist Biography." *AllMusic*. n.d. Accessed October 30, 2018. https://www.AllMusic.com/artist/the-stooges-mn0000562304/biography.

Eudeline, Christian. *Nos années punk 1972–1978*. Paris: Denoël, 2002.

Exposito, Suzy. "The Story of Feminist Punk in 33 Songs: Vulpes: 'Me Gusta Ser una Zorra.'" *Pitchfork*. August 8, 2016. https://pitchfork.com/features/lists-and-guides/9923-the-story-of-feminist-punk-in-33-songs/?page=2.

Faraci, Devin. "Smash Your Head on the Punk Rock: Bikini Kill—Rebel Girl." *Birth. Movies. Death*. March 22, 2013. https://birthmoviesdeath.com/2013/03/22/smash-your-head-on-the-punk-rock-bikini-kill-rebel-girl.

Farber, Jim. "D.O.A. by Lech Kowalski; Breaking Glass by Davina Belling, Clive Parsons and Brian Gibson." *Cinéaste* 11(3) (1981): 36–37.

Farber, Jim. "Laura Jane Grace: 'Punk Was More Closed-Minded Than the Church.'" *The Guardian* [London]. November 10, 2016. https://www.theguardian.com/music/2016/nov/10/laura-jane-grace-against-me-tranny-memoir.

A Fat Wreck. Shaun M. Colón, dir. 2016.

Faulk, Barry J., and Brady Harrison. *Punk Rock Warlord: The Life and Work of Joe Strummer*. Abingdon, UK: Routledge, 2014.

Fear, David. "Julien Temple on 'Lost' Pistols Film, Punk Docs & Joe Strummer's Socks." *Rolling Stone*. July 30, 2015. https://www.rollingstone.com/music/music-news/julien-temple-on-lost-pistols-film-punk-docs-joe-strummers-socks-45065.

Fee, Gayle. "Kudos for Dropkicks' Good Deeds." *Boston Herald*. May 17, 2016. https://www.bostonherald.com/2016/05/17/kudos-for-dropkicks-good-deeds.

Feminist Majority Foundation. "Rock for Choice." 2014. https://feminist.org/rock4c/index.html.

"50 Best Albums of 2014." *Rolling Stone*. December 1, 2014. https://www.rollingstone.com/music/music-lists/50-best-albums-of-2014-143954/yob-clearing-the-path-to-ascend-2-176452.

"The 50 Best Albums of 2014." *SPIN*. December 9, 2014. https://www.spin.com/2014/12/50-best-albums-2014.

"50 Greatest Punk Albums of All Time." *Revolver*. May 24, 2018. https://www.revolvermag.com/music/50-greatest-punk-albums-all-time#49-gun-club-%E2%80%94-fire-love.

Filmage: The Story of Descendents/All. Deedle LaCour and Matt Riggle, dirs. 2013.

The Filth and the Fury. Julien Temple, dir. 2000.

Filth and Wisdom. Madonna, dir. 2008.

Finding Joseph I. James Lathos, dir. 2017.

Finney, Ross. *A Blank Generation: Richard Hell and America's Punk Rock*. Thesis, University of Notre Dame, American Studies. 2012. https://americanstudies.nd.edu/assets/91769/finney_thesis.pdf.

Fiorello, Vinnie. "The 10 Best Ska-Punk Bands of the 90s." *Louder*. July 14, 2015. https://www.loudersound.com/features/the-10-best-90s-ska-punk-bands-by-less-than-jake-s-vinnie-fiorello.

Fisher, Kieran. "The 9 Best Documentaries about Punk Rock." *Nonfics*. 2018. https://nonfics.com/best-documentaries-punk-music.

"5 Criminally Overlooked Indie Bands You Need to Love." *What Culture*. May 4, 2013. http://whatculture.com/music/5-criminally-overlooked-indie-bands-you-need-to-love?page=6.

"The 500 Greatest Albums of All Time: 100–1." *NME*. October 25, 2013. https://www.nme.com/photos/the-500-greatest-albums-of-all-time-100-1-1426116.

Flintoff, Corey. "In Russia, Punk-Rock Riot Girls Rage against Putin." *NPR*. February 8, 2012. https://www.npr.org/2012/02/08/146581790/in-russia-punk-rock-riot-girls-rage-against-putin.

Foley, Michael Stewart. *Dead Kennedys' Fresh Fruit for Rotting Vegetables (33 1/3)*. New York: Continuum, 2015.

Foxton, Bruce. "Bruce Foxton: 'There's No Need for the Jam to Get Back Together.'" *The Telegraph* [London]. July 17, 2015. https://www.telegraph.co.uk/culture/culturenews/11736628/Bruce-Foxton-Theres-no-need-for-the-Jam-to-get-back-together.html.

Freek, Jim. "The Muffs." *Phoenix New Times*. January 20, 2000. https://www.phoenixnewtimes.com/music/the-muffs-6417854.

Freeman, Chris. "Bio." *Chris Freeman*. 2017. Accessed December 29, 2018. http://christophermarkfreeman.com/bio.

Freeman, Hadley. "How a Gypsy Punk Inspired a Whole New Catwalk Look." *The Guardian* [London]. January 17, 2008. https://www.theguardian.com/lifeandstyle/2008/jan/17/fashion.worldmusic.

Frere-Jones, Sasha. "Hanna and Her Sisters." *The New Yorker*. November 26, 2012. http://www.newyorker.com/arts/critics/musical/2012/11/26/121126crmu_music_frerejones.

Fresh Fruit for Rotting Eyeballs. Eric S. Goodfield, dir. 2005.

Frey, Hillary. "Kathleen Hanna's Fire." *The Nation*. December 23, 2002. Accessed September 21, 2020. https://www.thenation.com/article/archive/kathleen-hannas-fire/..

Fricke, David. "*Dookie* at 20: Billie Joe Armstrong on Green Day's Punk Blockbuster." *Rolling Stone*. February 3, 2014. https://www.rollingstone.com/music/music-news/dookie-at-20-billie-joe-armstrong-on-green-days-punk-blockbuster-241694.

From the Back of the Room. Amy Oden, dir. 2014.

"Fugazi." In *The Rolling Stone Encyclopedia of Rock and Roll*, 3rd ed., 358. Edited by Holly George-Warren and Patricia Romanowski. New York: Fireside, 2001.

"Fugazi Is a Benchmark, a Signpost and an Example of How It Could and Should Be Done." *Westword*. January 31, 2013. https://www.westword.com/music/fugazi-is-a-benchmark-a-signpost-and-an-example-of-how-it-could-and-should-be-done-5680146.

Gabel, J. C., Brian Roettinger, and Kristine McKenna, eds. *Slash: A Punk Magazine from Los Angeles: 1977–1980*. Los Angeles, CA: Hat & Beard Press, 2016.

Gaines, Donna. *Why the Ramones Matter*. Austin: University of Texas Press, 2018.

Garcia, Danny. *Looking for Johnny: The Legend of Johnny Thunders*. Hollywood, CA: Punk Hostage Press, 2018.

Garcia, Danny. *The Rise and Fall of the Clash*. London: Thin Man Press, 2012.

Garner, Dwight. "It's Mr. Hell on the Line." *New York Times*. March 19, 2013. https://www.nytimes.com/2013/03/20/books/richard-hells-i-dreamed-i-was-a-very-clean-tramp.html.

Garnett, Robert. "Too Low to Be Low: Art Pop and the Sex Pistols." In *Punk Rock. So What? The Cultural Legacy of Punk*, 17–30. Edited by Roger Sabin. London: Routledge, 2002.

Gendron, Bernard. *Between Montmartre and the Mudd Club: Popular Music and the Avant-Garde*. Chicago: University of Chicago Press, 2002.

George, Cassidy. "The Forgotten Story of Pure Hell, America's First Black Punk Band." *Dazed*. August 8, 2018. https://www.dazeddigital.com/music/article/40942/1/pure-hell-first-black-american-punk-band-history.

Gerstenzang, Peter. "Queer Rock 'n' Roll Pioneers Pansy Division Have Been Out, Proud, and Loud for 25 Years." *Esquire*. September 9, 2016. https://www.esquire.com/entertainment/music/q-and-a/a48457/pansy-division-interview.

Gessen, Masha. *Words Will Break Cement: The Passion of Pussy Riot*. New York: Riverhead Books, 2014.

Gibson, Christine. "Elvis on the Ed Sullivan Show: The Real Story." *Elvis Presley Australia*. n.d. Accessed August 26, 2020. https://www.elvispresleymusic.com.au/pictures/1956-september-9-ed-sullivan-show.html.

Gil de Rubio, Dave. "Resurrecting the Dead Boys." *Long Island Weekly*. October 23, 2017. https://longislandweekly.com/resurrecting-dead-boys.

Gimarc, George. *Punk Diary: The Ultimate Trainspotter's Guide to Underground Rock 1970–1982*. Lanham, MD: Backbeat Books. 2005.

Gimme Danger. Jim Jarmusch, dir. 2016.

Ginoli, Jon. *Deflowered: My Life in Pansy Division*. San Francisco, CA: Cleis Press, 2009.

Gioia, Ted. *Music: A Subversive History*. New York: Basic Books, 2019.

Giordano, Madea. "R.I.P. Warped Tour. At Least We Still Have Vans." *New York Times*. July 3, 2018. https://www.nytimes.com/2018/07/03/style/warped-tour-vans.html.

Glasper, Ian. *Burning Britain: The History of UK Punk, 1980–1984*. London: Cherry Red, 2004.

Glasper, Ian. *The Day the Country Died: A History of Anarcho Punk 1980 to 1984*. Chicago: Cherry Red Books, 2007.

Godfathers of Hardcore. Ian McFarland, dir. Showtime. 2017.

Gogol Bordello. "Immigraniada (We Comin' Rougher)." *YouTube*. February 4, 2012. https://www.youtube.com/watch?v=aKpgb2WrGo0.

Gogol Bordello. "Saboteur Blues (Official Lyric Video)." *YouTube*. June 4, 2017. https://www.youtube.com/watch?v=E81R3eod8ok.

Gogol Bordello. "Trans-Continental Hustle (Official Video)." *YouTube*. March 7, 2012. https://www.youtube.com/watch?v=cvB0TIs-2EE.

Gogol Bordello Nonstop. Margarita Jimeno, dir. 2008.

Gold, Andrew. "How Bad Religion Transcended the Ages of American Punk Rock." *Nashville Scene*. March 14, 2013. https://www.nashvillescene.com/music/article/13047368/how-bad-religion-transcended-the-ages-of-american-punk-rock.

Gold, Jeff, Iggy Pop, and John Savage. *Total Chaos: The Story of the Stooges*. Nashville, TN: Third Man Books, 2016.

Gold, Jonathan. "Darby's Last Stand." *LA Weekly*. June 24, 2010. https://www.laweekly.com/music/darbys-last-stand-2165657.

Goldberg, Michael. *San Francisco Chronicle and Examiner*. 1982. The Richard Hell Papers; Series 3 3, Sub AD; Box 19; Folder 1411.

Goldman, Vivien. *Revenge of the She Punks: A Feminist Music History from Poly Styrene to Pussy Riot*. Austin: University of Texas Press, 2019.

Goldman, Vivien. "The Story of Feminist Punk in 33 Songs." *Pitchfork*. August 8, 2016. https://pitchfork.com/features/lists-and-guides/9923-the-story-of-feminist-punk-in-33-songs.

Gomez, Melissa. "Pro-Trump Fan of Social Distortion Says Lead Singer Punched Him at Concert." *New York Times*. August 16, 2018. https://www.nytimes.com/2018/08/16/us/social-distortion-singer-beating-trump.html.

Gonzales, Michelle Cruz. *The Spitboy Rule: Tales of a Xicana in a Female Punk Band*. Oakland, CA: PM Press, 2016.
Good Vibrations. Lisa Barros D'Sa, Glenn Leyburn, dirs. 2012.
Goodman, William. "Green Day: 'We Love the Who and Cheap Trick.'" *SPIN*. May 11, 2009. https://www.spin.com/2009/05/green-day-we-love-who-and-cheap-trick/.
Gordon, Kim. *Girl in a Band*. New York: Dey Street Books, 2015.
Gorman, Paul. *The Look: Adventures in Rock and Pop Fashion*. Croydon, UK: Adelita, 2006.
Gottleib, Akiva. "Political Punk: Rage against the Band." *The Nation*. September 28, 2007. https://www.thenation.com/article/archive/political-punk-rage-against-band/.
Grace, Laura Jane. *Tranny: Confessions of Punk Rock's Most Infamous Anarchist Sellout*. New York: Hachette, 2016.
Graffin, Greg, and Steve Olson. *Anarchy Evolution: Faith, Science, and Bad Religion in a World without God*. New York: IT Books, 2009.
Graffin, Greg, and Steve Olson. *Population Wars: A New Perspective on Competition and Coexistence*. New York: Thomas Dunne Books, 2015.
Grand Theft Auto: San Andreas, 2004.
Gray, Marcus. *Last Gang in Town: The Story and Myth of the Clash*. London: Fourth Estate, 1995.
Gray, Marcus. *Route 19 Revisited: The Clash and London Calling*. New York: Soft Skull Press, 2010.
The Great Hunger: The Life and Songs of Shane MacGowan. Mike Connolly, dir. 1997.
Green, Al. "Ramones." *Rhino Insider*. January 21, 2014. https://www.rhino.com/article/ramones.
Green, Johnny. *A Riot of Our Own: Night and Day with the Clash*. London: Faber and Faber, 1999.
Green Room. Jeremy Saulnier, dir. 2015.
Greene, Andy. "Exclusive: The Dropkick Murphys Throw a Wild Irish Party in 'Going Out in Style.'" *Rolling Stone*. March 1, 2011. https://www.rollingstone.com/music/music-news/exclusive-the-dropkick-murphys-throw-a-wild-irish-party-in-going-out-in-style-2-192408.
Greene, James. *This Music Leaves Stains: The Complete Story of the Misfits*. New York: Scarecrow Press, 2013.
Greene, Jo-Ann. "Gypsy Punks: Underdog World Strike (Review)." *AllMusic*. n.d. Accessed July 10, 2018. https://www.AllMusic.com/album/gypsy-punks-underdog-world-strike-mw0000313458.
Greene, John. "Never Mind the Sex Pistols: Here's French Punk or Why Didn't *le punk français* Go Global?" *Journal of Popular Music Studies* 29 (2017): 122–144.
Gregory, Nina. "The 150 Greatest Albums Made by Women: Siouxsie and the Banshees: *The Scream* (Polydor, 1978)." *NPR*. July 24, 2017. https://

www.npr.org/2017/07/24/538378166/turning-the-tables-150-greatest-albums-made-by-women-page-3.

Grierson, Tim, Sam Adams, David Fear, and Elizabeth Garber-Paul. "25 Greatest Punk Rock Movies of All Time." *Rolling Stone*. August 6, 2019. https://www.rollingstone.com/movies/movie-lists/25-greatest-punk-rock-movies-of-all-time-103577/times-square-1980-104995.

Griffiths, Emma. "Remembering the Notting Hill Riot" *BBC News*. August 25, 2006. http://news.bbc.co.uk/2/hi/uk_news/england/london/5275542.stm.

Gross, Joe. *Fugazi's In on the Kill Taker (33 1/3)*. New York: Continuum, 2018.

Gross, Terry. "Music Interviews: For Laura Jane Grace, Punk Was a Form of Armor." *NPR*. April 4, 2017. https://www.npr.org/2017/04/04/522581237/for-laura-jane-grace-punk-was-a-form-of-armor.

Grow, Kory. "How Bad Brains Are Staying Positive and Moving Forward." *Rolling Stone*. December 14, 2016. https://www.rollingstone.com/music/music-features/how-bad-brains-are-staying-positive-and-moving-forward-123117.

Grow, Kory. "Sex Pistols' Steve Jones Looks Back: 'It Just Seemed Doomed.'" *Rolling Stone*. January 13, 2017. https://www.rollingstone.com/music/music-features/sex-pistols-steve-jones-looks-back-it-just-seemed-doomed-190912.

Grow, Kory. "X Look Back on 40 Years of Punk Iconoclasm." *Rolling Stone*. September 5, 2017. https://www.rollingstone.com/music/music-features/x-look-back-on-40-years-of-punk-iconoclasm-125843.

The Guardian [London]. "Grundy Banned." December 3, 1976. https://www.theguardian.com/theguardian/1976/dec/03/greatinterviews.

Guarisco, Donald A. "Clampdown" *AllMusic*. n.d. Accessed August 26, 2020. https://www.AllMusic.com/song/clampdown-mt0001940929.

Gullian, Charlotte. *Punk: Music, Fashion, Attitude!* Mankato, MN: Raintree, 2010.

Haas, Ann P., et al. "Suicide Attempts among Transgender and Gender Non-Conforming Adults." American Foundation for Suicide Prevention and the Williams Institute. January 2014. https://williamsinstitute.law.ucla.edu/wp-content/uploads/AFSP-Williams-Suicide-Report-Final.pdf.

Haenfler, Ross. *Straight Edge: Hardcore Punk, Clean Living Youth, and Social Change*. New Brunswick, NJ: Rutgers University Press, 2006.

Handel, Sarah. "The 150 Greatest Albums Made by Women: Against Me!: *Transgender Dysphoria Blues* (Total Treble, 2014)." *NPR*. July 24, 2017. https://www.npr.org/2017/07/24/538371651/turning-the-tables-150-greatest-albums-made-by-women-page-5.

Hanna, Kathleen. *Bikini Kill* (blog). n.d. Accessed June 18, 2018. https://bikinikillarchive.wordpress.com.

Hannon, Sharon M. "Punk Rock Was Not a Boys' Club." *Please Kill Me*. November 2, 2017. https://pleasekillme.com/punk-rock-not-boys-club.

Hannon, Sharon M. "Punk Rock Was Not a Boys' Club, Part 2." *Please Kill Me*. January 3, 2018. https://pleasekillme.com/punk-rock-not-boys-club-2.

Hannon, Sharon M. *Punks: A Guide to an American Subculture*. Santa Barbara, CA: ABC-CLIO, 2010.

Hanson, Kyra. "Where to Be Punk in London." *The Londonist*. December 6, 2016. https://londonist.com/london/features/where-to-be-punk-in-london.

Harbour, Dave. Personal Interview. June 25, 2018.

Hard Core Logo. Bruce McDonald, dir. 1996.

The Harder They Come. Perry Henzell, dir. 1972.

Hardy, Phil. *The Encyclopedia of Rock*. Vol. 2. London: MacDonald Orbis, 1976.

Harrington, Jon. "The Damned: *Damned, Damned, Damned* Expanded Edition." *Record Collector*. Issue 344. March 2007. https://recordcollectormag.com/reviews/damned-damned-damned-expanded-edition.

Harrington, Richard. "A Punk Legacy Takes a New Form." *Washington Post*. August 4, 2006. http://www.washingtonpost.com/wp-dyn/content/article/2006/08/03/AR2006080300435.html.

Harris, James. "29 Things You Didn't Know about Punk Style." *Complex*. May 6, 2013. https://www.complex.com/style/2013/05/29-things-you-didnt-know-about-punk-style.

Harry, Debbie. *Face It: A Memoir*. New York: Dey Street Books, 2019.

Harry, Debbie, Chris Stein, and Victor Bockris. *Making Tracks: The Rise of Blondie*. New York: Da Capo Press, 1989.

Harvey, Chris. "London Calling at 40: How the Clash Shattered Punk Orthodoxy and Created a Masterpiece." *The Independent* [London]. November 13, 2019. https://www.independent.co.uk/arts-entertainment/music/features/clash-london-calling-40-birthday-anniversary-museum-joe-strummer-a9201746.html.

Hated: GG Allin and the Murder Junkies. Todd Phillips, dir. 1993.

Hazzan, Dave. "A Report from South Korea." *Maximum Rocknroll*. August 12, 2012. http://maximumrocknroll.com/south-korea-report.

Heaney, Gregory. "Bad Religion: *Christmas Songs*." *AllMusic*. n.d. Accessed July 26, 2018. https://www.AllMusic.com/album/christmas-songs-mw0002581000.

Heart Like a Hand Grenade. John Roecker, dir. 2015.

Hebdige, Dick. *Subculture: The Meaning of Style*. New York: Routledge, 1979.

Hell, Richard. *I Dreamed I Was a Very Clean Tramp: An Autobiography*. New York: Ecco, 2013.

Heller, Jason. "From Dischord to Lookout, Punk Record Labels Sparked Change in the '90s." *AV Club*. March 11, 2014. https://music.avclub.com/from-dischord-to-lookout-punk-record-labels-sparked-ch-1798267613.

Heller, Jason. "Where to Start with the Righteous Noise of Dischord Records." *AV Club*. November 18, 2014. https://music.avclub.com/where-to-start-with-the-righteous-noise-of-dischord-rec-1798274575.

Heller, Jason. "With Zines, the '90s Punk Scene Had a Living History." *AV Club*. November 15, 2013. https://music.avclub.com/with-zines-the-90s-punk-scene-had-a-living-history-1798241222.

Heller, Joe. "Misfits: *Walk among Us*." *Pitchfork*. October 31, 2017. https://pitchfork.com/reviews/albums/misfits-walk-among-us.

Hendrickson, Matt. "Green Day and the Palace of Wisdom." *Rolling Stone*. February 24, 2005. https://www.rollingstone.com/music/music-news/green-day-and-the-palace-of-wisdom-245640.

Henry, Tricia. *Break All the Rules: Punk Rock and the Making of a Style*. Ann Arbor, MI: UMI Press, 1989.

Here to Be Heard: The Story of the Slits. William E. Badgley, dir. 2017.

Herrero, Rebeca. "Las Vulpes: 'Me gusta ser una zorra' ('I Like Being a Whore')." *Actipedia*. March 31, 2013. https://actipedia.org/project/las-vulpes-me-gusta-ser-una-zorra-i-being-whore.

Hewitt, Ben. "Siouxsie Sioux at 60: More Than a Monochrome Goth-Pop Priestess." *The Guardian* [London]. May 26, 2017. https://www.theguardian.com/music/2017/may/26/siouxsie-sioux-banshees-60-goth-pop-singer.

Heylin, Clinton. *Babylon's Burning: From Punk to Grunge*. New York: Penguin Books, 2006.

Heylin, Clinton. *From the Velvets to the Voidoids: The Birth of American Punk*. Chicago: Chicago Review Press, 2005.

Hiebert, Paul Ryan. "What Is Punk? 25 Definitions from People Who Should Know." *Flavorwire*. June 21, 2010. https://www.flavorwire.com/99393/what-is-punk-25-definitions-from-people-who-should-know.

Hilburn, Robert. "Iggy Pop Reaches Back to 'Raw Power.'" *Los Angeles Times*. May 9, 1997. http://articles.latimes.com/1997-05-09/entertainment/ca-56921_1_pop-raw-power.

Hillsbery, Thom Kief. *What We Do Is Secret*. New York: Villard, 2005.

Hilsum, Lindsey. "Battle of the Balaclavas: The Young Feminists Taking on Putin." *Chanel 4* [London]. February 18, 2012. https://www.channel4.com/news/battle-of-the-balaclavas-the-young-feminists-taking-on-putin.

Himes, Geoffrey. "Dropkick Murphys Stumble upon a Sonic Pot of Gold." *Houston Chronicle*. March 5, 2006. https://m.chron.com/entertainment/music/article/Dropkick-Murphys-stumble-upon-a-sonic-pot-of-gold-1891904.php.

"A History of South Korean Metal and Hardcore Punk, Part 1." *Invisible Oranges*. September 15, 2015. http://www.invisibleoranges.com/a-history-of-south-korean-metal-and-hardcore-punk-part-1.

Hochman, Steve. "Mojo Nixon Offers No Apologies." *Los Angeles Times*. September 26, 1987. https://www.latimes.com/archives/la-xpm-1987-09-26-ca-2622-story.html.

Hockenos, Paul. *Berlin Calling: A Story of Anarchy, Music, the Wall, and the Birth of the New Berlin*. New York: New Press, 2017.

Hodge, Will. "The 30 Best Punk Cover Songs." *Paste Magazine*. July 10, 2017. https://www.pastemagazine.com/articles/2017/07/the-30-best-punk-cover-songs.html.

Hodgkinson, Will. "John Lydon: Soundtrack of My Life." *The Guardian* [London]. October 31, 2009. https://www.theguardian.com/music/2009/nov/01/sexpistols.

Hodgkinson, Will, and Alexis Petridis. "The World Was Not Ready for Iggy and the Stooges." *The Guardian* [London]. March 10, 2010. https://www.theguardian.com/music/2010/mar/11/iggy-and-the-stooges-raw-power.

Hogan, Jon. "A Korean Punk Band's Struggles with Censorship." *Hyperallergic*. July 10, 2017. https://hyperallergic.com/389657/a-korean-punk-bands-struggles-with-censorship.

Holden, Stephen. "Screen: Return of the Living Dead." *New York Times*. August 16, 1985. https://www.nytimes.com/1985/08/16/movies/screen-return-of-the-living-dead.html.

Holden, Stephen. "Mojo Nixon Uses Satirical Humor in Rock to Root Out Pretentiousness." *The Chicago Tribune*. September 6, 1990. https://www.chicagotribune.com/news/ct-xpm-1990-09-06-9003140889-story.html.

Holley, Santi Elijah. "'We Still Need to Be Seen': Behind the Rise of Black Punk Culture." *The Guardian*. August 15, 2019. https://www.theguardian.com/music/2019/aug/15/we-still-need-to-be-seen-behind-the-rise-of-black-punk-culture.

Holmstrom, John. *The Best of Punk Magazine*. New York: IT Books, 2012.

Holter, Andrew. "The Last American Band: X Made It in Los Angeles, but They Flourished in the Heartland." *The Outline*. February 25, 2019. https://theoutline.com/post/7119/x-band-album-reissues-los-angeles-wild-gift-fat-possum-review.

Home, Stewart. *Cranked Up Really High—Genre Theory & Punk Rock*. New York: Codex Books, 1999.

Howe, Zoe. Street. *Typical Girls? The Story of the Slits*. London: Omnibus Press, 2009.

Hsu, Bill. "Spew: The Queer Punk Convention." *Postmodern Culture* 2(1) (September 1991).

Hudson, Alice. *Understanding the Politics of Punk Clothing from 1976 to 1980 Using Surviving Objects and Oral Testimony*. B.A. Thesis, University of Brighton, 2006.

Huey, Steve. "Dead Kennedys: *Fresh Fruit for Rotting Vegetables*." *AllMusic*. n.d. Accessed July 17, 2018. https://www.allmusic.com/album/fresh-fruit-for-rotting-vegetables-mw0000189736.

Huey, Steve. "The Donnas." *AllMusic*. n.d. Accessed July 27, 2018. https://www.AllMusic.com/artist/the-donnas-mn0000784535.

Huey, Steve. "Joey Ramone: Biography." *AllMusic*. n.d. Accessed June 15, 2018. https://www.AllMusic.com/artist/joey-ramone-mn0000173487.

Huey, Steve. "The Misfits: Biography." *AllMusic*. n.d. Accessed July 7, 2018. https://www.AllMusic.com/artist/misfits-mn0000891063.

Huey, Steve. "Mojo Nixon: Biography." *AllMusic*. n.d. Accessed December 13, 2019. https://www.AllMusic.com/artist/mojo-nixon-mn0000578028.

Huey, Steve. "Rancid: Biography." *AllMusic*. n.d. Accessed July 25, 2018. https://www.AllMusic.com/artist/rancid-mn0000335747.

Huey, Steve. "Social Distortion: Biography." *AllMusic*. n.d. Accessed July 1, 2018. https://www.AllMusic.com/artist/social-distortion-mn0000038302/biography.

Huey, Steve. "X-Ray Spex: *Germfree Adolescents*." *AllMusic*. July 25, 2018. https://www.AllMusic.com/album/germ-free-adolescents-mw0000088203.

Hull, Robert A. "The Sound and Fury of the Clash." *Washington Post*. September 28, 1979. https://www.washingtonpost.com/archive/lifestyle/1979/09/28/the-sound-and-fury-of-the-clash/86728564-3ab3-4032-af63-570b3a9b4781.

Hurchalla, George. *Going Underground: American Punk 1979–1989*. Oakland, CA: PM Press, 2016.

Hurley, Bri. *Making a Scene: New York Hardcore in Photos, Lyrics & Commentary 1985–1988*. Harrisburg, PA: Butter Goose Press, 2011.

Hurt, Andy. "A Whip Round with the Pogues." *Sounds*. August 17, 1985: 18–19.

"Hüsker Dü." In *The Rolling Stone Encyclopedia of Rock and Roll*, 3rd ed., 454–455. Edited by Holly George-Warren and Patricia Romanowski. New York: Fireside, 2001.

Hussey, Eric. "Liberty, Fraternity, Anarchy—Le Punk Francais." *BBC Sounds*. March 3, 2011. BBC Radio. https://www.bbc.co.uk/programmes/b00yz3h8.

"Ian MacKaye Interview." *Approaching Oblivion*. March 22, 2011. http://approachingoblivion.blogspot.com/2011/03/ian-mackaye-interview-minor-threat.html.

Idov, Michael. "Putin v. the Punk Rockers." *New York Times*. August 7, 2012. https://www.nytimes.com/2012/08/07/opinion/on-trial-putin-v-pussy-riot.html.

If I Should Fall from Grace from God: The Shane MacGowan Story. Sarah Share, dir. 2001.

Iggy and the Stooges Raw Power. 2020. https://iggyandthestoogesmusic.com..

Ignorant, Steve. *The Rest Is Propaganda*. London: Southern Records, 2010.

im-dead. "The Cramps: *Songs the Lord Taught Us*." *PunkNews.org*. September 25, 2005. https://www.punknews.org/review/4432/the-cramps-songs-the-lord-taught-us.

Ingham, Jonh. "*La belle dame sans merci*: Patti Smith: *Horses* (Arista Import)." *John Ingham—My Back Pages*. June 14, 2014. http://jonh-ingham.blogspot.com/2014/06/la-belle-dame-sans-merci-patti-smith.html.

Invasion of the Body Snatchers. Don Siegel, dir. 1956.

Ioffe, Julia. "Pussy Riot v. Putin: A Front Row Seat at a Russian Dark Comedy." *National Review*. October 27, 2012. https://newrepublic.com/article/105846/how-punk-rock-show-trial-became-russias-greatest-gonzo-artwork.

Irvine, Lindesay. "Mud, Music and Mayhem: Why the Slits' Cut Is Still Up for a Fight." *The Guardian* [London]. June 13, 2016. https://www.theguardian.com/music/musicblog/2016/jun/13/the-slits-cut-punk-music-vinyl-rerelease.

Irwin, Colin. "Pogue Mahone: The Story of the Pogues." *BBC: Radio 2*. n.d. Accessed July 7, 2018. https://www.bbc.co.uk/radio2/r2music/documentaries/pogues.shtml.

It Changed My Life: Bikini Kill in the UK. Lucy Thane, dir. 1993.

"It's the End of the World as Clear Channel Knows It." *Slate*. September 17, 2001. https://slate.com/news-and-politics/2001/09/it-s-the-end-of-the-world-as-clear-channel-knows-it.html.

Jackson, Jhoni. "Alice Bag Is a Chicana Punk Icon, but She's about to Release Her Very First Album." *Remezcla*. January 15, 2016. https://remezcla.com/features/music/alice-bag-chicana-punk-icon-interview.

Jackson, Jhoni. "Latinx Punk Fest Is Uniting Punks of the Latin American Diaspora." *Remezcla*. August 2, 2018. https://remezcla.com/lists/music/latinx-punk-fest-preview-2018.

The Jam: About the Young Idea. Bob Smeaton, dir. 2015.

"The Jam/Paul Weller/The Style Council." In *The Rolling Stone Encyclopedia of Rock and Roll*. 3rd ed., 480–481. Edited by Holly George-Warren and Patricia Romanowski. New York: Fireside, 2001.

Janovitz, Bill. "X: Los Angeles." *AllMusic*. n.d. Accessed December 20, 2019. https://www.AllMusic.com/song/los-angeles-mt0031907282.

"Jello Biafra Sues Dead Kennedys." *Billboard*. March 26, 2002. https://www.billboard.com/articles/news/76340/jello-biafra-sues-dead-kennedys.

Jenkins, Mark. "Punk History, Embroidered Here and There." *NPR*. October 10, 2013. https://www.npr.org/2013/10/10/228490858/punk-history-embroidered-here-and-there.

Jenkins, Mark. "*Taqwacores*: Muslim, Misfit and Making a Noise." *NPR*. October 21, 2010. https://www.npr.org/templates/story/story.php?storyId=130645554.

Jergovic, Miljenko. "What Punk Rock Meant to Communist Yugoslavia." *New York Times*. September 18, 2017. https://www.nytimes.com/2017/09/18/opinion/punk-rock-communist-yugoslavia.html.

"Jimmy Cliff on Career 'Rebirth' and the Nature of Success." *NPR: All Things Considered*. August 3, 2012. https://www.npr.org/2012/08/04/158102277/jimmy-cliff-on-career-rebirth-and-the-nature-of-success.

"Joe Strummer." *The Times* [London]. December 24, 2002. https://www.thetimes.co.uk/article/joe-strummer-hldszrqww5m.

Joe Strummer: The Future Is Unwritten. Julien Temple, dir. 2007.

Johns, Brian. *Entranced: The Siouxsie and the Banshees Story*. London: Omnibus Press, 1989.
Johnson, Ian. *The Wild, Wild World of the Cramps*. London: Omnibus Press, 1990.
Johnson, Zac. "The Donnas: *Spend the Night*." *AllMusic*. n.d. Accessed July 27, 2018. https://www.AllMusic.com/album/spend-the-night-mw0000662159.
Johnstone, Nick. *Patti Smith: A Biography*. London: Omnibus Press, 1997.
Jon. "The Germs: 'Forming/Sexboy' [Single] (1977)." *PunkNews.org*. November 12, 2017. https://www.punknews.org/review/15376/the-germs-forming-sex-boy-single.
Jones, Steve. *Lonely Boy: Tales from a Sex Pistol*. London: Da Capo Press, 2017.
Jones, Terry L. "The Fighting Irish Brigade." *New York Times*. December 11, 2012. https://opinionator.blogs.nytimes.com/2012/12/11/the-fighting-irish-brigade.
Joseph, John. *The Evolution of a Cro-Magnon*. New York: PUNKHouse Press, 2007.
Jubilee. Derek Jarman, dir. 1978.
Jurek, Thom. "Death . . . For the Whole World to See." *AllMusic*. n.d. Accessed June 1, 2018. https://www.AllMusic.com/album/for-the-whole-world-to-see-mw0000809362.
"Juvenalian Satire." *Encyclopedia Britannica*. n.d. Accessed June 17, 2018. https://www.britannica.com/art/Juvenalian-satire.
Kalarah, Kurosh Amoui. "Arabian Knights: Punk Islam and Selected Works by Michael Muhammad Knight." M.A. Thesis., The University of British Columbia, 2013.
Kane, Daniel. "From Poetry to Punk in the East Village." In *The Cambridge Companion to the Literature of New York*, 189–201. Edited by Cyrus R. K. Patell and Bryan Waterman. Cambridge, UK: Cambridge University Press, 2010.
Kaufman, Dave. "Ravers." *Colorado New Wave/Punk Rock*. September 2000. http://scarletdukes.com/colpunk/ravers.shtml.
Kaye, Ben. "Jackie Fox Issues New Statement Regarding Her Rape by Kim Fowley." *Consequence of Sound*. July 13, 2015. https://consequenceofsound.net/2015/07/jackie-fox-issues-new-statements-regarding-her-rape-by-kim-fowley.
Kaye, Lenny. "Raw Power." *Rolling Stone*. May 10, 1973. https://www.rollingstone.com/music/music-album-reviews/raw-power-102970.
Keefe, Michael. "The Damned: *Damned Damned Damned* (30th Anniversary Expanded Edition)." *PopMatters*. December 2, 2007. https://www.popmatters.com/the-damned-damned-damned-damned-30th-anniversary-expanded-edition-2498-2496195435.html.
Kemp, Mark. "Bradley Norwell: Life after Death." *Rolling Stone*. December 25, 1997. https://www.rollingstone.com/music/music-news/bradley-nowell-life-after-death-250120.

Kennedy, David. "*Frankenchrist* versus the State: The New Right, Rock Music and the Case of Jello Biafra." *Journal of Popular Culture* 24(1) (Summer 1990): 131–148.

Kenney, Shawna. "Most Notorious Punk Venues." *GRRR! Green Room Radio*. April 12, 2019. http://greenroom-radio.com/2016/04/12/most-notorious-punk-venues.

Kenney, Shawna, and Rich Dolinger. *Live at the Safari Club: A History of harD-Core Punk in the Nation's Capital 1988–1998*. Los Angeles, CA: Rare Bird Books, 2017.

Kester, Marian. *Dead Kennedys: The Unauthorized Version*. San Francisco, CA: Last Gasp of San Francisco, 1983.

Khanna, Vish. "Patti Smith Fights the Good Fight." *Exclaim*. May 2007. http://exclaim.ca/music/article/patti_smith_fights_good_fight.

Khidekel, Marina. "My First Year as a Woman." *Cosmopolitan*. April 9, 2013. https://www.cosmopolitan.com/entertainment/celebs/news/a4311/laura-jane-grace-first-year-as-a-woman.

Kholi, Manek. "Changing the Rules of Rhythm: Have You Heard of Math Rock?" *The News Minute*. November 3, 2015. https://www.thenewsminute.com/article/changing-rules-rhythm-have-you-heard-math-rock-35676.

Kielty, Martin. "30 Years Ago: Jello Biafra 'Wins' Obscenity Trial." *Diffuser*. August 27, 2017. https://diffuser.fm/jello-biafra-obscenity-trial.

Kirby, Jon. "Band in D.C.: Out of the Nation's Capital, Bad Brains Came with Extraordinary Positivity." *Wax Poetics*. July 28, 2015. https://www.waxpoetics.com/blog/features/articles/bad-brains-came-with-extraordinary-positivity/?src=longreads.

Knight, Michael Muhammad. *The Taqwacores*. New York: Soft Skull Press, 2009.

Koester, Megan. "You Can Eat Brunch in Black Flag's Old Practice Space (If You're Terrible)." *Vice*. December 24, 2013. https://www.vice.com/en_us/article/exmn9e/you-can-eat-brunch-in-black-flags-old-practice-space-if-youre-terrible.

Konan, Aude. "20 Black Punk Bands You Need to Listen To." *Okay Africa*. October 8, 2019. https://www.okayafrica.com/black-punk-bands-need-listen-to.

Kot, Greg. "Rebel Recall." *Chicago Tribune*. February 13, 2000. https://www.chicagotribune.com/news/ct-xpm-2000-02-13-0002130301-story.html.

Kramer, Wayne. *The Hard Stuff: Dope, Crime, the MC5, and My Life of Impossibilities*. New York: Da Capo Press, 2009.

Kristal, Hilly. *CBGB's & OMFUG*. New York: Harry H. Abrams, 2005.

Krosoczka, Jarrett J. *Punk Farm*. New York: Dragonfly Books, 2010.

Krosoczka, Jarrett J. *Punk Farm on Tour*. New York: Dragonfly Books, 2015.

Kugelberg, Johan, and Jon Savage. *Punk: An Aesthetic*. New York: Rizzoli, 2012.

Kuhn, Gabriel. *Sober Living for the Revolution: Hardcore Punk, Straight Edge, and Radical Politics*. Oakland, CA: PM Press, 2006.

Ladies and Gentlemen the Fabulous Stains. Lou Adler, dir. 1982.

Lahicky, Beth. *All Ages: Reflections on Straight Edge*. New York: Revelation Books, 1997.

Laing, Dave. *One Chord Wonders: Power and Meaning in Punk Rock*. Oakland, CA: PM Press, 2015.

Laing, Dave. "Punk Rock." In *The Encyclopedia of Rock*, vol 2, 222. Edited by Phil Hardy. Glasgow: Panther Books, 1976.

Landmark: Green Day. Spotify. 2017.

Langerholc, Emily. "Genre Studies: Punk Rock." *Rebel Music Teacher* (blog). January 23, 2017. http://www.rebelmusicteacher.com/blog/2017/1/23/genre-studies-punk-rock.

Larger than Life and in 3D. Lawrence Jordan, dir. 2009.

"Laura Leighton/Rancid." *Saturday Night Live*. Season 21, episode 6. Aired November 18, 1995 on *NBC*.

Law, Glenn. "Richard Hell." In *The Rough Guide to Rock: The Definitive Guide to More Than 1200 Artists and Bands*. 3rd ed. Edited by Peter Buckley. London: Rough Guides, 2003.

Leblanc, Lauraine. *Pretty in Punk: Girls' Gender Resistance in a Boys' Subculture*. New Brunswick, NJ: Rutgers University Press, 1999.

Lecaro, Lina. "'Mandy' Dives Is Pushed into the Mosh Pit." *Los Angeles Times*. June 28, 2001. http://articles.latimes.com/2001/jun/28/entertainment/ca-15838.

Lecaro, Lina. "The 10 Best Punk Rock Documentaries of All Time." *Paste*. July 23, 2015. https://www.pastemagazine.com/articles/2015/07/the-10-best-punk-rock-documentaries-of-all-time.html.

Lee, Michelle. "Oh Bondage Up Yours! The Early Punk Movement—And the Women Who Made It Rock." *Off Our Backs*. November/December 2002.

Lefebvre, Sam. "Bay of Punks: Remembering When Punk Rock Invaded San Francisco." *The Guardian*. February 23, 2017. https://www.theguardian.com/music/2017/feb/23/punk-rock-san-francisco-jim-jocoy-order-of-appearance.

Legaspi, Althea. "Germs Bassist Lorna Doom Dead at 60." *Rolling Stone*. January 16, 2019. https://www.rollingstone.com/music/music-news/germs-bassist-lorna-doom-dead-780323.

Leigh, Mickey. *I Slept with Joey Ramone: A Family Memoir*. New York: Simon and Schuster, 2009.

Leigh, Nathan. "'WTF Is Punk?': Afropunk Bands Fight for the Genre's Soul, and for Our Communities." *Afropunk.com*. August 27, 2017. http://afropunk.com/2017/08/wtf-punk-afropunk-bands-fight-genres-soul-communities.

Leight, Elias. "Pussy Riot Slam Donald Trump in 'Make America Great Again' Video." *Rolling Stone*. October 27, 2016. https://www.rollingstone.com/music/music-news/pussy-riot-slam-donald-trump-in-make-america-great-again-video-126889.

Leland, John. "Tribute: A Star of Anti-Charisma, Joey Ramone Made Geeks Chic." *New York Times*. April 22, 2001. https://www.nytimes.com/2001/04/22/style/tribute-a-star-of-anti-charisma-joey-ramone-made-geeks-chic.html.

Leopold, Todd. "The Worst Song of All Time, Part II." *CNN.com*. April 27, 2006. http://www.cnn.com/2006/SHOWBIZ/Music/04/25/worst.songs/index.html.

Lester, Paul. "The Original Junkie-Punk Richard Hell Revisits *Destiny Street*." *The Guardian*. November 26, 2009. https://www.theguardian.com/music/2009/nov/26/richard-hell-destiny-street-repaired.

Levin, Rachel P. *Feminist Punk Rockers and New Media Fan Communities: How Patti Smith and Carrie Brownstein's Music and Memoirs Kindle a Generation of Music Rebels*. B.A. Thesis, University of California Davis. 2016.

Lim, Louisa. "Louisa Lim: 'I Wanted to Discover How Chinese People Became Complicit in an Act of Mass Amnesia.'" *The Guardian*. July 21, 2015. https://www.theguardian.com/books/booksblog/2015/jul/21/louisa-lim-the-peoples-republic-of-amnesia-tiananmen-revisited-china.

Lipman, Masha. "The Absurd and Outrageous Trial of Pussy Riot." *The New Yorker*. August 7, 2012. https://www.newyorker.com/news/news-desk/the-absurd-and-outrageous-trial-of-pussy-riot.

Liquid Sky. Slava Tsukerman, dir. 1982.

Lister, Kate. "Anarchy in the U.K.: A Brief History of Punk Fashion." *Marie Claire*. October 26, 2015. https://www.marieclaire.co.uk/fashion/a-brief-history-of-punk-fashion-79145.

Little, Michael H. "Graded on a Curve: Richard Hell and the Voidoids, *Blank Generation*." *Vinyl District*. March 27, 2015. http://www.thevinyldistrict.com/storefront/2015/03/graded-on-a-curve-richard-hell-and-the-voidoids-blank-generation.

Lloyd, Richard. *Everything Is Combustible: Television, CBGB's and Five Decades of Rock and Roll: The Memoirs of an Alchemical Guitarist*. Mount Desert, ME: Beech Hill Publishing, 2017.

Lodi, Marie. "Joan Jett and Cherie Currie Respond to Jackie Fox's Rape Allegations." *Jezebel*. July 12, 2015. https://jezebel.com/joan-jett-and-cherie-currie-respond-to-jackie-foxs-rape-1717399575.

Loftus, Johnny. "Green Day: *American Idiot*." *Pitchfork*. September 23, 2004. https://pitchfork.com/reviews/albums/3568-american-idiot.

London Town. Derrick Borte, dir. 2016.

Lovedolls Superstar. David Markey, dir. 1986.

L7: The Beauty Process. Krist Novoselic, dir. 1998.

"L7 Chart History (Alternative Songs)." *Billboard*. June 11, 2018. https://www.billboard.com/music/l7/chart-history/alternative-songs.

Ludwig, Jamie. "From Dead Boy to Plowboy: Cheetah Chrome Says It Like It Is." *Vice: Noisey*. May 16, 2014. https://www.vice.com/en_us/article/rz7ky6/from-dead-boy-to-plowboy-cheetah-chrome-says-it-like-it-is.

Ludwig, Jamie. "Shocking Omissions: The Raw Rock Devotion of the Cramps' 'Songs the Lord Taught Us.'" *NPR*. September 11, 2017. https://www.npr.org/2017/09/11/549725379/shocking-omissions-the-raw-rock-devotion-of-the-cramps-songs-the-lord-taught-us.

Lydon, John. *Anger Is an Energy: My Life Uncensored*. New York: Dey Street Books, 2016.

Lydon, John. *Rotten: No Irish, No Blacks, No Dogs*. London: Hodder & Stoughton, 1993.

Lynskey, Dorian. "Euro Clash." *Sydney Morning Herald*. December 10, 2005. https://www.smh.com.au/entertainment/music/euro-clash-20051210-gdmlll.html.

Lynskey, Dorian. "Green Day: *American Idiot*." *The Guardian* [London]. September 16, 2004. https://www.theguardian.com/music/2004/sep/17/popandrock.shopping2.

Lynskey, Dorian. "Meet the Pro-Bush Punks." *The Guardian* [London]. July 7, 2004. https://www.theguardian.com/music/2004/jul/07/uselections2004.popandrock.

Lyons, Daniel Jack, Cenan Pirani, and Eve Lyons. "The New Punks of Los Angeles." *New York Times*. November 4, 2018. https://www.nytimes.com/2018/11/03/style/new-punks-los-angeles.html.

Lyons, Patrick. "How Bad Brains Created the Best Funk Metal Album 30 Years Ago." *Vice*. December 10, 2016. https://www.vice.com/en_us/article/ypv5kv/bad-brains-created-best-funk-metal-album-30-years-ago.

M., Jordan. "The Stooges: Raw Power." *Sputnik Music*. February 17, 2017. https://www.sputnikmusic.com/review/72941/The-Stooges-Raw-Power.

MacGowan, Shane. *A Drink with Shane MacGowan*. New York: Grove, 2001.

Mackey, Robert, and Glenn Kates. "Russian Riot Grrrls Jailed for 'Punk Prayer.'" *New York Times*. March 7, 2012. https://thelede.blogs.nytimes.com/2012/03/07/russian-riot-grrrls-jailed-for-punk-prayer.

Madani, Doha. "Singer Stops Festival Show to Call Out Sexual Assault in the Crowd." *HuffPost*. August 19, 2017. https://www.huffingtonpost.com/entry/architects-sam-carter-sexual-assault-speech_us_59985ba6e4b0a2608a6ca4d8.

Mahr, Krista. "'We Rebel against the System': Inside Soweto's Thriving Punk Scene." *The Guardian*. December 30, 2017. https://www.theguardian.com/inequality/2017/dec/30/we-rebel-against-the-system-inside-sowetos-thriving-punk-scene.

Maine, Samantha. "Campaign Launched in Support of Tribute Statue to Buzzcocks Frontman Pete Shelley." *NME*. December 16, 2018. https://www.nme.com/news/music/pete-shelley-tribute-statue-2421800.

Mapes, Jillian. "Pop-Punk Keeps Forgiving Sexual Harassers, to the Detriment of Its Teen Girl Fanbase." *Flavorwire*. July 16, 2015. http://flavorwire.com/528083/pop-punk-keeps-forgiving-sexual-harassers-to-the-detriment-of-its-teen-girl-fanbase.

Marchesse, David. "Johnny Marr on the Stooges Record That Changed His Life." *SPIN*. November 27, 2012. https://www.spin.com/2012/11/smiths-johnny-marr-stooges-raw-power-golden-age-vinyl.

Marcus, Greil. *In the Fascist Bathroom: Punk in Pop Music*. Cambridge, MA: Harvard University Press, 1999.

Marcus, Greil. *Lipstick Traces: A Secret History of the 20th Century*. Cambridge, MA: Harvard University Press, 1989.

Marcus, Greil. *Ranters and Crowd Pleasers: Punk in Pop Music 1977–1992*. New York: Doubleday, 1993.

Marcus, Sara. *Girls to the Front: The True Story of the Riot Grrrrl Revolution*. New York: Harper Collins, 2014.

Margasak, Peter. "Various Artists International Pop Underground Convention." *Chicago Tribune*. December 10, 1992. https://www.chicagotribune.com/news/ct-xpm-1992-12-10-9204220588-story.html.

Marr, Johnny. *101 Essential Rock Records: The Golden Age of Vinyl from the Beatles to the Sex Pistols*. Berkeley, CA: Gingko Press, 2013.

Marsh, Dave. "Richard Hell and the Voidoids." In *The Rolling Stone Record Guide*, 1st ed., 168. Edited by Dave Marsh and John Swanson. New York: Random House, 1979.

Marszalek, Julian. "As American as Capote: The Cramps' *Songs the Lord Taught Us* Revisited." *The Quietus*. March 9, 2015. https://thequietus.com/articles/17343-cramps-songs-the-lord-taught-us.

Martin, Dan. "'I Guess This Is Growing Up': Pop Punk Comes of Age (Maybe)." *The Guardian*. August 15, 2016. https://www.theguardian.com/music/2016/aug/15/pop-punk-green-day-blink-182-descendents.

Maslin, Janet. "Miss Spheeris's Punk Verite." *New York Times*. July 5, 1981. https://www.nytimes.com/1981/07/05/movies/miss-spheeris-s-punk-verite.html.

Masseria Faresalento Agriturismo. "Pizzica: The Traditional Dance of Salento." n.d. Accessed September 23, 2018. http://www.agriturismofaresalento.com/categoria-salento.asp/l_en/id_4/pizzica-the-traditional-dance-of-salento.html.

Matheu, Robert, and Jeffrey Morgan. *The Stooges: The Authorized and Illustrated Story*. New York: Harry N. Abrahams, 2009.

Mattioli, Heath, and David Spacone. *Disco's Out . . . Murder's In!: The True Story of Frank the Shank and L.A.'s Deadliest Punk Rock Gang*. Port Townsend, WA: Feral House Publishing, 2015.

McCarthy, Amy. "Punched, Groped, Beer Thrown in My Face: Being a Woman at a Concert Can Be Terrifying." *Salon*. May 6, 2015. https://www.salon.com/2015/05/06/punched_groped_beer_thrown_in_my_face_being_a_woman_at_a_concert_can_be_terrifying/.

McCarthy, Kerry. "Inside the Pussy Riot Trial." *HuffPost*. August 10, 2012. https://www.huffingtonpost.co.uk/kerry-mccarthy/inside-the-pussy-riot-trial_b_1757581.html?guccounter=1.

McClain, Buzz. "Rechanneling Their Passion." *Washington Post*. March 11, 2007. https://www.washingtonpost.com/wp-dyn/content/article/2007/03/09/AR2007030900491.html.

McDonnell, Evelyn. "Bikini Kill, Then and Now: A Front-Row View of a Punk Revolution." *New York Times*. May 3, 2019. https://www.nytimes.com/2019/05/03/arts/music/bikini-kill-live.html?action=click&module=RelatedLinks&pgtype=Article.

McDonnell, Evelyn. *Queens of Noise: The Real Story of the Runaways*. New York: Da Capo Press, 2013.

McDonnell, Evelyn, and Ann Powers, eds. *Rock She Wrote: Women Write about Rock, Pop, and Rap*. New York: Dell, 1995.

McDonnell, Evelyn, and Elizabeth Vincentelli. "Riot Grrrl United Feminism and Punk: Here's an Essential Listening Guide." *New York Times*. May 26, 2019. https://www.nytimes.com/interactive/2019/05/03/arts/music/riot-grrrl-playlist.html.

McGartland, Tony. *Buzzcocks: The Complete History*. London: John Blake Publishing, 2017.

McLeese, Don. *The MC5's Kick Out The Jams (33 1/3)*. New York: Continuum, 2005.

McLeod, Kimbrew. *Blondie's Parallel Lines (33 1/3)*. New York: Continuum, 2016.

McMahon, James. "Buzzcocks: The Brilliant Punk Band's Ten Best Songs." *NME*. December 13, 2018. https://www.nme.com/blogs/nme-blogs/buzzcocks-10-best-greatest-songs-tracks-singles-2420137#1qespV456fOg8t1c.99.

McMahon, James. "Pete Shelley: A Musical Pioneer Who Gave Us Lusty, Essential Punk Pop." *NME*. December 7, 2018. https://www.nme.com/blogs/nme-blogs/pete-shelley-musical-pioneer-gave-us-lusty-essential-punk-pop-2417762.

McNeil, Donald G. "Pornography and AIDS: A History." *New York Times*. November 5, 2012. https://www.nytimes.com/2012/11/06/health/porn-and-aids-a-history.html.

McNeil, Legs, and Gillian McCain. *Please Kill Me: The Uncensored Oral History of Punk*. New York: Grove Press, 1996.

Me First and the Gimmie Gimmies. "'Danny's Song' (Official Video)." *YouTube*. March 8, 2012. https://www.youtube.com/watch?v=cJ3M7DgBqA0.

"Me First and the Gimmie Gimmies." *Fat Wreck Chords*. Accessed October 6, 2020. https://fatwreck.com/collections/me-first-and-the-gimme-gimmes?view=artist.

Me First and the Gimmie Gimmies. "'I Believe I Can Fly' (Official Video)." *YouTube*. March 11, 2013. https://www.youtube.com/watch?v=vV3XQcCyyPc.

"Me First and the Gimme Gimmes: Chart History." *Billboard*. September 13, 2018. https://www.billboard.com/music/me-first-and-the-gimme-gimmes.

"Meet Me at 9:30: A History of DC's 9:30 Club." *Washington DC*. Accessed January 22, 2020. https://washington.org/visit-dc/930-club-history-washington-dc.

Mejia, Paula. "The 150 Greatest Albums Made by Women: X-Ray Spex: *Germfree Adolescents* (EMI, 1978)." *NPR*. July 24, 2017. https://www.npr

.org/2017/07/24/538354042/turning-the-tables-150-greatest-albums-made-by-women-page-10.

Mendock, Clark. "Trump's Sexual Assault Allegations: The Full List of Women Who Have Accused the President." *The Independent* [London]. December 2, 2019. https://www.independent.co.uk/news/world/americas/us-politics/trump-sexual-assault-allegations-all-list-misconduct-karen-johnson-how-many-a9149216.html.

Metcalf, Stephen. "Debunking Punk: What the Clash Meant to Rock 'n' Roll." *Slate*. February 22, 2005. https://slate.com/culture/2005/02/the-clash-less-punk-than-you-think.html.

Metcalf, Stephen. "The Messy History of Postpunk." *Slate*. March 6, 2006. https://slate.com/culture/2006/03/the-messy-history-of-postpunk.html.

Miller, Gary. *Anarcho Punk Albums: The Band's Story behind Anarchist Punk Music*. n.p.: Independently Published, 2018.

The Million Eyes of Sumuru. Lindsay Shonteff, dir. 1967.

Miret, Roger. *My Riot: Agnostic Front, Grit, Guts & Glory*. New York: Lesser Gods Books, 2017.

Mirovalev, Mansur. "A Guide to Pussy Riot's Oeuvre." *Washington Times*. August 18, 2012. https://www.washingtontimes.com/news/2012/aug/18/a-guide-to-pussy-riots-oeuvre.

"Mission." *Gogol Bordello*. December 12, 2018. http://www.gogolbordello.com.

Moeschen, Sheila. "Pussy Riot Proves We Are Not Having a Post-Feminist Moment." *HuffPost*. February 21, 2014. https://www.huffpost.com/entry/pussy-riot-proves-we-are-not-having-a-post-feminist-moment_b_4832117.

Mohr, Tom. *Burning Down the Haus: Punk Rock, Revolution, and the Fall of the Berlin Wall*. New York: Algonquin Books, 2018.

Molon, Dominic. *Sympathy for the Devil: Art and Rock and Roll Since 1967*. New Haven, CT: Yale University Press, 2007. 76.

Monk, Clair. "'Now What Are We Going to Call You? Scum! . . . Scum! That's Commercial! It's All They Deserve!': Jubilee, Punk and British Film in the Late 1970s." In *Seventies British Cinema*. Edited by R. Shail. London: BFI/Palgrave MacMillan, 2008.

Moore, Thurston. "Thurston Moore's Top 10 Punk Rock Films." *BFI*. June 8, 2018. https://www.bfi.org.uk/news-opinion/sight-sound-magazine/features/thurston-moores-top-10-punk-rock-films.

Moran, Chris. "Social Distortion: White Light, White Heat, White Trash (1996)." *Punknews.org*. December 17, 2002. https://www.punknews.org/review/1510/social-distortion-white-light-white-heat-white-trash.

Moran, Fran. "Rum, Sodomy, and the Lash." *The Parting Glass: An Annotated Pogues Lyrics Page*. January 28, 2005. http://www.poguetry.com/rsl.htm.

Moran, Lee. "Protestors Want Green Day's 'American Idiot' to Top UK Chart for Trump Visit." *HuffPost*. May 1, 2018. https://www.huffpost.com/entry/donald-trump-uk-visit-american-idiot_n_5ae8334ee4b055fd7fcf4fab.

Moreland, Quinn. "Alice Bag: *Alice Bag*." *Pitchfork*. July 5, 2016. https://pitchfork.com/reviews/albums/22069-alice-bag/.

Morley, Paul. "Siouxsie Sioux: 'I've Always Felt on the Outside'—A Classic Interview from the Vaults." *The Guardian* [London]. October 16, 2012. https://www.theguardian.com/music/2012/oct/16/siouxsie-banshees-classic-interview.

Morris, Keith. *My Damage: The Story of a Punk Rock Survivor*. Cambridge, MA: Da Capo Press, 2016.

Morse, Eric, and Anny Yi. *What Is Punk?* Jacksonville, FL: Black Sheep Books, 2015.

Moskowitz, David V. *Caribbean Popular Music*. Westport, CT: Greenwood Press, 2006.

Moss, Corey. "Reznor, Kayne, Green Day Reflect on Disaster, Inspire Relief for MTV Special." *MTV News*. September 10, 2005. http://www.mtv.com/news/1509302/reznor-kanye-green-day-reflect-on-disaster-inspire-relief-for-mtv-special.

Mott, Toby. *Oh So Pretty: Punk in Print 1976–1980*. New York: Phaidon Press, 2016.

MTV News Staff. "Jim Carroll Guests on New Rancid Album." May 4, 1995. http://www.mtv.com/news/505915/jim-carroll-guests-on-new-rancid-album.

Mullen, Brendan. "Annihilation Man." *LA Weekly*. December 27, 2000. https://www.laweekly.com/news/annihilation-man-2132852.

Mullen, Brendan. *Lexicon Devil: The Fast Times and Short Life of Darby Crash and the Germs*. Port Townsend, WA: Feral House, 2002.

Mullen, Brendan. *Live at the Masque: Nightmare in Punk Alley*. Berkeley, CA: Gingko Press, 2007.

Mullen, Brendan, and Marc Spitz. "Sit on My Face, Stevie Nicks!: The Germs, Darby Crash, and the Birth of SoCal Punk." *SPIN* 17(5) (May 2001): 106.

Muñoz, José Esteban. "'The White to Be Angry': Vaginal Davis's Terrorist Drag." *Social Text* (52/53) (1997): 81–103.

Murphy, John L. "Imagine If Crass Was Funny: Dead Kennedys: *Fresh Fruit for Rotting Vegetables*." *PopMatters*. June 13, 2014. https://www.popmatters.com/182738-alex-oggs-dead-kennedys-fresh-fruit-for-rotting-vegetables-the-early-2495649731.html.

Murphy, Tom. "Mojo Nixon: 'I Am Here to Set the World Straight about Tim Tebow and His Invisible Friends!'" *Westword*. April 11, 2012. https://www.westword.com/music/mojo-nixon-i-am-here-to-set-the-world-straight-about-tim-tebow-and-his-invisible-friends-5678585.

Murray, Charles Shaar. "No Pop, No Style Poly Styrene Is Still Strictly Roots." *NME*. May 13, 1978. Archived on the *Wayback Machine* October 27, 2009. https://web.archive.org/web/20091027102504/http://www.geocities.com/vintageinterviews/xrayspex.html.

Murray, Charles Shaar. "Weird Sounds inside Gasoline Alley." *NME*. November 1975. http://www.oceanstar.com/patti/crit/7511nme.htm.

Murray, Noel. "The Taqwacores." *AV Club*. October 21, 2010. https://film.avclub.com/the-taqwacores-1798166303.

Muther, Chris. "Shonen Knife Makes Its Point with Positive Punk." *Boston Globe*. March 9, 2005. http://archive.boston.com/ae/music/articles/2005/03/09/shonen_knife_makes_its_point_with_positive_punk.

Myers, Michele. "The 150 Greatest Albums Made by Women: X: *Los Angeles* (Slash/Rhino, 1980)." *NPR*. July 24, 2017. https://www.npr.org/2017/07/24/538357708/turning-the-tables-150-greatest-albums-made-by-women-page-7.

Nark, Jason. "Remembering Philly's Legendary, All-Black Punk Pioneers." *The Inquirer* [Philadelphia]. February 27, 2017. https://www.inquirer.com/philly/news/pennsylvania/Remembering-pure-hell-Phillys-Black-punk-pioneers.html.

National Coalition for the Homeless. "LGBT Homelessness." 2018. Accessed December 31, 2018. https://nationalhomeless.org/issues/lgbt.

Natural Born Killers. Quentin Tarantino, dir. 1994.

Needs, Kris, and Dick Porter. *Blondie Parallel Lives*. London: Omnibus Press, 2019.

New York Doll. Greg Whiteley, dir. 2005.

Nichols, Natalie. "Black Flag in Weekend Salute to Early Years." *Los Angeles Times*. September 15, 2003. http://articles.latimes.com/2003/sep/15/entertainment/et-nichols15.

Night of the Living Dead. George A. Romero, dir. 1968.

Nikita. "Dropkick Murphys Announce New Album and Brixton Academy Show." *PlanetMosh*. November 3, 2016. https://planetmosh.com/dropkick-murphys-announce-new-album.

1991: The Year Punk Broke. Dave Markey, dir. 1992.

"1997 Fruitopia Commercial." *YouTube*. December 9, 2011. https://www.youtube.com/watch?v=gKcrzy8acj4.

NOFX. *NOFX: The Hepatitis Bathtub and Other Stories*. Cambridge, MA: Da Capo Press, 2016.

Noisey Staff. "Top 25 Albums of 2014." *Vice: Noisey*. December 19, 2014. https://www.vice.com/en_us/article/rgpppy/noisey-staff-top-25-albums-of-2014-10-to-1.

O'Brien, Lucy. *She Bop: The Definitive History of Women in Rock, Pop and Soul*. New York: Penguin, 1996.

O'Brien, Lucy. *She Bop II: The Definitive History of Women in Rock, Pop, and Soul*. New York: Continuum, 2002.

O'Connor, Alan. "Punk Subculture in Mexico and the Anti-Globalization Movement: A Report from the Front." *New Political Science* 25(1) (2003): 43–53.

O'Connor, Mickey. "The 100 Best Album Covers Ever." *Entertainment Weekly*. March 19, 2001. https://ew.com/article/2001/03/19/100-best-album-covers-ever.

O'Falt, Chris. "Kathleen Hanna on Riot Grrrl, Feminism and New Doc 'The Punk Singer' (Q&A)." *Hollywood Reporter*. November 29, 2013. https://www.hollywoodreporter.com/news/kathleen-hanna-riot-grrrl-feminism-660601.

Official Charts. "Damned." Accessed November 5, 2019. https://www.officialcharts.com/artist/17625/damned.

Ogg, Alex. *Dead Kennedys: Fresh Fruit for Rotting Vegetables: The Early Years*. Oakland, CA: PM Press, 2014.

O'Hara, Craig. *The Philosophy of Punk: More Than Noise*. Chico, CA: AK Press, 2001.

Ohlheiser, Abby. "'I Can't Breathe': Pussy Riot's First Song in English Is about Eric Garner." *Washington Post*. February 18, 2015. https://www.washingtonpost.com/news/arts-and-entertainment/wp/2015/02/18/i-cant-breathe-pussy-riots-first-song-in-english-is-about-eric-garner.

O'Meara, Caroline. 2003. "The Raincoats: Breaking Down Punk Rock's Masculinities." *Popular Music* 22(3): 299–313.

"100 Best Albums of the Eighties." *Rolling Stone*. November 16, 1989. https://www.rollingstone.com/music/music-lists/100-best-albums-of-the-eighties-150477/xtc-skylarking-67641.

"100 Greatest Artists: The Clash." *Rolling Stone*. December 2, 2010. https://www.rollingstone.com/music/music-lists/100-greatest-artists-147446/the-clash-91542.

"100 Greatest Guitarists of All Time." *SPIN*. May 3, 2012. https://www.spin.com/2012/05/spins-100-greatest-guitarists-all-time.

"1,000 Albums to Hear before You Die." *The Guardian* [London]. November 23, 2007. https://www.theguardian.com/music/2007/nov/23/1000toheartbeforeyoudie.

O'Neil, Luke. "No More Silence: Sexual Harassment in the Scene." *AltPress*. October 26, 2015. https://www.altpress.com/features/no_more_silence_sexual_harassment_in_the_scene.

Organization for Security and Co-Operation in Europe. "Russia's Presidential Election Marked by Unequal Campaign Conditions, Active Citizens' Engagement, International Observers Say." March 5, 2012. https://www.osce.org/odihr/elections/88661.

Osgerby, Bill. "Silver Screen Sedition: Auteurship and Exploitation in the History of Punk Cinema." In *Fight Back: Punk, Politics, and Resistance*, 205–231. Edited by the Subcultures Network. Manchester, UK: Manchester University Press, 2014.

The Other "F" Word. Andrea Blaugrund Nevins, dir. 2011.

Our Nation: A Korean Punk Rock Community. Stephen Epstein and Timothy R. Tangherlini, dirs. 2002.

Ozzi, Dan. "Major Label Debut: Punk's 'Sell Out' Albums Revisited." *Vice: Noisey*. April 2, 2015. https://www.vice.com/en_us/article/rkqwqy/major-label-debut-punks-sell-out-albums-revisited.

Ozzi, Dan. "Raise Your Fist and Blood Pressure with War on Women's 'Capture the Flag.'" *Vice: Noisey*. April 9, 2018. https://www.vice.com/en_us/article/vbxyqb/war-on-women-capture-the-flag-album-stream.

Palaniuk, Chuck. *Fight Club*. New York: W. W. Norton, 1996.

Pansy Division: Live in a Gay Rock Band. Michael Carmona, dir. 2008.

Panzar, Javier. "It's Official: Latinos Now Outnumber Whites in California." *Los Angeles Times*. July 8, 2015. https://www.latimes.com/local/california/la-me-census-latinos-20150708-story.html.

Pappademas, Alex. "Green Day: The 2004 'American Idiot' Cover Story." *SPIN*. September 25, 2014. Originally published in *SPIN* in November 2004. https://www.spin.com/2014/09/green-day-2004-american-idiot-cover-story.

Pareles, Jon. "Pop Review: No Debutant, Blondie Returning to Its Roots." *New York Times*. February 25, 1999. https://www.nytimes.com/1999/02/25/arts/pop-review-no-debutante-blondie-returns-to-its-roots.html.

Parmar, Priya, Anthony J. Nocella, Scott Robertson, and Martha Diaz. *Rebel Music: Resistance through Hip Hop and Punk*. Charlotte, NC: Information Age Publishing, 2014.

Partridge, Kenneth. "The Clash's *London Calling* at 35: Classic Track-by-Track Album Review." *Billboard*. December 13, 2014. https://www.billboard.com/articles/review/album-review/6406102/the-clashs-london-calling-at-35-classic-track-by-track-album-review.

Paytress, Mark. *Siouxsie and the Banshees: The Authorized Biography*. London: Sanctuary Publishing, 2003.

Peake, Steve. "Top 10 X Songs." *LiveAbout*. December 20, 2019. https://www.liveabout.com/x-songs-80s-10422.

Peake, Tony. "*Jubilee*." Criterion Collection. May 26, 2003. https://www.criterion.com/current/posts/267-jubilee.

Pell, Nicholas. "Unpopular Opinion: How Can Anyone Not Love Me First and the Gimme Gimmes?" *LA Weekly*. January 31, 2017. https://www.laweekly.com/unpopular-opinion-how-can-anyone-not-love-me-first-and-the-gimme-gimmes.

Pelly, Jenn. "Hundreds of Punks Hit the Desert: The Modern Music Festival Was Born." *New York Times*. January 24, 2019. https://www.nytimes.com/2019/01/24/arts/music/desolation-center-punk-desert-concert-film.html.

Pelly, Jenn. "The Raincoats' Debut Album Is a Classic DIY Document." *Pitchfork*. September 26, 2017. https://pitchfork.com/features/article/the-raincoats-debut-album-is-a-classic-diy-document.

Pelly, Jenn. *The Raincoats' The Raincoats (33 1/3)*. New York: Continuum, 2017.

Pelly, Jenn. "War on Women: *Capture the Flag*." *Pitchfork*. April 17, 2018. https://pitchfork.com/reviews/albums/war-on-women-capture-the-flag.

Pelly, Jenn. "X-Ray Spex: Germfree Adolescents." *Pitchfork*. January 15, 2017. https://pitchfork.com/reviews/albums/22316-germfree-adolescents.

Penny, Laurie. "Pussy Riot: 'People Fear Us because We're Feminists.'" June 22, 2013. *New Statesman*. https://www.newstatesman.com/politics/2013/06/pussy-riot-people-fear-us-because-were-feminists.

Petridis, Alexis. "Misunderstood or Hateful? Oi!'s Rise and Fall." *The Guardian* [London]. March 18, 2010. https://www.theguardian.com/music/2010/mar/18/oi-cockney-rejects-garry-bushell-interview.

Petridis, Alexis. "The Slits' Viv Albertine on Punk, Violence, and Doomed Domesticity." *The Guardian* [London]. June 1, 2014. https://www.theguardian.com/music/2014/jun/01/the-slits-viv-albertine-punk-violence-domesticity.

Petrusich, Amanda. "A Transcendent Patti Smith Accepts Bob Dylan's Nobel Prize." *The New Yorker*. December 10, 2016. https://www.newyorker.com/culture/cultural-comment/a-transcendent-patti-smith-accepts-bob-dylans-nobel-prize.

Petrusich, Amanda. "Where Punk Rock Begins." *The New Yorker*. September 15, 2016. https://www.newyorker.com/culture/cultural-comment/where-punk-rock-begins.

Phares, Heather. "X: The Unheard Music." *AllMusic*. n.d. Accessed December 20, 2019. https://www.AllMusic.com/song/the-unheard-music-mt0008900587.

Phillip, Abby. "Unearthing a Deadly Secret: Were 57 Irish Workers Murdered in 1832 Pennsylvania?" *Washington Post*. October 8, 2015. https://www.washingtonpost.com/news/morning-mix/wp/2015/10/08/unearthing-a-deadly-secret-were-57-irish-workers-murdered-in-1832-pennsylvania.

Phillips, Amy, and Evan Minsker. "Bikini Kill Announce Reunion Tour." *Pitchfork*. January 15, 2019. https://pitchfork.com/news/bikini-kill-announce-reunion-tour.

Phillips, Lior. "The 50 Albums That Shaped Punk Rock: Sixouxie and the Banshees: *The Scream* (1978)." *Consequence of Sound*. January 7, 2018. https://consequenceofsound.net/2018/01/the-50-albums-that-shaped-punk-rock/2.

Piccoli, Sean. "Sound and Fury of the Clash Continues with a Vast Legacy." *SunSentinel* [Broward and Palm Beach, Florida]. January 3, 2003. https://www.sun-sentinel.com/news/fl-xpm-2003-01-03-0212311010-story.html.

Pickard, Joshua. "Record Bin: The Relentless Hardcore Frenzy of Bad Brains' Self-titled Debut." *Nooga Today*. March 19, 2016. https://noogatoday.6amcity.com/record-bin-the-relentless-hardcore-frenzy-of-bad-brains-self-titled-debut.

Pitchfork. "Staff Lists: Top 100 Albums of the 1970s." June 23, 2004. https://pitchfork.com/features/lists-and-guides/5932-top-100-albums-of-the-1970s.

Plagenhoef, Scott. "Blondie: *Parallel Lines: Deluxe Edition*." *Pitchfork*. July 22, 2018. https://pitchfork.com/reviews/albums/12058-parallel-lines-deluxe-edition.

Plagenhoef, Scott. "Staff Lists: Top 100 Albums of the 1970s." *Pitchfork*. June 23, 2004. https://pitchfork.com/features/lists-and-guides/5932-top-100-albums-of-the-1970s/?page=9.

"The Pogues." In *The Rolling Stone Encyclopedia of Rock and Roll*, 3rd ed., 767–768. Edited by Holly George-Warren and Patricia Romanowski. New York: Fireside, 2001.

Poly Styrene: I Am a Cliché. Paul Sng, dir. In production.

Pop, Iggy. *'Til Wrong Feels Right: Lyrics and More*. New York: Clarkson Potter, 2019.

Pop, Iggy, and Anne Wehner. *I Need More: The Stooges and Other Stories*. Los Angeles: 2.13.61 Publishing, 1997.

Popoff, Martin. *Punk Tees: The Punk Revolution in 125 T-Shirts*. New York: Sterling, 2016.

Porter, Dick. *The Cramps: A Short Rock n Roll History*. Medford, NJ: Plexus 2007.

Porter, Dick. *Journey to the Centre of the Cramps*. London: Omnibus Press, 2015.

Porter, Dick, and Kris Needs. *Blondie: Parallel Lives*. London: Omnibus Press, 2016.

Portwood, Jerry. "Pansy Division's Jon Ginoli on Gay Punk Band's 25th Anniversary, New LP." *Rolling Stone*. August 6, 2016. https://www.rollingstone.com/music/music-features/pansy-divisions-jon-ginoli-on-gay-punk-bands-25th-anniversary-new-lp-115903.

Post-Punk.com. "Spatsz from French Coldwave Duo Kas Product Has Passed Away." February 2, 2019. https://www.post-punk.com/spatsz-from-french-coldwave-duo-kas-product-has-passed-away.

Potter, John. *The Cambridge Companion to Singing*. Cambridge, UK: Cambridge University Press, 2000.

Powell, Mike. "The Raincoats." *Pitchfork*. July 9, 2013. https://pitchfork.com/features/secondhands/9166-the-raincoats.

Powers, Ann. "No Longer Rock's Playthings." *New York Times*. February 14, 1993. https://www.nytimes.com/1993/02/14/arts/pop-music-no-longer-rock-s-playthings.html.

Powers, Ann. "Songs That Say 'Me Too.'" *All Songs Considered*. NPR. October 17, 2017. https://www.npr.org/sections/allsongs/2017/10/17/558098166/songs-that-say-me-too.

Powers, Ann. "Turning the Tables: The 150 Greatest Albums Made By Women (As Chosen By You)." *NPR*. July 24, 2017. https://www.npr.org/2018/04/09/600116052/turning-the-tables-the-150-greatest-albums-made-by-women-as-chosen-by-you.

Prato, Greg. "Dead Boys: Biography." *AllMusic*. n.d. Accessed December 18, 2019. https://www.AllMusic.com/artist/dead-boys-mn0000140689/biography.

Prato, Greg. "Dead Boys Come to Life." *Rolling Stone*. January 25, 2005. https://www.rollingstone.com/music/music-news/dead-boys-come-to-life-107351.

Prato, Greg. "Dead Kennedys' East Bay Ray on Their Explosive Live Legacy—And His Hopes for Jello Biafra." *Billboard*. April 10, 2019. https://www.billboard.com/articles/columns/rock/8506510/dead-kennedys-east-bay-ray-dk40-live.
Prato, Greg. "Paul Simonon: Biography." *AllMusic*. n.d. June 23, 2018. https://www.allmusic.com/artist/paul-simonon-mn0000026250/biography.
Prato, Greg. "Topper Headon: Biography." *AllMusic*. n.d. June 23, 2018. https://www.allmusic.com/artist/topper-headon-mn0000134739/biography.
Prato, Greg. "X: *Los Angeles*." *AllMusic*. n.d. December 20, 2019. https://www.AllMusic.com/album/los-angeles-mw0000319061.
Prindle, Marc. "A Tribute to Tributes to the Ramones." *SPIN* (April 2009): 62.
Proefrock, Stacia. "Gogol Bordello: Biography." *AllMusic*. n.d. June 19, 2018. https://www.allmusic.com/artist/gogol-bordello-mn0000670273/biography.
Punk. Jesse James Miller, dir. Epix. 2019.
Punk: Attitude. Don Letts, dir. 2005.
Punk: Chaos to Couture. Metropolitan Museum of Art. New York. 2013. https://www.metmuseum.org/exhibitions/listings/2013/punk.
Punk in Africa. Deon Maas and Keith Jones, dir. 2013.
The Punk Rock Movie. Don Letts, dir. 1978.
Punk77. "Dead Boys." n.d. Accessed December 18, 2019. http://www.punk77.co.uk/groups/deadboys.htm.
Punk77. "Siouxsie and the Banshees." n.d. Accessed August 26, 2020. http://www.punk77.co.uk/groups/banshees.htm.
The Punk Singer. Sini Anderson, dir. 2013.
The Punk Syndrome. Jukka Kärkkäinen and Jani-Petteri Passi, dirs. 2012.
Punk's Not Dead. Susan Dynner, dir. 2007.
Pussy Riot. "Chaika." *YouTube*. February 3, 2016. https://www.youtube.com/watch?v=VakUHHUSdf8.
"Pussy Riot Found Guilty of Hooliganism by Moscow Court." *The Guardian*. August 17, 2012. https://www.theguardian.com/world/2012/aug/17/pussy-riot-found-guilty-hooliganism.
Pussy Riot. "Gig at Christ the Savior Cathedral (Original Video)." *YouTube*. July 2, 2012. https://www.youtube.com/watch?v=grEBLskpDWQ.
Pussy Riot. "Organs." *YouTube*. October 26, 2016. https://www.youtube.com/watch?v=dTmNxp3e4m4.
Pussy Riot. "Original Protest Videos: Obscurity Stunt." *YouTube*. September 6, 2012. https://www.youtube.com/playlist?list=PLM-gAbrrlEaU1p1rkai8D4GdA09wZgE_x.
Pussy Riot: A Punk Prayer. Mike Lerner and Maxim Pozdorovkin, dirs. 2013.
Pussy Riot! A Punk Prayer for Freedom. New York: Feminist Press, 2013.
Pussy Riot. "Straight Outta Vagina." *YouTube*. October 26, 2016. https://www.youtube.com/watch?v=Bp-KeVBNz0A.
Quantick, David. *The Clash: Kill Your Idols*. London: Unanimous, 2000.

Queens of British Pop. BBC One. April 1, 2009.
Queer as Punk. BBC Radio 6.
Queercore: How to Punk a Revolution. Yony Leyser, dir. 2017.
Rabid, Jack. "Bad Religion: *Stranger Than Fiction*." *AllMusic*. n.d. Accessed December 20, 2019. https://www.allmusic.com/album/stranger-than-fiction-mw0000121096.
Rachalis, Kit. "Plastic Letters." *Rolling Stone*. April 7, 1982. https://www.rollingstone.com/music/music-album-reviews/plastic-letters-121381.
Raggett, Ned. "The Damned: 'Neat, Neat, Neat.'" *Allmusic*. November 2, 2019. https://www.allmusic.com/song/neat-neat-neat-mt0014023343.
Raggett, Ned. "Misfits: Walk among Us." AllMusic. n.d. Accessed July 7, 2018. https://www.allmusic.com/album/walk-among-us-mw0000197473.
Raha, Maria. *Cinderella's Big Score: Women of the Punk and Indie Underground*. Emeryville, CA: Seal Press, 2005.
"The Raincoats." In *The Rolling Stone Encyclopedia of Rock and Roll*, 3rd ed., 801. Edited by Holly George-Warren and Patricia Romanowski. New York: Fireside, 2001.
Ramirez, AJ. "Green Day—All about Dookie, 'Longview.'" *PopMatters*. December 4, 2009. https://www.popmatters.com/116819-green-day-all-about-dookie-longview-2496133631.html.
Ramirez, AJ. "Nice Guys Finish Last: The Top 15 Green Day Songs." *PopMatters*. September 19, 2012. https://www.popmatters.com/162725-nice-guys-finish-last-the-top-15-green-day-songs-2495820460.html.
Ramirez, Carlos. "War on Women Get Their Sports on in 'Capture the Flag' Music Video (Premiere)." *No Echo*. May 7, 2019. https://www.noecho.net/features/war-on-women-capture-the-flag.
Ramone, Dee Dee. *Lobotomy: Surviving the Ramones*. New York: Thunders Mouth Press, 2000.
Ramone, Johnny. *Commando: The Autobiography of Johnny Ramone*. New York: Harry N. Abrams, 2012.
Ramone, Marky. *Punk Rock Blitzkrieg: My Life as a Ramone*. New York: Atria, 2016.
"Ramones." *Rock and Roll Hall of Fame*. 2002. https://www.rockhall.com/inductees/ramones.
Rankin, Jennifer. "Pussy Riot Case Likened to Stalin Show Trials." *Irish Times* [Dublin]. August 9, 2012. https://www.irishtimes.com/news/pussy-riot-case-likened-to-stalin-show-trials-1.533129.
Raposa, David. "Metal Urbain: *Anarchy in Paris!*" *Pitchfork*. February 8, 2005. https://pitchfork.com/reviews/albums/11785-anarchy-in-paris-tokio-airport.
Raw Power. CBS Records. 1997. Liner notes.
Ray, Ruby. *Ruby Ray: Kalifornia Kool: Photographs 1976–1982*. New York: Trapart Books, 2019.

"Reader's Poll: Green Day's Best Songs." *Rolling Stone*. September 26, 2012. https://www.rollingstone.com/music/music-lists/readers-poll-green-days-best-songs-10928/1-jesus-of-suburbia-223286.

Redding, Dan. "Fugazi Still Performs Privately, According to Ian MacKaye." *Culture Creature*. January 19, 2017. https://www.culturecreature.com/fugazi-reunion.

Reddington, Helen. *The Lost Women of Rock Music: Female Musicians of the Punk Era*. Farnham, UK: Ashgate Publishing, 2007.

Reed, Ryan. "See Pussy Riot's Nadya Take Literal Blood Bath in 'Organs' Video." *Rolling Stone*. October 26, 2016. https://www.rollingstone.com/music/music-news/see-pussy-riots-nadya-take-literal-blood-bath-in-organs-video-107353.

Reich, Wilhelm. *The Function of Orgasm: Discovery of the Orgone*. New York: Orgone Institute Press, 1942.

Reighley, Kurt B. "French-Fried Punk: Métal Urbain: The Seminal Act Few Have Heard." *The Stranger*. March 25, 2004. https://www.thestranger.com/seattle/french-fried-punk/Content?oid=17564.

Reilly, Nick. "Buzzcocks Back Campaign to Get 'Ever Fallen in Love . . .' to Number One after Pete Shelley's Death." *NME*. December 10, 2018. https://www.nme.com/news/music/buzzcocks-back-campaign-to-get-ever-fallen-in-love-with-someone-you-shouldntve-to-number-one-after-pete-shelleys-death-2418717.

Repo Man. Alex Cox, dir. 1984.

Rettman, Tony. *NYHC: New York Hardcore 1980–1990*. New York: Bazillion Points, 2014.

Rettman, Tony. *Straight Edge: A Clear-Headed Hardcore Punk History*. New York: Bazillion Points, 2017.

Rettman, Tony, and Tesco Vee. *Why Be Something That You're Not: Detroit Hardcore 1979–1985*. New York: Revelation Records, 2010.

Return of the Living Dead. Dan O'Bannon, dir. 1985.

Reynolds, Simon. "The First Sensitive Punk: Remembering Buzzcocks' Pete Shelley." *Pitchfork*. December 8, 2018. https://pitchfork.com/features/afterword/the-first-sensitive-punk-remembering-buzzcocks-pete-shelley.

Reynolds, Simon. *Rip It Up and Start Again: Postpunk 1978–1984*. London: Faber and Faber, 2009.

Reynolds, Simon. *Sex Revolts: Gender, Rebellion, and Rock 'n' Roll*. Cambridge, MA: Harvard University Press, 1996.

Reynolds, Simon. *Totally Wired: Postpunk Interviews and Overviews*. London: Faber and Faber, 2009.

Richards, Chris. "Bikini Kill Was a Girl Punk Group ahead of Its Time." *Washington Post*. September 18, 2012. https://www.washingtonpost.com/lifestyle/style/bikini-kill-was-a-girl-punk-group-ahead-of-its-time/2012/11/18/3fdc61bc-31d8-11e2-bfd5-e202b6d7b501_story.html.

Riefe, Jordan. "Slash: The LA Punk Fanzine That Was Too Snotty to Live." *The Guardian*. September 23, 2016. https://www.theguardian.com/music/2016/sep/23/slash-los-angeles-punk-fanzine.

Riot on the Dance Floor. Steve Tozzi, dir. 2014.

"Rip It to Shreds: A History of Punk and Style." *Pitchfork*. Accessed January 14, 2020. https://pitchfork.com/features/from-our-partners/9943-rip-it-to-shreds-a-history-of-punk-and-style.

The Rise and Fall of the Clash. Danny Garcia, dir. 2012.

Rivera, Erica. "Erica Rivera Interviews Shonen Knife." *Erica Rivera, Writer*. September 16, 2014. http://www.ericarivera.net/2014/09/.

Roach, Martin. *This Is It: the First Biography of the Strokes*. London: Omnibus Press, 2003.

Robb, John. *Punk Rock: An Oral History*. Oakland, CA: PM Press, 2012.

Robbins, Ira. "Black Flag." *Trouser Press*. July 27, 2018. http://trouserpress.com/entry.php?a=black_flag.

Roberts, Randall. "'Nobody in That Room Knew What to Do': Former Runaways Bassist Jackie Fox Discusses Rape Allegations." *Los Angeles Times*. July 15, 2015. https://www.latimes.com/entertainment/music/la-et-ms-0715-jackie-fox-runaways-fowley-rape-interview-20150715-story.html.

Roberts, Randall. "On Alice Bag's New Album, *Blueprint*, an Original L.A. Punk Sets Out to Correct the Historical Record." *Los Angeles Times*. March 27, 2018. https://www.latimes.com/entertainment/music/la-et-ms-alice-bag-20180327-story.html.

Robinson, Charlotte. "So Tough: The Boy behind the Sid Vicious Myth." *PopMatters*. June 14, 2006. https://www.popmatters.com/060809-sidvicious-2496104849.html.

"*Rock 'n' Roll High School* (1979)." *Rotten Tomatoes*. Accessed June 15, 2018. https://rottentomatoes.com/m/1017745_rock_n_roll_high_school.

Rockwell, John. "Experimental Rock. Vigorous in Britain." *New York Times*. January 14, 1979. https://www.nytimes.com/1979/01/14/archives/experimental-rock-vigorous-in-britain.html.

Rockwell, John. "Patti Smith: Horses." *Rolling Stone*. February 12, 1976. https://www.rollingstone.com/music/music-album-reviews/horses-90476/.

Rockwell, John. "The Pop Life; *London Calling* Helps the Clash Live up to Billing." *New York Times*. January 4, 1980. https://www.nytimes.com/1980/01/04/archives/the-pop-life-london-calling-helps-the-clash-live-up-to-billing.html.

Roffman, Michael. "R. I. P. Pete Shelley, Frontman of the Buzzcocks Dead at 63." *Consequence of Sound*. December 6, 2018. https://consequenceofsound.net/2018/12/pete-shelley-buzzcocks-dead.

Rolling Stone. "500 Greatest Albums of All Time." May 31, 2012. https://www.rollingstone.com/music/music-lists/500-greatest-albums-of-all-time-156826.

Rolling Stone. "500 Greatest Songs of All Time." December 9, 2004. https://www.rollingstone.com/music/music-lists/500-greatest-songs-of-all-time-151127.

Rollins, Henry. *Get in the Van.* Los Angeles: 2.13.61, 1995.

Romanawski, George, and Patricia Warren. *Rolling Stone Encyclopedia of Rock and Roll.* Rev. ed. New York: Touchstone, 2001.

Rombes, Nicholas. *New Punk Cinema.* Edinburgh, UK: Edinburgh University Press, 2005.

Rombes, Nicholas. *The Ramones' Ramones (33 1/3).* New York: Continuum, 2005.

Rosen, Steven. "Might the Sonics Be the Great American Rock Band?" *HuffPost.* April 30, 2015. https://www.huffpost.com/entry/might-the-sonics-be-the-great-american-rock-band_b_7174168.

Roth, Matthue. "Formal Punk." *Forward.* May 18, 2010. https://forward.com/culture/128091/formal-punk.

Rowley, Scott. "The Damned: An Epic Tale of Fast Living and Faster Music." *Louder.* October 26, 2017. https://www.loudersound.com/features/the-damned-an-epic-tale-of-fast-living-and-faster-music.

Rubin, Mike. "This Band Was Punk Before Punk Was Punk." *New York Times.* March 12, 2009. https://www.nytimes.com/2009/03/15/arts/music/15rubi.html.

Rude Boy. Jack Hazan and David Mingay, dirs. 1980.

Ruhlmann, William. "Blondie: *Parallel Lines.*" *AllMusic.* n.d. Accessed July 22, 2018. https://www.allmusic.com/album/parallel-lines-mw0000011984.

The Runaways. Floria Sigismondi, dir. 2010.

"The Runaways." *Punk77.* n.d. Accessed September 3, 2018. http://www.punk77.co.uk/groups/runaways.htm.

Runtagh, Jordan. "Elvis Presley on TV: 10 Unforgettable Broadcasts." *Rolling Stone.* January 28, 2016. https://www.rollingstone.com/music/music-news/elvis-presley-on-tv-10-unforgettable-broadcasts-225225.

Runtagh, Jordan. "Ramones' Debut LP: 10 Things You Didn't Know." *Rolling Stone.* February 4, 2016. https://www.rollingstone.com/music/music-news/ramones-debut-lp-10-things-you-didnt-know-234045.

Rupert, Dylan Tupper. "Revolution Girl Style, Still: Bikini Kill Thrill at First Show in 22 Years." *Rolling Stone.* April 26, 2019. https://www.rollingstone.com/music/music-live-reviews/bikini-kill-reunion-show-los-angeles-review-827695.

Rutter, Barry. "Break-Up of the Jam Was Bitterest Pill for Rick Buckler." *Woking News and Mail* [Woking, UK]. March 7, 2012. https://www.wokingnewsandmail.co.uk/?p=365.

Ryzik, Melana. "Joan Jett: 'My Lot in Life Is to Battle.'" *New York Times.* September 27, 2018. https://www.nytimes.com/2018/09/27/movies/joan-jett-bad-reputation-documentary.html.

Sabin, Roger. *Punk Rock, So What?: The Cultural Legacy of Punk.* New York: Routledge, 2002.

Saeed, Sana. "The Very Black History of Punk Rock." *AJ+*. February 25, 2018. https://www.youtube.com/watch?v=WgIWDZ1xxdM.
Saincome, Matt, Bill Conway, and Krissy Howard. *The Hard Times: The First 40 Years*. Boston, MA: Mariner Books, 2019.
Salad Days: A Decade of Punk in Washington, DC. Scott Crawford, dir. 2014.
Salewicz, Chris. *Redemption Song: The Ballad of Joe Strummer*. New York: Macmillan, 2006.
Saltet, Thierry. *Le Massacre des bébés skaï: Punk Rock Festival Mont de Marsan 1976 & 1977*. Montpellier, France: Julie Editions, 2013.
Sandford, Daniel. "Pussy Riot Trial: Muscovites Reflect on Divisive Case." *BBC News*. July 30, 2012. https://www.bbc.com/news/world-europe-19041458.
Sartwell, Crispin. "Book Review: Phases and Stages." *Austin Chronicle*. May 31, 2002. https://www.austinchronicle.com/music/2002-05-31/93942.
Saunders, Hilary. "Meet Baltimore Feminist Hardcore Band War on Women." *Bitch*. Bitch Media. February 13, 2015. https://www.bitchmedia.org/post/meet-baltimore-feminist-hardcore-band-war-on-women.
Savage, Jon. *England's Dreaming: The Sex Pistols and Punk Rock*. London: Faber and Faber, 1992.
Savage, Jon. "High Priestess." *SPIN* (June 1986): 66.
Savage, Jon. *Punk 45: Original Punk Rock Singles Cover Art*. London: Soul Jazz Books, 2013.
Savage, Jon. *This Searing Light, the Sun and Everything Else: Joy Division: The Oral History*. London: Faber and Faber, 2019.
Savage, Jon, William Gibson, Gee Vaucher, and Linder Sterling. *Punk: An Aesthetic*. New York: Rizzoli, 2012.
Sawyer, Miranda. "Spellbound: Siouxsie and the Banshees." *BBC Sounds*. BBC Radio 4. October 2012. https://www.bbc.co.uk/programmes/b01n9z0v.
Sayej, Nadja. "'Punk Never Dies': Celebrating the Revolutionary Art of an Era." *The Guardian*. April 25, 2019. https://www.theguardian.com/artanddesign/2019/apr/25/punk-never-dies-celebrating-the-revolutionary-art-of-an-era.
Schatz, Lake. "Pussy Riot Announce First-Ever North American Tour." *Consequence of Sound*. January 31, 2018. https://consequenceofsound.net/2018/01/pussy-riot-announce-first-ever-north-american-tour.
Schemmer, Cynthia. "40 Years of Fairytales: A Retrospective of the Raincoats." *She Shreds*. July 13, 2017. https://sheshredsmag.com/40-years-fairytales-retrospective-raincoats.
Schild, Matt. "Pansy Division's Jon Ginoli." *AV Club*. April 11, 2009. https://music.avclub.com/pansy-divisions-jon-ginoli-1798216254.
Schinder, Scott. "Ramones." In *Icons of Rock: An Encyclopedia of the Legends Who Changed Music Forever*, vol. 2, 535–564. Edited by Scott Schinder and Andy Schwartz. Westport, CT: Greenwood Press, 2008.

Schnipper, Matthew. "Black Flag: *Damaged*." *Pitchfork*. April 14, 2017. https://pitchfork.com/reviews/albums/23077-black-flag-damaged.

Sebra, Matt. "The 11 Essentials of Punk Style." *GQ*. May 2, 2013. https://www.gq.com/gallery/the-11-essentials-of-punk-style.

Serial Mom. John Waters, dir. 1994.

The Sex Pistols. *Never Mind the Baubles—Christmas '77 with the Sex Pistols*. Julien Temple, dir. 2013. *YouTube*. December 27, 2013. https://www.youtube.com/watch?v=mXpSrT7jVb0.

Seymour, Corey. "*Punk*—A New 4-Part Documentary—Aims to Tell the Whole Truth and Nothing but the Truth about Punk Rock." *Vogue*. March 11, 2019. https://www.vogue.com/article/punk-documentary-epix-review.

Seymour, Corey. "Pussy Riot's Nadya Tolokonnikova on Her New Guide to Activism, Raising the Next President of Russia, and Her 'Holy War' on Fairy Tales." *Vogue*. October 12, 2018. https://www.vogue.com/article/pussy-riot-guide-to-activism.

Shaw, Chris. "Black Flag Waves On: Black Flag's Reunion Leaves Some Wondering Why." *Memphis Flyer*. July 10, 2014. https://www.memphisflyer.com/memphis/the-flag-waves-on/Content?oid=3701626.

Shaw, Phillip. *Patti Smith's Horses*. New York: Continuum, 2008.

Shea, Christopher D. "Forty Years On, What Does Punk Rock Mean?" *New York Times*. August 16, 2016. https://www.nytimes.com/2016/08/15/arts/music/punk-rock-defined-buzzcocks-henry-rollins.html.

Shea, Christopher D. "Hey Ho, It's Old: England Embraces Punk 40 Years Later." *New York Times*. August 14, 2016. https://www.nytimes.com/2016/08/15/arts/music/punk-rock-anniversary.html.

Sherman, Maria. "13 Mexican Punk Bands You Need to Hear Right Now." *Fuse*. May 5, 2016. https://www.fuse.tv/2014/04/mexican-punk-bands.

Sherman, Maria. "20 All-Female Bands You Need to Know." *Billboard*. March 6, 2015. https://www.billboard.com/articles/pop-shop/girl-group-week/6494444/20-female-bands-sleater-kinney-ex-hex-girlpool.

Shonen Knife. "Banana Chips." *YouTube*. October 25, 2011. https://www.youtube.com/watch?v=eVxmQ1pimKo.

Shonen Knife. "Pop Tune." *YouTube*. May 14, 2012. https://www.youtube.com/watch?v=ADo6wawOUFo.

Shorthand, Agony. "Agony Shorthand Talks Electronically with Alice Bag." *Agony Shorthand* (blog). March 18, 2005. http://agonyshorthand.blogspot.com/2005/03/agony-shorthand-talks-electronically.html.

Sid & Nancy. Alex Cox, dir. 1986.

"*Sid & Nancy*." *Rotten Tomatoes*. Accessed December 25, 2019. https://rottentomatoes.com/m/sid_and_nancy.

Silverman, Carol. *Romani Routes: Cultural Politics and Balkan Music in Diaspora*. Oxford, UK: Oxford University Press, 2012.

Simmons, Todd. "Limping with the Stooges in Washington Heights." *Brooklyn Rail*. May 2, 2007. https://brooklynrail.org/2007/5/music/limping-with-the-stooges-in-washington-h.

Simpson, Dave. "Anarchy in Huddersfield: The Day the Sex Pistols Played Santa." *The Guardian* [London]. December 23, 2013. https://www.theguardian.com/music/2013/dec/23/sex-pistols-anarachy-film-huddersfield-never-mind-baubles.

Simpson, Dave. "How We Made: Heart of Glass." *The Guardian* [London]. April 29, 2013. https://www.theguardian.com/music/2013/apr/29/how-we-made-heart-glass.

Simpson, Dave. "Poly Styrene: An Optimist to the Last" *The Guardian* [London]. April 26, 2011. https://www.theguardian.com/music/musicblog/2011/apr/26/poly-styrene-x-ray-spex.

Simpson, Dave. "Poly Styrene: The Spex Factor." *The Guardian* [London]. March 23, 2011. https://www.theguardian.com/music/2011/mar/23/poly-styrene-interview.

Sinclair, Tom. "How Green Day Saved Rock—And Their Own Career." *Entertainment Weekly*. September 5, 2014. https://ew.com/article/2014/02/05/how-green-day-saved-rock-and-their-own-career.

Sinclair, Tom. "The 25th Anniversary of a Seminal Punk Album." *Entertainment Weekly*. September 24, 2004. https://ew.com/article/2004/09/24/25th-anniversary-seminal-punk-album.

Singh, Lavanya. "The Korean Rock Bands Shaking up the Status Quo." *Dazed*. June 29, 2018. https://www.dazeddigital.com/music/article/40528/1/the-korean-rock-bands-shaking-up-the-status-quo.

Sinker, Daniel. *We Owe You Nothing: Expanded Edition: Punk Planet: The Collected Interviews*. Chicago: Punk Planet Books, 2007.

Sladen, Mark, and Ariella Yedgar. *Panic Attack!: Art in the Punk Years*. London: Merrell, 2007.

SLC Punk. James Merendino, dir. 1998.

Sloan, Rachel. "A Girl in the Pit." *Medium*. October 18, 2018. https://medium.com/the-establishment/a-girl-in-the-pit-6aeacaf96ca8.

The Slog Movie. Dave Markey, dir. 1982.

Small, Doug. *Green Day*. London: Omnibus Press, 2005.

Smith, Chris. *101 Albums That Changed Popular Music*. Oxford, UK: Oxford University Press, 2009.

Smith, Gareth Dylan, Mike Dines, and Tom Parkinson, eds. *Punk Pedagogies: Music, Culture and Learning*. New York: Routledge, 2017.

Smith, Patti. *Just Kids*. New York: Echo, 2010.

Smith, Pennie. *Poly Styrene (Marian Elliot)*. London: National Portrait Gallery, 1978.

Smith, Peter. *Sex Pistols: The Pride of Punk*. Lanham, MD: Rowman & Littlefield, 2018.

Smith, R. J. "Punk Rock on Trial." *Spin* (February 2000): 73–78.

Smith, Sid. "Richard Hell and the Voidoids' *Blank Generation* Review." *BBC Music*. 2007. https://www.bbc.co.uk/music/reviews/fv63.

Smithereens. Susan Seidelman, dir. 1982.

Snapes, Laura. "The 150 Greatest Albums Made by Women: The Raincoats: *The Raincoats* (Rough Trade, 1979)." *NPR*. July 24, 2017. https://www.npr.org/2017/07/24/538357126/turning-the-tables-150-greatest-albums-made-by-women-page-8.

Snapes, Laura. "The 150 Greatest Albums Made by Women: The Slits: *Cut* (Island Records, 1979)." *NPR*. July 24, 2017. https://www.npr.org/2017/07/20/538373376/turning-the-tables-150-greatest-albums-made-by-women-page-4.

Snowden, Don, ed. *Make the Music Go Bang!: The Early L.A. Punk Scene*. New York: Macmillan, 1997.

Sokol, Brett. "Forsaking the Punk Clubs of His Youth for a Well-Stocked Library." *New York Times*. November 7, 2017. https://www.nytimes.com/2017/11/07/arts/forsaking-the-punk-clubs-of-his-youth-for-a-well-stocked-library.html.

Sommer, Tim. "Post-Punk 101: What Is Post-Punk?" *The Observer*. June 10, 2016. https://observer.com/2016/10/post-punk-101-what-is-post-punk.

Sommerlad, Joe. "Sid Vicious Is Still Punk's Biggest Mystery, 40 Years after His Death." *The Independent*. February 2, 2019. https://www.independent.co.uk/arts-entertainment/music/features/sid-vicious-40th-anniversary-sex-pistols-nancy-spungen-murder-heroin-john-lydon-malcolm-mclaren-a8757761.html.

Spicer, Al. *The Rough Guide to Punk*. New York: Penguin, 2006.

Spitz, Mark. *Nobody Likes You: Inside the Turbulent Life, Times, and Music of Green Day*. New York: Hachette Books, 2007.

Spitz, Mark. *We Got the Neutron Bomb: The Untold Story of L.A. Punk*. New York: Three Rivers Press, 2001.

Staff, Harriet. "Richard Hell: By the Book." *Poetry Foundation*. November 8, 2017. https://www.poetryfoundation.org/harriet/2017/11/richard-hell-by-the-book.

Stanley, Kyle. "Warped Tour Already Planning Reunion at Riot Fest 2020." *Hard Times*. August 10, 2018. https://thehardtimes.net/music/warped-tour-planning-reunion-riot-fest-2020.

Stassen, Murray. "I Started a Punk Zine in Racist Rural South Africa." *Vice: Noisey*. October 24, 2013. https://www.vice.com/en_us/article/vdpg9x/i-started-a-punk-rock-zine-in-rural-south-africa-where-nobody-liked-punk-rock.

Steen, Andreas. "Long Live the Revolution? The Changing Spirit of Chinese Rock." In *Popular Music and Human Rights*. Vol. 2, World Music, 131–146. Edited by Ian Peddie. Surry, UK: Ashgate Press, 2011.

Stefanko, Frank. *Patti Smith: American Artist*. San Rafael, CA: Insight Editions, 2006.

Stein, Chris. *Chris Stein/Negative: Me, Blondie, and the Advent of Punk*. New York: Rizzoli, 2014.
Stein, Chris. *Point of View: Me, New York City, and the Punk Scene*. New York: Rizzoli, 2018.
Stewart, Allison. "Against Me Tells an Intensely Personal Story on 'Transgender Dysphoria Blues.'" *Washington Post*. January 20, 2014. https://www.washingtonpost.com/entertainment/music/against-me-tells-an-intensely-personal-story-on-transgender-dysphoria-blues/2014/01/20/9c1fe210-7fc9-11e3-93c1-0e888170b723_story.html.
Stipe, Michael. *Two Times Intro: On the Road with Patti Smith*. New York: Little and Brown, 1998.
Stiv: No Compromise, No Regrets. Danny Garcia, dir. 2019.
St. John, Warren. "A Big Surprise: Fright-Wing Support." *New York Times*. March 21, 2004. https://www.nytimes.com/2004/03/21/style/a-bush-surprise-fright-wing-support.html.
Stooge. Madeleine Farley, dir. 2017.
"Stooges, The." *The Rolling Stone Encyclopedia of Rock and Roll*. New York: Simon and Schuster, 2001.
Stories from She Punks. Gina Birch and Helen Reddington, dirs. 2019.
Strongman, Phil. *Pretty Vacant: A History of Punk*. Chicago: Chicago Review Press, 2008.
Strummer, Joe, Mick Jones, Paul Simonon, and Topper Headon. *The Clash: Strummer, Jones, Simonon, Headon*. London: Atlantic Books, 2008.
"Strummer's Lasting Culture Clash." *BBC News*. December 23, 2002. http://news.bbc.co.uk/2/hi/entertainment/2600955.stm.
Sullivan, Caroline. "How We Made Cut (the Slits)." *The Guardian* [London]. June 24, 2013. https://www.theguardian.com/music/2013/jun/24/how-we-made-cut-the-slits.
Sullivan, Jim. "Dead Boys Resurrected—The 1970s American Punk Rockers Are on Tour." *WBUR: The ARTery*. September 15, 2017. https://www.wbur.org/artery/2017/09/15/dead-boys-punk-rock.
Sweeting, Adam. "Joe Strummer." *The Guardian* [London]. December 24, 2002. https://www.theguardian.com/GWeekly/Story/0,3939,866686,00.html.
Sweeting, Adam. "Lux Interior: Co-Founder of the Cramps, Exponents of Trash Culture and 'Psychobilly' Music." *The Guardian*. February 5, 2009. https://www.theguardian.com/music/2009/feb/06/obituary-lux-interior.
Sweeting, Adam. "Poly Styrene Obituary: One of the Punk Era's Original Talents, She Fronted the Band X-Ray Spex." *The Guardian* [London]. April 26, 2011. https://www.theguardian.com/music/2011/apr/26/poly-styrene-obituary.
Swensen, Andrea. "NPR's 150 Greatest Albums Made by Women." *BrooklynVegan*. July 26, 2017. http://www.brooklynvegan.com/nprs-150-greatest-albums-made-by-women.
Swenson, Kyle. "When Punk Rock Raged, Pete Shelley of Buzzcocks Stuck with Love Songs and Changed Music History." *Washington Post*. December 7,

2018. https://www.washingtonpost.com/nation/2018/12/07/when-punk-rock-raged-pete-shelley-buzzcocks-stuck-with-love-songs-changed-musical-history.

Sylvian, Sylvian. *There's No Bones in Ice Cream: Sylvain Sylvain's Story of the New York Dolls*. London: Omnibus Press, 2018.

Tank Girl. Rachel Talalay, dir. 1995.

The Taqwacores. Eyad Zahra, dir. 2010.

Tarr, Joe. *The Words and Music of Patti Smith*. New York: Praeger, 2008.

Tayler, Jeffrey. "What Pussy Riot's 'Punk Prayer' Really Said." *The Atlantic*. November 8, 2012. https://www.theatlantic.com/international/archive/2012/11/what-pussy-riots-punk-prayer-really-said/264562/.

Taylor, Steven. *False Prophet: Field Notes from the Punk Underground*. Middletown, CT: Wesleyan University Press, 2003.

Thill, Scott. "'I'm Not an Ad Man': Jello Biafra Breaks Down the Current Dead Kennedys Swindle." *Morphizm*. June 17, 2018. http://morphizm.com/css/new-musical-express-and-consequence-of-sound-loves-my-jello.

Thomas, Pauline Weston. "1970s Punk Fashion History Development." *Fashion Era*. Accessed January 3, 2019. https://www.fashion-era.com/punks_fashion_history1.htm.

Thompson, Dave. *Bad Reputation: The Unauthorized Biography of Joan Jett*. Lanham, MD: Backbeat, 2011.

Thompson, Dave. *Dancing Barefoot: The Patti Smith Story*. Chicago: Chicago Review Press, 2011.

Thompson, Dave. *London's Burning: True Adventures on the Front Lines of Punk, 1976–1977*. Chicago: Chicago Review Press, 2000.

Thompson, Dave. "X-Ray Spex: *The Anthology*." *AllMusic*. n.d. Accessed July 25, 2018. https://www.allmusic.com/album/the-anthology-mw0000658579.

Thompson, Stacy. "Punk Cinema." *Cinema Journal* 43(2) (2004): 47–66.

Thompson, Stacy. *Punk Productions: Unfinished Business*. New York: State University of New York Press, 2004.

Thompson, Stephen. "Pansy Division: Interview." *AV Club*. September 16, 1998. https://www.avclub.com/pansy-division-1798207936.

Thompson, Stephen. "Review: Against Me!, 'Transgender Dysphoria Blues.'" *NPR Music: First Listen*. January 12, 2014. https://www.npr.org/2014/01/12/261095666/first-listen-against-me-transgender-dysphoria-blues.

Threadgould, Michelle. "We're Not Going Anywhere: Growing Up Latino and Punk in America." *Observer*. January 28, 2016. https://observer.com/2016/01/were-not-going-anywhere-growing-up-latino-and-punk-in-america.

"The 300 Best Albums of the Past 30 Years (1985–2014)." *SPIN*. May 11, 2015. https://www.spin.com/2015/05/the-300-best-albums-of-the-past-30-years-1985-2014.

Times Square. Alan Moyle, dir. 1980.

Tolokonnikova, Nadya. *Read & Riot: A Pussy Riot Guide to Activism*. New York: Harper One, 2018.

"Tom Gabel of Against Me! Comes Out as Transgender." *Rolling Stone.* May 9, 2012. https://www.rollingstone.com/music/music-news/tom-gabel-of-against-me-comes-out-as-transgender-175477.

"Top 50 Albums of 2014." *Consequence of Sound.* December 11, 2014. https://consequenceofsound.net/2014/12/albums-of-the-year-2014.

"Top 100 Albums of the 1980s." *Pitchfork.* November 21, 2002. https://pitchfork.com/features/lists-and-guides/the-top-100-albums-of-the-1980s/?page=1.

Torres, Greg. "Pansy Division and the Evolution of Openly Queer Bands." *Pitchfork.* July 15, 2015. https://pitchfork.com/thepitch/823-pansy-division-and-the-evolution-of-openly-queer-bands.

Trakin, Roy. "Two New Docs, 'Punk' and 'Godfathers of Hardcore,' Prove the Genre's Not Dead." *Variety.* March 11, 2019. https://variety.com/2019/music/news/punk-godfathers-of-hardcore-documentaries-epix-iggy-pop-1203159756.

"Transcript: Sex Pistols v. Bill Grundy." *The Guardian* [London]. February 4, 2004. https://www.theguardian.com/media/2004/feb/04/realitytv.broadcasting1.

Travis, Tiffini A., and Perry Hardy. *Skinheads: A Guide to an American Subculture. From San Francisco Hardcore Punks to Skinheads.* Santa Barbara, CA: ABC-CLIO, 2002.

Trendell, Andrew. "Green Day's *American Idiot* Movie Has 'Green Light from HBO.'" *NME.* October 6, 2016. https://www.nme.com/news/music/green-day-347-1191635.

Tricarico, Antonia, Joan Jett, Amy Farina, and Tara Jane O'Neil. *Frame of Mind: Punk Photos and Essays from Washington, DC, and Beyond, 1997–2017.* New York: Akashic Books, 2019.

True, Everett. *Hey Ho Let's Go: The Story of the Ramones.* London: Omnibus Press, 2010.

True, Everett. "The Raincoats Were the Original Rock Gods All Along." *Vice.* November 15, 2019. https://www.vice.com/en_uk/article/gyz7pq/the-raincoats-40th-anniversary-tour-review.

Truly, Madly, Deeply Vale. David Nolan, producer. Granada Productions. 2004.

Trynka, Paul. *Iggy Pop: Open Up and Bleed.* New York: Crown Archetype, 2007.

Tucker, Ken. "Parallel Lines." *Rolling Stone.* November 3, 1982. https://www.rollingstone.com/music/music-album-reviews/parallel-lines-113070.

Turcotte, Bryan Ray, Michelle Carr, and Gary P. Dent. *It All Dies Anyway: L.A., Jabberjaw, and the End of an Era.* New York: Rizzoli, 2015.

Turcotte, Bryan Ray, and Christopher T. Miller. *F*%ked Up + Photocopied: Instant Art of the Punk Rock Movement.* Berkeley, CA: Gingko Press, 2002.

Turcotte, Bryan Ray, and Doug Woods. *Punk Is Dead: Punk Is Everything!* Berkeley, CA: Gingko Press, 2007.

Turn It Around: The Story of East Bay Punk. Corbett Redford, dir. 2017.

"TVE Considera 'Hipócritas' las Críticas a la Canción de Las Vulpes." *El País* [Madrid]. April 28, 1983. https://elpais.com/diario/1983/04/28/radiotv/420328803_850215.html.

24 Hour Party People. Michael Winterbottom, dir. 2002.

Tyler, Kieron. *Smashing It Up: A Decade of Chaos with the Damned*. London: Omnibus Press, 2017.

UK/DK: A Film about Punks and Skinheads. Christopher Collins, dir. 1983.

United Press International. "Album Cover Prompts Suit from Shriners." October 3, 1986. *Sun Sentinel* [Orlando, FL]. https://www.sun-sentinel.com/news/fl-xpm-1986-10-03-8602280346-story.html.

"Unpublished Disposition Melvin J. Morris, et al., Plaintiffs-appellants, v. Eric Boucher, et al., Defendants-appellees, 875 F.2d 866 (6th Cir. 1989)." May 23, 1989. US Court of Appeals for the Sixth Circuit, 875 F.2d 866 (6th Cir. 1989). *Justia US Law*. https://law.justia.com/cases/federal/appellate-courts/F2/875/866/179513/.Accessed June 17, 2018.

Valentine, Gary. *New York Rocker: My Life in the Blank Generation with Blondie, Iggy Pop and Others 1974–1981*. London: Sidgwick & Jackson, 2002.

Vallely, Sasha. "Japanese Pop-Punk All-Girl Band Shonen Knife: Writing, Touring and Guitar Gear." *Guitar Girl Magazine*. July 11, 2017. https://guitargirlmag.com/interviews/japanese-pop-punk-girl-band-shonen-knife-writing-touring-and-guitar-gear.

Van Duser, Natasha. "The 11 Most Punk Films of All Time." *AltPress*. March 3, 2017. https://www.altpress.com/features/the_11_most_punk_films_of_all_time.

Veal, Michael E., and E. Tammy Kim, eds. *Punk Ethnography: Artists & Scholars Listen to Sublime Frequencies*. Middletown, CT: Wesleyan University Press, 2016.

Vee, Tesco. *Touch and Go: The Complete Hardcore Punk Zine '79–'83*. New York: Bazillion Points, 2010.

Velichko, Anna. "The Case of Creative Representation in Pussy Riot's 'Punk Prayer.'" *Medium*. November 17, 2016. https://medium.com/@annavelichko/the-case-of-creative-representation-in-pussy-riots-punk-prayer-4684c003756b.

Vice Staff. "South Korea—Punk Here Is Like It Is Everywhere Else." May 7, 2009. https://www.vice.com/en_us/article/kwgnzy/south-korea-punk-here-is-like-it-is-everywhere-else.

Vincent, Alice. "Kim Fowley, Runaways Manager, Dies at 75." *The Telegraph* [London]. January 16, 2015. https://www.telegraph.co.uk/culture/music/music-news/11349964/Kim-Fowley-Runaways-manager-dies-aged-75.html.

Vitale, Tom, "Joe Strummer's Life after Death," *NPR: Morning Edition*. December 20, 2012. https://www.npr.org/2012/12/20/167651279/joe-strummers-life-after-death.

Wakeman, Jessica. "Flashback: Nancy Spungen Found Dead at Chelsea Hotel." *Rolling Stone*. October 12, 2017. https://www.rollingstone.com/culture/culture-news/flashback-nancy-spungen-found-dead-at-chelsea-hotel-118648.

Walker, Matt. *Gainesville Punk: A History of Bands & Music*. Charleston, SC: History Press Library Editions, 2016.

Wanshel, Elyse. "Green Day's 'American Idiot' Is Topping UK Charts upon Trump's Visit." *HuffPost*. July 9, 2018. https://www.huffpost.com/entry/greendays-american-idiot-is-topping-uk-charts-upon-trumps-visit_n_5b43c593e4b07aea75430e90.

Wassup Rockers. Larry Clark, dir. 2006.

Watts, Halina. "Paul Weller Insists the Jam Will Never Reunite as It's 'Against Everything We Stood For.'" *Daily Mirror*. August 22, 2015. https://www.mirror.co.uk/3am/celebrity-news/paul-weller-insists-jam-never-6319736.

We Are the Best! Lukas Moodysson, dir. 2013.

Weingarten, Christopher R., et al. "50 Greatest Pop-Punk Albums." *Rolling Stone*. November 15, 2017. https://www.rollingstone.com/music/music-lists/50-greatest-pop-punk-albums-122677/.

We Jam Econo: The Story of the Minutemen. Tim Irwin, dir. 2005.

Webb, Robert. "Story of the Song: 'Hong Kong Garden,' Siouxsie and the Banshees (1978)." *The Independent* [London]. August 21, 2009. https://www.independent.co.uk/arts-entertainment/music/features/story-of-the-song-hong-kong-garden-siouxsie-and-the-banshees-1978-1775005.html.

Weigel, Brandon. "Feminists Fight Back: Hardcore Band War on Women Mocks the Haters on Its Self-titled New Album." *Baltimore Sun*. February 3, 2015. https://www.baltimoresun.com/citypaper/bcp-feminists-fight-back-hardcore-band-war-on-women-mocks-the-haters-on-its-selftitled-new-album-20150203-story.html.

Weingarten, Christopher R., et al. "50 Greatest Pop-Punk Albums." *Rolling Stone*. November 15, 2017. https://www.rollingstone.com/music/music-lists/50-greatest-pop-punk-albums-122677.

Weisbard, Eric. "Young, Loud, and Snotty." *SPIN* (10) (September 1994): 69–71.

Welch, John. "Anarchy in the UK and the Tour They Tried to Ban." *BBC News*. December 3, 2016. https://www.bbc.com/news/uk-england-norfolk-38165091.

"Welcome to the Club: An Oral History of D.C.'s 9:30 Club on Its 30th Anniversary." *Washington Post*. April 18, 2010. https://www.washingtonpost.com/wp-dyn/content/article/2010/04/16/AR2010041602110.html.

Wendell, Eric. *Patti Smith: America's Punk Rock Rhapsodist*. Lanham, MD: Rowman & Littlefield, 2014.

Westcott, Lucy. "War on Women Fuses Feminism and Hardcore Punk." *Newsweek*. October 20, 2016. https://www.newsweek.com/war-women-hardcore-punk-feminism-511714.

What We Do Is Secret. Rodger Grossman, dir. 2007.
WHIMN. "Singer Stops Show to Call Out Sexual Assault in Crowd." *New York Post*. August 21, 2017. https://nypost.com/2017/08/21/singer-stops-show-to-call-out-sexual-assault-in-crowd.
White, Josh. "Why a History of Punk Rock Matters." *HuffPost* [UK]. January 20, 2012. https://www.huffingtonpost.co.uk/josh-white/punk-rock-history_b_1103667.html.
Whitney, Jon. "Metal Urbain: *Anarchy in Paris!*" *Brainwashed*. January 3, 2004. http://brainwashed.com/index.php?option=com_content&task=view&id=2913&Itemid=96.
"Who Is Poly Styrene?" *BBC Four: Arena*. Season 4, episode 10. Ted Clisby, dir. January 20, 1979. https://www.bbc.co.uk/programmes/b01jn409.
Who Killed Nancy. Alan Parker, dir. 2010.
Wild, David. "Shonen Knife Cuts Like a Knife." *Rolling Stone*. April 15, 1993. https://www.rollingstone.com/music/music-news/shonen-knife-cuts-like-a-knife-94526.
Williamson, Eugenia. "Punk's Not Fed: I Ate at the CBGB Newark Airport Restaurant and It Sucked." *Vice: Noisey*. January 27, 2016. https://www.vice.com/en_us/article/gqm7gq/punks-not-fed-i-ate-at-the-cbgb-newark-airport-restaurant-and-it-sucked.
Willman, Chris. "Classic Lineup of Punk Band X Returns to Studio for First Time in 34 Years." *Variety*. January 15, 2019. https://variety.com/2019/music/news/original-lineup-punk-band-x-new-record-1203109031.
Winwood, Ian. *Smash!: Green Day, the Offspring, Bad Religion, NOFX, and the '90s Punk Explosion*. Cambridge, MA: Da Capo Press, 2018.
Wolf, Naomi. *The Beauty Myth: How Images of Beauty Are Used against Women*. New York: Harper Perennial, 2002.
Woolever, Lydia. "Female Trouble: Shawna Potter of War on Women Talks Music and the #MeToo Movement." *Baltimore*. April 2018. https://www.baltimoremagazine.com/2018/3/30/shawna-potter-of-war-on-women-talks-music-and-metoo-movement.
"World Cup: Pussy Riot Protesters Jailed over Pitch Demonstration." *BBC News*. July 17, 2018. https://www.bbc.com/news/world-europe-44846446.
Worley, Matthew. *No Future: Punk, Politics, and British Youth Culture, 1976–1984*. Cambridge, UK: University of Cambridge Press, 2017.
Worley, Matthew. "Punk, Politics and British (Fan)zines, 1976–84: 'While the World Was Dying, Did You Wonder Why?'" *History Workshop Journal* 79(1) (April 2015):76–106.
Wuelfing, Amy Yates. *No Slam Dancing, No Stage Diving, No Spikes: An Oral History of the Legendary City Gardens*. Morrisville, PA: DiWulf Publishing, 2014.
"X: 40 Years of Punk in Los Angeles." Grammy Museum. Accessed December 20, 2019. https://grammymuseum.org/event/x-40-years-of-punk-in-los-angeles.

X: The Unheard Music. W. T. Morgan, dir. 1986.
"X-Ray Spex." *Punk77*. Accessed September 3, 2018. http://www.punk77.co.uk/groups/x_ray_spex.htm.
Yanick, Joseph. "Movies about Punk: the Good, the Bad, and the Other." March 20, 2014. *Vice: Noisey*. https://www.vice.com/en_us/article/6vnma6/movies-about-punk-the-good-the-bad-and-the-other.
Yeung, Neil Z. "Dropkick Murphys: *11 Short Stories of Pain and Glory*." *AllMusic*. n.d. Accessed July 3, 2018. https://www.allmusic.com/album/11-short-stories-of-pain-glory-mw0002995052.
Zan Gibbs Riot Grrrl Zine Collection, 1987–2003. Fales Library and Special Collections. New York University.
Zavella, Patricia. "Beyond the Screams: Latino Punkeros Contest Nativist Discourses." *Latin American Perspectives* 39(2) (March 2012): 27–41.
Zhuk, Sergi I. "Fascist Music from the West: Anti-Rock Campaigns, Problems of National Identity, and Human Rights in the 'Closed City' of Soviet Ukraine, 1975–84." *Popular Music and Human Rights*. Vol. 2, *World Music*, 147–159. Edited by Ian Peddie. Surry, UK: Ashgate Press, 2011.
Ziegler, Jay. "Dusting 'Em Off: The Clash—*Cut the Crap*." *Consequence of Sound*. March 8, 2009. https://consequenceofsound.net/2009/03/dusting-em-off-the-clash-cut-the-crap.
Žižek, Slavoj, and Nadya Tolokonnikova. *Comradely Greetings: The Prison Letters of Nadya and Slavoj*. New York: Verso, 2014.

Index

"A Bout de Souffle" (Marie et les Garçons), 60
Activism. *See* Political activism
Adolescents, The, 142, 175, 186
"Adventures Close to Home" (The Raincoats), 110
Adverts, The, 35, 178
Afro-punk, 18–20, 52–55, 183
Against Me!, 4, 8, 10, 13–15, 184–187
Against the Grain (Bad Religion), 22
"Age" (X-Ray Spex), 168
Age of Unreason (Bad Religion), 22
Agnostic Front, 175
Ain't Love Grand (X), 166
"Ain't Nothing to Do" (Dead Boys), 48
Airport, Jak, 167
Albertine, Viv, 36, 135–138, 159
"Alcohol" (Gogol Bordello), 70
Alexander, Dave, 145, 148
Alice Bag (Alice Bag), 15–18
Alice Cooper (band), 47, 53, 86
Alien Kulture, 150
"Alien She" (Bikini Kill), 24
Alive! in Osaka (Shonen Knife), 128–132
Alkaline Trio, 171
All Ages (Drew Stone, Dir.), 175

All Bagged Up (The Bags), 16
"All for Nothing" (The Muffs), 93
"All Hell Breaks Loose" (Misfits), 88
"All I Want for Christmas" (Shonen Knife), 104
"All I Want for Christmas Is You" (My Chemical Romance), 120
Allin, GG, 49, 175
"All My Loving" (Me First and the Gimmie Gimmies), 84
"All This and More" (Dead Boys), 47–48
"All You Can Eat" (Shonen Knife), 131
"Alone and Forsaken" (Social Distortion), 143–144
Alternative rock, 11, 71, 108, 132, 181, 186
Alternative Tentacles records, 52
Al-Thawra (band), 149–150
Alyokhina, Maria, 105–107
American Hardcore (Paul Reichman, Dir.), 175
American Idiot (Green Day), 71–74
"American Idiot" (Green Day), 73–74
"American Jesus" (Bad Religion), 5
"American Nights" (The Runaways), 123
"American Prayer" (Jim Morrison), 141

American punk, 13–32, 39–41, 46–58, 62–67, 71–74, 77–80, 82–98, 101–124, 138–146, 151–154, 164–167
"American Wedding" (Gogol Bordello), 70
AM radio/rock, 76, 82–85. *See also* 1950s and 1960s pop and rock
"Anarcha" (War on Women), 153–154
Anarcho-punk, 41–44
"Anarchy in the UK" (Sex Pistols), 5, 44, 124, 126
. . . And Out Come the Wolves (Rancid), 114–117
Angry Red Planet (Ib Melichor, Dir.), 87
Angry Snowmans, 5, 103–104
"Another Day" (The Muffs), 92–93
Another Kind of Tension (Buzzcocks), 34
"Another World" (Richard Hell and the Voidoids), 120
Ant, Adam, 67, 158
Anti-musicianship, 64–67, 124–128
Anti-romance songs, 3–4, 28–36, 48, 66, 75, 80–82, 92–94, 110, 136–137, 146–147, 165
Anti-war music, 49–50, 73–74, 79, 105
"Antonio Baka Guy" (Shonen Knife), 132
Ari Up, 135–138
Armendariz, Alicia. *See* Bag, Alice
Armstrong, Billie Joe, 71–74
Armstrong, Tim, 114–117, 171–172
"Art-I-Ficial" (X-Ray Spex), 168
"Art School" (The Jam), 75
Asheton, Ron, 145, 148
Asheton, Scott, 145, 148
Asian Dub Foundation (band), 150
Aspinall, Vicky, 109
Astigarraga, Begoña, 80
"As Wicked" (Rancid), 116

"Asylum" (Crass), 41–43
A 3 dans le WC (band), 61
Au Pairs, 110, 159
"Avenues and Alleyways" (Rancid), 117
"Away from the Numbers" (The Jam), 75

Babes in Toyland, 122, 132
"Baby Go Round" (The Muffs), 92–94
"Bad Brain" (Ramones), 19
Bad Brains, 18–20, 26, 52, 62, 88, 148, 175, 179, 183, 186
"Bad Luck Song" (Shonen Knife), 131–132
Bad Religion, 4–5, 8, 10, 20–22, 102, 114, 175, 181, 183, 185–187
Bag, Alice, 15–18, 159, 173, 183
Bag, Pat, 16
Bags, The, 15–16, 159
Bailey, Steven. *See* Severin, Steven
Baker, Brian, 84
"Bakersfield" (Social Distortion), 144
"Ball and Chain" (Social Distortion), 142
"Banana Chips" (Shonen Knife), 131
Bangles, The, 78, 159
Bangs, Lester, 119, 147
Banke, Richard. *See* Roper, Skid
"Banned in DC" (Bad Brains), 19
Barber, Tony, 34
Barker, Phil, 34
"Basket Case" (Green Day), 72
"Batman Theme" (The Jam), 77
Bator, Steven John. *See* Bators, Stiv
Bators, Stiv, 46–49
Baudelaire, Charles, 140
BBC, 33–34, 97, 101–102, 119, 127–128, 135–136, 163, 170, 180, 184
"BBQ Party" (Shonen Knife), 131
Beaham, Paul. *See* Crash, Darby
"Bear up Bison" (Shonen Knife), 131

Index **251**

Beatles, The, 32, 45, 76, 84, 94, 112–113, 118, 128, 131, 133–134, 147
"Beat on the Brat" (Ramones), 113
"Beat Surrender" (The Jam), 77
Becvare, Adam, 49
Bedtime for Democracy (Dead Kennedys), 51
"Beercan Boy" (Pansy Division), 96
Bentley, Jay, 20, 85
"Bermuda Triangle Blues (Flight 45)" (Blondie), 30–31
"Betrayal Takes Two" (Richard Hell and Voidoids), 120
"Better Off Dead" (Bad Religion), 21
"Better Than Me" (The Muffs), 93
B-horror and science fiction films, 39–41, 85–88
Biafra, Jello, 8, 49–52, 91, 125, 187
"Big Mouth" (The Muffs), 94
Bikini Kill, 5, 7–9, 18, 22–25, 78, 108, 110, 122, 162–163, 175, 181, 183–184, 186–187
Billboard, 36–37, 55, 64, 78, 94, 116, 145
Birch, Gina, 108–110
"Birdland" (Patti Smith), 140
"Black and White" (The Raincoats), 110
"Black Christmas" (Poly Styrene), 170
Black Coal for Rotten Children (Angry Snowmans), 104
Black Flag, 10, 25–28, 45, 62, 158–159, 162, 174–175, 186
"Blackmail" (The Runaways), 123
"Black Me Out" (Against Me!), 15
Black Sabbath, 128, 131
"Blank Generation" (Richard Hell and the Voidoids), 118
Blank Generation (Richard Hell and the Voidoids), 117–121
Blink 182, 103
Blitz, Johnny, 46–49
"Blitzkrieg Bop" (Ramones), 112
Blondie, 28–32, 141, 179, 186
"Blood One" (Bikini Kill), 24
"Blow Shit Up" (The Kominas), 150
Blue, Vicki, 122, 124
"Blue Christmas" (Misfits), 102
Blueprint (Alice Bag), 18
"Blueprint" (Fugazi), 64
Blues, 28, 89–90, 118, 142–146, 164
Bo-Day-Shus!!! (Mojo Nixon and Skid Roper), 88–91
Bogosian, Eric, 166
Bolles, Don, 65–67
Bollocks to Christmas (various artists), 103
Bonebrake, D[onald] J., 164
"Born to Kill" (The Damned), 45
Bouicher, Eric Reed. *See* Biafra, Jello
"Boulevard of Broken Dreams" (Green Day), 73–74
Bowie, David, 65, 146, 148
Bragg, Billy, 6–7, 116, 186
"Brains for Dinner" (Misfits), 87
"Brand New Cadillac" (The Clash), 37
Bratmobile, 18, 162
Brats on the Beat (various artists), 114
Breaking Glass (Brian Gibson, Dir.), 155–156
"Breaking Windows" (Warm Gun), 62
"Break It Up" (Patti Smith), 140–141
Breeders, The, 4, 129
Breton, André, 2, 59
"Bricks and Mortar" (The Jam), 76
Bricks Are Heavy (L7), 77–80
British Invasion bands, influence of on punk, 45, 76, 112
British punk, 32–48, 41–46, 75–77, 108–110, 124–128, 132–138, 167–170
"Broken Hymns" (Dropkick Murphys), 57

Brooks, Harlan, 151
B-science fiction films. *See* B-horror and science fiction films
Buckler, Rick, 75
Burchill, Julie, 162
Burk, Clem, 31
Burkett, Michael John. *See* Fat Mike
Burns, Raymond Ian. *See* Captain Sensible
Burroughs, William, 141
Business, The (band), 102
Butchies, The, 172
Butthole Surfers, 4
Buzzcocks, 4, 32–35, 94, 179, 186

Caiafa, Jerry. *See* Only, Jerry
Caiafa, Paul. *See* von Frankenstein, Doyle Wolfgang
Calcinator, 61
"California Hustle and Flow" (Social Distortion), 143
"California Über Alles" (Dead Kennedys), 5, 50–51
"Can't Take It with You" (Social Distortion), 143
Cape, Joey, 82–83
Capitalism, critiques of, 41–44, 49–52
"Ça Plane pour Moi" (Plastic Bertrand), 60
Captain Sensible, 44–46
"Capture the Flag" (War on Women), 153
Capture the Flag (War on Women), 151–154
"Carcass" (Siouxsie and the Banshees), 133–134
Carroll, Jim, 4, 116
Cash, Johnny, 99, 142, 144
Cassey, Ken, 58
"Caught with the Meat in Your Mouth" (Dead Boys), 48
"Cautious Lip" (Blondie), 31
Cavalier, Dave, 151

Cayetana, 163
CBGB (New York), 10, 19, 28–29, 39, 44, 47–49, 60, 90, 114, 117–119, 138, 141, 155, 178–179, 181, 185
CBGB (Randall Miller, Dir.), 155
Celtic punk, 5, 55–58, 98–103, 183
Censorship, 33, 50–52, 72, 76, 80–81, 102, 187
Cervenka, Exene, 159, 164–166
Cervenkova, Christine. *See* Cervenka, Exene
"Chaika" (Pussy Riot), 107
"Chalice and the Blade, The" (War on Women), 154
Chalk Circle (band), 159
Chanukah songs, 104
Chapman, Mike, 28
Charles de Goal (band), 61
Cheetah Chrome and the Casualties, 49
Chefs, The, 110
"Chemical Warfare" (Dead Kennedys), 50–51
"Cherry Bomb" (The Runaways), 122–123
Childbirth (band), 163
"Childbirth" (War on Women), 153
Chimes, Terry, 35
"China Girl" (David Bowie), 148
China White (band), 142
Chinese punk, 187
Christian punk, 172
Christmas, 101–104; Japanese Christmas, 104
"Christmas Has Been X-ed" (NOFX), 103
Christmas music. *See* Punk Christmas
"Christmas Night of the Zombies" (MxPx), 103
Christmas Songs (Bad Religion), 22, 102
"Christmas Time for My Penis" (The Vandals), 103

Chrome, Cheetah, 46–49, 155
Circle Jerks, The, 4, 158, 174–175, 179, 183, 186
"City of New Orleans" (Me First and the Gimmie Gimmies), 84–85
"Clampdown" (The Clash), 36
Clash, The, 28, 31, 35–38, 39–41, 43–46, 49, 59, 75–76, 89, 98, 108, 114–115, 135–136, 138, 149, 156, 159–160, 162, 175, 177, 179–180, 186–188
Clash: Westway to the World, The (Don Letts, Dir.), 175
Cliff, Jimmy, 115–116
"Climbing a Chair to Bed" (Dropkick Murphys), 55–58
Cobain, Kurt, 35, 128–129
Cola, Casey, 67
Coldpunk, 61
Coltrane, John, 139
Colvin, Douglas Glenn. *See* Ramone, Dee Dee
Combat Rock (The Clash), 38
Cometbus (zine), 174
Confrontation dressing, 8, 176–177
Conscious Clit (zine), 174
Conscious Consumer (X-Ray Spex), 170
"Contact in Red Square" (Blondie), 30–31
Cook, Paul, 124, 126–128
Cool, Tré, 71–74
Coon, Caroline, 59, 126, 132, 162
Cooper, Alice. *See* Alice Cooper
Corman, Rodger, 114, 158–159
Costello, Elvis, 99, 158
Country music, 83–84, 90, 142–144, 164
County, Jane, 158
Covers. *See* Punk covers
Cow punk, 39–41, 88–91, 143, 183
Cox, Alex, 99, 126, 154, 158
Cramps, 4, 39–41, 86, 147, 179, 183
Crash, Darby, 16, 65–67, 155

Crass, 8, 41–44, 49, 162, 187
Crass, Chris, 92
"Crimson and Clover" (Joan Jett and the Blackhearts), 123
"Cruel" (Dropkick Murphys), 56–57
"Cruel to Be Kind" (Shonen Knife), 131
Crust punk, 150, 172, 174
Cruz, Brandon, 52
Crystals, The, 128
Cummings, John William. *See* Ramone, Johnny
Cummings, Sue, 78, 163
Currie, Cherie, 121–124, 155
Curse, The (zine), 174
Cut, The (The Slits), 135–138
Cut the Crap (The Clash), 38

Dadaism, 2, 59
Dallion, Susan. *See* Sioux, Siouxsie
Daltrey, Roger, 34
"Daly City Train" (Rancid), 116
Damaged (Black Flag), 25–28
"Damaged I" (Black Flag), 27
"Damaged II" (Black Flag), 27
Damned, Damned, Damned (The Damned), 44–46
Damned, The, 35, 41, 44–46, 47, 59, 86–87, 179, 183, 186
Dandy Warhols, 102
Danell, Dennis, 142
"Danny's Song" (Me First and the Gimmie Gimmies), 83
"*Dans le Labyrinthe*" (Charles de Goal), 61
Danzig, Glenn, 85–88
Darby Crash (band), 67
da Silva, Ana, 108
Davis, Clive, 53
Davis, Don, 53
"Day the World Turned Day-Glo, The" (X-Ray Spex), 168
Dead Bhuttos, 149–150
Dead Boys, 4, 18, 46–49, 155, 175, 179
"Dead End Justice" (Runaways), 123

"Dead Friend" (Against Me!), 15
Dead Kennedys, 4–5, 8, 49–52, 157, 179, 183, 187
Dead Milkmen, 186
Dean, Paul, 167
Death (band), 4, 8, 52–55, 185, 187
"Death of Jail, Freedom to Protest" (Pussy Riot), 106
"Death or Glory" (The Clash), 37
"Death Trip" (The Stooges), 147
"Debbie Gibson Is Pregnant with My Two-Headed Love Child" (Mojo Nixon and Skid Roper), 90
Debord, Guy, 1, 59
Débris, Eric, 61
Decline of Western Civilization, The (Penelope Spheeris, Dir.), 16, 65, 165, 174
"Deeds Not Words" (Dropkick Murphys), 56–57
"Deep Water" (Pansy Division), 97
Deep Six (band), 172
Deflowered (Pansy Division), 94–98
Dekker, Desmond, 115
"Denis" (Blondie), 29–30
"Denny" (Pansy Division), 97
"Depression" (Black Flag), 27
Descendents, The, 175, 186
Descloux, Lizzy Mercier, 2
"Desperado" (Me First and the Gimmie Gimmies), 84–85
Destiny Street (Richard Hell and the Voidoids), 120
Destiny Street Repaired (Richard Hell and the Voidoids), 121
Destri, James, 31
"Detroit 442" (Blondie), 31
"Devil's Whorehouse" (Misfits), 87
DEVO, 61
Devoto, Howard, 32
D. I. (band), 157
Diacritical (band), 150
"Diamond in the Rough" (Social Distortion), 143

Dickies, The, 18, 45, 102
Dicks, The, 4
Dictators, The, 114
"Diet Pill" (L7), 79
Diggle, Steve, 32, 34
Dirnt, Mike, 71–74
"Dirty Old Town" (The Pogues), 99–100
Dischord Records, 62, 64, 171
"Disorder and Disarray" (Rancid), 117
"Dispatch from Mar-a-Lago" (L7), 80
Distillers, The, 186
"Divisive Shit" (War on Women), 153
DK40 (Dead Kennedys), 52
DOA (band), 175
D. O. A.: A Rite of Passage (Lech Kowalski, Dir.), 174–175
Documentaries about punk, 16, 20, 44, 46, 49, 52, 55, 65, 71, 74, 77, 80, 91, 98, 101, 108, 110, 114, 124, 138, 150, 163, 165, 167, 170, 174–176, 179–180. *See also* Films about punk and punks
Doe, John, 164–166
Dogs, The, 61
Dolly Mixture (band), 110
Donnas, The, 171, 186
"Don't Drag Me Down" (Social Distortion), 142
"Don't Want No Foo Foo Haircut on My Head" (Mojo Nixon and Skid Roper), 89–90
Dookie (Green Day), 71–74
Doom, Lorna, 65–67
Doors, The, 85, 166
"Do They Owe Us a Living" (Crass), 42–53
"Double Dare Ya" (Bikini Kill), 25
"Down at the Rock and Roll Club" (Richard Hell and the Voidoids), 120
"Down in Flames" (Dead Boys), 46
Downtown Boys, 163

Index **255**

"Dragon Lady" (Germs), 66–67
Dream Wife, 4, 163
"Drinking with the Jocks" (Against Me!), 14
Dr. Know, 18–20
Dr. Know (band), 52
Dropkick Murphys, 5, 8, 55–58, 98, 101, 103, 172, 183, 187
"Drug Me" (Dead Kennedys), 51
Drunken Butterfly, 163
Dub[step] 62, 71, 135–138
"Dub the Frequencies of Love" (Gogol Bordello), 71
Duchac, John. *See* Doe, John
Dylan, Bob, 84, 141

East Asian punk, 148–151
East Bay Ray, 52
Eastern European music, 67–71
East Infection (Gogol Bordello), 71
Electric Callas (band), 60
"*Électrifié*" (Calcinator), 61
Electropunk, 60, 135
"Elegie" (Patti Smith), 141
"11th Hour" (Rancid), 117
Elliott-Said, Marianne Joan. *See* Styrene, Poly
"Eloise" (The Damned), 46
"Elvis Is Everywhere" (Mojo Nixon and Skid Roper), 88–89
Elvis Presley (Elvis Presley), 38
End of the Century: The Story of The Ramones (Jim Fields and Michael Gramaglia, Dirs.), 175
"End Result" (Crass), 42
Eno, Brian, 61
Erdeyl, Thomas. *See* Ramone, Tommy
ESG (band), 159
"*Euthanasie*" (Les Olivensteins), 61
"Ever Fallen in Love (With Someone You Shouldn't've)" (Buzzcocks), 4, 33–34
"Everglade" (L7), 78–79

Every Band Has a Shonen Knife Who Loves Them (various artists), 132
"Everybody's Happy Nowadays" (Buzzcocks), 34
"Every Single Thing" (The Muffs), 92, 94
Everything Went Black (Black Flag), 27–28
"Everywhere I Go" (The Muffs), 92–93
Experimental punk, 135–138
"Eye to Eye" (The Muffs), 92, 94

"Fairytale in the Supermarket" (The Raincoats), 109–110
"Fairytale of New York" (The Pogues), 102
Fall Out Boy, 103
"Fan Club" (The Damned), 45
Fantomes, the, 62
Fanzines. *See* Zines
"Far Side of Nowhere" (Social Distortion), 143
Fat Mike, 8–10, 82–83, 171, 186
Fat Wreck Chords, 82, 171
Fear (band), 103, 158, 162
Fearless Iranians in Hell (band), 150
Feedback. *See* Fuzz and feedback
Feeding of the 5000, The (Crass), 41–44
"Feel the Pain" (The Damned), 46
Feminism, 5, 13, 22–25, 77–80, 104–110, 122, 135–138, 151–154, 156, 159–163, 167, 174, 180
Feminist Majority Foundation, 78, 163, 180, 186
Festivals, 180–181
"Fever" (Cramps), 40
'50s rock and roll. *See* 1950s and 1960s pop and rock
Fight Rosa Fight, 163
Filmage: The Story of Descendents/All (Deedle LaCour and Matt Riggle, Dirs.)

Films about punk and punks, 154–158, 174–176. *See also* Documentaries about punk
Filth and the Fury, The (Julian Temple, Dir.), 175
Finch, Jennifer, 77
Finding Joseph I (James Lathos, Dir.), 20
"Fish" (The Damned), 45
"Five Years" (David Bowie), 65
Flogging Molly, 5, 98, 186
Flores, Lysa, 18
"Fluffy City" (Pansy Division), 97
Fluoride, Klaus, 52
"FM" (The Slits), 137
Food, songs about, 128–132
Foo Fighters, 82–83
"Forces of Victory" (Gogol Bordello), 71
Ford, Lita, 122
Forster, Ariane Daniela. *See* Ari Up
For the Whole World to See (Death), 52–55
"Forward to Death" (Dead Kennedys), 51
"Four Horsemen" (The Clash), 37
Fowley, Kim, 16, 121–124, 155, 161
Fox, Jackie. *See* Fuchs, Jackie
Foxton, Bruce, 75
Frankenchrist (Dead Kennedys), 50–52
Frederiksen, Lars, 114, 116
Freeman, Chris, 94–96
Freeman, Matt, 114
"Free Money" (Patti Smith), 140
French language punk, 1–2, 61
French punk, 1–2, 58–62, 179
French surrealism and symbolism, 2, 59–60, 140
Fresh Fruit for Rotting Vegetables (Dead Kennedys), 49–52
"Freydele" (Golem), 104
Frischmann, Justine, 166
"From Your Girl" (The Muffs), 92, 94

Fuchs, Jackie, 121–124
"Fuck Authority" (Pennywise), 4
"Fuck Christmas" (Fear), 103
"FUCKMYLIFE666" (Against Me!), 15
"Fuck You Up" (Dream Wife), 4
Fugazi, 8, 62–64, 163, 179, 181, 183, 187
Fun-Da-Mental, 150
Fun House (The Stooges), 145–146
Funk music, 18, 53
"Funland at the Beach" (Dead Kennedys), 51
Futureheads, 34
"FUU" (Dream Wife). *See* "Fuck You Up" (Dream Wife)
Fuzz and feedback, 39–41, 92–94

Gabba Gabba Hey: A Tribute to the Ramones (various artists), 114
Gabel, Tom. *See* Grace, Laura Jane
Gang Green, 175
Garbage (band), 4
"Garbage Dump" (He Yong), 187
"Garbageman" (Cramps), 40
Garcia, Danny, 175
Gardner, Suzi, 77
Garner, Eric, 107
Garratt, Nicky, 172
Gaslight Anthem (band), 14
Gazoline (band), 61
Gearhead (zine), 174
Geiger, H. G., 51–52
Gender norms, challenges to, 8, 13–15, 29, 33–34, 36, 39–42, 69, 77–82, 93–94, 132–139, 149–154, 159–163, 167, 178
"General Bacardi" (Crass), 43
Generation X (band), 174
"Generator" (Bad Religion), 82
Genet, Jean, 2, 59–60, 139
"Genetic Engineering" (X-Ray Spex), 169
"Germfree Adolescents" (X-Ray Spex), 168, 183

Germfree Adolescents (X-Ray Spex), 167–170, 183
Germs, 4, 16, 45, 64–67, 82, 115, 155, 173–174, 179, 183
Germs Incognito. *See* Germs
GI (Germs), 64–67
Giant Kitty, 132, 163
Gibson, Brian, 155
Gilkyson, Tony, 166
"Gimme Danger" (The Stooges), 146–147
"Gimme the Sweet and Lowdown" (Social Distortion), 143–144
"Gimmie, Gimmie, Gimmie" (Black Flag), 27
"Gin Guzzlin' Frenzy" (Mojo Nixon and Skid Roper), 89
Ginn, Greg, 26–28
Ginoli, Jon, 94–98
Girard, Marie, 60
Girl Germs (zine), 174
Girl's Guide to Taking over the World, A (zine), 174
"girls to the front" policy, 22, 78, 152, 162
Give 'Em Enough Rope (The Clash), 35
"Gloria" (Patti Smith), 140
Go Betty Go, 163, 186
Godfathers of Hardcore (Ian McFarland, Dir.), 175
God Is My Co-Pilot (band), 94
"God Rest Ye Merry Gentlemen" (Bad Religion), 102
"God Save the Queen" (Sex Pistols), 5, 124, 126–127, 157
Gogol Bordello, 8, 67–71, 185–187
Go-Gos, The, 128, 159, 179
"Going Out in Style" (Dropkick Murphys), 56
Going Out in Style (Dropkick Murphys), 55–58
Golem (band), 104
Goorjian, Michael, 156

Gordon, Kim, 78, 159
Gore, Tipper, 51–52
Gossip (band), 162
Goth music, 44–46, 132, 135
Grace, Laura Jane, 13–15, 163
Graffin, Greg, 20
Graham, Terry, 16
Grammy Awards, 71, 148, 157
Great Rock and Roll Swindle, The (Julian Temple, Dir), 127–128
"Greed" (Fugazi), 63–64
Green Day, 4, 8, 10, 14, 71–74, 96, 114, 171, 179, 184–187
Green Room (Jeremy Saulner, Dir.), 157, 187
"Green Tangerine" (Shonen Knife), 131
Greystone Hall (Detroit), 88
"Grimly Fiendish" (The Damned), 46
"Groovy Underwear" (Pansy Division), 96
Grossman, Rodger, 67, 155
Grundy, Bill, 5, 44, 81, 126, 132
Grunge music, 71, 77–78, 146, 178
"G's Song" (Crass), 42–43
Guerilla performances, 104–108
Guilty Razors, 62
"Gun for Christmas, A" (The Vandals), 103
"Guns of Brixton, The" (The Clash), 5, 37
Gurewitz, Brett, 20, 117, 171
Gutsy, Suzi, 135
Gypsy punk, 5, 67–71, 183

Hackney, Bobby, 52–55
Hackney, Dannis, 52–55
Hackney, David, 52–55
Halmagy, Jeff. *See* Magnum, Jeff
"Handshake, The" (Bad Religion), 21–22
"Hang 'Em High" (Dropkick Murphys), 56–57
"Hanging on the Telephone" (Blondie), 28

"Hang Myself from the Tree" (The Vandals), 103
Hanna, Kathleen, 8, 18, 22–25, 92, 151–153, 162–163, 174–175, 183
Happy Birthday, Baby Jesus (various artists), 103
"Happy Holidays You Bastard" (Blink 182), 103
Hardcore punk, 6, 18–22, 25–28, 44–45, 49, 52, 62–67, 114–115, 148, 151–154, 158, 163, 172, 174–175, 178–180
"Hardest Mile, The" (Dropkick Murphys), 57, 101
Hard Times and Nursery Rhymes (Social Distortion), 142–145
"Harem in Tuscany" (Gogol Bordello), 70
"Hark! The Herald Angels Sing" (Bad Religion), 102
"Harmony in My Head" (Buzzcocks), 34
Harry, Deborah, 28–31
"Hatebreeders" (Misfits), 88
Hated: GG Allin and the Murder Junkies (Todd Phillips, Dir.), 175
"Hats off to Larry" (Me First and the Gimmie Gimmies), 84–85
"Havana Affair" (Ramones), 113–114
Headon, Nicky "Topper," 35–38
HeartattaCk (zine), 173–174
Heartbreakers, The. *See* Johnny Thunders and the Heartbreakers
Heartfield, John, 134
"Heart of Glass" (Blondie), 28
Heavens to Betsey (zine), 174
Heavens to Betsey, 162, 174
Hell, Richard, 2, 28, 60, 117–121, 156, 177
Hellcat Records, 117, 172
"Helter Skelter" (Siouxsie and the Banshees), 134
Hendrix, Jimi, 53, 61

Henley, Darren. *See* Peligro, D. H.
"He's So Sorry" (Alice Bag), 17
"Hey Little Girl" (Dead Boys), 48
Hey Zeus! (X), 167
"Highly Inflammable" (X-Ray Spex), 168
"High Tension Wire" (Dead Boys), 47
"Hired Gun" (Bad Brains), 19
"History Lesson Part 2" (Minutemen), 6
"Ho Ho Ho Chi Minh" (Showcase Showdown), 103
Hole, 4, 78, 162, 179, 181
"Holiday" (Green Day), 73–74
Holiday, Billie, 144
"Holiday in Cambodia" (Dead Kennedys), 50
Holmstrom, John, 28, 155, 173–174
"Homecoming" (Green Day), 73–74
"Homo Christmas" (Pansy Division), 4, 103–104
Homocore (zine), 174
Homophobia, 5, 16–17, 162. *See also* LGBTQ rights
"Homosapien" (Pansy Division), 97
"Homosapien" (Pete Shelley), 34, 97
"Hong Kong Garden" (Siouxsie and the Banshees), 134–135, 160
"Hooray for Me" (Bad Religion), 21
"Hooray for Santa Claus" (Sloppy Seconds), 103
Horror films. *See* B-horror and science fiction films
Horror punk, 39–41, 46, 85–88, 184
Horses (Patti Smith), 138–142, 161, 164
"House of Suffering" (Bad Brains), 19
H. R., 18–20, 88, 175
Hudson, Earl, 18–20
Hudson, Paul D. *See* H. R.
Huggy Bear (band), 162
Hurbier, Charlie, 61

Hurding, Paul "B. P.," 167
Hurrah! Die Butter Ist Alle (Hurray! The Butter Is Gone!) (John Heartfield), 134
"Hurts and Noises" (Guilty Razors), 62
Hüsker Dü, 32
Hussain, Sena, 150
Hütz, Eugene, 67–71
Hymen, Jeffrey Ross. *See* Ramone, Joey
Hynde, Chrissie, 178

"I Against I" (Bad Brains), 19
I Against I (Bad Brains), 18–20
"I Ain't Gonna Piss in No Jar" (Mojo Nixon and Skid Roper), 89
"I Am a Cliché" (X-Ray Spex), 169–170
"I Am a Poseur" (X-Ray Spex), 170
"I Believe I Can Fly" (Me First and the Gimmie Gimmies), 83–84
"I Can't Breathe" (Pussy Riot), 107
"I Can't Do Anything" (X-Ray Spex), 169–170
"Identity" (X-Ray Spex), 168
"I Didn't Have the Nerve to Say No" (Blondie), 31
Idiot, The (Iggy Pop), 148
Idol, Joey, 87
"I Don't Believe in Santa" (The Vandals), 103
"I Don't Mind" (Buzzcocks), 33
"I Don't Wanna Be Rich" (Guilty Razors), 62
Ieperfest (Ypres, Belgium), 180
"I Fall" (The Damned), 45–46
If I Were a Carpenter (Shonen Knife and various artists), 129
"I Fought the Law" (The Clash), 31
Iggy and the Stooges. *See* Stooges, the
"I Got by in Time" (The Jam), 75
"I Heard It through the Grapevine" (The Slits), 137
"I Kill Children" (Dead Kennedys), 51
"I Live Off You" (X-Ray Spex), 168–169
"I'll Be Your Maccabee" (Schmekel), 104
"Ill in the Head" (Dead Kennedys), 51
"I'm a Man You Don't Meet Every Day" (The Pogues), 99–100
"I'm Cramped" (Cramps), 41
"I'm Gonna Dig Up Howlin' Wolf" (Mojo Nixon and Skid Roper), 89
"I'm Gonna Love You Too" (Blondie), 28
"I'm Shipping Up to Boston" (Dropkick Murphys), 58
"Incomplete" (Bad Religion), 20–21
Independent record labels, 6, 171–172
"Individual" (Bad Religion), 21
"I Need Lunch" (Dead Boys), 48
"I Need Somebody" (The Stooges), 146
"I Need You" (The Muffs), 94
Inesperado Adiós (Alice Bag), 17–18
"Infected" (Bad Religion), 4, 21–22
"In Love" (The Raincoats), 110
"Inner Logic" (Bad Religion), 21
Insomniac (Green Day), 73
"Instant Hit" (The Slits), 137
Interior, Lux, 39–41
Interrupters, The, 163
"In the City" (The Jam), 76–77
In the City (The Jam), 75–77
"I Only Want to Be with You" (Me First and the Gimmie Gimmies), 85
Iraq War, 10, 73, 186
Irish/Irish-American history and culture, 55–58, 98–101
Irish punk, 98–101. *See also* Celtic punk
"Irish Rover, The" (Dropkick Murphys), 56, 58

"Is It Day or Night?" (Runaways), 123
Islam/Islamaphobia, 148–151, 184
It's Alive (Ramones), 183
"It's a New Find" (Shonen Knife), 131
"It's Gonna Be a Punk Rock Christmas" (The Ravers), 101–102
"I Turned into a Martian" (Misfits), 87
"I've Changed My Address" (The Jam), 75
"I Wanna Be Sedated" (Ramones), 4
"I Wanna Be Your Boyfriend" (Ramones), 113
"I Wanna Be Your Dog" (Fantomes), 61
"I Wanna Be Your Dog" (Sid Vicious), 146
"I Wanna Be Your Dog" (The Stooges), 61, 81, 146
"I Was a Teenage Anarchist" (Against Me!), 13
"I Was a Teenage Werewolf" (Cramps), 40
"I Won't Be Home for Christmas" (Blink 182), 103

Jam, The, 35, 75–77
James, Brian, 44–46, 49
"James Bondage" (Pansy Division), 96
"jamming econo," 6
Japanese punk, 128–132
Jarmusch, Jim, 148, 158
Jazz, 18, 28, 36
Jenifer, Daryl, 18–20
Jeroan Drive (band), 48
"Jesse James" (The Pogues), 99–100
"Jesus of Suburbia" (Green Day), 73
Jett, Joan, 22, 24, 66, 78, 92, 121–124, 179, 181, 186
"Jigsaw Feeling" (Siouxsie and the Banshees), 133

"Jimmy Jazz" (The Clash), 37
Jingle Punks, 104
Joan Jett and the Blackhearts, 123, 179
Joanna Gruesome (band), 163
"Johnny Hit and Run Pauline" (X), 165
Johnny Thunders. *See* Johnny Thunders and the Heartbreakers
Johnny Thunders and the Heartbreakers, 44, 49, 117–118, 144, 174
"Jolene" (Me First and the Gimmie Gimmies), 84–85
"Jolly Old Saint Nick" (SSD), 102
Jones, Grace, 158
Jones, Mick, 35–38, 136
Jones, Steve, 124–125, 128
Joy Division, 133, 135
Jubilee (Derek Jarman, Dir.), 156–158
"Judy Is a Punk" (Ramones), 113
Julie Ruin (band), 25
"Jump into the New World" (Shonen Knife), 131
"Junkie Man" (Rancid), 116

Karren, Billy, 22–25
KaS Product, 61
Kawakubo, Rei, 178
Kawano, Risa, 131
"Keep on Knockin'" (Death), 54
Khan, Shahjehan, 149
"Kidnapper" (Blondie), 31
"Kids Are Alt-Right, The" (Bad Religion), 22
"Kill Me Two Times" (Electric Callas), 60
"Kill the Poor" (Dead Kennedys), 50
Kill the Sexist (Pussy Riot), 104–108
"Kimberly" (Patti Smith), 140
Kindell, Ty. *See* Zoom, Billy
Kiss (band), 86, 128
"Kissed" (Pansy Division), 97

Index **261**

"Kiss Them for Me" (Siouxsie and the Banshees), 135
Kleenex (band), 159
Klezmer punk, 5, 104
Knight, Michael Muhammad, 148–150, 157, 184
Kominas, The, 149–151, 184
Korus, Kate, 135
Kottwitz, Jason, 49
Kristal, Hilly, 10, 47, 118, 155, 178–179
"Kropotkin Vodka" (Pussy Riot), 106

Laborers and labor unions, support of, 8, 58, 101, 186–187
Ladies and Gentlemen the Fabulous Stains (Lou Adler, Dir.), 156
"Land" (Patti Smith), 141
"Land of Treason" (Germs), 65
Landscape #XX (H. G. Geiger), 51–52
"Last Caress" (Misfits), 87–88
Las Vulpes, 80–82, 162
Latinx punk, 15–18, 80–82, 162
Leave Home (Ramones), 183
"Leave Mine to Me" (Bad Religion), 21
Lee, Craig, 16
"Legend of Pat Brown, The" (The Vandals), 157
Lemeshev, Yuri, 68
Les Olivensteins, 61
Le Tigre, 25, 162, 175
"Let Me Help" (Bad Brains), 19
"Let's Lynch the Landlord" (Dead Kennedys), 50–51
"Let's Pretend" (Germs), 66
"Let's Submerge" (X-Ray Spex), 169–170
Lett, David. *See* Vanian, Dave
Letts, Don, 174–175
Levine, Keith, 128
"Lexicon Devil" (The Germs)
LGBTQ punk. *See* Queercore

LGBTQ rights, 5, 13–15, 187
"Liars Beware" (Richard Hell and the Voidoids), 120
"Life of Pain" (Black Flag), 27
Liles, Brent, 142
"Lil Red" (Bikini Kill), 24
Limp Wrist, 18
"Lincoln Logs" (Mojo Nixon and Skid Roper), 90
"Lion's Share" (Germs), 67
Literal Bitch (zine), 174
Little Bob Story (band), 59
"Little Drummer Boy, The" (Bad Religion), 102
"Little Drummer Boy, The" (Dandy Warhols), 102
"Little Hypocrite" (Alice Bag), 17
Livermore, Larry, 171
Loaded (The Runaways), 123
Logic, Lora, 167, 170
Lollapalooza (music festival), 10–11, 78, 117, 129, 185
"London Calling" (The Clash), 36
London Calling (The Clash), 35–41
London punk scene, 35–41, 44–46, 60–61, 75–77, 108–110, 114, 124–128, 132–136, 155–159, 167–170, 173–174, 176–180, 184, 186
London SS (band), 35, 44
"Lone Wolves" (War on Women), 153
"Longview" (Green Day), 72
Lookout Records, 96, 171, 173
Lords of the New Church, 46, 49
"Los Angeles" (X), 165
Los Angeles (X), 164–167, 183
Los Angeles punk scene, 15, 25–26, 64–67, 77–78, 92, 111, 129, 142, 158–159, 164–167, 173, 179
Los Crudos, 18
"Lost in the Supermarket" (The Clash), 36
Love, Courtney, 99, 154, 158

"Love and Romance" (The Slits), 136–137
"Love at the Pier" (Blondie), 31
Love Bites (Buzzcocks), 33
"Love Comes in Spurts" (Richard Hell and the Voidoids), 120
"Lovers" (The Runaways), 123
Love songs, 56, 73, 143–144. *See also* Anti-romance songs
"Love You More" (Buzzcocks), 34
Lowe, Nick, 44–45, 131
L7, 4–5, 8–10, 77–80, 114, 122, 132, 162–163, 180–181, 184, 186–187
"Lucky Guy" (The Muffs), 92–93
Lunachicks, 132, 181, 186
Lust for Life (Iggy Pop), 148
Lyall, Geoffrey. *See* Fluoride, Klaus
Lydon, John, 109, 128, 135, 167. *See also* Rotten, Johnny

MacColl, Ewan, 100
MacColl, Kristy, 100, 102–103
MacGowan, Shane, 99, 102–103
"Machine Gun Blues" (Social Distortion), 143–144
MacKay, Steve, 148
MacKaye, Ian, 22, 62–64, 171
Madansky, John. *See* Blitz, Johnny
"Mad Daddy, The" (Cramps), 40
Magnum, Jeff, 46–48
"Mahogany" (Me First and the Gimmie Gimmies), 82
"Make American Great Again" (Pussy Riot), 107
Malkmus, Stephen, 166
Manzarek, Ray, 164, 166
Mapplethorpe, Robert, 139–140
Marcus, Greil, 136
Marie et les Garçons, 60
Marley, Dave, 174
Marr, Johnny, 146
Masque, The (Los Angeles), 16, 44, 65, 173, 179
Math rock, 25–28

Matlock, Glen, 124, 128
Maximum Rocknroll (zine), 173
"Maxwell Murder" (Rancid), 115
May 1968 demonstrations (France), 1, 59
McArdle, Alanna, 163
MC5, 47, 54, 61, 89, 175
McKay, John, 133
McKenzie, Scott, 84
McLaren, Malcolm, 1, 43–44, 59–60, 117, 119, 124–125, 127–128, 132
McMillan, Neill Kirby, Jr. *See* Nixon, Mojo
McNeil, Legs, 173
McNeish, Peter. *See* Shelley, Pete
"Media Blitz" (Germs), 66
Me First and the Gimmie Gimmies, 5, 77, 82–85, 186
Me Gusta Ser (Las Vulpes), 80–82
"Me Gusta Ser Una Zorra" (Las Vulpes), 80–81, 161
Mellor, John Graham. *See* Strummer, Joe
Melvin, Eric, 85
"Memorial Day" (Dropkick Murphys), 57
"Merchandise" (Fugazi), 63–64
"Merry Christmas (I Don't Wanna Fight Tonight)" (Ramones), 103
"Merry Christmas, I Fucked Your Snowman" (Showcase Showdown), 103
Metal Boys, 60–61
Metallic KO (The Stooges), 147
Metal Machine Music (Lou Reed), 61
Metal music, 18, 25, 28, 85–88
"Metal Postcard (Mittageisen)" (Siouxsie and the Banshees), 134
Métal Urbain, 60–61
Meyers, Richard Lester. *See* Hell, Richard
Millar, Christopher John. *See* Rat Scabies
Miller, Gary. *See* Dr. Know

Miller, Jesse James, 175
Miller, Randall, 155
Miller, Thomas. *See* Verlaine, Tom
Mind Power (band), 18–19
Minor Threat, 62–64, 159, 171, 175, 179
Minor Threat (Minor Threat), 62–64
Minutemen, 6, 175
"Mirage" (Siouxsie and the Banshees), 134
Misfits, the, 4, 40–41, 46, 85–88, 102, 179, 183–184, 186
"Modern Day Virgin Sacrifice" (Alice Bag), 17
Mod-revival punk, 75–77
"Mommy Can I Go Out and Kill Tonight" (Misfits), 87
Mommy's Little Monster (Social Distortion), 142
"Monster" (L7), 79
Mont-de-Marsan, France, 1, 58–59, 180
Morimoto, Emi, 129
Morrison, Jim, 140–141
"Move On" (Shonen Knife), 131
"Mr. Integrity" (L7), 79
MTV, 22, 72, 90–91, 116, 129
Muffs, The, 92–94
Muffs, The (The Muffs), 92–94
"Muhammad Was a Punk Rocker" (Kourosh Poursaehi), 149
Murphy, John E. "Dropkick," 55
Music business, alternative models of, 3–7
MxPx, 103
My Chemical Romance, 4, 102
"My Favorite Things" (Me First and the Gimmie Gimmies), 82
"Mystery Plane" (Cramps), 40–41
"My Strange Uncles from Abroad" (Gogol Bordello), 71
"My Way" (Frank Sinatra), 5, 77, 128
"My Way" (Sid Vicious), 5, 77, 128

Nakatani, Michie, 128
"Nausea" (X), 166
"Navigator" (The Pogues), 100–101
Nazi imagery, 49–51, 134–135
Nazi punks, 157, 187
"Nazi Punks Fuck Off" (Dead Kennedys), 4, 157
"Neat, Neat, Neat" (The Damned), 45
"Negative Queen" (Pansy Division), 96–97
Neon Boys, 117–118
Ness, Mike, 142–145
Never Mind the Baubles (Julian Temple, Dir.), 101
Never Mind the Bollocks: Here's the Sex Pistols (Sex Pistols), 124–128
"New Pleasure" (Richard Hell and the Voidoids), 120
"New Rose" (The Damned), 44–45
New Wave, 28–29, 48, 60–61, 75–76, 135–136
New York Dolls, The, 47, 61, 118
New York punk scene, 1–2, 19, 28–32, 44, 46–52, 59–60, 87, 114, 117–119, 136, 138–142, 156, 159, 163, 173
"Nicotine Stain" (Siouxsie and the Banshees), 134
"Night of the Living Dead" (Misfits), 87
Night of the Living Dead (George Romero, Dir.), 86–87, 158
Night of the Living Dead Boys (Dead Boys), 47
"Nike-a-Go-Go" (Misfits), 87
Nimrod (Green Day), 73
9/11, 73–74, 149–151
9:30 Club (Washington, D. C.), 179–180
1950s and 1960s pop and rock, 28–29, 40, 76–77, 82–88, 92, 110–114, 128–129
"1953" (Dropkick Murphys), 56

Nirvana, 35, 79–80, 108, 110, 129, 167
Nissen, Melanie, 173
Nitzsche, Jack, 67
Nixon, Mojo, 4, 88–91, 114, 183
NME, 33–34, 161
"No Fun" (Sex Pistols), 146
"No Fun" (The Stooges), 146
NOFX, 9–10, 82–85, 103, 175, 186
"No Imagination" (Blondie), 31
Nolan, Jerry, 118
"No Looking" (The Raincoats), 110
"No Means No" (Alice Bag), 17
"No More" (Black Flag), 27
"Non-Stop Dancing" (The Jam), 76
"North Pole" (The Muffs), 94
"Not Anymore" (Dead Boys)
"Not Like Me" (The Muffs), 92–93
Novoselic, Krist, 80
"Now I Wanna Sniff Some Glue" (Ramones), 173

O'Brien, Derek, 142
Obscenity, prosecution for. *See* Censorship
"Obsessed with You" (X-Ray Spex), 168
"O Chanukah" (Jingle Punks), 104
O'Connor, Eugene Richard. *See* Cheetah Chrome and the Casualties
October, Gene, 158
"Off Duty Trip" (The Raincoats), 110
Official Kathleen Hanna Newsletter, The, 174
Offspring, 10, 114, 163, 181, 185–186
"Oh Bondage, Up Yours!" (X-Ray Spex), 167–170
"O Holy Night" (Phenobarbidols), 103
Oi! punk, 114–117, 171–172, 183, 187

Oi to the World (The Vandals), 103
"Old Main Drag, The" (The Pogues), 99
"Olympia, WA" (Rancid), 116
101's, The, 35
100 Club (London), 44, 61, 125, 179–180
"1 of 2" (The Damned), 45
"One Way or Another" (Blondie), 28
Only, Jerry 86, 88
Only Lovers Left Alive (The Wanderers), 48
Open Market record shop (Paris, France), 59–60
Operation Ivy, 114, 171
"Organs" (Pussy Riot), 107
"Orgasm Addict" (Buzzcocks), 4, 33
Osaka Ramones (Shonen Knife), 114
"Osama bin Laden as Crucified Christ" (Against Me!), 14
Osborne, Joan, 78
Osterberg, James Newell. *See* Pop, Iggy
Other F Word, The (Andrea Blaugrund Nevins, Dir.), 175
"Other Newest One, The" (Germs), 66
"Our Way" (Germs)
"Out of Step" (Minor Threat), 62
Outpunk (zine), 174
"Overground" (Siouxsie and the Banshees), 133
"Over the Rainbow" (Me First and the Gimmie Gimmies), 84–85

"Padded Cell" (Black Flag), 27
"Pair of Brown Eyes, A" (The Pogues), 99
Palmolive, 109, 135–138
Pandoras, The, 92
Pansy Division, 4–5, 8, 94–98, 103–104, 184, 187
Parallel Lines (Blondie), 28–30
"Paralytic States" (Against Me!), 14–15

Index 265

"Paris Marquis" (Métal Urbain), 61
Pavement (band), 166
"Pay Rent" (The Slits), 137
Pearlman, Sandy, 35
"Peek-a-boo" (Siouxsie and the Banshees), 135
Peel, John/Peel Sessions, 34, 128–129, 134–136, 138
Peepshow (Siouxsie and the Banshees), 135
"Peg o' My Heart" (Dropkick Murphys), 57–58
Peligro, D. H., 52
"Penetration" (The Stooges), 147
"People Who Died" (Jim Carroll), 4
Pepperell, Raymond John. *See* East Bay Ray
Perfect Pussy (band), 163
Perry, Mark, 172–173
Petrol Girls, 163
Phair, Liz, 78, 92, 163
Phantasmagoria (The Damned), 46
Phenobarbidols (band), 103
Picciotto, Guy, 63
"Picture This" (Blondie), 28
"Pigs Are Haram" (The Kominas), 150
"Pistol for Paddy Garcia, A" (The Pogues), 99
Pitchfork, 26, 33, 64, 101, 109
Plakas, Demetra, 77
"Plan, The" (Richard Hell and the Voidoids), 120
Plan 9 from Outer Space (Ed Wood, Dir.), 87
"Planté Comme un Privé" (Asphalt Jungle), 61
"Plastic Bag" (X-Ray Spex), 168–169
Plastic Bertrand, 60
Plastic Letters (Blondie), 28–32
"Pleasure and the Beast" (War on Women), 154
Poets/poetry, 2, 117–121, 138–142, 164
Pogues, The, 5, 98–101, 102, 158, 183

"Poisoned Seed" (Alice Bag), 17
"Police and Thieves" (The Clash), 31
Police brutality, 27, 42, 107
"Police Story" (Black Flag), 27
Political activism, 8–10, 41–44, 55–58, 73, 77–80, 104–108, 151–154, 162, 180–181, 186–188
Political music and lyrics, 5, 20, 35–38, 41–44, 49–52, 55–58, 73, 76, 104–108, 120, 151–154
"Politicians in My Eyes" (Death), 53–54
"Polka Polka, The" (Mojo Nixon and Skid Roper), 90
Pollitt, Tessa, 135–138
Pop, Iggy, 31, 47, 65, 128, 145–148, 154, 163, 181, 183
Pop music. *See* 1950s and 1960s pop and rock
"Pop Tune" (Shonen Knife), 131
"Positively Bodies Parking Lot" (Mojo Nixon and Skid Roper), 89
Positive Mental Attitude, 18–20
Post-punk, 36, 132–133, 135, 159, 183–184
Potter, Shawna, 151–154
Poursaehi, Kourosh, 149
Prairie Home Invasion (Mojo Nixon and Jello Biafra), 90
Prank (band), 172
"Predator in Chief" (War on Women), 152
Presley, Elvis, 37, 51, 76–77, 86, 90
Pretenders, 178, 180
"Pretend We're Dead" (L7), 5, 78
Pretty Mess, A (band), 163
"Pretty Vacant" (Sex Pistols), 119
Profane Existence (independent record label and zine), 172–174
"Programmed" (Alice Bag), 17
"Promises" (Buzzcocks), 34
Protopunk, 35, 40, 44, 46, 52–55, 145, 158
Psychedelic rock, 40, 145

Psychobilly, 39–41, 86, 88–91, 183
Public Image Ltd. (band), 128
Pub rock, 2–3, 6, 35, 59
Punk (Don Letts and Jesse James Miller, Dirs.), 175
Punk: Attitude (Don Letts and Jesse James Miller, Dirs.), 175
"Punk Christmas" (Impact), 103
Punk Christmas music, 5–6, 101–104, 170
Punk covers, 5, 55–58, 82–85, 102–103, 123, 129, 134, 137, 142–144, 146, 166
Punk fashion, 7–8, 162, 175–178
Punk 45: Les Punks, The French Connection (various artists)
"Punk Is Dead" (Crass), 43
Punk journalism/journalists, 162, 172–174
Punk Magazine, 28, 155, 173
Punk Planet (zine), 174
Punk pop, 28, 71–74, 155, 173, 184
"Punk Prayer, A" (Pussy Riot), 104–108, 188
"Punk Rock Chanukah Song" (Yidcore), 104
Punk Rock Movie, The (Don Letts, Dir.), 174
Punk Singer, The (Sini Anderson, Dir.), 175
Punk's Not Dead (Susan Dynner, Dir.), 175
PunkVoter, 9–10, 58, 186
"Pure" (Siouxsie and the Banshees), 133
Purkhiser, Erick. *See* Interior, Lux
Pussy Riot, 4–5, 8–9, 104–108, 188
Pussy Whipped (Bikini Kill), 22–25
Putin, Vladimir, 9, 104–108, 188
"Putin Ignites the Fires of Revolution" (Pussy Riot), 107
"Putin Zassal" (Pussy Riot), 106–107
"Pyramid Power" (Shonen Knife), 131

Queens of Noise (The Runaways), 123
Queercore, 13–15, 18, 32–35, 94–98, 104, 172, 174, 184
Quine, Robert, 118, 120

"Rachbottomoff" (Pansy Division), 97
Racine, Pamela, 68
Racism, 165; accusations of, 134–135; anti-racism, 5, 13, 20, 35, 142, 149, 153, 180, 187
Radio, Radio, Radio (Rancid), 114
"Rainbow Connection" (Me First and the Gimmie Gimmies), 84
Raincoats, The, 5, 9–10, 108–110, 162, 183
Raincoats, The (The Raincoats), 108–110
Rainone, Patricia. *See* Bag, Pat
Rake It In: The Greatest Hits (Me First and the Gimmie Gimmies)
Ramone, C. J., 85
Ramone, Dee Dee, 49, 111–112
Ramone, Joey, 9, 46–47, 111–113, 144, 187
Ramone, Johnny, 9, 111–112, 187
Ramones, 4–5, 9–10, 19, 28, 46–47, 54, 80, 82, 92, 94, 96, 102–103, 110–114, 124, 128–130, 133, 136, 141, 155, 158–159, 164, 166, 172–173, 175–177, 179–181, 183, 185, 187
Ramones (Ramones), 110–114
Ramone, Tommy, 111
Ranchera music, 17
Rancid, 4, 41, 46, 103, 114–117, 163, 171, 174–175, 181, 183, 186
Rancid News (zine), 174
R & B. *See* Rhythm and blues
Rankin, Andrew, 98
Rape/rape culture, 16–17, 23–24, 110, 121–124, 151–152, 165
"Rare Old Mountain Dew, The" (Irish folk song), 102

Rastafarianism, 18–20, 115
Rat Scabies, 44–46
Raun, Dave, 82
Ravers, The, 101–102
Raw Power (The Stooges), 145–148
"Reality Asylum" (Crass), 42.
 See also "Asylum" (Crass)
Really, Really Happy (The Muffs), 94
"Rebel Girl" (Bikini Kill), 22–25
"Reciprocate" (Pansy Division), 97
Reddington, Helen, 110
Red Kross, 132
"Redondo Beach" (Patti Smith), 140
Reed, Brett, 114
Reed, Lou, 61, 123, 141
Reggae, 18–20, 35–38, 62, 114–117
"Re-ignition" (Bad Brains), 19
"*Rein a Dire*" (Marie et les Garçons), 60
"Reject of Society" (Crass), 42
"Release the Cobblestones" (Pussy Riot), 106
Religion, critiques of, 4–5, 20, 43, 51, 70, 104–108, 139–140, 154
Repeater (Fugazi), 62–64
"Repeater" (Fugazi), 63–64
Repo Man (Alex Cox, Dir.), 157–158
Reproductive freedom, 5, 23, 78, 151–154, 163, 180, 187
"Reprovisional" (Fugazi), 64
Return of the Living Dead (Dan O'Bannon, Dir.), 158
"Return to Heaven" (Bad Brains), 19
Re-Volts (band), 82
"Revolution Rock" (The Clash), 37
Rhodes, Bernard, 1, 38, 59
Rhodes, Zandra, 178
Rhythm and blues, 35, 40, 53, 76
Richard Hell and the Voidoids, 28, 117–121, 179
"Richie Dagger's Crime" (Germs), 45, 66, 82, 115
"Riding on the Rocket" (Shonen Knife), 131

Rimbaud, Arthur, 2, 59–60, 117, 139–140
"Ring of Fire" (Social Distortion), 142
Riot Fest (Chicago, Illinois), 10–11, 20, 25, 181, 186
Riot grrrl, 9–10, 22–24, 77–80, 162–163, 172, 174, 180–181, 183–184
Riot Grrrl (zine), 174
"Rise Above" (Black Flag), 26–27
Rise and Fall of the Clash, The (Danny Garcia, Dir.), 175
Ritchie, Simon John. See Sid Vicious
Ritter, Rob, 16
"Road Zombie" (Social Distortion), 143
Rockabilly, 28, 31, 35–37, 39–41, 50, 61, 86, 90, 131, 142, 164
Rock against Racism concerts (London, U.K.), 9, 167, 180, 186–187
Rock against Sexism concerts (London, U.K. and U.S.A.), 180
"Rock & Roll" (The Runaways), 123
"Rock & Roll" (Velvet Underground), 123
Rock and Roll Hall of Fame, 20, 38, 71, 112, 126, 141, 148
"Rock and Roll T-shirt" (Shonen Knife), 131
Rock Animals (Shonen Knife), 129
Rocket from the Tombs, 46, 54
Rock for Choice concerts, 9–10, 78, 163, 180–181, 186
Rock 'n' Roll High School (Rodger Corman, Dir.), 114, 158–159
"Rock on the Moon" (Cramps), 40
"Rock on the Moon" (Jimmy Stewart), 40
Rock opera, 71–74
Rocksteady music, 37, 115
Rodrigol, Mamen, 80
Rolling Stone, 13, 15, 22, 24, 30, 33, 44, 71, 88, 101, 112, 119, 133, 135, 139, 146, 180

Rolling Stones, The, 112
Rollins, Henry, 26–27, 174
Romero, Paloma. *See* Palmolive
"Room 13" (Black Flag), 27
Root Hog or Die (Mojo Nixon and Skid Roper), 90
"Roots Radical" (Jimmy Cliff), 115
"Roots Radicals" (Rancid), 115
Roper, Skid, 88–91
Rorschach, Poison Ivy, 39–41
"Rose Tattoo" (Dropkick Murphys), 55
Rotten, Johnny, 32, 124–125, 128, 135, 177–178. *See also* Lydon, John
Roxy, The (London), 61, 136, 174
"Ruby Soho" (Rancid), 115–116
Rude Boy (Jack Hazan and David Mingay, Dirs.), 156
"Rudie Can't Fail" (The Clash), 37
Ruin Johnny's Bar Mitzvah (Me First and the Gimmie Gimmies), 85
Rum, Sodomy, and the Lash (The Pogues), 98–101
Runaways, The, 7, 16, 66, 121–124, 130, 132, 136, 155, 161, 179
Runaways, The (The Runaways), 121–124
Runaways, The (Floria Sigismondi, Dir.), 155
Russian punk, 104–108, 187–188
Ruthenberg, Georg. *See* Smear, Pat
Ryan, Barry, 46
Ryan, Teresa. *See* Doom, Lorna

"Sacred Love" (Bad Brains), 19–20
Sagg Taqwacore Syndicate, 150
Saints, The (band), 54
"Sally MacLaenne" (The Pogues), 99
"Salted City" (84 Flesh), 61
Salt-N-Pepa, 78, 163
Samiam (band), 172
Samutsevich, Yekaterina, 105–107
Sanders, Mike, 94

"San Francisco" (Me First and the Gimmie Gimmies), 84–85
San Francisco punk scene, 49, 71, 94–96, 127
Sartre, Jean Paul, 139
Savages (band), 133
"Saying Goodbye" (The Muffs), 92–93
"Say It" (War on Women), 151–152
Schmekel (band), 104
Scream, The (Siouxsie and the Banshees), 132–135
Screamers, The, 173, 179
Screeching Weasel, 171
"Search and Destroy" (Sid Vicious), 146
"Search and Destroy" (The Stooges), 146–147
"Season's Upon Us, The" (Dropkick Murphys), 103
"Secrets" (The Runaways), 123
Secret Trial Five (band), 149–151, 184
"Securior" (Crass), 43
"See Her Tonight" (The Damned), 45
See How We Are (X), 166
"77" (Alice Bag), 18
7 Year Bitch (band), 181
"Sex and Dying in High Society" (X), 165
Sexism, 22–25, 78–82, 104–110, 134–138, 149, 151–154, 168–169; in the music industry 16, 22–25, 48, 78, 138–139, 141, 156, 159–163. *See also* Feminism
Sex Pistols, 4–5, 19–20, 28, 32, 35, 44–49, 59, 61, 64–65, 75–76, 81, 96, 101, 109, 115, 117, 119, 124–128, 132, 135–136, 145–146, 148, 154, 156–157, 159, 174–175, 177, 179, 186
Sexual assault. *See* Rape
Sexual harassment of female punks, 23–24, 80–82, 151–154, 160–161, 174

Sexuality, women's, 23, 29, 80–82, 122–123, 154, 161
7 Seconds (band), 175
Severin, Steven, 132, 158
"Shake Appeal" (Sid Vicious), 146
"Shake Appeal" (The Stooges), 146–147
Sham 69 (band), 175
"Sharia Law in the U.S.A." (The Kominas), 150
Shattered Faith (band), 142
Shattuck, Kim, 92–94
"She" (Green Day), 72–73
Shelley, Pete, 4, 32–34, 97
Shiflett, Chris, 82–83, 85
Shiflett, Scott, 85
"Shitlist" (L7), 4, 79
Shonen Knife, 4–5, 104, 114, 128–132, 163, 184
"Shoplifting" (The Slits), 137
Showcase Showdown, 103
"Shut Down (Annihilation Man)" (Germs), 67
"Shut the Door" (Fugazi), 64
"Sick Bed of Cúchulainn, The" (The Pogues), 98
"Sick Boys" (Social Distortion), 143
Sid and Nancy (Alex Cox, Dir), 126, 154–155, 158
Signed and Sealed in Blood (Dropkick Murphys), 55
"Silence Is the Gift" (War on Women), 153–154
"Silent Night" (The Dickies), 102
Simonon, Paul, 35–38, 135
Sinatra, Frank, 5, 77, 128
Singles Going Steady (Buzzcocks), 32–35
Sioux, Siouxsie, 125, 132–135, 158, 176
Siouxsie and the Banshees, 28, 35, 132–135, 159–160, 179
Situationist International collective, 1, 59

"Six Pack" (Black Flag), 27
Six Weeks (band), 172
'60s pop. *See* 1950s and 1960s pop and rock
Ska, 36, 71, 103, 114–117, 136
Skinned Teen (band), 163
Skinny Girl Diet (band), 163
Skrewdriver (band), 187
Skulls (band), 179
"Skulls" (Misfits), 87
Slash (zine), 173
Slash Records, 78, 164
"Slave, The" (The Germs), 67
Slawson, Spike, 82–85
SLC Punk (James Merendino, Dir.), 156
Sleater-Kinney, 110, 163
Slits, The, 35–36, 75, 108–110, 115, 135–138, 152, 159–160, 187
Slog Movie, The (Dave Markey, Dir.), 174
"Sloop John B" (Me First and the Gimmie Gimmies), 82–85
Sloppy Seconds (band), 103
"Slow Down" (The Jam), 76–77
Slug and Lettuce (zine), 174
"Slumber" (Bad Religion), 21
Smear, Pat, 65–67
Smith, Patti, 2, 47, 59–60, 108, 118, 138–142, 159, 161, 163–164, 179, 183, 186
Smithereens (Susan Seidelman, Dir.), 156
Smiths, The, 135, 146
Smoking Popes, 186
Sniffin' Glue, 6–7, 172–173
Social Distortion, 142–145, 179, 183–184, 186
Social Distortion (Social Distortion), 143
"So Messed Up" (the Damned), 45
"Song of Remembrance for Old Boyfriends, A" (Pansy Division), 97
Song Ramones the Same, The (various artists), 114

Songs the Lord Taught Us (Cramps), 39–41
"Sonic Reducer" (Dead Boys), 48
Sonic Youth, 108, 129, 132, 159
Sorrondeguy, Martin, 18
"Soul Kitchen" (X), 166
"Sounds from the Street" (The Jam), 75
South Korean punk, 188
"So What?" (Crass), 42–43
"Space Christmas" (Shonen Knife), 104
"Space Zombies" (Misfits), 87
"Spanish Bombs" (The Clash), 5, 36–37
Spanish punk, 80–82
Sparks, Donita, 77
"Spend, Spend, Spend" (The Slits), 137
Spheeris, Penelope, 16, 65, 157, 165, 174
SPIN Magazine, 15, 64, 79
Spinnerettes, The, 163
Spiral Scratch (Buzzcocks), 32
"Spray Paint" (Black Flag), 27
Springsteen, Bruce, 55, 58
Spungen, Nancy, 126, 128, 154, 175
SSD (band), 102, 175
SST Records, 27–28
"Stab Yor Back" (The Damned), 45–46
Stafford, Jack. *See* Airport, Jak
"Stagger Lee" (Lloyd Price), 37
"Stand by Me" (The Clash). *See* "Train in Vain" (The Clash)
"Star Bellied Boy" (Bikini Kill), 24
Starwood Hotel (Los Angeles), 67, 173
"Stealing People's Mail" (Dead Kennedys), 51
Steineckert, Brandon, 117
"Stepping into Christmas" (The Business), 102
Stewart, Jimmy, 40

Stiff Little Fingers (band), 102
Stilettos, The, 49
"Still Alive" (Social Distortion), 143
Stinky Toys, 170
Stooges, the, 45, 53–54, 61–62, 80–81, 145–148, 175, 186
Stooges, The (the Stooges), 145–146
"Straight Edge" (Minor Threat), 62
Straight-edge punk, 62–64, 188
"Straight Outta Vagina" (Pussy Riot), 107
Straight to Hell (Alex Cox, Dir.), 99, 158
"Stranger Than Fiction" (Bad Religion), 21
Stranger Than Fiction (Bad Religion), 20–22
Stranglers (band), 179
Street Harassment: An Open Letter to Women and Girls, and Why Aren't Boys Called Sluts? (zine), 174
Strummer, Joe, 32, 35–38, 98, 136, 144, 158
"Strychnine" (Cramps), 4, 40
"Stupid Jerk" (The Muffs), 94
Styrene, Poly, 4, 23, 30, 162–163, 167–170, 178
"Styrofoam" (Fugazi), 64
Subterraneans, The, 44
"Suburban Home" (Alice Bag), 17
"Suburban Relapse" (Siouxsie and the Banshees), 134
Suburbia (Eric Bogosian, Dir.), 166
Suburbia (Penelope Spheeris, Dir.), 157
Subway Sect, 108, 179
"Sucks" (Crass), 43
"Sugar" (Bikini Kill), 24
"Sugarlight" (X), 166
Suicidal Tendencies, 158, 186
"Suicide Bomb the Gap" (The Kominas), 150
Suicide Machines, 186

Index 271

"Summertime" (Me First and the Gimmie Gimmies), 83–84
"Sunday Girl" (Blondie), 28–30
"Sunday Hardcore Matinee" (Dropkick Murphys), 58
"Sunglasses After Dark" (Cramps), 40
"Super Group" (Shonen Knife), 131
Superstition (Siouxsie and the Banshees), 135
Super Taranta! (Gogol Bordello), 67–71, 82, 132
"Super Taranta!"(Gogol Bordello), 69
"Supertheory of Supereverything" (Gogol Bordello), 70
Surf music, 39, 50, 83, 89, 92
"Sushi Bar Song" (Shonen Knife), 131
"Sweet Christmas" (Shonen Knife), 104
"Sweet Marilyn" (Metal Boys), 61
"Switch" (Siouxsie and the Banshees), 134

"Take 'Em Down" (Dropkick Murphys), 57
"Take Me Home Country Roads" (Me First and the Gimmie Gimmies), 84
"Takin' My Love" (The Jam), 76
Talking Heads, 132
Taneda, Ritsuko, 129
Taqwacore, 148–151, 157, 184
Taqwacores, The (Eyad Zahra, Dir.), 149, 157
Taqwacores, The (Michael Muhammad Knight), 148–149, 157, 184
Taylor, Vince, 37
Team Dresch, 94, 163, 172
"Tear It Up" (Cramps), 40
Ted Leo and the Pharmacists, 171
"Teenage Lobotomy" (Ramones), 82
"Teenage Whore" (Hole), 4
Television (band), 28, 47, 60, 117–119, 141, 179
"Television" (Bad Religion), 20–21
"Television" (X-ray Spex), 66
"Tell Me So" (Bikini Kill), 24
Temple, Julian, 101, 127–128, 175
"Tessie" (Dropkick Murphys), 55
"That's So Gay" (Pansy Division), 5
"They've Got a Bomb" (Crass), 42
"Thirsty and Miserable" (Black Flag), 27
39/Smooth (Green Day), 71
"Thunders" (The Runaways), 123
Thunders, Johnny, 49, 118, 144
Tiananmen Square massacre, 187
"Time Bomb" (Rancid), 115
"Time for Truth" (The Jam), 75–76
Time Machine, The (Me First and the Gimmie Gimmies fan site)
Times Square (Allan Moyle, Dir.), 156
"Times They Are a-Changin', The" (Me First and the Gimmie Gimmies), 84
"Tiny Voices" (Bad Religion), 21–22
Today show, 5, 45, 81, 126, 132
Tolokonnikova, Nadezhda, 105–108
"Tomato Head" (Shonen Knife), 129
"Too Drunk to Fuck" (Dead Kennedys), 4
Top of the Pops, 30, 32, 42
"Top of the World" (Shonen Knife), 129
"Touch I Crave, The" (Alice Bag), 17
Townshend, Pete, 53
Trade Test Transmission (Buzzcocks), 34–35
Trafford, Howard. *See* Devoto, Howard
"Train in Vain" (The Clash), 36
Transgender Dysphoria Blues (Against Me!), 13–15
Transphobia, 13–15. *See also* LGBTQ rights

272 Index

Trapped Animal (The Slits), 138
"Tribal Connection" (Gogol Bordello), 70
Tribe 8 (band), 163
Trippple Nippples, 163
"True Trans Soul Rebel" (Against Me!), 14–15
TSOL (band), 157
Tubes, The, 156
"Turn It Up" (Alice Bag), 18
"Turnover" (Fugazi), 63
"Turn Those Clapping Hands into Angry Balled Fists" (Against Me!), 13
Tuts, The, 163
"TV Party" (Black Flag), 26
"TV Set" (Cramps), 40
"20 Eyes" (Misfits), 87
"21st Century Digital Boy" (Bad Religion), 5, 20–22
"Twist Barbie" (Shonen Knife), 131
"Two Beats Off" (Fugazi), 64
"Two Coffins" (Against Me!), 15
"Typical Girls" (The Slits), 36, 136–138

UK/DK (Christopher Collins, Dir.), 175
U.K. Subs, 172
"Ultimate" (Gogol Bordello), 70
Unclogged (X), 167
"Unconditional Love" (Against Me!), 14
"Unheard Music, The" (X), 166
Unlimited (Mojo Nixon and Skid Roper), 90
"Unprotected Sex with Multiple Partners" (Against Me!), 4
"Uptown Girl" (Me First and the Gimmie Gimmies), 84–85
Usmani, Basim, 149–150

Vail, Tobi, 22–25, 162
Valenzuela, Francisca, 18

Vammen, Melanie, 92
"Vampira" (Misfits), 87
Vandals, The, 103, 157, 186
Vanian, Dave, 44–46, 86
Vans Warped Tour. *See* Warped Tour
Vázquez, Loles, 80
Vázquez, Lupe, 80, 82
Vega, Autoro, 111
Velvet Underground, 61, 123, 175
Venues, 178–180
Verlaine, Paul, 2, 60, 118–119
Verlaine, Tom, 2, 60, 118–119
Versace, Gianni, 178
Vibrators, The, 179
Vicious, Sid, 4–5, 49, 65, 77, 124–128, 146, 154–155, 175, 179
Vig, Butch, 79
Village Voice, 119, 139, 141
"Violence of Bureaucracy, The" (War on Women), 153
Vito, Jennifer, 151
"Viva Las Vegas" (Dead Kennedys), 51
Voidoids, The. *See* Richard Hell and the Voidoids
Voids, The, 163
von Frankenstein, Doyle Wolfgang, 88
Vote Hezbollah (band), 149–151, 184

"Wake Me Up When September Ends" (Green Day), 73–74
Walk among Us (Misfits), 85–88
"Walking on the Water" (Richard Hell and the Voidoids), 120
Wallace, Christine. *See* Rorschach, Poison Ivy
"Waltzing Matilda" (The Pogues), 99–100
Wanderers, The, 48
"Wargasm" (L7), 79
Warhol, Andy, 119, 141
Warm Gun (band), 62
Warning (Green Day), 73
War on Women, 151–154

Index

War on Women (War on Women), 151
Warped Tour, 10, 78, 181, 186
"Warrior in Woolworth" (X-Ray Spex), 169
"Wars End, The" (Rancid), 116
"Wasabi" (Shonen Knife), 131
Washington, D. C. punk scene, 18–20, 24, 159, 179
"Wash No Dishes No More" (Mojo Nixon and Skid Roper), 89
Waters, John, 48, 79–80
Wayne County and the Electric Chairs, 158, 174
"We Gotta Have More Soul" (Mojo Nixon and Skid Roper), 89
We Have Come for Your Children (Dead Boys), 47
We Jam Econo: The Story of the Minutemen (Tim Irwin, Dir.), 175
"Welcome to Paradise" (Green Day), 72–73
Weller, Paul, 75–77
"We Must Bleed" (Germs), 66
Werner, Suzanne, 151
West, Sandy, 122
Westwood, Vivienne, 8, 125, 162, 178, 184
"What a Shame" (Crass), 42
"What Do I Get?" (Buzzcocks), 4, 33
"What I See" (Black Flag), 27
What Is Punk? (Morse and Yi), 184
"What Love Is" (Dead Boys), 48
"What's Behind the Mask" (Cramps), 41
What We Do Is Festive (Angry Snowmans), 104
"What We Do Is Secret" (Germs), 66
What We Do Is Secret (Rodger Grossman, Dir.), 67, 155
"When I Come Around" (Green Day), 72–73
"When Ya Get Drafted" (Dead Kennedys), 50
Whitby, Susan. *See* Logic, Lora

"White Christmas" (Stiff Little Fingers), 102
White Heat, White Light, White Trash (Social Distortion), 142
"White People for Peace" (Against Me!), 13
Who, The, 22, 34, 53, 146
Whoop Dee Do (The Muffs), 94
"Who Says?" (Richard Hell and the Voidoids), 120
"Wide Open" (Mojo Nixon and Skid Roper), 89
Wilcox, Kathi, 22–25
"Wildcats of Kilkenny, The" (The Pogues), 99
Wilden, William. *See* Zero, Jimmy
Wild Gift (X), 164
Williams, Hank, 143–144
Williamson, James, 146–148
Wilson, Tony, 1, 32–33, 59
Wolfe, Alison, 18, 162
"Women" (Crass), 43
Women in punk, 13–18, 22–25, 28–32, 39–41, 58–62, 67–68, 77–82, 92–94, 100–110, 121–124, 128–142, 150–154, 159–163, 164–170, 173–174
Women's health. *See* Reproductive freedom; Sexuality, women's
"Wonderlust King" (Gogol Bordello), 60
"World's a Mess; It's in My Kiss, The" (X), 165
"World Up My Ass" (Circle Jerks), 4
"Writing on the Wall" (Social Distortion), 144
"Wrong 'Em Boyo" (The Clash), 37

X (band), 159, 164–167, 173, 179, 183, 186
"Xmas Eve (She Got Up and Left Me)" (Rancid), 103
X-Ray Spex, 4–5, 23, 30, 35, 60, 66, 76, 109, 159, 162, 167–170, 179, 183

Yamano, Atsuko, 128
Yamano, Naoko, 92, 128, 131
"YDTMHTL" (War on Women), 153–154
Year Zero punk bands, 9, 28–49, 58–62, 64–67, 75–77, 80–82, 108–114, 117–128, 132–142, 145–148, 154–170, 172
Yidcore punk. *See* Klezmer punk
Yong, He, 187
"You Drive Me Wild" (The Runaways), 123
Young, Loud, and Snotty (Dead Boys), 46–49
"You Pay" (Crass), 42
"Your Country" (Gogol Bordello), 70
"You're a Mean One, Mr. Grinch" (Misfits), 102
"Your Emotions" (Dead Kennedys), 50
"Your Phone's Off the Hook, but You're Not" (X), 166

"Your Pretty Face Is Going to Hell" (The Stooges), 147
"You Say You Don't Love Me" (Buzzcocks), 33
"Youth Nabbed as Sniper" (Blondie), 30–31
Yoyo A Go Go punk and independent music festival (Olympia, Washington), 181
Y Pants (band), 159
"Yule Shoot Your Eye Out for Christmas" (Fall Out Boy), 103

Zahra, Eyad, 157
Zermati, Marc, 59–60, 184
Zero, Jimmy, 46
"Zina-Marina" (Gogol Bordello), 70
Zines, 7, 172–174
Ziskrout, Jay, 20
Žižek, Slavoj, 106
"Zombie Dance" (Cramps), 40
Zombies, 40, 87, 103, 158
Zoom, Billy, 164, 166

About the Author

JUNE MICHELE PULLIAM teaches courses in horror fiction and film, adolescent literature, and gender studies at Louisiana State University in Baton Rouge. One of her deepest regrets is arriving in Baton Rouge six months too late to see the Sex Pistols during their only visit to the city.

www.ingramcontent.com/pod-product-compliance
Lightning Source LLC
Chambersburg PA
CBHW060945230426
43665CB00015B/2072